T0083579

ZUZANA JURKOVÁ ET AL.
PRAGUE SOUNDSCAPES

CHARLES UNIVERSITY IN PRAGUE
KAROLINUM PRESS 2014

Reviewed by Miloš Havelka (Prague)
Speranţa Rădulescu (Bucarest)

Authors:
Peter Balog
Hana Černáková
Jakub Jonáš
Pavla Jónssonová
Zuzana Jurková – authorial team head
Veronika Seidlová
Filip Schneider
Zita Skořepová Honzlová
Jan Stehlík
Veronika Svobodová

ISBN 978-80-246-2515-7
ISBN 978-80-246-2596-6 (online: pdf)

CONTENTS

LISTENING TO THE MUSIC OF A CITY
Zuzana Jurková

Prague Soundscapes is about the music in Prague through the ears of ethnomusicologists. As my student Petra once said, "When someone has been through ethnomusicological schooling, he never listens to music the same way as before." This apparently banal truth (after all, every experience we have changes further ones) is particularly valid in the case of music: we perceive it so intimately, and are so used to approaching through the categories of "like" vs. "don't like" that we experience a change in approach as an attack on our personal integrity. However, this is exactly how ethnomusicology works: whether or not you like certain music is not the main issue. You have to understand *why* it is the way it is. For an ethnomusicologist, listening means trying to understand.

From our point of view, ethnomusicology is more or less synonymous with musical anthropology. We thus seek the answer to that WHY in human society – in its behavior, values, and relationships. However, as is often the case in science, there is no universal theory, or even a universal concept clarifying what exactly music is. From the ethnomusicological perspective, it is not only sound, but also – and in fact primarily – the people who produce and listen to it and the way in which they do so, that is fundamental. It is the world around sound. The musical world.

Imagining this is not always entirely simple. In order to clarify our perspective, we begin this book with theoretical considerations. In the second part of the first chapter, we then describe the process of writing this book. Each of the following six chapters is connected to a single anthropological phenomenon which we are convinced is related to the shape of music. And in fact, these connections are the main theme of our book.

A bonus awaits attentive and empathetic readers: it often happens (and it has also repeatedly happened to us) that when we understand why music sounds exactly the way it does, we like it. It becomes our music.

FOR THOSE WHO DO NOT WANT TO WASTE TIME ON THEORY

We imagined music in Prague as a set of musical worlds (for which the word *soundscapes* is sometimes used): worlds of people who perform and listen to a certain type of music; worlds whose boundaries are, however, vague. In addition to having unclear boundaries, these worlds are permeated from various sides by global factors both those of a technical and economic character and those of thoughts and images. And so the Prague soundscape is full of streams of individuals, all of which are constantly merging and influencing one another, the sounds they produce, and meanings with which they connect those sounds.

FOR THOSE WHO ARE NOT AFRAID OF THEORY

Our topic originally appeared to be simply arranged along three axes: people (who listen) – music (which they listen to) – and place (where they listen). It looked as though we wanted to describe a three-dimensional reality – certainly not an easy task, but at least an understandable and transparent one. Besides, concepts for this reality exist that may help us, at least a bit.

The key concept, in the English-language literature (and also in several Czech texts), is called soundscape. It combines the word *sound* with the morpheme *-scape,* which refers most directly to the word *landscape.* However, it carries connotations not of solidity associated with mountains and meadows that form a landscape, but rather, of a process of creation or formation. For that matter, Kay Kaufman Shelemay, speaking about her idea of *soundscape* (which is similar to ours and about which we will speak a little later), refers to seascape, *which provides a more flexible analogy to music's ability both to stay in place and to move in the world today, to absorb changes in its content and performance styles, and to continue to accrue new layers of meanings.*[1]

The word *soundscape* was first popularized in the 1970s in the work of the Canadian composer and sound ecologist Raymond Murray Schafer and his colleagues. In their concept, a soundscape is comprised of the sound characteristics of a concrete environment, some sort of sound parallel to a landscape, including the sounds of cars, bells, footsteps and birds singing... Schafer and his team considered this sound landscape, the sound environment, both as a research topic (being primarily interested in people's perceptions of it) and also as a special sort of artistic work. In this approach, they were not far from John Cage, who is discussed in the third chapter.

---

1   Shelemay 2006: XXXIV.

In 2000, the word *soundscape* was used by the Harvard ethnomusicologist Kay Kaufman Shelemay in the title of her book. While the form of the term itself was inspired by the cultural anthropologist Arjun Appadurai,[2] in the content Shelemay followed up on the well-known three-part analytical model of the classic ethnomusicologist Alan Merriam (1964). In it, Merriam, a trained anthropologist (and passionate musician) suggested how to research music from the anthropological perspective – as a product of human activity. What we are accustomed to calling "music itself" (and what Merriam calls "sound phenomenon") is a product of human behavior – the movement of fingers on strings, the vibration of vocal chords – and also of the interaction of the audience when it spontaneously joins the performing group e.g. by clapping in rhythm. The review of an operatic performance that the critic writes for an influential newspaper also belongs here: this "verbal behavior" can cause the soprano, Madam X., whose vibrato was criticized by the reviewer, not to sing the main role next time.

Verbal behavior also belongs in this category, whether in the form of a written review of an operatic performance or oral disagreement with the playing of a local cymbalom band at a wedding. All of this influences the sound of music now or in the future.

The above-mentioned types of human behavior, however, are not accidental; on the contrary, they are deeply rooted in human ideas, values and concepts – be they about music or, more broadly, about the world in general. The ancient Indians, convinced of the spiritual effects of sound, tried with all their might to avoid mistakes during the performance of ritual chanting. Therefore, they created the first known musical notations and established one social stratum especially for the performance of these sacred texts. And thus it is still possible to listen to their ancient (sometimes very complicated) melodies today. Musicians in a punk band, convinced of the rottenness of the majority society, express their revulsion, their rebellion, their negation in various ways: with simple crudeness against the cultivated and complicated classics, with amateurism available to everyone against specialization (including musical), and by wearing rumpled and even torn pants, socks and jackets with unfriendly and prickly-looking decorations against refined, fancy clothing.

As far as people are concerned, Merriam's model, like the cultural and social anthropology of the time, assumed a relatively simple world of more or less isolated, homogeneous, and, moreover, static groups.[3] It is exactly because of this unrealistic view that Shelemay emphasizes that dynamic similarity to the *seascape* which makes it possible to grasp changes in the sound world and in

---

2   His concept of -scapes appears in the book *Modernity at Large*, 1996.
3   Regarding terminology, the English-language literature most often uses the term "community."

How can we listen to the music of the whole city? Prague from the Petřín Hill lookout tower

the world of people. We use the expression "musical world" as a synonym for soundscape for such an idea of music in the most various contexts.[4]

Both concepts clearly differentiate in their musical ties; while Schafer's concept binds sounds to a place, Shelemay connects them primarily to people – to those who produce music as well as those who listen to and appreciate it. The latter concept is understandably closer to us as musical anthropologists. We also agree with Merriam's and/or Shelemay's understanding of music: following the ethnomusicological tradition (and perhaps somewhat limited by a tradition of historical musicology), we understand music as an intentional human creation. Concretely: we would not unequivocally agree with the classical musicological assertion that music is (only) a sound structure which bears esthetic information. We know that phenomena we would designate as music have (and, as is apparent in the music of Prague, not only in rather exotic cultures) various meanings in different cultures and in many cases it would not occur to the "users" of these phenomena to ask if the music is "lovely." Nevertheless, we constantly oscillated between Blacking's thesis that music is "humanly organized sound" (which we understood as "*intentionally* humanly organized sound"), and a newer concept, highly popularized by Christopher Small, that music is actually human activity,[5] which is not too far from Merriam's understanding.

---

4   It is beyond scope of this text to deal with different meanings and variants of the term "musical world" in the texts of other authors; we have just tried to find a meaningful equivalent to "soundscape." These include Becker's (1982) *Art Worlds*, or "musical worlds" (or "musical pathways" used in the same sense) by Ruth Finnegan (1989).

5   Small 1998: 2.

Thus, decisive for us is the intentionality which connects sound to people. The idea of Schafer and his followers that the sound of passing trams, random footsteps and slamming doors could be perceived as art or music is alien to us, not only because we are not such limited traditionalists, but also because it is closer to the anthropological point of view of understanding music as an intentional human creation than as a product of place.

But what can we do if the concept of music, its most crucial intention, becomes unintentionality, thus the unintentionality of the resulting sound shape, and, on the contrary, the intentional connection to the random sounds of a place? That was exactly the case of a special type of concert – a "sound-specific performance" (as the organizers called it) – in the Bubeneč sewage disposal plant, which we will discuss later, and other Prague musical events. One dimension of our three-dimensional research reality – the dimension of music – gradually became foggy.

Moreover, inside the unclearly bounded phenomenon called music, there are, as we knew from our own research and that of other ethnomusicologists, very permeable borders of categories called genre or style. And, thus, what is called a mantra in two different places sounds completely different in each. Or the music sounds similar, but it means something different to those who play it and those who listen to it. Jazz could be an example: so full of meaning for the Czech youth at the very beginning of World War II (as Škvorecký writes about it), meaning so far from that of the Afro-American fathers of jazz a half century earlier. This is exactly the accruing of new layers mentioned by Shelemay.

The fogginess, related at first to the concept of music and its categories, is also applicable to the second axis of our interest: people. Like Merriam, thinking about the rather simple reality of isolated homogeneous societies, the world was viewed in the same way by many sociologists and cultural anthropologists.[6] When they became interested in groups of people who differed from others (usually in an urban environment), groups that they began to call subcultures, they realized that their common element was often musical style. Sometimes musical style directly generates such groups,[7] sometimes it strikingly indicates them,[8] and sometimes this process is a two-way street. Punk subculture is usually mentioned as an especially famous example. Our experience – be it from the musical style itself (and thus, from the sound of the

---

6   This homogeneous approach began to change, especially in the 1990s.

7   Turino 2008: 187 mentions the example of the American contra-dance movement, when a community is created around the musical activity itself. In her extensive article about community (2011), Shelemay convinces us that music plays a basic role in forming communities of different types. (pp. 367–370).

8   For example, various features of hip-hop specifically belonged to certain age groups of Afro-American urban ghettos at the time of its origin.

The smallest musical world
is the individual

music) or from the people we met – revealed a world less "homogenized" and less clearly segmented. The majority of today's teenagers would most likely say that they belong MORE OR LESS (and this is meant literally: sometimes more and sometimes less, sometimes only fleetingly) to one subculture or another.[9]

Some of today's philosophers and sociologists agree. While in traditional societies people had, according to Anthony Giddens, a relatively fixed majority of social roles and ways to fulfil them (and thus possibilities for their own self-creation were limited), for our "late modernity" an overwhelming offer of possibilities is significant, and everyone can always chose an answer to the question, "Who am I and how shall I behave?"[10] The picture of homogeneous subcultures crumbles. This approach is taken to the extreme by Mark Slobin,[11] according to whom everyone is a unique musical culture. Most ethnomusicologists would rather, however, identify with Kay Shelemay, who says, *We do not*

---

9   And some would, on the contrary, emphasize that they are not connected to one or another style and subculture, which is, however, actually the sign of another distinctive group.

10   Giddens 1991: 70.

11   Slobin 1993: IX.

study a disembodied concept called "culture" or a place called "field," but rather a stream of individuals.[12] We thus perceive a human world metaphorically as a mass of individuals carried by the same stream. Some are closer to the center of the stream; some are more on the side; some get out and climb on the bank. Sometimes the stream splits or, on the contrary, merges with another one. We can apply the thesis of Zygmunt Bauman about liquid modernity,[13] including that of musical worlds. Or we can use the idea of the universe with galaxies, orbits, and individual planets. The closer we look, the more detailed are the worlds which open to us, until we reach the world of each human individual.

For the understanding of such **individual worlds**, Timothy Rice offers a model which is similarly three-dimensional to the one we thought about at the beginning. Its axes are, however, different: time, place and metaphor.[14] On the axis of time, chronological as well as historical (how a musical composition flows, in which "objective" time its performance is set), is interwoven with the phenomenological, experiential one (how I perceive it – most likely in a different way from the first time, etc.). On the axis of place, Rice leaves an idea of a concrete, "natural," physical place (*we and our subjects increasingly dwell not in a single place but in many places along a locational dimension of some sort*[15]) and accepts the idea that it is a social construct in which a social event is set into the most varied coordinates. (Where, in my personal history, did that happen?). Here Rice comes close to the socio-geographic method of mental maps which some researchers use to try to understand how people perceive their environment.[16] How would Prague look on the mental map of a techno fan and, on the other hand, of a singer of Gregorian chant?

The third dimension is *metaphor*. Rice uses this term to mean ...*the fundamental nature of music expressed in metaphors in the form "A is B" that is, "music is x."*[17] This is not a rhetorical figure, but a way of thinking: metaphors as special forms of images emphasize some details while suppressing others and, in doing so, express the structure of our thinking. When we say that good news is "music to my ears" we reveal substantial values which we attribute to music. (The clever reader certainly realized that this axis of Rice's is almost identical with the deepest layer of Merriam's model.)

Although Rice discusses music as a personal experience and the musical world of an individual, as an ethnomusicologist he does not ignore the in-

12   Shelemay 1997: 201.
13   Bauman 2000.
14   Rice 2003.
15   Rice 2003: 160.
16   For example, Shobe and Banis 2010.
17   Rice 2003: 163.

disputably collective nature of music. He suggests closer understanding of individual musical worlds because of our better understanding of the character of musical collectivity – and also human collectivity: how close are the listeners of the same operatic performance in their experiencing of the music and how close are those of a rock concert or participants in a Hare Krishna procession? Equally? Unequally? Why?

We still have not addressed the third axis: **place**. It is possible to think about the local anchoring of music in several principal directions. The most striking and loudest one comes from the idea of massive territorialization,[18] the phenomenon torn off from one concrete physical place as an accompanying feature of modernity. All of us are daily witnesses to this: not only the omnipresence of Coca Cola and Shell gas stations, but also souvenirs from Greece made in Indonesia... Arjun Appadurai adds further consequences of modernity to this, especially the influence of imagination in our lives (and possibilities of realizing this imagination to a large degree)[19], and tension between the global and the local. The cocktail mixed from these ingredients makes every place specific.

For investigation of this specificity, Appadurai offers five dimensions of "global cultural flows". They are not meant as different types of influences which form today's reality. Appadurai speaks about *deeply perspectival constructs.*[20] They are building stones of what he calls "imagined worlds," thus worlds which are established by historically constituted ideas of people and groups around the whole world.

The five dimensions are (a) *ethnoscapes* (by this Appadurai means...*persons who constitute the shifting world in which we live: tourists, immigrants, refugees, exiles, guest workers...); (b) technoscapes (...the global configuration... of technology and the fact that technology... now moves at high speeds across various kinds of previously impervious boundaries...); (c) financescapes (... the disposition of global capital that is now a more mysterious, rapid, and difficult landscape to follow than ever before...)*[21] These three dimensions are connected in an unforeseeable way or – regarding many other influences – even separated.

Both of the other -scapes are closely connected to the world of the imagination: (d) *mediascapes (... the distribution of electronic capabilities to produce and disseminate information (newspapers, magazines, television stations, and film-production studios... and the images of the world created by these media... while... they provide... large and complex repertoires of images, narratives, and ethnoscapes to*

---

18   Concept elaborated by Appadurai 1996, also discussed by Rice 2003.
19   In doing so, he follows Anderson 1983 and his concept of "imagined communities", i.e. communities created on the basis of imagination, not physical closeness.
20   Appadurai 1996: 33.
21   Appadurai 1996: 33.

viewers throughout the world, in which the world of commodities and the world of news and politics are profoundly mixed); (e) ideoscapes are related to the ideologies of states and the counter-ideologies of movements explicitly oriented to capturing state power or a piece of it... These ideoscopes are composed of elements of the Enlightenment worldview, which consists of a chain of ideas, terms, and images, including freedom, welfare, rights, sovereignty, representation, and the master term **democracy...**[22]

Appadurai's conception suited us for two reasons. The first was a certain convergence of points of view: we also saw technology (in the chapter on electronic dance music), commerce (in the chapter on commodification) and migration (in the chapter on identity) as important contemporary social phenomena which are strikingly expressed in music.

In addition, Appadurai's conception of a deep perspectival construct also suits freer application because it corresponds to the "metaphoric" nature of music, as it is called by Rice[23]. In other words, it is possible to look at music and also at phenomena that influence it from different perspectives. We used it in the introduction of different theoretical views, different schools.

We do not, however, want to give up the idea of local anchoring of music. (Here Appadurai's idea of tension between the local and the global, which characterizes different places, suits us well. For us, it means the possibility of looking for the specific character of Prague musical worlds.) Our initial decision to understand music not only as sound, but also as a social phenomenon, i.e. the sounds and people who produce and accept them, is substantial. In this case, we are primarily interested in how the people of our Prague musical worlds are connected to a concrete place, including the meanings they attribute to it. At the same time, we are convinced of the non-randomness of the location of a musical event: the shape of the space where music sounds is not random – musicians and listeners have chosen it and, moreover, physical boundaries co-form the event; the environment of the event is not random (as is shown in our "Walk along the Royal Road"); and, finally, the broad stage of Prague is certainly not random. This non-randomness, however, is formed by influences of different dimensions (historical, social, economic...) – and also our perspectives. We certainly do not present the Prague musical world in its constantly changing plasticity: we did not, in fact, intend to do so. Hopefully we have grasped some of its moments and perspectives.

---

22   Appadurai 1996: 35–36.
23   Rice 2003.

WRITING ABOUT THE MUSIC OF A CITY, SPECIFICALLY PRAGUE

Zuzana Jurková

For years I have been teaching a musical anthropology seminar at the Faculty of Humanities. In it the students learn how to research music as a social activity rather than as a "sound object." Because the faculty is located in Prague – and it is necessary to have "material" at hand – the majority of the research takes place in this city. Some like ethnomusicology so much that they continue with a bachelor's thesis, master's study in anthropology focusing on ethnomusicology, and sometimes even a doctorate. Thus we have assembled a lot of material about what is going on with music in Prague and also various ways of looking at it. At the same time, a sort of free platform[24] was formed at which we discussed various questions of ethnomusicology for years, where we invited guests[25] and where we organized various events,[26] so necessary for the acquisition of experience of broad horizons – because the ethnomusicologist must see that the music he listens to and understandably (!) considers to be the best is not the only right one. The fact that classmates like a completely different kind (or, even worse, only a slightly different kind) is not necessarily an expression of snobbism, ignorance or contemptible unmanliness. He must experience what Timothy Rice formulates in the following minimalist way: Music is X. That music is something different for everybody.

In 2009 or 2010 we decided that our "thesaurus" was sufficient for sharing. We wanted to share both the exciting amount of material and the various musics and surrounding "worlds" and also the exciting variety of views on it. From earlier experience we knew that writing "collectively" has its numerous

---

24   Recently formalized as the Institute for Ethnomusicology of the Faculty of Humanities, Charles University.

25   Our long-term lecturer is Adelaida Reyes (USA); Speranta Radulescu (Rumania), Victor Stoichita (France) and Irén Kertész-Wilkinson (UK) have repeatedly lectured here. Particularly legendary was a series of lectures by Bruno Nettl (2010). Since I do not keep a systematic database/chronicle of guests, I have likely forgotten someone.

26   Students were directly involved in the organization of several international conferences: Romani Music at the Turn of the Millennium (2003), Music and Minorities (2008), round-table Theory and Method in Urban Ethnomusicology (2011), international doctorate seminar (2011), International Summer School with students of the University of Pittsburg (2012).

At an ethnomusicology seminar

and sharp crags.[27] On the other hand, however, we wanted to preserve the distinctiveness of individual perspectives. Therefore – and also inspired by many ethnomusicological texts which use so-called interperspectivity or intersubjectivity[28] – we decided to combine two basic genres in the text of the book.

The first of these are like snapshots. In them, the authors attempt to transmit the experience of a musical event. And because the experience is always very subjective, we allow the personal voices of those who participated in the events to be heard. (Sometimes the personal history of learning the described musical world surfaces which, in our opinion, can help draw the reader in and also enlighten the personal perspective through which the author sees the world. We are aware that sometimes the very different tones of the texts can be confusing but we think that the transfer of the feeling of teamwork, in which the experience of the individuals is not lost, is worth a bit of effort in reading.) The snapshots, however, are not only verbalized emotion or mechanical description: in them, we try to capture those aspects of the event that we consider to be relevant for the perspective from which we present the event. At the same time, we begin with the presumption that the reader is not at home in the described world (in anthropological terminology, he is not an "insider"). Therefore, the description can sometimes seem very naïve, like some sort of

---

27 As a team, we wrote *Roads of Romani Music* in 2004 and, in 2008, texts and catalogue for the *Musika Etnika* exhibition for the National Museum.

28 A method using as many perspectives as possible. It is also proclaimed in the textbook which we use for our ethnomusicological seminar: Stone Sunstein – Chiseri-Strater, 2007.

school writing assignment. However, we have experienced that at least some world is completely unknown to everyone, and thus we needed and valued such "basic" description. A similar genre, however, is used in the majority of ethnographic or anthropological works. It enables us to look at the event through the eyes of an outsider and, at the same time, the author chooses the facts which s/he considers important from the overwhelming number of facts overall. For the best mediation of the event, we also add photographs. However, not all research sites were appropriate for taking pictures and not all the authors are good photographers, which is why the pictures vary in quality and quantity.

The second genre, presented for the most part in boxes distinguished by color, is "theoretical lenses". These most often communicate theoretical concepts through which we look at a musical event. It is self-evident that what happens can be viewed from various angles. Applied to research, this means the possibility of using different theories. The suitability of using a concrete theory, however, is proven by its explanatory power. We have thus chosen from an arsenal of available ethnomusicological or anthropological theories those which, in our opinion, illuminated these phenomena well. In some cases – e.g. in Lomax's case, used in connection with opera – we didn't want to avoid the presentation of a theory which already, in current ethnomusicological discourse, is rather deep beyond the horizon, but in its time it was very important. In the interest of a homogeneous style it was I who wrote all of the theoretical texts. Those which relate to the research of other authors, however, were collaborative efforts. The entire text was also discussed with all of the authors.

Aside from the fact that we structured the text into the two above-mentioned genres, we further stratified them so that the more detailed information, for example about musicians, is set off in small lettering and completely marginal comments appear in the form of footnotes along with references to the literature or other sources. We thus wanted to achieve the possibility of reading the book – perhaps repeatedly – on various levels: first, e.g., as fleeting familiarization with everything one can hear in Prague, then with an interest in understanding the ethnomusicological perspective, later with attention to accessible details. In our opinion, the division of the text also simplifies orientation –where to look for which type of information. Basic instructions concerning this paragraph to the reader are as follows: do not be afraid to skip over the small lettering to theoretical texts for explanations if you are not interested in the details.

WRITING ABOUT THE PRAGUE SOUNDSCAPE(S)

As is apparent from the introductory text, Prague and its soundscapes do not yet appear in clear contours, as a clearly profiled model. So our writing is also more of an examination of the topic; it is similar to the groping of blind men trying to know and describe an elephant.[29] The topics we use to introduce Prague - the elephant - definitely do not represent systematic categories, because we are unable to provide such profound systematicity.

At the same time, it is not a random ("aleatoric") choice of topics (although even such a choice would show something substantial). We set a few criteria. As mentioned above, our intention is to show music in Prague through the eyes and ears of an ethnomusicologist. That is why we tried, on the one hand, to capture events which take place here more frequently, and, at the same time, those in which, at least from our perspective, musical language and a musical event are very explicable through the cultural values of the community. The third criterion was a certain diversity regarding the presented styles as well as the discussed topics in order to show Prague as multidimensional as possible. However, it is clear from the following pages that none of the topics are isolated, just as no music - whether we think about its language or an event - is untouched by what is happening around it in contemporary Prague. This is exactly the interlocking that ascertained that we, groping blind men, are touching the same elephant. And with enough patience, the contours will appear more and more clearly.

Besides a certain representativeness, appropriateness (homogeneity of musical style and its cultural context) and diversity, we targeted one more goal. In addition to Prague musical events themselves, we also intend to introduce ethnomusicology - a discipline which aims to understand people through music and music through people. Individual topics provided the occasion to introduce various theoretical concepts which are, in the history of (musical) anthropology, of different degrees of importance, but, in our opinion, relevant for the given soundscape.

We step into the Prague soundscape as anthropology and ethnomusicology used to do, that is to say, by focusing on "those others." However, this is not because we consider the worlds of minorities and foreigners more interesting or important than the others. But here it is possible to observe several basic phenomena that will also be important for the other chapters. As for the material concerning Romani/Gypsy music, it is clear that the musical "world" arises through some sort of negotiation between musicians and listeners (whom Lévi-Strauss calls the "silent performers"). And here it is also apparent how musical language reflects those "negotiated" cultural values.

In the second part of the chapter, we focus on recent migrants. We concentrate on the fact that their musical production is a manifestation of their attempts to join the new environment. And because belonging is an important

---

29 This metaphor is used by Bruno Nettl in one of his books, Nettl, 2012: XIV.

component of personality, we come close to the term "identity," that is, to the deep question of what music can express about who we are.

The next three chapters are interconnected. The first of them deals with **music in relation to social stratification and the specialization connected to it**. If Prague tries to (re)present[30] itself by means of music (and mainly at the beginning of our research we were surprised at how little takes place in comparison to other metropolises),[31] then it is through art music. The simplest explanation seems to be the emphasis on the presentation of Prague as primarily a historical city. The ideal intersection of this representativeness of art music and the emphasis on nationhood, which is always so present in the Prague space, can be, for example, a performance of the opera *Rusalka* by Antonín Dvořák (the very same Dvořák who – at least in the Czech imagination – conquered the New World, and a recording of his symphony even reached the moon, a fact which the Czech media enjoy repeating) in the National Theater on National Avenue in the very center of the city at the most prestigious address. Here, one can view the musical style of the opera genre through Lomax's *cantometrics* method: it almost perfectly corresponds to the characteristics of a stratified and specialized society used in this method. Although today *cantometrics* is considered mainly as a sort of historical curiosity,[32] it would be a pity to disregard it, especially in connection to a topic that refers so much to history.

An accompanying feature of social stratification is usually **specialization**. While, until the beginning of the 20th century, this specialization in art music was manifested mainly in the sphere of interpretation, starting about 1920, the specialization also extends to the area of reception of art. "Modern" or "contemporary" art music becomes – because of its still unaccepted concepts – the preserve of specialists. The central figure in the introduction of these new concepts was John Cage. A beautiful illustration of the use of Cage's "new" approach to music, new sounds and emphasis on the specificity of place can be the "site-specific performance" of *The Lucid Dreams of Mr. William Heerlein Lindley* in the former sewage treatment plant in Bubeneč. The fact that there were only a few dozen attendees confirms the "special character" of such an event.

---

30 By this formulation I mean partly to point out the titles of events in Prague (Prague Spring, Prague Autumn, Music of the Prague Castle…) and also official events such as anniversary celebrations, where classical music is not exclusive, but it does dominate. Thirdly, there are events designated for not particularly interested tourists, that is, a sort of musical souvenir of Prague. We will discuss these in the chapter on musical commodification.

31 In the past years we have hardly ever come across the use of musical symbols as positive metaphors for non-musical reality, which is very common, for example, in Vienna. Only recently there appeared, e.g., the ad for Czech Airlines: "The Czech Republic, a Symphony of the Senses."

32 Lomax's philosophical starting point corresponded to inter-war comparative approaches, which compared cultural phenomena with only little regard to context.

The second topic, the topic of **music and rebellion**, is closely connected to the previous one through Turner's theory of *communitas* as a mode of social existence, complementary to a common stratified society. The theory of *communitas* can very easily be applied to the most famous phenomenon in the history of Czech musical rebellion, the group *The Plastic People of the Universe*. In the texts of the speaker of the group, Ivan "Magor" Jirous, can be found the concept of the **underground** as its *own special world existing apart from established society with a different internal charge, a different esthetic and consequently also a different ethic.*[33] Esthetics understandably corresponds to a peculiar musical language; ethics, among others, with social humiliation and a certain local exclusion which can even be seen in today's punk events at the Modrá Vopice Club or on Parukářka hill.

One everlasting question is related to musical rebellion: How rebellious is music if it maintains features of a rebellious musical style, but fills stadiums with listeners – members of the very system against which the music protests (and here and there even with its representatives)? When (thanks to the functioning system) it fills the bank accounts of its performers? Quietly and from a very official and non-rebellious place – the New Scene of the National Theater – Tom Stoppard answers this question with his play *Rock 'n' Roll* – a play which is, among other things, about the *Plastic People of the Universe*, a play in which the *Plastics* play "live", not only in Prague performances, but also in premieres abroad.

It is this last question which introduces the next chapter, which discusses the **commodification of music**, that is, the process by which music becomes primarily a product intended for earning money. We begin the chapter with Petr Zelenka's entertaining (and mildly frightening) film "Mňága: Happy End." This opens the key topics of the chapter: the influence of money (financial corporations are seen not only in the film but also in reality) both on the inhabitants of that world and on the shape of the music. The functioning of such a world is possible because of the new life philosophy of man (and also the understanding of music) as well as specific mechanisms connected with the dissemination of music. Part of it was described in the 1930s and 1940s by Theodor Adorno and, a half century later, the musicians of the KLF band made fun of them. Our snapshots confirm that these mechanisms are resistant to all ridicule – at least temporarily.

The variable which forms the basis of the sixth chapter is technology, specifically electronically generated sound, which substantially changed the shape

---

33 Jirous 2008: 7.

of music in many ways. Out of all of the forms of electronic music, we choose two genres of **electronic dance music (EDM)**, freetekno and psytrance. In them, we show two forms of an attempt to escape from the commercial reality described in the preceding chapter and to establish a non-commercial, non-anonymous, "free" world. A world created in closest symbiosis with technology – a sort of musical realization of Appadurai's *technoscape*. In connection with this attempt to escape, and also as a bridge to the following chapter, we acquaint the reader with Judith Becker's book *Deep Listeners*, which is a very complex and unconventional way of dealing with the relationships between music, emotion and trance.

It would be possible to discuss the connection between **music** and **spirituality**, which is the subject of the 7th chapter, from many angles. We open this chapter with a *harinam*, the procession of devotees of Hare Krishna through Prague. This event (by way of an unexpected link through techno music in a videoclip about the Prague Krishnas) connects this chapter to the preceding one. In addition, we take note of several phenomena in the *harinam* which are otherwise unusual in the Czech environment: the objectivistic understanding of the effect of music, the public presentation of spirituality, and the like.

Using the musical occasions of the autumn St. Wenceslas Festival, we show the dichotomy of "specialization" vs. generality (laity) which in today's Christian context to a certain extent overlaps with the concept of "music as art" vs. "music as spiritual practice." The activity around a gospel workshop opens up another dichotomy connected with the performance of music, that is, (in the words of Thomas Turino) the participants vs. presentation model. The way of performing music reveals the prevalent reasons why music actually sounds the way it does. In addition, here – mainly at a closing concert – a very evident snowballing of meanings or a relabeling of the musical genre. And along with this change in meaning for musicians and the public, the shape also changes. The eternal musical metamorphosis.

Although we did not create a sufficiently systematic theoretical model for the description of Prague musical worlds and the musical world of Prague, a few basic features emerged through the exposition of topics chosen on the basis of various criteria. The first of these is the blurring of various borders (in the concept of music, in style/genre, in the concept of musical sound...). This is a consequence of the merging of individual worlds or influences that cross the worlds, which is an unavoidable situation in a city – a dense and dynamic environment. It also justifies our concept of Prague as, to a certain extent, an integrated whole which we view from various perspectives.

A second significant finding is that new "worlds" arise through the attempt of the inhabitants to separate themselves – whether as a supporter of "new" music, which uses the language of concrete sounds thus far unused; as an aggressively shouting punk rebel protesting against the system; as a dancer at a techno party, escaping from the world of commerce, anonymity and limits to his own autonomous world created in symbiosis with technology; or as a participant in a Krishna procession trying, with the singing of mantras, to extricate himself from this ephemeral world... From this perspective, musical events of the new immigrants are the picture of a dynamic process in which its actors are looking for the shape of their own world. All of this corresponds well to the findings of a number of ethnomusicologists that music strengthens group identity by fostering internal values as well as separating them from their surroundings.

We have already published some of the texts in this book in various versions. Most were in the faculty journal *Lidé města/Urban People*: the introductory theoretical text Listening to the Voices of a City (Jurková 2012a), Myth of Romani Music (Jurková 2010), The Makropulos Case as a semiotic experience (Jurková-Jonssonová 2010) and Harinam in the Prague streets (Jurková-Seidlová 2011). Zita Skořepová Honzlová's texts in this book are also closely connected with her article in *Urban People* (Skořepová Honzlová 2012). Passages from the theoretical text about identity are part of my chapter in a book about national identity in Czech music (Jurková 2012b),and part of the texts about the lucid dreams of Mr. William Heerlein Lindley and John Cage were published in the *Journal of Urban Culture Research* (Jurková 2012c).

ACKNOWLEDGEMENTS

From the preceding text, it is clear that environment at the Faculty of Humanities of Charles University and its long-term financial support were of essential importance for the origin of this book.

For the writing of the texts we consulted a few colleagues, mainly those who understand the given fields most thoroughly. They were Petr Jansa, Jana Vozková, Dana Bittnerová, Hedvika Novotná, Michael Pospišil, Marek Šlechta, Jan Chmelarčík, Lily Císařovská, and Adelaida Reyes. We thank all of them sincerely. Many students took part in the discussions about the texts and in the proofreading – some of them for a longer period of time, some for only one or two semesters. Their participation is varied, but, in any case, not negligible. We are also grateful to them.

Not only the English version of this book, but also many of the original Czech versions of the text as well quite a few of our ethnomusicological activities would not have come into being without the selfless and patient work of Valerie Levy. We are eternally grateful to her for this.

MUSIC AND IDENTITY
Zuzana Jurková

In addition to music, the subject of this chapter is *identity* – a word which some would rather exclude from discussion because of its equivocality, almost amorphousness, while for others it is a key term in the social sciences. What deserves greater attention than to ascertain (or at least to attempt to ascertain) who we actually are?

Although, we sometimes waver between two positions, this time we will try to defend the second one. Before we go into a more detailed discussion of our understanding of identity, we would like to anticipate two of its basic features which influenced the shape of this chapter. The first is that identity binds a person to "his" group (while "his" has various meanings according to the dimensions of identity). The German historian and religious studies scholar Jan Assmann connects identity with so-called *connective structure:* "It establishes connections and commitments in two dimensions: social and temporal. It binds a person to his neighbor through a symbolic world of meaning which creates a shared space of experience, expectation and behavior whose connecting and obligatory power contributes to the development of understanding and intimacy... and, by that, establishes belonging or identity, which enables the individual to speak of 'us.'"[1]

The question of the connection of an individual to a group is crucial for ethnomusicologists – otherwise we would be able to speak only of musical preferences or activities of individuals (similarly, historical musicology until recently dealt mainly with the so-called great white men). However, we are convinced that individuals are connected (let us call it connective structure) to the "shared space of experience... and intimacy" with which they identify themselves.

The second basic feature of identity is the fact that concurrently with how it both *connects* – "us who are talking to each other" and also *separates* – "us" from "those others," those we do not understand. The dividing line is what we perceive as "other." And in fact, the question of what we perceive as distinctive

---

1   Assmann 2001: 20.

(the color of hair? eyes? religion? history?) provides important information about ourselves. [2]

As it will be apparent later, we do not accept Thomas Turino's[3] concept of identity uncritically, but will mention it here. Turino differentiates between the terms *self* and *identity. Self* is composed "of an entire quantity of *habits* (tendencies to repeat behavior, thinking or reactions under similar circumstances.)" In contrast to *self, identity* includes "a partial and changeable choice of habits and characteristics that we use for our own representation (shaped) both for oneself as well as for others and also those aspects which are perceived as characteristic of ourselves or others." And thus for Turino – as for us – the basis of identity is the aspiration to show who we are to those around us and to recognize those who do not belong to us.

The first part of this chapter, "The myth of Romani music in contemporary Prague," is primarily an example of which aspects non-Roma consider representative of Roma – those closest and oldest "others" – and how "Romaniness" moved and moves into the hands of Roma.

In the second part, which arises from Zita's long-term research on the musical activities of foreigners in Prague, we wish to understand what the musical representation of various migrants says about their "negotiation" of their own identity with those around them.

WHAT IS IDENTITY ACTUALLY ABOUT?

In the past decade many researchers in the social sciences and the humanities agree with Rogers Brubaker that **identity** is a term which is *too ambivalent, too torn between a "hard" and a "soft" meaning, essentialist connotation and constructivist qualifier for it to be conveniently able to serve demands for social analysis.*[4] Let us briefly look at its developmental stages so that we can then try to find a shape which could be useful for the understanding of some Prague musical events.[5]

Credit for the popularity of the question of identity goes to the psychoanalyst Erik H. Erikson, for whom personal identity is the inner and deep "core" of the human personality, a core which evolves, but whose basis is feeling... *enabling the individual to experience his own I as something that defines continuity*

---

2   The book "Ethnic Groups and Boundaries," edited by Fredrik Barth (1998) is the classic text on this subject.

3   Turino 2008: 101–102.

4   Brubaker 2004: 29.

5   I am grateful to Zita Skořepová Honzlová for many materials on the topic of identity.

and identity and to act accordingly.[6] After Erikson, the term identity switches over to the realm of the social sciences: it asserts itself in the theory of referential groups (Merton), in social constructivism (Berger and Luckmann), among the interactionists (mainly Erving Goffman) and in social anthropology. There – understandably – a strong accent on the collective side of identity is found which necessarily has to do with the dynamics that form identity by means of inter-human relations. Because – according to Jenkins – the basis of humanity is relationships and interactions, meetings with other people are therefore the fundamentals for shaping identities: According to Berger and Luckmann, identity is always the result of *the dialectics of the relation of the individual and society*[7] and in regard to the constant socialization of man, his identity is constantly renewing and changing.

What Erikson and others after him drew attention to is worth recalling: that the "problem of identity" is a problem of the (post-) modern world. Judith Howard,[8] for example, presumes that identity, based earlier rather on ascribed statuses than achieved ones[9], does not present the individual with possibility of choice and thus of both frustration and lack of clarity which are connected with choice. In other words: the more we ask about identity, the more complex and complicated the answer is.

Similarly, although based on other data, authors from the field of inter-cultural psychology see a change of identity: real "subcultures" appear only in connection with industrialization, so there is mutual influence and acculturation among them.[10] Their members, exposed to manifestations and values of various subcultures, must take a position or choose from among them: they become active agents. At this moment, **identity as a dynamic process**, which is the result of individual consideration, evaluation and behavior, appears. The above-mentioned Erving Goffman with his famous text *The Presentation of Self in Everyday Life* often appears in connection with this term.[11] In it, the author

---

6   Erikson 2002: 41.

7   Berger, Luckmann 1999: 171.

8   Howard 2000.

9   The American anthropologist R. Linton began to use the term "status" for man's position in the social system. He differentiates between statuses which are ascribed, more or less unchanged (sex, age…) and achieved (education…).

10   In agreement with Herskowitz (1936) I define it thus: "Acculturation comprehends those phenomena which result when groups of individuals having different cultures come into continuous first-hand contact with subsequent changes in the original culture pattern on either or both groups."

11   It is as if the Czech translation of the title *We All Play Theater* considered Goffman's critics right to state that he presents people as cynical and superficial. Let us emphasize that Goffman's metaphor is sociological, not psychological and Goffman does not understand "play acting" as some sort of pretending something that is not, but as choosing from one's

presents a dramatic metaphor of society in which the individual plays the role of self-presentation for others, who are his audience, and with whom the image of his role is negotiated. At the same time each is, however, also a member of the audience, who evaluate and thus influence others' performance of their roles. It is self-evident that the "role of an actor" and the "role of the audience" refer not only to the behavior of the individual, but basically determine the behavior of the entire collective.

This concept of identity, with its emphasis on immediate change and also on the agreement of the "players" and "audience" is narrowly connected with questions of "ascribed" and "achieved/appropriated" music, which Speranta Radulescu discusses in her article about Romani music. She claims that *identification, attribution and assumption of the ethnic attribution of musics are only local and temporary... which, however, does not mean that they are less worthy of our attention for that reason.*[12] How is the **relationship between music and identity** considered from the ethnomusicological perspective?

Apart from the fact that music is considered an important means of the integration of man with himself on the individual level,[13] it is also – as a social activity *par excellence* – ideal for expressing collective identity.[14] As ethnomusicologists[15] often prove, sometimes it even serves as a foundation for this collective identity; in any case, it is an important "agent."

Furthermore: if we use the vocabulary of the interactionists, including Goffman, identity is relational and situational: it depends on the relationship with whom and when we claim a given element. (If we looked through the semiotic optic of Peirce and Turino – as mentioned in the next chapter – the same would be expressed by an *interpretant* which determines the relationship between the sign and the object. This also closely copies the above-mentioned assertion of Speranta Radulescu.) From the available arsenal of musical styles, ways of interpretation, etc., I choose the ones that I wish to represent myself

---

own "repertoire of roles": the role of the mother of a small child, the role of a certain professional position, the role of a customer, etc.

12   Radulescu 2003: 84.

13   Turino 2008: 3 ff. presents several arguments about the integrative role of art. One comes from the anthropologist Bateson (1972) and his ideas of perceptions of the world on various levels, further from the concept of *flow* by the psychologist Csikszentmihaly about the extra-rational experiences during the pursuit of art, mainly music. The third circle of arguments is connected with the philosopher and semiotician G.S. Peirce. Turino sees the basis of personal integration in "semantic snowballing": the same musical activity style evokes various reactions on various occasions and has various meanings to the listener. At the same time, however, previous meanings are not quite lost, and thus during the repeated emergence of the composition, the listener connects various historical levels of personality.

14   *Music and dance are key to identity formation because they are often public presentations of the deepest feelings and qualities that make a group unique.* Turino 2008.

15   E.g., Turino 2008, Shelemay 2001.

and about which I am convinced that the others – the "audience of my identity performance" – accept as my calling card. If that happens, it connects me with those who have the same calling cards and it differentiates me from the others. However the connection will be valid only for here and now (or at least temporarily).

It is not surprising that Erik Erikson (1902–1994) – the illegitimate child of a Jewish mother in pre-war Germany, refugee in Denmark and later in the USA – highlighted the question of identity. The experiences related of many migrants and the literature proclaim repeatedly how closely man is tied to that "shared space of experience and intimacy" and how essentially deracination weighs down on them. With a change of environment – not only territorial, but mainly social – it is necessary to a certain degree to create a new identity for oneself: for a new "audience" and with new ways which are understandable to the environment. A basic element of the newly created identity is also the relationship to its previous home as well as to its current location.[16]

---

16 Adelaide Reyes (1999) deals with this problem using the example of Vietnamese refugees in the United States.

THE MYTH OF ROMANI MUSIC IN CONTEMPORARY PRAGUE

Zuzana Jurková

I. MYTH

It should be clear that this text is about Romani music that is played in Prague today. First, however, I would like to explain how I understand the word "myth." Here it has two – almost contradictory – meanings. The first one is its most common/colloquial use: something unreal, opposing reality (whatever we understand by "reality"), some sort of chimera, and thus, in connection with Romani music, what non-Roma naively and erroneously imagine by the term "Romani music." It would be possible to present many examples. Here is a striking one from a recent ethnomusicological conference: Speranta Radulescu asked two Romani musicians to listen to two pieces of music by two famous non-Romani composers intended as explicit "representations" of Romani music: Ravel's Rhapsody *Tzigane* and the introductory section of Enescu's *Impressions*. Neither one perceived them at all as "Gypsy."[17] And in fact, this text partially deals with non-Romani concepts of Romani music.

At the same time, however, we use the term "myth" the way Bronislaw Malinowski (1884–1942) used it. According to Malinowski, myths are a kind of "charter for today". "These stories create an integral part of culture…, dominate and rule many cultural features, create the dogmatic (primitive) backbone of civilization."[18] As we shall see, the more or less dogmatic concept of what Romani music is has co-created and continues to co-create its shape.

II. THE MYTH OF MUSIC

In 1923, Leoš Janáček (1854–1928) composed his first string quartet, the "*Kreutzer Sonata*." Although originally (based on sketches of the composition worked on starting in 1909) he wrote a composition for violin and piano, eventually he

---

17   Radulescu 2009.
18   From the lecture "Myth in Primitive Psychology", 1925, cited by Bowie 278.

wrote it for a classical quartet. This quartet of strings – two violins, viola and cello – was used by composers for more than one hundred years as a "diarist" ensemble, to which it was possible to entrust the most intimate thoughts. In addition, the next Janáček string quartet, one of his last compositions, was called "Intimate Letters" (originally "Love Letters") and it was the most emotional declaration of the old composer to his last love, Kamila Stösslová. Indeed, it is not possible to imagine a more appropriate interpreter for a most personal message: the homogenous instrumental combination evokes the impression of uninterrupted intimacy; string instruments capable of reacting to the player's slightest impulse seem perfectly ideal for the expression of those most subtle emotions. Janáček subscribed to this concept. He used the classical instrumental make-up and also the common four-movement form. However, he handled the individual movements his own way – not only as far as tempo is concerned, but in his entire musical language: his work with musical motifs,[19] harmony and generally work with color,[20] and primarily a maximum of expression. Each tone sounded as if it expressed the most varied shades of joy or sadness, despair or resignation. As Milan Kundera writes precisely (and expressively): *for Janáček only tone that is an expression, that is an emotion, has a right to exist.*[21]

Janáček's string quartet, the *"Kreutzer Sonata,"* was already the third link in the chain – a chain which very clearly encompasses a change in the concept of music during the last century and a half.

At its beginning, in 1803, Ludwig van Beethoven (1770–1827) the last classical composer with an inclination toward Romanticism, composed the *"Kreutzer Sonata"* for violin and piano. The composition is famous for its technical demands; however, despite the fact that Beethoven's musical language was no longer symmetrical in the Classicist style, like the music of his predecessors, only rarely today would this sonata be called unusually emotional or even passionate.

The second link in the chain is the eponymous novella by Leo Tolstoy (1829–1910). One of the basic themes here is passion, against which the narrator of the book argues for his life story in which passion, at first pretended, then let out like a genie from a bottle and nourished by music, ruins lives. At the end of the book, the main character is emotionally (understand erotically) aroused by Beethoven's composition, during which she plays the piano accompaniment

19 Janáček uses some themes of the Beethoven sonata to work with them in his own distinct way, almost as with living beings.
20 In the fourth movement there is, for example, a passage which is markedly reminiscent of the last scene of Katya Kabanova, the solo aria of Katya and the backstage chorus.
21 Kundera: 2004: 26.

for a friend with whom she begins an extra-marital relationship; the husband
– similarly emotionally aroused – kills her.

Tolstoy appears here like a prophet warning against the destructive effects of passion, passion evoked and strengthened by the music. Too late. In 1889, there was no longer the strength that would conquer the idea, maximally developed and supported by Romanticism, about both sovereignty and the "sanctification" of emotion/passion – and also of their close connection to music.

Even if we did not know anything about Janáček's such romantically empathetic relationship to the heroines of his operas Katya, Jenufa and Emilia, and even if we did not know the line from his correspondence relating to his first string quartet, *I had in mind a poor woman, abused, beaten, beaten to death, as the Russian writer Tolstoy wrote about her in his Kreutzer Sonata*,[22] from the first notes of the music – the painful chord of the string instruments, and in general the entire Janáček language, full of dynamic and tempo changes which are the very essence of emotion – clearly convey whose side he is on. Away with Apollonian discipline! Feeling/passion/emotion is everything.[23]

It is difficult to imagine anything else: Janáček's personality, as if it were the embodiment perhaps of all the main Romantic ideas – from the close connection to folk culture through maximally personal and creative individualism and long-term social non-recognition to numerous emotional outbursts at women. (Incidentally, Janáček's composition was not the last in the above-mentioned chain; in 2000 the Dutch writer Margriet de Moor wrote a romantic novel with the same title, referring to all of its "predecessors.")

But why am I presenting Janáček and the whole chain leading to the rise of his first string quartet in the context of music and myth? (My own interest in Janáček's music is certainly not a sufficient reason to set him apart in an essay about the myth of music in an urban environment.) For two reasons. The first of them is the assumption that music DEFINITELY DOES NOT HAVE TO BE a "language of feeling," but it may be almost anything else (as is shown, by the way, in many places in this book). Thus the connection between music and emotion or even passion is one of those petrified ideas that shape human behavior – it is one of the dominant myths of our time.

The Gregorian chant, Johann Sebastian Bach with his contemporary relevant approach to music praising the glory of God (... *as with all music, so in the basso continuo there should be nothing else but the final and last goal which is*

---

22 Quoted according to Havlík 2000.
23 I also agree, however, with Kundera's characterizing Janáček as an "antiromantic" – but in the strict sense of Kundera, who understands romanticism as a false, "romantic" view of the world.

God's glory and recreation of thought. Where this is not respected, no real music will arise, but only hellish noise, and bad fiddling will be heard)[24], or – along with many others – the unemotional conceptualism of John Cage, whom we will discuss in the next chapter. And, of course, numerous examples come from outside of Europe: music as sound realization of the heavenly order, that is, of the universal order in China; music as a kind of transformation from one type of being to another among the Amazon Indians; music as bringing memories of people or places among the Northern European Saami into the present or as an objective device for reaching the coveted "illumination" of thought.

A second reason for the introduction of the Janáček example is the illustration of the complexity of the musical phenomenon according to the Merriam model. Music, at least artistic music, has in the past century become an event which is excluded from the common, profane (in the Romantic concept of the low and pragmatic) world, and it has reached the "higher" world of "sacred" emotions. This concept can be read well in the sphere of human behavior relating to music, for example, of a festive environment in which music is performed, or from the clothing of the musicians and listeners. (Tailcoats or morning coats of musicians during afternoon concerts sometimes strike the eye.) Another striking related characteristic is the sophistication of the musical language. The creation of a musical work is not commonly accessible to amateurs – it demands special training, just like the performance of the pieces these specially trained composers created. Extraordinariness, exclusion from normal life is expressed here, both with technical demands on the performer (who thus stands as a romantic hero outside of the majority society) and also a special "unnatural" quality of musical sound (one is strongly aware of it when one unexpectedly hears opera singing: in a daily environment a surprising sound, unlike anything else).

In the resulting musical sound both tendencies, which are to a certain extent contradictory, are present in our concept of music: disciplined refinement on the one hand, and declared – in the framework of convention performed – emotionality on the other hand.

It is now possible to insert a picture of what is presented in Prague today as Romani/Gypsy music and dance into these initial thoughts about the character of music in general and its form in Western artistic music tradition specifically.

---

24   J. S. Bach 1738 – see Michels 2000: 101.

III. THE MYTH OF ROMANI MUSIC IN PRAGUE

In 2008 (I did my research from May to November), I decided to investigate what was playing in Prague under the heading Romani/Gypsy music (songs, dances) and materials written in English as Gypsy/Gipsy music.[25] In other words, I am interested in what Praguers imagine Romani/Gypsy music to be or what they call it. An attempt at possible delimitation through genre or style based on our preconceptions would necessarily founder, as we point out not only using examples from collected material, but also the older experience of other authors.[26] My point of departure was publicly available materials (cultural programs, flyers, Internet ads) announcing live performances. It is surely possible that I was unaware of some performances, but I presume this did not happen often.

The other type of material that interested me consisted of available recordings, in whose title or genre category the word Romani/Gypsy/Gipsy appeared.

Events that were connected with Gypsy/Romani music were of two types: 1) regularly repeated performances and 2) one-time performances.

1.

a) Once a year, during the last week in May, the World Romani *Khamoro* festival takes place in Prague. It is one of the five category A metropolitan festivals such as the Prague Spring. In 2008 *Khamoro's* tenth anniversary took place May 25–31. Besides seven concerts (the premiere with two Czech groups, three called Gypsy jazz, three concerts of traditional Romani music; in them there were 13 bands from eight countries), there were also a Music and Minorities international ethnomusicological conference, a Spanish flamenco workshop in the Zambra studio,[27] four exhibitions and two film showings.[28]

b) Once a week, on Sundays, the popular Lesser Quarter music club Popocafépetl presents so-called *Gipsy Nights*, during which two rompop bands, *Bengas* and *Gitans*,[29] alternate.

c) Also once a week, on Thursdays, in the Zambra dance center in Vinohrady women from 21 to 48 years old meet and eagerly learn "Gypsy dancing."[30]

---

25 In this text I do not deal with an analysis of the terms "Gypsy/Romani", though I am convinced that this is a promising research topic.

26 e.g. Reyes 1982.

27 We will also discuss the Zambra studio in connection with Gypsy dance courses; flamenco courses are not usually advertised in connection with Romani/Gypsy music.

28 For details, see www.khamoro.cz.

29 For details, see www. popocafepetl.cz.

30 I have details about the Gypsy dance course at Zambra from my student Pavlina Holcová,

World Roma festival Khamoro

d) Every week from Wednesday to Sunday in the restaurant "U sedmi andělů" on Jilská Street in the Old Town there is a trio of Roma who play violin, cimbalom and double bass. The evenings are advertised as *Today Live Gipsy music.*

2.

a) In August, the Theater without Balustrades reprised[31] the musical *Gypsies Go to Heaven.* To a great extent, the performance copies the famous Russian film from 1976 which can also still be bought on DVD. A CD of the performance has been published with the songs from the show. Ida Kelarová is credited in the program as the author of the musical arrangement; her band *Romano Rat* also accompanies the singers on the CD.

b) As part of the "Prague Autumn" classical music festival,, three concerts of the Budapest Gypsy Symphony Orchestra, also called A Hundred Gypsy Violins, took place on September 20 and 21. This orchestra has been part of the "Prague Autumn" every year since 2003.[32]

---

who not only goes dancing there, but is also carrying out research about Gypsy dance for her bachelor's thesis.

31 The premiere took place on April 15, 2004.

32 After the first concert there appeared in *Romano Džaniben* an interview with the band leader and first violinist, Sándor Rigó-Buffó, see *Romano Džaniben*, jevend 2003, pp. 208–211.

c) On October 18 the Strašnice Theater premiered a "dance-theater project/ social specific theater"[33] – "Gypsy Suite". In the performance, several songs by the late Romani singer Jan Áču Slepčík are heard; the performance was dedicated to him.

d) On November 8, in the Abaton club in Libeň, the autumn part of the well-known musical festival Sázava Fest (the more popular part of which was held in the summer) took place. As the main performer, the popular Romani rapper Gipsy.cz appeared here with a repertoire from his two latest CDs (see below).[34]

The second field was music media. I was interested in what was immediately for sale in physical form (thus avoiding getting entangled in global Internet shopping); my basic idea was that recordings that were available demonstrated greater interest.

In the category of "Romani music", I found recordings of a favorite Slovak band *Diabolské husle,* "Devil's violin of Berky-Mrenica: Gypsy Dance" and "Devil's violin: Greetings from Slovakia."

The term "Gypsy" is connected with two performers of Dvořák and Bendl's *Gypsy songs* and *Gypsy melodies* (Roman Janál[35] and Magdalena Kǒzená[36]), the Brno funky band *Gulo čar* CD entitled *Gipsy Goes to Hollywood,* altogether seven different recordings of the French *Gipsy Kings,* the pop band *Triny* with its *Gypsy Streams* CD, three CDs of the above-mentioned rapper *Gipsy.cz,* that is, *Rýmy a blues, Romano hip hop* and *Reprezent,* and also Lagréne Birelli, an exponent of Gypsy jazz.

Labeled as "romano" are the CD *Staré slzy,* one of the latest CDs of Ida Kelarová and *Romano Rat,* a mixture of genres and performers of the "Most beautiful Gypsy songs/ *Jekhšukareder Romane giľa,*" and *Gipsy Way,* the newest CD of the violinist Pavel Šporcl and *Romano stilo.*

Besides the above-mentioned categories, but clearly presented as Romani music, are also the two latest recordings of Věra Bílá and her group *Kale* (who, however, have not played together since 2005), *Rovava* and *C'est comme ça,* and also a CD entitled *Dža* by the *Bengas* band.

---

33 Quoted from the invitation: To the question of what it means, the authors of the production explained that it is a theatrical work which strikingly reflects a social theme, here the Romani question (from the historiographic and comparative perspective)."

34 The popularity of Gipsy.cz culminated in the first half of 2009, when he played and sang at the Days of European Culture in Prague (Get a Taste of Europe) in March in Prague. He was sent via Czech television as a representative of the Czech Republic to the international musical competition, the Eurovision Song Contest, etc.

35 *Gypsy Melodies.*

36 *Songs My Mother Taught Me.*

SOUNDSCAPES

At first glance it seems that what I gathered represents a whole continuum of possible musical approaches to the "Gypsy" topic. Despite this, I will try to sort them out according to Kay Kaufman Shelemay's above-mentioned concept of *soundscapes*. The resulting groups show a certain coherence, from the basic concepts, to human behavior and to the musical sound. At the same time, however, it is true that the basic feature of *soundscapes*, relating to their continual variability, is their mutual influence.

In the material presented, I see three *soundscapes* that have existed for some time and one newly forming (at least in the Czech lands). I label it according to the original performer-listener pair. This pair, however, determined the goal of the music performed – and it formed (among others) the basic features of musical language.

"WHO FOR WHOM" AS KEY

We can locate a *soundscape* most easily through an encounter with a specific musical performance... (The best tangible traces of *soundscape* in human behavior and musical sound are there. Here one can deduct much about basic concepts.) To better understand a *soundscape*, we need to attend repeated events and to gather a range of additional information about their sound, setting, and significance.[37]

1. GADJE FOR GADJE ABOUT ROMA
Magdalena Kožená: *Songs My Mother Taught Me*

Magdalena Kožená, undoubtedly the most famous Czech opera and concert singer abroad today, chose songs by composers from her native land for her "personal" CD. Near its beginning there are three songs from the famous Dvořák cycle *Gypsy Melodies*, op. 55: "Songs My Mother Taught Me," "The Strings are Tuned" and "And the Wood is Quiet All Around."

On the recording can be heard, first, the mournful motif of the piano; then it is repeated and developed by the highly cultivated voice of the famous singer (so unlike untrained or folk singing); she sings of the feelings of a Gypsy mother, song, music and dance, sadness, nature and freedom. It is easy to imagine a live performance during which this beautiful and always perfectly

---

37 Kaufman Shelemay 2006: xxxv.

dressed woman leans on a shiny concert grand piano played by a man in a black jacket. The audience in the hall, dressed somewhat less elegantly than the performers, listens quietly; some have a program in their laps in which they can check the text (which is not always easy to understand). For the majority of the listeners, the music undoubtedly evokes some emotions, apart from the fact that the listeners are enthusiastic about the singer's performance and at the end they applaud enthusiastically.

This *soundscape* is undoubtedly the oldest of those discussed: Goethe (1749–1832) and Pushkin (1799–1837) had already written about what Gypsies experienced (more precisely, how non-Gypsies imagine what Gypsies experienced). The image of Gypsies/Roma ideally corresponded to the Romantic values of the time: passion, abandon – and frequent professional connection to music, which in the contemporary point of view meant their status as "artists" strengthened this Romantic image even more. It is not surprising that Gypsy literary inspiration appealed so much to the Romantic composers Carl Maria von Weber (1786–1826) and Mikhail Glinka (1804–1857) to begin with, and in our times ending, e.g., with Sylvie Bodorová (b. 1954) and her composition *Gila Rome* (1980). In addition, the famous Russian film *Gypsies Go to Heaven* (1976), based on the novel *Makar Chudra* (1892) by Maxim Gorky and its subsequent innumerable variations are proof of the long-lasting popularity of this romantic myth.

The musical language of this *soundscape* is initially closely attached to mainstream musical language: not only do Antonín Dvořák in his songs or Giuseppe Verdi in his operas (Troubadour) not use Romani music idioms, but Janáček also does not deviate from his musical speech in his later The Diary of One Who Disappeared (1916) in the singing of the Gypsy girl Zefka. Specific musical language in connection with the Roma appears in the music of Franz Liszt (1811–1886): exotic intervals or scales with augmented second (since his time in musical theory denoted as "Gypsy major" and "Gypsy minor") evokes the Romantic image of some extraordinary thing, use of rubato rhythm which is not subjugated to regular meter, i.e. the free treatment of time. Liszt's relation to the music of the Roma was, however, exceptional, mainly thanks to his connection to Hungarian culture. In it, Romani musicians had the exceptional position of bearers and guardians of the (musically expressed) national specificity. Besides, Liszt was in relatively close contact with the contemporary expansion of Hungarian "Gypsy bands," whose style of playing he minutely detailed in the first systematic book about the music of the Roma.[38]

---

38   Liszt 1859.

Liszt's influence is important for this *soundscape* in one more sense: in his welcoming opening to the "other." This way, more or less strong influences of music of the Roma inspired classical composers, e.g., Liszt's compatriot Béla Bartók.

The essence of this *soundscape* nevertheless remains emotionally satisfying to listeners more or less accustomed to the idioms of classical music and, at the same time, expecting something exotic. Therefore, for example, in *Gypsy Suite*, which is dedicated to the memory of the Romani songster Jan Áču Slepčík, his music and singing are not sufficient: for a "real" impression the directors had to supplement it with a romantic solo violin played, moreover, by a Rom in red shoes.

2. ROMA FOR GADJE
One hundred Gypsy violins
Rudolfinum, September 20, 2008, at 4 p.m.

Within the framework of the "Prague Autumn" classical music festival, in the Rudolfinum, the most prestigious concert hall in Prague, three concerts of the *Budapest Gypsy Symphonic Orchestra*, also called *One hundred Gypsy violins*,[39] are taking place. Like every year, all three are sold out in advance, and this is even despite the fact that tickets in the orchestra cost about a thousand crowns.

The audience is extraordinarily varied, from parents and grandparents with children to youths to senior citizens. There are only a few Roma in the auditorium.

With a ten-minute delay, which is not too common in classical music concerts, 100 musicians, among them two women – in white shirts, black pants or skirts and red or blue vests – arrive on stage. (Later it will become clear that the blue vests belong to the soloists – besides violinists, there is also one clarinet player and one cimbalom player.) For the second half of the evening, the players put on classic black suits. Except for nine clarinets, the orchestra contains only string instruments: six large Hungarian cimbaloms, and mainly violins, violas, cellos and double basses.

The majority of the compositions on the program can be heard at classical music concerts, but most often as encores or as "light" concert numbers: Monti's Czardas, Sarasate's *Gypsy Melodies [Zigeunerweisen]*, the *Thunder and Lightning* polka or The *Blue Danube* waltz by Johann Strauss or the *Radetsky*

---

39   The orchestra, founded in 1985, was originally called the "100-strong Budapest Gypsy Orchestra."

The Budapest orchestra One Hundred Gypsy Violins

March by Johann Strauss, Sr., and Khachaturian's *Saber Dance* from the ballet *Gayaneh*. The second type of compositions are those written by contemporary composers especially for the orchestra (e.g., *Gypsy Fire* by Zoltán Horwath) which show the specific qualities of the orchestra, mainly their instrumental virtuosity balancing on the edge of performability combined with proverbial (perhaps well feigned) temperament.

Numerous members of the audience enthusiastically applauding after every number confirm the constant attraction of the tradition whose roots are in Hungarian and Slovak restaurants and coffee houses of the 19th century. Still today it is possible to find isolated groups with that original, chamber-like appearance in Prague. The context of the city of the 21st century, however, gives it a rather different character and meaning.

TODAY LIVE GIPSY MUSIC AT 8 P.M.
Restaurant U 7 andělů (Seven Angels), Jilská Street, Old Town
November 22, 2008

If you type "Live Gypsy music in Prague" into Google, the first result will not be the web page of the Romani festival *Khamoro* or some popular Romani group, but rather, "Prague's Best Restaurants."[40] Of these fourteen restaurants, undoubtedly aimed primarily at foreign clientele, twelve of them offer "live music." My personal research, however, revealed that "live Gypsy music" (in any shape) is not offered by any of them. On the internet advertisement for "Prague's Best Restaurants", the offer of live Gypsy music is clearly part of their image.

"Live Gypsy Music," however, is surely possible to track down in Prague. It is announced on a board (in English) on the door of the *Seven Angels* restaurant, which is in the most historic center of Prague, only a few yards from Old Town Square. It is hard to imagine a place with a greater concentration of foreign tourists – and obviously the announcement is meant for them. The main room to the right of the entrance is evidently supposed to impress you in two ways: through its antiquity (the date 1392 above the entrance is in bold, patinated painting, the whole place with historic (or historicized) furnishings; and luxury (most of the little tables are only for two, but are closely lined up so that the impression of *séparé* is hardly convincing; large, richly decorated mirrors reflect the flames of candles; in comparison to the little tables, strikingly large wine glasses...). The relatively high prices for average food and mainly for drinks correspond to this.

We are the only Czechs among the guests. Couples in ordinary clothing prevail; a group of youths are dining at the larger table. In a little alcove off the main room, at the entrance to the cloakroom, there are three musicians in dark suits and white shirts: a cimbalom player at a large Hungarian pedal instrument; behind him a bass player; in front – nearest to the guests – a violinist. He also reacts to the (sparse and lukewarm) reactions of the guests. During one of the breaks, I learn in an interview with the musicians that they are brothers from a musical family from the Slovak-Hungarian border.

Their repertoire is very similar to the repertoire of the Budapest Gypsy Symphony Orchestra. The *Radetsky March*, the *Blue Danube* waltz, a melody from *Carmen*, and the Jewish *Hava nagila* which is popular even among Gypsy bands of this type... and, in addition, jazz compositions and Suk's *Song of Love*.

The *soundscape* around Gypsy coffee-house cimbalom bands (which sometimes play with a clarinet or its metal cousin, the *tárogato*, as another melodic instrument) has a rather different character. The music in it is not art that communicates emotion, but a craft – a craft serving to give the guests of the coffee houses or restaurants a good time. An auditorily undemanding repertoire is connected to this purpose. Listeners value Romani musicians for their perfect

40 www.pragueexperience.com/restaurants/highlights/restaurants_live_music.asp (June 12, 2009).

technique and then for the mastery of their craft (even if an adequate dose of emotion, mediated by Roma as their romanticized incarnation, is also expected). The Romani community traditionally valued its coffee-house musicians for their ability to earn a relatively high financial reward.

In Prague at the beginning of the 21st century, this *soundscape* takes various shapes. Symphonic music listeners are satisfied with a less demanding repertoire. The violin virtuoso and showman Pavel Šporcl spices up his performances (and discographies) with something unusual, that is, playing along with a real "Gypsy cimbalom band"[41]; their repertoire is easy to predict: Monti, Sarasate, Khachaturian, Strauss... And it also accommodates tourists looking for "genuine, old-fashioned atmosphere" in Prague with which, perhaps in their imaginations, the Austro-Hungarian coffee-house band can distantly correspond.

41   See booklet CD Pavel Šporcl + *Romano Stilo*.

3. ROMA (NOT ONLY) FOR THEMSELVES: ROMPOP[42]
Gipsy Nights: *Bengas*
Popocafépetl Club
October 26, 2009, at 8 p.m.

Popocafépetl on Újezd in the Lesser Quarter of Prague has several namesakes, but this is the only one to have regular music programs: on Mondays, Havana Nights, on Fridays and Saturdays, Friday/Saturday Dance Fever, and on Sundays, Gipsy Nights. On these nights, two rompop bands – *Gitans* and (the better known) *Bengas* alternate.

The club occupies the whole basement of an old house on the main Lesser Quarter street, right next to an elegant Thai restaurant. But despite its attractive location, its interior resembles many of the usual music clubs: unplastered stone walls, bare wooden tables with the club logo. The main room with a bar (where prices are surprisingly low) and only a hint of a stage at the shorter wall; in an alcove, the mixer. The next room is acoustically connected to the main room. On the other side of the staircase, where the music sounds much weaker, there are two quieter rooms marked as a "wine cellar", which today are almost empty.

A half hour before the beginning, the main room is completely full. Most of the audience consists of young people between 20 and 25 years old, often in hip hop hoodies, but also in shiny disco tops. In addition to Czech, you can hear English and French; the club is a frequent destination of foreign students who are in Prague on an Erasmus exchange program. Shortly before the announced beginning, two groups of Roma arrive and clamor to be seated in front of the stage.

Bengas[43] (Devils) are playing this time with three guitars, one bass guitar, a keyboard and three different sets of percussion instruments. Although the group acknowledge various sources of inspiration,[44] their musical language is relatively homogeneous: a dense fabric of guitar sound; above it solo masculine singing in Romani, the choruses alternating with parallel part singing. There are short instrumental introductions and interludes in which there may be virtuoso playing. Lucid phrasing, no great dynamic or tempo changes. The musical style of the group is undoubtedly influenced by the *Gipsy Kings*, with whom *Bengas* played in 2004 during their Prague concert.

---

42 I have already devoted a separate in-depth article to an analysis of rompop – Jurková 2008.
43 See www.bengas.net.
44 On their web pages they mention, in addition to their own compositions, "Eastern chastushki, czardases, Russian and Hungarian songs of the Roma, Balkan folklore, Arab and Spanish rhythms" as part of their repertoire (July 15, 2009).

After 8 p.m., not only are all the places taken (including a few newly placed tables and room at the bar), but people are also standing between the tables. During the music they sway to the rhythm. After each composition they applaud or whistle favorably. Today *Bengas* are clearly the most popular group playing *rompop*. This term[45] originated in the 1970s and refers to a fusion of traditional music played and sung by the Roma for themselves with elements of contemporary Western popular music, specifically pop music. In the broad stream of *rompop*, two main styles loom large. The first of these, reminiscent of the musical expression of ethno-emancipating attitudes, consciously links to their own local tradition and combines its special characteristic musical elements with elements of international pop music (mainly in the field of instrumental accompaniment, but also rhythm and its realization…). Pioneers of this style, sometimes labeled as the *ethnic mainstream*[46] in Central Europe are the Hungarian *Kalyi Jag*.

Much more popular both among the majority public and, chiefly, among Roma, is the style that consciously does not use (or at least not to such a striking degree) local music idiom, but often lets itself be inspired by other examples, first and foremost, the enormously popular French (but with Spanish roots) *Gipsy Kings*. In the Romani environment this style – both as recorded music and as music actively performed – has the classic function of *bashaviben*, played and sung for their own entertainment, accompanying social gatherings, often connected to dance. In the past two decades, however, *rompop* has also often been discovered in the non-Romani environment: at concerts of world music, in "classical" music clubs such as Popocafépetl or Roxy, but also at high-level events.[47] The spectrum of bands that have turned to it is very broad. If we compare the social background of the groups with their musical language, we arrive at a remarkable correlation. On the one hand, there are groups that formed as amateurs, generally on a family basis. They initially played only for themselves and their closest surroundings, and gradually rose from this local level, perhaps even to the international scene. They play mainly their own compositions, and their own musical language – although the musicians acknowledge various influences – has features similar to those described above: a dominating distinctive melody, "dense" and energetic accompaniment and

---

45   Katalin Kovalcsik (2003) uses synonymously *Roma pop*.

46   Hemetek 1998. Kovalcsik (2003) labels it *ethnic music culture* (p. 92 n.).

47   In the year 1990, rompop groups such as *Točkolotoč* played at the benefit concert "SOS Racism," organized by President Havel and at which Paul Simon performed; in the summer of 2006, *Terne čhave* performed at a garden concert organized by the Senate of the Czech Republic.

perfectly mastered part singing, which is mainly made up of parallel melodic lines. This can be reminiscent of the sound realization of what Michael Steward, in his famous book *The Time of the Gypsies,* calls the timeless brotherhood of Roma. Věra Bílá[48] and her accompanying group *Kale* (Blacks),[49] as the first and most striking representatives of this genre in the Czech Republic have all of the above-mentioned features, as do the East Bohemian *Točkolotoč* and *Terne Čhave* (Young Boys)[50] and the Prague *Bengas.*

There is a different type of group which arose, as it were, from the outside with dramaturgical or commercial intentions. Their members are not dominantly Roma; they do not have any links other than musical ones, and their *raison d' être* are not entertainment realized through music as with the preceding groups, but musical products. This very different musical concept is – unsurprisingly – reflected in their musical language, which is much more artistic, for example, with complex sequences[51] of playing with timbre. The differing point of departure is also clear in the composition of the repertoire, which contains mostly old Romani songs. In this category are both Ida Kelarová and her projects and mainly the group *Triny* (Three),[52] whose rise can be attributed to the experienced producer Ivan Král.

The rompop *soundscape* confirms the attentive listener's realization that the basic concept, or WHAT music represents for the musicians, is straightforwardly and clearly reflected in HOW the music finally sounds – without regard to a uniform label.

4. ROMANO HIP HOP
Get a Taste of Europe: performance of the group Gipsy.cz
Wenceslas Square, March 6, 2009

One of the events accompanying the Czech presidency of the European Union was the three-day "Festival of European Regions" Get a Taste of Europe, March 5–7, 2009. It took place at the so-called Golden Cross, that is, the place where the main communication arteries meet: Wenceslas Square and Příkopy. On a small stage on Příkopy one could see and hear folk music groups; a large stage on the lower part of Wenceslas Square was occupied by various genres of popular music.

---

48 http://romani.uni-graz.at/rombase/ > personalities > Bílá, Věra; official Web page: www.verabila.com.
49 In the year 2005, however, Věra Bílá and *Kale* separated and today they sing alone.
50 www.ternechave.net.
51 E.g canon in the song *Phadžiľa, Phadžiľa* on *Triny* CD.
52 www.triny.cz.

While the preceding band, the Greek hip hoppers *SIFU Versus and DJ WAXWORK*, did not attract the interest of many Praguers or tourists, several hundred people gathered in front of the stage for the group *Gipsy.cz*: not only homeless people (some of whom were a bit drunk) and not only tourists: mainly Czechs, mostly young. A couple of dozen Roma.

First to step into the effective colorful lighting are the black-clothed Surmaj brothers (a guitarist and an electric double-bass player), the violinist Vojta "Béla" Lavička, and finally – with the enthusiastic applause and whistling of the audience – the slight Radek Banga – "Gipsy" in a typical hip hop outfit: a jacket with a hood trimmed with fur, a cap and wide pants. During his arrival you can hear the chorus of his first song – *Romano hip hop*. It has a striking and memorable melody with only a few words ("Romano hip hop in the house, šunen savore, Gipsy.cz in the house); the musicians interpolate the words with rhythmic syllables (hop, hop, chit, chip) in off-beat, as is frequent in the traditional music of Vlach Roma and in the music of contemporary groups, e.g. the Hungarian *Kalyi Jag*. The showy passages of the violin copy the melody; they are also sometimes heard in the interlude.

The chorus alternates with rapping, that is, quickly recited passages to the rhythm of musical accompaniment. "Come in the rhythm, whether you are a Rom or not. Dance savore! Piki piki piki piki piki pom! I want all to know that I am a Rom. That my band is Romani, dark, that it plays blackly. So come, chip hop, come with us, we don't care if you are a gadjo. But nobody is perfect, you f... idiot, it is all about romano hip hop." The second verse is in Romani; he concludes again in Czech. Gipsy dominates not only in singing (other musicians join in the choruses), but the whole stage: he moves easily, comments on songs and verbally and non-verbally communicates with the audience. Soon the first listeners begin to move to the rhythm, clap and join in the singing of the chorus...

Most of the songs from the latest CDs (*Romano hip hop* and *Reprezent*) have a similar character: they combine rapping with distinctive, but not trivial, melodies in the chorus or accompaniment, their texts (generally less playful but more aggressive than in *Romano hip hop*) alternate languages: Czech predominates; after it, "Romanes" is represented (which Romani scholars call the specific language of Gipsy.cz) and then somewhat oddly-pronounced English.

The fact that *Gipsy.cz* was chosen to be the Czech representative in international competitions is not especially surprising: in the previous year the Czech minister for human rights named Gipsy ambassador for the European Union's European Year of Equal Opportunities and, shortly after the Get a Taste of Europe festival, Czech television publicized the fact that it chose the group (in contrast with the usual approach whereby the national representative selected though a vote by television viewers) to represent the Czech Republic in the international Eurovision Song Contest. It seems as if *Gipsy.cz* and mainly Radek Banga were chosen from the outside to be the representatives of the Romani community. They are popular enough among the majority (although sometimes their song texts are criticized) and, at the same time, they can appear to be a suitable example for young Roma to follow.

There is no doubt that the picture of the "good Rom everyone praises"[53] comes primarily from the love for Gipsy's musical style. From this point of view, the non-standard approach of Czech television was quite legitimate: none of the regularly chosen representatives of the previous years had advanced even to the semifinals. On the contrary, the official esteem of the CD *Romano hip hop*,[54] along with a great number of votes for Gipsy in the national European round in the past years, enabled Czech TV to presume that this original and popular group would be successful. The fact that they ultimately were not any more successful than their predecessors in no way lessened the popularity of their style, which, however, has only little in common with hip hop.

Gipsy (this pseudonym has been used since their musical beginnings by the *Kalo rikonos* group) began, however, as a genuine hip hopper, more precisely a rapper (see below) in the group *Syndrom Snopp*. He recorded three CDs[55]: *Syndrom Snopp* - 1997, *Syndrom separace* - 2001 and *Syndrom Snopp 3.0*-2003. They have the same basic features as the original hip hop of Afro-American ghettos of the 1970s. His point of view was strong social and racial frustration for which aggressive recitation is more suitable than song (called *rap* - radical anarchistic poetry) to the rhythm of usually recorded music. This musical background arises most often with mixed music on a turntable, which is, along with *breakdance* and *graffiti*, a moving and graphic element, considered the main components of hip hop. Somewhat later *beatbox*, recorded rhythmic oral sounds, appeared.

At the time of authentic hip hop, however, this tendency already appeared in Gipsy's music, which can be ascribed both to his extraordinary ambition (also expressed verbally - both in song texts,[56] and in interviews[57]) as well as to the long-past tendency of Romani musicians to manage easily with stylized

53   Title of an article by Karel Veselý in *A2* 27/2008: 13.

54   The CD was awarded the Golden Disc for the sale of 10,000 copies.

55   For suggestions relating to Gipsy, mainly his time with Syndrom Snopp, I am grateful to my student Tomáš Dočkal - see Dočkal 2007.

56   For example, in the song *I can* "In Prague and almost in all Bohemia I proved to many ones that I can be same and even better than millions!" CD *Ya favourite CD Rom*. This album, sung entirely in English, has the obvious ambition of penetrating beyond Czech listenership.

57   One recent example: "Do not categorize me; I did not lower myself... in short an entirely new species in evolution." *Lidové noviny*, June 12, 2009.

Gipsy.cz

and genre borders. In 1999 – that is, between two hip hop CDs – he recorded the CD *Ramonis*, characterized as a "soul pop hip hop disk with a gentle breath of jazz" with the prestigious publishing firm BMG.[58] In 2005[59] he then recorded in the style of R 'n' B the album *Rýmy a blues* (with extraordinarily vulgar texts, which is typical of rap rather than of R 'n' B). After these came the two popular albums mentioned earlier: *Romano hip hop* and *Reprezent*.

It was actually these – with their gentle criticism and acceptable originality – that earned Gipsy such popularity.[60] At the same time, however, there was a void among authentic hip hoppers.

Still, a tempting question remains: Is the image of the social situation of the Czech Roma and the Afro-American ghetto reflected in similar musical expression? A positive response seems obvious in so far as some authors simply consider it as a given.[61] The reality, though, is different. In contrast with Slo-

---

58 http://skola.romea.cz/cz/index.php?id=hudba/28 (July 10, 2009).

59 The date is not mentioned on the CD; I took it from Dočkal. It is also confirmed in an internet review from the same year.

60 It seems significant to me, andon www.gipsy.cz (July 13, 2009) none of their preceding CDs is even mentioned.

61 Radostný more naively formulates it in an exemplary way (2008).

vakia, where the hip hop scene is dominated by the recognized Romani rapper Rytmus with the group *Kontrafakt,* in the Czech lands there is nobody similar. Nor in various types of contests or workshops has any outstanding Romani rap talent[62] appeared – and those who do rap do it mainly in Czech.

At the same time, one cannot disregard the large number of Romani children and young people (mainly boys) who have taken up breakdancing and beatbox. When I once asked a certain breakdancer from Rokycany how often he practiced, he answered: "We practice all the time – in school and afterwards, too". Field workers confirm the omnipresence of both hip hop elements and, actually, they are from the socially most marginalized places. It seems, so to speak, that a certain part of the hip hop soundscape of the American ghettos has found resonance in a similar environment in our country and fulfills a similar task, while its rap element has successfully joined the broad stream of popular music.

CODA

As is clear at first glance and hearing, the term "Romani music" can be found in contemporary Prague in the most varied forms and in the most varied environments. For the most part, it is imbued with those mythical qualities which are attributed to it – and to the Roma in general – by romanticism: from emotionality to passion, individuality or love of freedom, and also the basic connection of Roma to music. At the same time, however, as is also confirmed by ethomusicological research in other urban environments[63] this label does not correspond to a clear-cut genre definition. The configurations of various shapes of the above-mentioned qualities, and also of the expectations of the public, create various musical images – *soundscapes.*

But it is essential that everyone – the musicians and the audience – and also those who are in other ways connected to the rise and existence of these images, for instance the restaurateurs of "Seven Angels" – are right in their concept. The myth of Gypsy/Romani music is thus inseparably interwoven in our networks of relations and consequences to which Clifford Geertz (1973) compares culture.

---

62 See, e.g., the Brno contest Street Sounds (www.street-sounds.cz) or the workshops mentioned above by Dočkal in Ústí nad Labem (Dočkal 2007: 83–84).

63 Reyes 1982.

FENG-YÜN SONG VOICE PAINTING[64]
U DŽOUDYHO
MARCH 24, 2010, 7 P.M.
Zita Skořepová Honzlová

At approximately one-month intervals since autumn 2009, a cycle of "exclusive therapeutic concerts"[65] called *Voice Painting* has taken place at the *U Džoudyho* center near I. P. Pavlova, one of the busiest Prague intersections. On March 24, 2010, a few people have been here since before 7 p.m. standing in line for tickets. Along with them, I descend the narrow staircase to a cellar space divided into a few rooms. I find myself not in a tea parlor, but in a shop and a neighboring bookstore. A glance into the shop window near the door, I notice, in addition to an ad for various types of meditation and relaxation, posters behind glass advertising a series of events taking place here. I am surprised by the variety and number of exhibitions, lectures on Taoism, meditation, interpretation of tarot cards, onovercoming the fear of death or introducing alternative therapeutic approaches, but also collective performances of various types – playing on shaman drums, circle dancing or singing of mantras.

In addition to all this, today's *Voice Painting* with Feng-yün Song is also featured. The shop is not dedicated only to tea or tea-related objects. In addition to these articles, one can purchase a wide spectrum of goods from incense sticks and moon stones to various "ethnic" jewels, cards, sidereal pendulums, curative wands, crystal balls and other esoteric gadgets to CDs with relaxation and meditation music, solar lamps, energy pictures, mandalas and a vast quantity of spiritual and esoteric literature. Without the colors of all the exhibited articles, the space would seem stark with its light, natural wood – it seems that the shop underwent a complete reconstruction not long ago. The air here, like that in other Prague tea houses I know, is steeped in the aroma of incense. After looking around for a while, I go and buy a ticket for today's event for 150 crowns and descend to the next room.

At 7:14, nine people are sitting on modern cushioned chairs placed in a circle. I recognize half of the public thanks to their regular attendance at this cycle's concerts. As at other times, today the audience is composed of a dis-

---

64 We use the form of the name Feng-yün Song uses in the Czech environment.
65 http://www.fengyunsong.cz/koncerty_archiv09.html (September 7, 2010).

parate group of people. They are mainly couples of women of various ages, two lone young men and a few pensioners. All are informally or only slightly formally dressed. Those who came with someone else whisper or talk in low voices. As always, I hear them mention of Feng-yün Song and her voice seminars, but also esotericism. The "loners" glance around the room, which has subdued lighting except for a few scattered solar lamps and candles. Objects are for sale here –meditation pictures, natural crystals, statues of Buddhas in glass cases, relaxation pillows on the floor and various African and "shaman" drums, a didgeridoo and a marimba in the corners of the room.

Feng-yün Song has already arrived. She walks around the room a couple of times and goes upstairs to talk something over with the staff. She is wearing a red turtleneck sweater, a tight dark skirt down to her knees and boots. At 7:37 she returns and, in a low voice, welcomes the guests. In perfect Czech, with only the slightest Chinese accent, she introduces today's concert as a "musical event" that will be "our mutual concert." Everyone quietly observes her and, with a smile, all nod their heads, thus signifying that the course of today's event is already known to them. Before Feng-yün Song herself begins to sing, she invites those present to join her in some way if they feel like it. The cellar room is now lit only by the warm glow of a solar lamp situated in a corner. Some of the audience members are clearly trying to induce a state of relaxation, and, closing their eyes, they concentrate on the coming moments. Others move their eyes back and forth from the singer to the other participants. The arrangement of the seats in a circle where everyone can see everyone else apparently helps this. Feng-yün Song stands at the head of the circle, closes her eyes, clears her throat slightly and, after taking a breath, begins a high, sometimes slightly nasal, tone which gradually gains strength. After a long while, a pentatonic melody begins to develop, initially resulting in an irregular meter and slow tempo. A series of sung tones is separated by Chinese syllables, the performance of which is very impressive for an audience unaccustomed to hearing singing in Asian languages. The quiet of the dusky cellar space is completely filled by the voice with a surprisingly broad range and varying dynamics. The breathing, the placement of the tones, the phrasing and the entire delivery unambiguously convince the audience of the absolute mastery of the technical and interpretational side of her art. Feng-yün Song sings sitting and standing with a permanent smile, sometimes reminiscent of a European classical singer, but her mouth moves so that it is possible to pronounce Chinese vowels. In higher positions, the voice sounds quieter and softer, but soon it slides into a surprisingly low register in which the softness of falsetto tones alternates sharply with the sonority of the chest register. When, after the end of the first song, a few people applaud, the singer, as usual, announces that today there will be no applause. If they like the composition the audience may nod their

Feng-yün Song, Prague, Ryba naruby (Backwards Fish) club (photo: Zita Skořepová Honzlová)

heads in agreement, which happens each time. At the beginning, a few songs are sung *a capella* or with the accompaniment of a gong-like resonant bowl. The singer provides basic information about each song: a Chinese, a Korean and a Mongolian song performed in Chinese, generally with a love or nature motif. Feng-yün Song uses a few single tones produced on a Chinese moon lute as accompaniment to the third song. In contrast to the dominant singing, it is apparent that her playing functions only as an elementary accompaniment. While some watch the singer with curiosity, others close their eyes while she sings and allow themselves to be completely carried away: it seems that for them, listening is really a certain kind of meditation.

After the first few solos, Feng-yün Song invites those present to sing or play something themselves. The first person to get up is a middle-aged woman. She timidly introduces herself and tells the others that she likes folk songs best and that she likes playing the clarinet. Right after that, she plays the well-known Moravian song "Kebych byla jahodú" (If I Were a Strawberry). She is followed by a young man who, with more self-confidence than the preceding singer, sings three Czech folk songs. After that, Feng-yün Song again takes the initiative and sings a few more songs. She invites the audience to join in two of them: they are supposed to clap or chant in certain sections according to a simple scheme. Between the songs she speaks about spring, which is the period of growth; the body awakens while the soul is still asleep. A word about the balance of yin and yang energy comes up and the audience learns a voice exercise that benefits the burdened liver in the spring. For a while, the musical performance changes into a lecture. Perfect mastery of the Czech language, cultivated diction and performance bring conviction to the singer's speech. Two retired women want to know how voice exercise can help the stomach, heart or skin. The next-to-last solo song of Feng-yün Song is a Korean lullaby, from the Chinese point of view apparently rather sentimental because the father in it cries over the cradle of his child.

As usual in the spaces of *U Džoudyho*, the whole performance ends with everyone present music making. The lights go out and the space is illuminated by only two solar lamps. Feng-yün Song stands in the circle with the others and begins improvised singing on various syllables. Meanwhile, one of the employees of the tea house arrives and stands in the middle of the circle with a shaman drum; at the beginning he quietly accompanies the singing with a simple rhythmic pattern. A few women and a jolly young man join him after a while with low humming. Two minutes later, everyone has already joined in the performance – by clapping or singing, and I note with surprise the consonance they achieve here. All are standing close to each other. Some of the women who arrived together hold hands and others begin to stamp to an ever-increasing tempo, and regular beats of the drum stimulate the activity of the individual participants. Now, the voice of Feng-yün Song, along with the sound of the drum, is complemented by twelve more voices and clapping. Spontaneous melodic and rhythmic alliances are being created here. It is evident that all the participants are having a strong experience from the joint performance of the music. During the fifteen-minute improvisation there are alternating gradations of tempo and dynamics and again their lessening. Seventeen minutes later, the joint "voice painting" ends with the silencing of all the voices and other sounds. A few seconds later, Feng-yün Song quietly bids farewell. Warm and long applause is heard. A few people stay to speak with the singer about further events. After 9:30 everyone leaves.

The singer Feng-yün Song comes from the town of Jiamusi in northeastern China, an area that calls itself the Chinese Siberia. Although she comes from a musical family and all of her siblings enjoy playing an instrument or singing, she is the only one who earns her living from music. She attended the family school of the Peking Opera, studying singing for twelve years with the singer Shang Chuej-min. At the same time, she pursued Czech studies in Peking at the Institute for the Study of Foreign Languages; later she earned a scholarship to study in the Czech Republic, where she finished her studies at the Philosophical Faculty of Charles University with a Ph.D. dissertation (1994). However, she also wanted to dedicate herself to music. In 1992, she began teaching Chinese opera in the drama department of the Jaroslav Ježek Conservatory where, as she says, she acquired experience with Czech students and audiences and discovered a way to pass down her specific knowledge. She still teaches in the musical theater department of the Prague Conservatory. On her website she presents herself as a "trainer and therapist"[66] because, along with singing, she dealt with traditional Chinese therapeutic methods for a long time and thus – quite unsurprisingly – she holds educational seminars and courses called "Autotherapy of the voice" for the public. In them she introduces and applies Chinese philosophical-therapeutic principles and breathing and voice techniques. On the flyers for "Voice tuning and therapy," the caption states, "About regulation of qi, breath, emotion and voice, knowledge of one's own self with Feng-yün Song" and "The road to the voice is the road to harmony, to the 'child' in us. Only the harmonious state of the soul and body enables free voice production." The courses are on two levels: "tuning through voice and breath" for beginners and "tonal therapy and numeric acupuncture" for advanced learners. Also on offer are complex "singing lessons" with breathing, voice and articulating exercises and song study. The events take several forms, from regular three- to five-hour lessons given once a month in evenings (at a price range from 500 to 1000 crowns per lesson), to one-time day or weekend seminars to the weekly Summer Voice School.

In addition to teaching, Feng-yün Song established the radio programs *Music roulette* and *Tea Room* on Czech Radio, which she conceptualized and also moderated and into which she inserted her own songs. With the help of Czech Radio, she organized the first public concert in the Roxy Club in which she appeared with the percussionist Alan Vitouš. In 2008, she organized the first yearly *Songfest*[67] music festival, which takes place yearly on the occasion of the celebration of the Chinese lunar new year, first in Prague and later in several other Czech cities.[68] She moderates the evenings along with the famous actor Jaroslav Dušek. They share the program with other musicians, dancers and other performers with various repertoires from European art music and acting improvisations to the Vietnamese Lion Dance and the art of the Japanese sword.[69]

Feng-yün Song collaborates both with Czech musicians of alternative genres (e.g. the experimental percussionists Jaroslav Kořán and Alan Vitouš) and performers of classical music, the Hradec Králové Philharmonic Orchestra, the pianist Lenka Navrátilová) and those who are inspired by jazz (Trio Puo). She tries to connect Chinese elements in song with piano, bass and a number of percussion instruments and she points them toward multi-genre and experimental musical styles. In her reper-

---

66 "Who is Feng-yün Song?" http://www.fengjunsong.cz/index.php/cs/o-feng-yun-song (Jan. 2, 2012).

67 www.songfest.cz (Jan. 2, 2012).

68 In Český Krumlov, Hradec Králové, Zlín and Brno.

69 E.g. pianist Kayoko Zemanová, didgeridoo player Ondřej Smeykal, guitarist Amit Chattarjee, but also groups like Čankišou, dancers Tina Ahmed and Tej Kumari Thakuri, members of the Peňa Flamenco Studio, etc. In 2011 in Český Krumlov the Central Asian group Jagalmay also performed. The fifth year – the year of the dragon 2012 – began to have international dimensions because of the virtuoso Gao Yingying, who plays the Chinese lute.

toire, however; she has compositions of Western art music (in solo recitals she also presents songs by, e.g., Dvořák and Janáček). These recitals with classical European repertoires take place in the Atrium in Žižkov while the *Songfest* is performed in the nearby Akropolis Palace. Voice painting and other chamber performances of the singer take place in smaller Prague venues; in addition to U Džoudyho, also in the Akropolis Palace, often in the Ryba naruby and Jedna báseň tea houses, the Potrvá coffee house, the Small Nostic Theater and the Small Vinohrady Theater. It is possible to learn about all the singing engagements, *Songfest*, and pedagogical activities on extensive, regularly updated and professionally operated Web pages. In addition, thanks to the cooperation of several of the above-mentioned musicians, seven CDs have already been issued.

NOWRUZ, TWICE IN A DIFFERENT WAY

Zita Skořepová Honzlová

CELEBRATION OF THE PERSIAN NEW YEAR
ABC Theater,
Sunday, March 21, 2010, 7:30 p.m.

Shahab Tolouie – guitarist, composer and singer from Iran. At concerts he presents his own works, which he introduces as "EthnoFlamenco," in other words, a fusion of elements of Spanish flamenco and Persian classical music. He works with several Czech musicians[70] who accompany him on the classical and the fretless guitar and various "ethnic percussions"[71]... He appears as a soloist, the leader and also the most important musician in the ensemble, uses the "flamenco guitar" and the Persian *setar* and is the only one who also sings. The compositions are either purely instrumental or complemented by Persian texts inspired by the works of Jalaleddin Rumi, Hafiz and other Persian classics. Tolouie is a professional musician. In addition to the Czech Republic, he performs in independent concerts or as a part of festivals in other countries (in 2010 and 2011 in Germany, an Eastern-European tour in Russia, Poland, Ukraine, Moldavia and Turkey). He pursues a cohesive style of self-presentation which is reflected in his striking exterior as well as in the concept of his web pages and other publicity materials.

The first spring day of 2010, Shahab Tolouie gives a concert on the occasion of *Nowruz* – "Persian", or, more precisely, Zoroastrian, "New Year". The event is organized at the ABC Theater on Vodičkova Street, one of the most frequently attended and famous Prague theaters. In the immediate surroundings of the theater there are no posters to be seen indicating today's program. Nevertheless, I did glimpse a few of them in streets in the center of Prague and here in the theater I notice them only after entering the foyer. However, I did receive one electronically along with a personal message from a musician who will also perform in today's concert. On a large poster with this month's program placed

---

70   He performs either with the "Shahab Tolouie Trio" or the "Shahab Tolouie Quartet."
71   The Czech musician Tomáš Reindl or the American Hearn Gadbois usually accompanies him on the Indian *tabla* and other percussion instruments used in Arab and Persian music.

Nowruz: Celebration of the Persian New Year, Prague, ABC Theater

in a display window in the area which also houses the theater's box office, there is mention of Sunday, March 21, 2010, with the title of today's concert, "Celebration of the Persian New Year" with a note that "this event is not a production of the Prague City Theaters" and thus no student or other discounts apply. All tickets cost 350 crowns. I later notice that in the MDP Magazine, copies of which are scattered around the lobby of the theater, the poster in reduced size appears on the pages reserved for advertisements. It captures Shahab Tolouie posing with a guitar in his usual concert clothing – a white shirt with a slightly open neck and long sleeves, black pants and, on his right arm, a silver bracelet which, during his performance, always throws bright reflections attracting the attention of the audience. Under his name are smaller letters introducing today's guest musicians – David Koller and Pavel J. Ryba; then, in even smaller letters, are all the others who are performing in the concert.[72]

Tickets go on sale a half hour before the beginning: today at 7 p.m. At this time, people are already standing in front of the box office. Before the beginning of the concert, some have coffee, some mineral water, wine or beer at the refreshment bar. At the stairs or in the halls are publicity stands of several

72 Tomáš Reindl, Tomáš Vychytil, Martin Kapusník, Hearn Gadbois; dancers Rena Milgrom and Petra Šťastná.

shops with musical instruments – partners or sponsors of today's event. At one stand, posters of A3 format hang announcing today's concert. Here interested parties can also buy the Shahab Tolouie CD. In the foyer and later, glancing at the people arriving in the auditorium, I recognize all of the ubiquitous five Iranians, but the general majority of the public is made up of Czechs and a few foreigners –tourists who happen to be attending the concert. People are elegantly, but also informally, dressed, mainly middle-aged; I guess the youngest of them are between twenty and thirty-five years old; there is a slight majority of women. The theatergoers come alone or in pairs, exceptionally in threes. In the hall there are only a few families with older children up to twelve years old. Most of the newcomers enter during the third and final bell at 7:30.

The curtains on the sides as well as the floor of the stage are black so that the number of musical instruments draws our attention; in addition to two guitars and a double bass there are a number of percussion instruments – I see a few shapes of Arab or Persian *darbukkas,* a few frame drums, an Indian *tabla* and a set of drums used in European popular music.

At 7:35, the light over the auditorium and the stage go down for a moment. A sharp beam of light soon cuts through the darkness and is aimed at the arriving presenter. She greets the audience and points out the "display of Persian-ethnic instruments" on the stage: She further mentions that today's concert is dedicated to the welcoming of the Persian New Year, *Nowruz (which means "a new spring"),* and she mentions some customs connected with this holiday. Gradually she introduces today's concert, a "Persian-Spanish fusion" and, mainly, Shahab Tolouie, his quartet and today's guest musicians – David Koller, Hearn Gadbois and Pavel Ryba. In conclusion, she thanks the sponsors.

The stage is again plunged into darkness: only a sign alternates on a screen with the picture of an icily silver night's full moon. The first tones of the Persian drum, the *dombak,* are heard in an improvised introduction with an irregular meter. After a while a chime and the double bass with a melismatic minor melody of "meditative" character are added. The first spotlight goes on at the moment Shahab Tolouie begins to play the guitar. He is sitting in the very middle of the stage, dressed as usual in a white shirt with an open neck and black pants. He plays the flamenco guitar, identifiable mainly by its penetrating sound. After a while, he also begins to sing. His singing reminds me of the style of Mohammed Reza Shadjarian, an outstanding representative of Persian classical singing. When the first composition is over, the audience applauds, as it does after the next two pieces. Shahab Tolouie always smiles and says "thank you." No further information about the individual compositions, or about today's program, is available.

During the next composition all of the musicians are illuminated – the second guitarist, the double bass player and the percussionists. At the same time, the picture on the screen changes; there now appears a photograph of a segment of a typical Persian rug pattern; it later alternates with a picture of embroidery on a blue background. The musicians play without music sheets; the compositions have clearly been thoroughly practiced beforehand, but they are partially improvised. It seems that all are very absorbed in their playing and they distinctly communicate with each other with glances and mime. The second percussionist Hearn Gadbois, who is sitting on the right side of the auditorium, joins the Indian *tabla* drums player Tomáš Reindl. Gadbois' long hair is entwined into a braid. He is wearing an Indo-Pakistani style *shalwar qameez*, that is, a black cotton tunic down to his knees and wide pants of the same color.

After the first three compositions, the dancer Rena Milgrom arrives on stage several times, each time in a different costume. When she enters, she places a pink flower in the center of the stage, as if she were invoking her graceful motion. Shahab Tolouie now trades the guitar for the *tar*, a Persian lute with a long neck. The playing now recalls Persian music – in the prelude the long, colorfully rich sound of vibrating strings alternates with a series of a rapid row of tones, sometimes at micro-intervals evoking an impression of a distant musical system to a number of the listeners. After the short prelude, Tolouie begins to sing accompanied by Hearn Gadbois on a clay *darbukka*, a goblet-shaped drum frequently used in folk and classical Middle-Eastern music. Tomáš Reindl has a solo in the following composition and he offers the public a "cadenza" on the *tabla*, in which he improvises on the basis of Indian rhythmic patterns while using diverse types of strokes; in a later drum duet with David Koller he demonstrates his art again. One number is also dedicated to flamenco; the Czech dancer Petra Šťastná is now accompanied by Shahab Tolouie in flamenco style. In the course of the concert Tolouie alternates two guitars, whose tuning he changes not only before the beginning of the composition, but sometimes during it.

Next come two "main" guest musicians, established professionals who have been around the Czech jazz-rock musical scene for a long time. First, the guitarist Pavel J. Ryba appears. He is a middle-aged man with long hair tied into a pony tail, a dark T-shirt and jeans. He has a jazz-like solo on a fretless guitar; the other musicians gradually join in. Then David Koller comes forward. He is famous as a former member of the well-known band Lucie. He and Shahab Tolouie sing – alternating Czech and Persian verses – the song "Dele man" from the CD *Tango Perso* known as "My Heart." This composition with a dramatic and distinctly memorable motif is often also heard in other performances. The concert ends just before 9:30. The musicians are rewarded with great applause; all bow together and each one receives a red rose from the employees of the theater.

NOWRUZ IN THE UZBEK COMMUNITY

Saturday, March 20, 2010, 6 p.m; Schwaiger Villa

Farhod Tashev – a drummer, *doira* frame drum player and member of the central Asian band *Jagalmay*. Farhod Tashev was born in 1979 in southeastern Uzbekistan. From his youth he was interested in music, partly because of his father's love of music. He completed his studies at the Tashkent Conservatory, where he specialized in Uzbek and South American percussion instruments. He sings and plays guitar. In the Czech Republic he earns his living as a manual worker and takes on various jobs, but he also makes money (not only as a member of *Jagalmay*, but also thanks to occasional performances with other musicians) by playing the *doira*, his favorite frame drum, considered to be the unforgettable instrument of Uzbek music.

 Ulugbek Samandarev – also a member of the *Jagalmay* band, in which he plays the *rebab*. He comes from the Uzbek province of Karakal-Pakistan,[73] where he was a farmer and where he left his wife and family. He came to the Czech Republic to earn money. He is currently working in a warehouse. In contrast to Farhod Tashev, he didn't have any professional musical schooling.

 Allamurad Rakhimov – an amateur singer and *dutar* player; he plays modern Central Asian music. He works in Prague as a radio announcer in the Turkmen section of Radio Free Europe.

On Thursday, March 18, 2010, I travel to Lysá nad Labem for another performance of the Central Asian band *Jagalmay* in the series of European contact groups, "Foreigners and Us". Farhod Tashev had already informed me before the beginning about another performance of theirs. It will be a meeting of the Uzbek community on the occasion of the celebration of *Nowruz*. I am to be at the Schwaiger Villa on Saturday, March 20, at 6 p.m. The ticket, which is at the same time a contribution to a party, will cost 500 crowns. I immediately recall that three months earlier I attended a Kyrgyz community celebration, the organization of which looked similar.

 On the designated day after six in the evening I head for Prague's Bubeneč. The Schwaiger Villa is slightly apart on the short, steep Schwaigerova Street; it takes me a while to find it. The surroundings appear relatively pretentious and the villa itself evokes the impression of a luxurious pension. In the parking lot there are several dark limousines and land rovers. There are no posters anywhere or any information about today's event (not that I had expected any). The entrance is guarded by two young Uzbeks in black jackets and jeans. When I announce that I am going to the *Nowruz* celebration, they ask in poor Czech

---

73 A mountainous desert area of northeastern Uzbekistan, the land of historic Khorezm.

Nowruz celebration, Prague, Villa Schwaiger (photo: Zita Skořepová Honzlová)

for either a special ticket, which one of the people before me had shown, or 500 crowns. At the reception I meet Farhod Tashev, who welcomes me and leads me through rooms. Apparently there will first be a short welcome and information about *Nowruz*, and only then will come the party and the musical performance. He leads me to a room –apparently usually the dining room for guests of the pension. A few elegantly dressed people are already sitting around tables there. I notice that the men are sitting with the men and the women with the women. He introduces me to another young man who is dressed in a dark suit. Together they seat me with two young women. These are speaking Russian, as are some of the other guests; the absolute majority of the guests are non-Europeans. Directly opposite me there is a screen on the wall. On the table are a few refreshments – sliced apple, sweet and salty pretzels.

In a while, a young man with a closely trimmed beard and frizzy black hair and wearing a white jacket and black pants arrives. He greets the people and with a broad smile shows a whole row of straight white teeth among which – in contrast to the others – there isn't a single gold one. First, he informs us about the *Nowruz* holiday. During his explanation, a PowerPoint presentation runs on the screen, alternating with photographs of famous Uzbek landmarks with details of shots of people in traditional clothing, snapshots of group dances and pictures of holiday dishes. Everything is complemented by descriptions in Uzbek. After the end of the presentation, a young man invites the audience to the feast which is interspersed with performances of the musicians of "traditional" and "folk" songs of Central Asia, among which a musical version of a poem by Omar Khayyam, the famous medieval mystic and man of letters who came from Uzbekistan, will also be heard.

Neither now nor later are any of the individual musicians introduced. I am thus curious to know who besides Farhod Tashev will perform today. The introductory speech of the young man is heard twice – first in Uzbek, then in Russian. Afterwards in a conversation with one of the musicians I learn that there are not only Uzbeks here, but also Turkmens, Tajiks, Kyrgs as well as other Central Asians who still use Russian first and foremost for mutual understanding.

Around seven, the people move to an elongated lounge with twelve tables. At one end of the room, a somewhat raised stage covered with an Afghan carpet has been prepared. The musicians are already in place and are rearranging the microphones. On the left, I see the percussionist Farhod Tashev in a white shirt and gray pants; he is tuning the *darbukka.* Lying on the floor are two *doiras,* a tambourine and a *dutar* which in central Asia is a popular two-string lute with a long neck and a small pear-shaped soundboard. Behind the drummer, an older musician sits at the keyboard. In the back I see Ulugbek Samandarev, who today will play the banjo instead of the usual Central Asian lute. In the corner on the right stands a young woman who is tuning a violin. I later learn that she comes from Ukraine and is the friend of one of the Central Asian musicians. In front of her at a small harmonium I see the last of today's band – the Turkmen musician Allamurad Rakhimov. In a shiny dark suit with a tie, he is the most formally dressed of them all. At the other end of the lounge there are a few tables from which the guests take all kinds of goodies: of course there are the typical Uzbek *plov,*[74] grilled lamb and roast chicken, steamed vegetables, a quantity of rice and pancakes, several kinds of salad, fruit, and Turkish-style sweets. On another table are water and all kinds of non-alcoholic beverages. At the bar, almost everyone buys beer or wine. Gradually, however, a few bottles of hard alcohol also make their way from table to table. But nobody gets completely drunk during the evening. Now I guess there are about sixty people here. Men predominate; some are also here with their Ukrainian girlfriends; there are also a few women originating from Central Asia.

The musical performance begins with a few recorded songs, to which Farhod Tashev improvises live on the *doira* or on the *darbukka.* Then the others join in. First they play songs "for listening" in a slower tempo. Allamurad Rakhimov

---

74 Pieces of lamb in rice with carrots and raisins; considered to be the Uzbek national dish.

sings touchingly in a Central Asian manner and his nasal voice sounds rather sharp in the microphone. At the same time, he alternates playing the *dutar* and the harmonium. Farhod Tashev accompanies him on the drum. Ulugbek Samandarev on the banjo is almost inaudible, like the Ukrainian violinist, who plays in unison with the singing. Meanwhile the guests are eating dinner at the tables; while some are concentrating on the music, others chat with the people at their table. There is applause after each song, but nobody is dancing yet. Apart from the first composition "Bahor" (Spring), which is tied to Nowruz, the others are non-specific love songs. Allamurad Rakhimov sings in several languages; on the program there are songs in Uzbek, Turkmen, Tajik, Azeri, Turkish and Farsi. Then he explains that for those Turkish- and Farsi-speaking Central Asians, all the songs are at least partly understandable.

As time passes, the musicians present musical compositions at a more and more lively tempo and the first dancing "competition": couples or groups of three young people get up and dance in a circle with their arms in the air, nudging each other and shouting and clapping. The older people don't dance, except for a middle-aged couple – parents of the presenter in a white jacket – who dance with him to a popular Azerbaijan song about the beauty Rihane. He is the only one to dance with a girl; otherwise no Uzbek girls dance. To me their dance is amazing. I admire the way they let themselves be completely devoured by the very lively, rich rhythm of the music. The girl dances with streaks of hair in her mouth and her animated spontaneity leads her to taking off her high-heeled shoes so she can dance better. Ukrainian girls whizz by the front of the stage twice – however without their Uzbek partners. They, in contrast to the Uzbek girl, are evidently not accustomed to dancing to this music and so, with some embarrassment, they try to imitate the movement of belly dances, which supplement a sort of discotheque dance.

Fahrhod Tashev's solo performance earns great attention and applause. He descends from the stage and puts on a black Uzbek cap; he wraps a half-folded checkered scarf around his belt and plays the *doira*. After eight it is also time for the popular "duel" on two *doiras*; Farhod thus competes with the other Uzbek drummer Ulugbek. Each one alternately plays the drum: the winner is the one who improvises more rapidly and with more embellishments. Their solos alternate, sometimes in shorter intervals, sometimes in longer ones, until they join in one complex rhythmic pattern whose metric structure is shaped by the mutual interaction of both musicians. At this time, the majority of the men stand up from the tables and with clapping and noisy shouting, raise their hands over their heads, join in a circle and dance to the rhythm of the playing of the two drums whose loud sound completely fills the space. Not only is it unnecessary for the other instruments to accompany them, but also they wouldn't be heard. The next part of the program also earns great affection when an elderly Uzbek player sits at the keyboard and sings songs in Russian *dumka* style, here cheerful *chatushkas*.

At 9:15 another musician, a Syrian Armenian named Miran, whom I know as a member of the *Allstar Refugee Band*, arrives with an *oud*, an Arab lute. He sits in the center of the stage, tunes his lute a while and at the same time improvises a prelude. Farhod accompanies him after a while on the *darbukka*, which he plays instead of the Uzbek *doira*. Miran then sings a well-known song in Turkish, Armenian and Arabic. After ten o'clock the program of "traditional music" ends. The Uzbek musicians – members of *Jagalmay* – leave, as do some of the guests. About twenty young people stay: a discotheque continues in the cellar rooms. From there, only recorded music can be heard – well-known English, but also Russian, song hits. I hear *"Otchi Tchornye"* as well as two Turkish songs by the pop singer Tarkan. The choice of songs is similar to what was played during the intermissions of live music at the Kyrgyz community celebration.

"ETHNIC" MUSIC FOR ENTERTAINMENT
Zita Skořepová Honzlová

CUBAN EVENINGS IN LA CASA DE LA HAVANA VIEJA
Opatovická 28, Prague 1

Every other Thursday on a board in front of "La Casa de la Havana Vieja – Classic Cuban Bar" in the center of Prague, a sign in white chalk and capital letters appears: "TODAY LIVE CUBAN MUSIC" or "8 P.M. CUBAN BAND." The board hangs next to the entrance, above which shines a neon sign with the words "Casa Havana." On the sides of the door, a view of the interior is provided by windows which, thanks to their inconspicuousness, someone walking along this New Town street would hardly notice. Immediately after entering, it is clear that the bar is one of the so-called "better" establishments: wood panels stylishly harmonize with dark red leather benches along the wall, with lights and decorative objects. The feeling of luxury with a touch of antiques is disturbed only by the fact that all of the newish furnishings lack the wear of years. The appropriateness of the first impression is consequently confirmed by the professionally appearing and behaving waiter and the menu with a rich offering mainly of brand-name rum, cocktails, cigars and small snacks. The prices also correspond to an attempt at better-than-average quality.

Early in the Thursday evenings of these weeks, some of the tables for two, four or more guests are already taken. The number of customers increases to around eight. They come mostly in pairs or groups of three, even fewer alone or, on the contrary, in numerous groups. Most of them are women and men of younger middle age in formal dress, suits that fit well, but also in expensive ready-made clothes inspired by recent fashion trends; on the tables, next to large calendars in leather folders, lie expensive cell phones. If there is room left, a few passers-by, often foreign tourists, sit without reservations. It is, however, clear that the absolute majority of the people don't come as accidental guests. Most of the guests are not sitting with a beer, the favorite Czech drink: apart from good hard alcohol, the waiters serve glasses of various shapes with cocktails of different colors and flavors. Around some of the tables you can smell the smoke of quality cigars.

Santy y su Marabú Trio, Prague, La Casa de la Havana Vieja (photo: Zita Skořepová Honzlová)

Before eight, three musicians from the *Santy y su Marabú* band arrive. While the bass player, Amador, is wearing black jeans, a red T-shirt and white tennis shoes, the other two players are dressed in dark suits. The drummer, Carlos, tries to find a good position between his knees for a *bongo*, the pair of unequal Afro-Cuban small drums with skin membranes, while the guitarist and band leader, Santiago, tunes his guitar. The *trés cubano*, or Cuban guitar, can attract your attention to the unusually large distances among its three pairs of strings. The musicians greet the bar personnel and chat merrily in Spanish while preparing their instruments and adjusting the microphones. Soon the sounds of Cuban percussion and guitars are heard. The more careful listener acquainted with their repertoire can recognize fragments of songs presented at other concerts. Meanwhile, a waiter brings glasses of beer and mineral water. The musicians are seated at the end of one of the benches across from the bar so that they are playing in the front, non-smoking part. The live music can also be heard well in the somewhat larger second room reserved for smokers, where the sound reverberates through small speakers placed in each corner at the ceiling. Practically precisely at the stroke of eight, the sound check flows into the performance of this evening. First the musicians warm up with improvisations on the guitar, *bongo* and bass guitar, still without singing. The melody of the *trés* accompanied by the bass guitar is colored by a few alternating Cuban rhythmic patterns played on the *bongo*. The drummer, Carlos, plays and modulates the rhythms with a nonchalant routine and only sometimes pays attention to what is happening around him. Spontaneously emerging improvised passages are joined with motifs or phrases used elsewhere in songs as interludes or solo cadences of the *trés* guitar. Quiet singing is added, often only choruses or parts of songs. Apart from the extracts from the repertoire performed in individual concerts of *Santy y su marabú*, the musicians also play their own arrangements of known pop songs like "Volare, cantare" or "Besame mucho." Flutes, trumpets and trombones, otherwise used for the group's individual concerts, are not used in this space because of their volume. Compositions in quicker and slower tempo alternate, but the singing and playing are quieter and calmer most of the time. In contrast to concerts where some members of the band stand, here they all sit. The bandleader, Santiago, sits close to the other players and limits himself to occasional nodding to the rhythm. He does not indulge in the pleasure of body movements as he does in clubs where he is confronted with a public eager to dance. I have the feeling that, for him, playing tonight is sometimes a routine activity. For a few moments, the musicians notice only each other and play as if they were rehearsing something new and took pleasure mainly in playing together without regard to the attention and reaction of their "public". From a glance at the musicians, it is apparent that over the course of the evening each one mainly follows his fellow players, at the very most with a friendly smile at some of those who are looking at him. The guests, however, pay only sporadic attention to the music. It surprises me that even the beginning of this performance passed without notice. Gradually, from time to time, someone looks up from his table partner at the musicians or taps his finger to the rhythm at the bar, but without ceasing to converse with his neighbor. At the end of the composition, some of the guests applaud a couple of times. But nobody gets up from the tables to dance.

After precisely half an hour of playing, it is time for a thirty-minute intermission. The musicians go to the bar and drink beer or mineral water while they chat among themselves and a bit with one of the employees. A similar half-hour of music alternates with an equally long intermission until eleven o'clock. During the evening, a magician in a black vest and pants and a white shirt and top hat also walks through the bar. He entertains some of the guests directly at their tables with a set of metal rings and other magic.

Santy y su Marabú is a band which, when all the members are present, is made up of a Cuban guitar (*trés cubano*), a keyboard, Afro-Cuban percussion (*bongo and congo*), a flute, a trumpet, a trombone, and a bass guitar. It was formed in 2002, soon after the arrival of the founder, the Cuban guitarist and composer Santiago F. Jiménez Smith, in Prague. From its beginnings, the group changed its name and composition a number of times. Since the beginning of my research in the autumn of 2009 the band has gone through several changes. With the exception of the Cuban "core" of the group represented by the band leader Santiago F. Jiménez Smith, the percussionist Juan Carlos Diaz and the keyboard player Andris Batista Tamayo, different players alternated, for example, on the bass guitar or percussion. Apart from two Czech trumpet and trombone players (František Kněžek and Štěpán Schejbal) and the Slovak percussionist Michal Bolčo there are two Mexican musicians, the bass player Luis Franco Reyes and the drummer Omar Rojas. Most of the musicians graduated from music schools; they present their ensemble as "talented, professional, Cuban musicians with great temperament and energy."[75] Their repertoire comprises both original compositions of the founder and band leader Santiago F. J. Smith and his own arrangements of Cuban "traditionals" – in other words, there are compositions by already legendary Cuban composers such as Eliseo Grenet, Arsenio Rodríguez, Marcelino Guerra, etc. The band is mainly oriented on *son*, but also on other genres which are not considered to be exclusively Cuban: *salsa, cha-cha, merengue, guaguanco*.

They perform in various Prague music clubs (in 2009 and 2010 regularly on Monday "Latin Nights" at the Popocafépetl Club, irregularly, e.g., in the Lucerna Music Bar, Rikatádo, Lávka Club, and Jazz Dock), as a smaller group in more luxurious restaurants and bars and also in the framework of "Cuban" or "multicultural" evenings, but also often at company events and parties, at balls (2008 – the Czech Television ball) and private wedding and birthday celebrations.

The band mainly play in their full number at festivals (2009 – e.g. Sázava Fest, Festival Kamenčák Chomutov, Jablonec Cultural Summer, and Febiofest Pardubice; 2008 – e.g., Prague the Heart of Nations). In addition to live performances, members of the band also offer music compositions to order, as well as instruction. Cuban traditions performed by *Santy y su marabú* from the "Rumberito" compilation can be used commercially by those interested as musical background, for example, for a film or advertisement.

KITITI
Confessions – Africa Music Bar, Šafaříkova 11, Prague 2
January 22, 2010, 8 p.m.

Besides the Cubans of *Santy y su Marabú*, another entertainer who played in Prague, mainly in 2010, was the Congolese musician Kalanda ("Elvis") Kititi. As he told me in

---

75   http://www.santymarabu.eu/o-kapele (August 31, 2010).

an interview, he was born on December 23, 1968, in the Democratic Republic of the Congo. Since the age of fourteen, he has actively played music; as he says, he first began with Christian music after he recovered from malaria. He taught himself to play the guitar and began to sing with a church gospel choir; he later moved on to secular music. He founded his first own band in 1987 when he was still in his native Congo; he formed a few other groups during the time he performed in Kenya. He has been living in the Czech Republic since 1998. In 2002, along with a few other musicians including Gambia percussionist Papis Nyass, he founded the *Tshikuna* band specializing in "modern rhythms from the capital, Kinshasa, such as *soukous*, but also other traditional styles, e.g., *mutwashi* and *zebola*." In 2010 and 2011, he appeared with bass guitarist Jiří Opička, the American guitarist Shel Gunther and the Slovak percussionist Dalibor Hoček in a formation named *KITITI* and played concerts once or twice a month in Prague clubs,[76] where he performed music based on "folklore and modern Congolese styles".[77] He also worked with other Czech musicians (e.g., Pavel Fajt and Alan Vitouš) and he wrote the music for the film of Dan Svátek, *Blízko nebe*. He has been living in Prague since 1999 and has two daughters with his Czech wife. Occasionally he performs abroad, mostly in Italy. He sings in Lingala, but also in Kikongo, that is, in the languages spoken in his native land. The texts of the songs, in his words, try to "give advice to people," but he also sings of love and everyday life. Even if the texts are intentionally sung in his mother tongue, which he currently considers the most natural, he believes that his music is also, with certain adjustments, acceptable to the Czech public. He most appreciates it when concertgoers enjoy themselves, which means mainly that they dance.

I learned about Kititi's regular performances of via the Internet – either from an invitation posted on a personal web presentation,[78] the Czech information portal about Africa,[79] internet club pages where he was performing,[80] or thanks to news sent over the social network *Facebook* a few days before a concert. Today's concert, like the previous ones, takes place at two-month intervals at Zvonařka in a space called the "Africa Music Bar."

The spot, called Confessions, is a not very large bar and, at the same time, a musical club in the cellar space of a Secession house. The name of the club is painted above a smallish double door. I notice a blackboard at the entrance, on

76 Regularly in the "African" club *Confessions – Africa Music Bar* (Prague 2) in the Lesser Quarter bar *Popocafépetl* in the framework of "African Nights," occasionally also elsewhere.
77 http://www.kititi.net/cs/bio/ (August 28, 2010).
78 www.kititi.net
79 www.afroportal.cz
80 www.popocafepetl.cz , www.myspace.com/confessionsbar , www.hushcafe.cz , www.chapeaurouge.cz, etc.

which "TODAY HIP HOP" is written in large blue chalk letters, which evidently do not correspond to the program announced for this evening. But nowhere is there mention that Kititi is playing today. I wonder if everyone who intended to come here knew about this performance in advance.

As I slowly descend into the cellar along a narrow, poorly lit and worn-out winding staircase, I feel like coughing: dust and the smoke from cheap cigarettes float in the air, their age making it even more acrid. Downstairs opposite the entrance there is a small bar behind which stand a young African and a rather stout young lady with a blond pony-tail. I looked for a drink menu in vain, but after a while I notice writing on the wall at the bar – "piña colada," "Cuba libre" and other names of these best-known cocktails and beer, everything without the price listed. All the same, everyone there orders beer and pays a price corresponding to the lowest Prague average.

The walls and the arched ceiling are painted in various colors reminiscent of a number of flags of African states, i.e. yellow, red, green and black prevail. On the opposite wall there is a portrait of Bob Marley. On the whole, the walls, bar chairs and tables of all sorts look considerably worn. On the right side of the bar, about five tables for four are facing the stage; on the left side there are only two small tables pushed together, behind which there are a number of small bar tables. Those who are not sitting at a table can put their glasses down on a counter at the wall. Possible dance space is modest; it is a "narrow aisle" between the small tables on the left and the tables on the right side of the bar.

Ten minutes before the announced beginning of the concert, that is, at 7:50, there are eleven people at the bar, fewer than half of whom are Czechs. Next to me an African is speaking loudly in broken Czech, his white sweater shining blue thanks to the special lighting. He is chatting with two Czech women. Like a number of attendees not only of Kititi's but also of other "African" concerts, the Czech women are very stout, dressed in tight-fitting shirtwaists with shiny patterns and conspicuously made up. The chairs around the little tables and the bar seats are gradually taken by groups of new arrivals – either Africans or Czech youths no older than 20. The majority of the Africans greet Kititi warmly, but they also greet each other and many Czechs exchange greetings and friendly hugs with some of the Africans. People who don't know anyone here apparently don't come.

The guests seated around the tables or at the little bar tables smoke, drink beer and more or less loudly speak Czech, but the Africans also speak French with occasional African expressions. Meanwhile the musicians check the sound system on stage – I recognize fragments of songs I have heard at previous performances.

At 8:45, the man in the white sweater stands up from his table and walks around to the guests. He takes 50 crowns from each one, the entrance fee for today's performance and he stamps a dark blue square on each person's hand. The "concert" really begins around nine o'clock. Kititi, standing in the center of the stage, greets the audience with a husky voice: "Bonsoir, hello, dobrý večer!" which is answered with noisy applause and shouting by the Africans there. Then in a low voice he invitingly says into the microphone, "This music is about love and life," and begins to play along with the other musicians.

The strong sound of amplified guitars fills the space. The rhythmic accompaniment is provided by a set of European drums which, however, as always are played in syncopated four- and six-beat meter that sound more complex than the parts for drums in ordinary popular music.

After a few minutes, Kalanda Kititi also begins to sing. His sonorous voice sings all of the songs of the evening in African languages. His personality, the whole time of his performance, definitely attracts the greatest attention, not only because he stands in the center of the stage and is in the brightest spot of this dim room. Without question, his appearance also attracts attention: compared to his informally dressed fellow players in sweat shirts, jeans or cargo pants, he is wearing a perfectly coordinated outfit. A form-fitting black T-shirt and jeans of the same color with a distinctive belt emphasize his athletic physique. At the same time, he is also the most distinctive musician in the group. The gestures, mimicry and movements of his body awaken the impression that he fully enjoys his own singing, guitar playing and interaction with his fellow players. It seems to me that the songs follow each other in a sequence I have heard elsewhere. A number of the Africans, whether or not they are dancing, sometimes sing aloud with Kititi or applaud between the individual songs and shout in deep voices, "Hee...Kititi....bravo....merci beaucoup".

The Czechs who are present stand in the background of all of the happenings. The young couple sitting the first little table in the front of the room rarely watch the dancing in the aisle of the club or only rarely looked toward the stage. Around nine, five Czech teenagers arrive. Like another couple, they just sit at a table and don't dance once all evening. It seems that the music is mere sound background for them. At 9:15, a middle-aged Czech woman in a red sweater and blue jeans joins me at my table. After a while, we begin to talk. She is the girlfriend of one of the musicians. Glancing at the dancing Africans, she admits to me that she would love to dance but *she is embarrassed.*

Around 9:30, like in the other club performances of Kititi's I've experienced, there is a roughly half-hour intermission. At this time there are only about 20 people here. During the intermission Kititi orders a beer and water at the bar and talks to the guests, mainly the Africans. The other members of the band stay in the front of the stage. Sounds of modern African music float from the loudspeakers – again apparently the same well-known songs. Some of the people are already slightly drunk; they merrily sing along with the loud speakers. Slightly after ten, most of the Czech guests leave, except for the foursome of young people at the first table. At the same time, another group of Africans arrive; there are now about thirty men and only one woman. All are wearing very modern clothing in a colorful spectrum of styles, including fleece winter coats and hip-hop caps and wide pants with crotches down to their knees.

The second half of today's concert begins at ten o'clock. Now, during each song, various Africans stand up from the tables and dance - either alone or in pairs or in fours. At those times I observe a nascent shared feeling of pleasure from the music, and listening to it strengthens the intoxication of dance. I admiringly follow the bodies of the dancers in constant spontaneous, but nevertheless perfectly synchronized, motion. The dancers moving with short steps comprised of stamping feet rotate with bent arms close to their bodies; they mainly pay the greatest attention to the wavy movements of their sides, which sometimes bump into someone else's. A smile is mirrored on their faces with closed or, on the contrary, merrily open eyes, complete with a lit cigarette.

The concert ends after eleven - because the bar is in an apartment building and after ten it is necessary to be quiet. Kalanda Kititi says good-by with a loud "Merci, merci beaucoup!"

MALANKA, THE UKRAINIAN BALL
BARRICADERS' CULTURAL HOUSE, SARATOVSKÁ 20, PRAGUE 10.
FEBRUARY 27, 2010, 7 P.M.
Zita Skořepová Honzlová

During my research I discovered that at community events in Prague during anniversaries and holidays some hundreds of members of foreign minorities gather, almost invisible to the Czech majority. This was the case of the Ukrainian ball, which is organized every year by the Ukrainian Initiative to celebrate St. Melanie's day. The ball took place in the Barricaders' Cultural House in Prague-Strašnice. The building itself, apart from the unappealing surroundings of a neighboring marketplace, is inconspicuous and rather run-down - from the exterior, but mainly from the interior, as if it were breathing the socialist atmosphere. On the inside, in addition to advertisements on Country Radio, posters of "Eva and Vašek" invite you. In contrast to the exterior view from the front, from which the Cultural House appears to be a small building,

Days of Ukrainian Culture, Prague (photo: Ukrainian Initiative)

Ukrainian ball Malanka, Prague,
Barricaders' Cultural Center
(photo: Ukrainian Initiative)

I am surprised at the vastness of the interior space, reminiscent at first glance of a large tavern. The walls are covered with wooden boards, and tables with red tablecloths with the name "Gambrinus" on them are arranged on the left and right sides in several long rows. Between them there is an empty space, which reminds us of the fact that there will obviously be dancing here. The air of the evening is pervaded with cigarette smoke. Scattered on the tables are the latest issue of the community magazine "Porohy" as well as flyers for a transportation company that dispatches buses to Ukraine and Moldavia. After seven o'clock, a great part of the guests arrive, many of whom are personally welcomed by the head of the Ukrainian Initiative, Viktor Rajčinec, and his son, Bohdan. Most of the people are of upper middle age, but there are also a few seniors and families with children. Everyone is dressed up; combinations, how-ever, evidently conform to criteria somewhat different from those of Czechs; at this and other Ukrainian events, they wear blouses or jackets of striking colors with a quantity of sequins, little red pumps with very high heels for the women and violet velvet jackets for the men. Generally it is possible to catch a glimpse of a few young men and women wearing Ukrainian folk blouses with typical regional embroidery in the audience. At 7:20, Bohdan Rajčinec takes the stage and presents the program in Ukrainian and then, in shortened form, in perfect Czech. As at other Ukrainian events, here, too, the youth ensemble Džerelo begin the evening with a dance scene of a "Village Wedding." Their performances – each time in different folk costumes, then alternated several

Ukrainian ball Malanka, Prague, Barricaders' Cultural Center (photo: Ukrainian Initiative)

times with the *Ruch* band, Ukrainian musicians from Poland who present "national songs in a modern rendition." Extensive applause is earned by Ukrainian women dancers, first for their belly dancing and then by a dancing duo impersonating an angel and a skeleton with hoops accompanied by abrasive metallic music and singing in German, and then an acrobat who dances in a special costume so that the optical illusion evokes a picture of two dancing sprites. As guests, the Prague vocal choir Gospel Limited perform; during their performance Bohdan Rajčinec notes that, according to some people, American songs are close to Ukrainian ones. This performance, however, does not invoke a great response; the public enjoy *Ruch* and then, mainly, *Ignis*, who appear after nine o'clock. This ensemble began forty years ago in Prague and Viktor Rajčinec, the head of the Ukrainian Initiative and concurrently co-organizer of the Malanka ball, still performs with his son in it. *Ignis* is dedicated to "national songs"[81] from the various regions of Ukraine; they are presented in arrangements for singing, two guitars, accordion and keyboard. Just as elsewhere, the musicians appeared at this ball in black pants and black or white folk shirts decorated with innumerable kinds of Ukrainian embroidery. On today's program there

---

81   See http://www.ukrajinci.cz/cs/kapela-ignis/ (February 20, 2012).

are about ten Ukrainian songs, which according to the cheering reactions of the public are quite well-known and popular –. A few slower nostalgic numbers alternate with invigorating dance compositions during which the musicians glow with pleasure and élan; mainly the band leader, Viktor Rajčinec, is in his element and with his temperament he surrenders himself to the atmosphere of the sustained good mood of the public. The people chat cheerfully; the dance floor fills with couples and dance groups mainly consisting of young people. I notice that a whole bottle of vodka has been consumed at the table next to mine. The *kolomeika* has great success; during it the dancers form a circle, thus filling the whole floor. In the course of my research and mainly on the basis of an interview with Viktor Rajčinec I learned that the *Ignis* musicians unambiguously prefer such a performance at events at least co-organized by the Ukrainian Initiative and do not intend to adjust their repertoire or the general character of their self-presentation in order to conform to other events or before another public. For two years, for example, the same compositions have been heard which, among the Ukrainian listeners present today (the absolute majority of whom are immigrants who had already come to the Czech Republic years ago and decided to stay) inspire the enthusiasm and nostalgia of "sweet memories" of the past, just like the *pizmonim* performed by Syrian Jews in Brooklyn[82] or performances of the Ziriab band for Arab listeners.[83]

82 Kaufman Shelemay 1998.
83 Skořepová 2010.

REFUFEST
KAMPA PARK, PRAGUE 1
FRIDAY, JUNE 18, 2010, 12 P.M. – 9 P.M.
Zita Skořepová Honzlová

At five minutes after noon I enter Prague's Kampa Park where, as in the previous years, the Refufest Festival is to take place. Its proclaimed aim is the "meeting of traditions and cultures."[84] The goal of the organizers – the NGO InBáze Berkat – is, however, broader: not only to introduce cultural performances, culinary or "typical" products of minorities and mainly migrant groups living in the Czech Republic, but also to point out bad practices in employment of foreigners and other problems that refugees and voluntary work migrants must face in the Czech Republic. I notice posters pinned on several trees, on which there is a picture of an Asian girl in a red folk costume with a string instrument that I can't identify.

At first, everyone notices a large outdoor stage on which a banner with the words "Refufest or a Holiday is Coming" and the logos of the organizations supporting the festival is fastened. On each side of the stage, there is a little tent village. On the left are small stands covered with blue cloths. Flags and signs with the names of countries are hanging in front of them. I notice Uzbekistan, Vietnam, Georgia, Armenia, Kyrgyzstan, Indonesia, Mongolia, Kalmykia, Ukraine, Belarus, Pakistan and Afghanistan. On the right of the stage, there are a number of oblong tables with a white cloth above them; on the tables the participants – mainly women – arrange plastic trays and plates with cold and warm refreshments. They offer various "national" vegetable and meat dishes, sweet and savory pastries and traditional bread. Like at the smaller stands to the left of the stage, signs with names have also been placed here at each table. I recognize a few African countries, Azerbaijan, Iraq and Armenia. Among the stands representing individual countries I also notice stands with the logos of the organizations InBáze Berkat, People in Need, The Organization for the Aid to Refugees, Amnesty International and Greenpeace. Apart from these, there are a few others without big signs or posters. They have small flyers on tables, free for the taking. Fixed on the back wall, one of these "unmarked" stands has a large hand-painted colorful poster with the words "Foreigners are not dispos-

---

84   www.refufest.cz . (November 19, 2012.)

Refufest: Prague, Kampa Park (photo: Zita Skořepová Honzlová)

able". In the space between the stands still below the cloth there are a few rows of tables and benches for those who wish to sit and eat. Near the stands with refreshments, there is a large board with a reproduction of a comics page that describes the difficult fate of Vietnamese, Mongolian and Algerian migrants in the Czech Republic.

According to the schedule, the program should start at any moment, but, in light of the morning rain, the beginning has been delayed and so the preparatory phase hasn't ended yet. This is manifested by the technicians bustling about with cables and sound technicians and participants who just now are readying their stands, exhibiting various objects, or beginning to cook. At a stand with the "Afghanistan" sign, I greet the operators of my favorite Afghan restaurant in the center of Prague. They tell me that they are here for the umpteenth time and, as I notice, they are offering a degustation of some of the dishes from their own menu. Apart from this, one can see here, next to photographs of the famous blue mosque in Mazari Sharif, the mountainous landscape of Hindu Kush and a reduced clay model of Bamiyan Buddhist statues, a few small hand-knotted carpets. A middle-aged man, a journalist who has been living in Prague for a long time, is decorating a paper kite with water colors; besides food and carpets, this year they want to introduce kite flying, an important Afghan tradition. Like this stand, the other ones also representing individual states offer, in addition to food tastings, various objects for sale – Vietnamese non-la hats, Uzbek puppets, hand-made clothing, head coverings, bags or decorative textiles; the strong aroma of incense sticks wafts from the "Pakistan" stand, mingling with the various aromas of the food that has just been prepared.

Around 12:30 the first visitors are already arriving; for the time being, they just stop at the individual stands and from time to time turn their attention to the currently empty stage. At 1:30 the program is officially opened; two moderators welcome the guests to the "multicultural Refufest festival which is also a street happening." A pair of City Police guards with a dog capture everyone's attention; they walk around the park twice and look over the stands strictly. However, they soon leave. In the meantime, the first couple – Tomáš Reindl and Jana Fabiánová – appear on stage. They play the cello and the Australian wind instrument, the didgeridoo, but scarcely twenty people are listening. Next, the journalist and writer František Kostlán alternates with the Romani youth dance ensemble *Cikáni jdou do nebe (Gypsies go to heaven)*. A few girls with long hair adorned with roses and colorful frilled skirts perform dances of Russian Roma accompanied by recorded music for the more numerous public. The moderators, except for a short intermission of the participants, draw the visitors' attention to the possibility to buy food and objects sold by people from the refugee camp in Kostelec nad Orlicí and to events at individual stands, e.g. a workshop of Afghan dance with Magdalena Hoškova at 3 p.m. František Kostlán calls on people to sign the petition "Together against racism and disrespect."

After three in the afternoon, hundreds of people of all ages are already circulating among the stands. Most are members of the younger and middle generations; there are only a few seniors; families with small children in carriages also walk around the park. I notice that some of the participants watch only one or two performances, stop at stands and leave, while a smaller part remain here; they sit with a beer or other refreshments in the space with tables and benches and alternate between looking around the stands and more or less concentrated watching of the acts on the stage. After a performance on an Indonesian *gamelan*, the Central Asian band *Jagalmay* appears on stage around 3:45. The members of the band arrive somewhat shyly, but with smiles: four Kyrgyz women and two Uzbek men. From the left stand the younger Gulsara, middle-aged Janyl and Elvira, and adolescent Sajara. They are wearing white, pink, red and light green dresses with rich frills on their skirts and sleeves, all made of semi-transparent synthetic material reminiscent of veils. At first glance, the beholder is captivated by the ornaments which are on their pointy hats and which border the edge of the black velvet vests in identical colors and style. It is obvious that these costumes, clearly inspired by some sort of regional folk costume, are colored variations of one model. The Uzbek musicians Farhod

Jagalmay at Refufest (photo: Zita Skořepová Honzlová)

and Ulugbek are wearing dark pants, wide white tunics and, at this moment, tall felt Kyrgyz caps.

They look around for a few seconds, smiles alternating with concentrated looks, and the three women standing at the end of the stage put the Kyrgyz Jew's harps (*temir komuz*) to their lips. The amplifying system somewhat deforms their own mysterious buzzing sound. Although rhythm has the central role in this composition, and the alternation of variously long tones squeezed out identically by all three Jew's harps plays the central role in this composition, there is a perceptible hint of a melody in the playing. The next number is sung in unison by the women, who perform a folk-like Kyrgyz song from 1916, "Jagalmay." Then Janyl removes a three-string lute, a *komuz,* with a long neck and a pear-shaped back, from its case: this is considered the Kyrgyz national instrument. She plays a solo composition in which the short introductory motif gradually develops. Janyl plays very skillfully – it is obvious that she is accustomed to this instrument, which she has been playing since her youth. Particularly impressive to me are the changes in the technique of vibrating the strings, and mainly the effective playing with the instrument "upside down," when, with a quick motion, she places the lute between her knees and holds it vertically with the neck downward toward the ground. The public reward this number not only with applause but also with several shouts of admiration. In the next act, Gulsara dances to the accompaniment of the *komuz* lute and the singing of Janyl and Elvira in unison. The constantly smiling dancer does pirouettes, raises her hands high and in her dance imitates the motion of *komuz* playing, thus similar to Janyl's playing the instrument.

Meanwhile, the people in the audience walk in front of the stage; some watch the performance while standing with a plastic cup in their hands; others sit on the grass because the sun is shining and the weather is lovely. Two children managed to lift an Afghan kite into the air, which now flies over the stands on the left side of the stage. To the right of the stage a seated young man has a Tajik *pakol* on his head that says "Lion of Panjsher," Ahmad Shah Massoud,[85] which he bought at one of the stands of a non-governmental organization. A few people close to the stage photograph or film the performers with their compact cameras or cell phones.

The following number is played by the male musicians with two Uzbek frame drums, *doyras*, whereas the female members of the group have gone backstage. During the previous number, the men had replaced their Kyrgyz head coverings with Uzbek caps and tied three-cornered colored scarves around their waists. The standing musicians hold their drums in the vertical position in front of their chests and vibrate the membranes with their fingers. A booming sound enriches the jangling and rattling of a number of metal rings placed under the membranes of the drum frames. It seems that they are performing something like a drum duel for the public. Both drums first begin to play the same rhythmic pattern in slow tempo; at a certain time, though, they separate and "answer" each other; the tempo and volume of the playing increase and diminish. Both drummers utilize different techniques and combine different rhythmic patterns, parts of them, and individual kinds of beats, dynamic possibilities of the instrument and timbre. The joint number concludes with a quick succession of richly ornamented whirling beats.

In the last two numbers, the female members of *Jagalmay* appear in Uzbek costumes. These are, compared to those of Kyrgyzstan, much more colorful. The tunics of shiny material with many-colored geometric patterns most often reminiscent of rhomboids reach down to the middle of their calves. Under them, tight pants in identical colors are visible. On their heads, they have four-sided hats. Round mirrors sewn on them reflect the glow of the lights as do a number of beaded tassels along the whole perimeter of the hats. In the next number, two *doyras* provide the instrumental accompaniment. Farhod sings in Uzbek while Janyl and Elvira clap and sing only in the choruses. In her dance,

---

85   An Afghan commander and politician of Tajik origin. In the 1980s he became famous as an anti-Soviet fighter. In the second half of the 1990s he became commander-in-chief of the so-called Northern Alliance, opponents of the Taliban movement. He was assassinated in 2001.

Farhod Tashev plays the dayereh
(photo: Zita Skořepová Honzlová)

Gulsara draws attention to the movements of her hand and shoulders and mainly to a special movement of her head as it goes from side to side with her chin thrust forward. As next to last the Azeri popular song "Rihane" is sung. Everyone sings, but only three of the four female members of the group dance. Ulugbek and Farhod stay in the background with the *doyras*. People in the audience enjoy watching the participants and clap to the rhythm with pleasure. Evidently, the quicker numbers with rhythmic accompaniment and dancing receive greater applause than the first song, "Jagalmay", for solo voice. At the very end, Sajara appears alone in a red costume with a black vest and sequins. This time, the musical accompaniment is a recorded popular Uygur song. The little beauty already skillfully master's a dancer's movements and coquettish expressions learned from television and the Internet; she theatrically spins in her long bell-shaped skirt and two thick black braids that reach down to the middle of her thighs twirl around her body. The thirty-minute performance of *Jagalmay* ends with mighty applause.

After *Jagalmay*, the girl from the poster appears on stage; she is a small musician from Mongolia. She performs in a red folk costume in which she presents a "Mongolian dance." The public also appreciatively applaud her skillful playing on the "horse violin", the *igil*, a two-string bowed instrument. Her playing style resembles cello playing. The instrument is characterized by a horse-head carving at the end of the neck.

Apart from bands whose members are only or for the most part foreigners, during the afternoon there also appear short performances of Czech groups like the women's vocal band *Yellow Sisters* and the *Džezvica* band that claims Balkan inspiration. In the early evening, a more numerous public, now roughly four-hundred people, enjoy the numbers of the ensemble of a Romani accordionist and the singer Mário Bihári. Starting at 7 p.m., the multinational group the "Allstar Refugee Band", takes the stage. With the passage of time, the productions become closer and closer to dance and popular music. I notice that the public has grown by roughly twenty foreigners who came to watch their friends – participants in the festival – and talk to them in front of the stands. At the conclusion of Friday's program, the Equator band, led by Iraqi drummer and singer Annas Younis, perform. Part of the public start to dance spiritedly to the music with accompaniment of the most common Arab rhythmic patterns after Annas Younis arouses them by calling out "I don't see you dancing. Are you tired? Hands up and dance!" and with an introductory adaptation of several popular Arab hits, e.g. "Habibi" by the Egyptian singer Amr Diab. A few minutes after eight, the show ends and the people disperse.

JAGALMAY

Jagalmay is the only musical group in the Czech Republic whose members are oriented toward Central Asian music and dance. The ensemble was founded in Prague in about 2000 by the journalist Janyl Chytyrbaeva, who comes from a Kyrgyz musical family. In the Czech Republic, through the activities of the *Jagalmay* group, she tries to play "traditional" Central Asian music. She is mainly interested in musical expressions considered in various regions of Central Asia as "original."[86] In the repertoire of the group, therefore, are compositions that are judged to have no or only minimal Russian influence. There are Kyrgyz, Kazakh, Uzbek and Uygur songs, instrumental and purely vocal compositions, and dance-music pieces coming from Central Asia or from the Caucasian region, performed in arrangements using of regionally "typical" instruments. In her short introductions during performances for the Czech public, Janyl Chytyrbaeva sometimes presents the music of Kyrgyzstan and Kazakhstan as "nomadic" or "shamanic," while she attributes Uzbek songs to their local "urban" culture. In the words of the moderators at various events and on printed programs

---

86   From the second half of the 19th century the gradual subjugation of Central Asian Khanates by the tzarist Russia was underway, the Russification reached its peak with the creation of the Soviet Union, when individual regions became republics, or districts.

Jagalmay at Refufest (photo: Zita Skořepová Honzlová)

and on posters, the band is characterized as playing "folk" or "traditional" "music and dance of Central Asia" or "Central Asian nations," "Central Asian folklore," etc.

Apart from the three Kyrgyz members Janyl, Elvira and Gulsara, that is, the stable core of the group, during the years of their existence the composition of the *Jagalmay* group has changed several times due to, for example, arrivals, shorter or longer participation and departures of members and partly unpredictable circumstances (the non-prolongation of a permanent residence visa or the departure from the Czech Republic for other reasons, etc.).The ages of the musicians vary in a relatively wide range. Elvira Jumajeva and Gulsara Bekbagysheva have children who grew up in the Czech Republic and for whom Czech is their primary language of communication. While the daughter of Elvira Jumajeva, Sajara, whose mother is Kyrgyz and whose father is Uygur, had considered herself Czech earlier, she has now, according to Janyl Chytyrbaeva, returned to her "roots" and mainly performs Uygur dance in *Jagalmay*. It is actually Kyrgyz songs and Uygur dances that provide a suitable possibility for acquainting Sajara with "her own" but now, paradoxically, more distant language and culture. Sajara learned to dance Central Asian dance by watching video recordings on the Internet and from the instructions of her mother and some of their Central Asian friends.

Often for a short time there are men and women in the group whose ages range from young adulthood to upper middle age with origins in various states (Kyrgyzstan, Kazakhstan, Uzbekistan, Turkmenistan, Afghanistan, and Azerbaijan) and with different musical backgrounds ranging from self-taught to graduates of music-education institutions such as conservatories. With the change of the member base of the band there are also changes in its repertoire and arrangements. Janyl Chytyrbaeva has the main task of directing the activities of the band. Apart from singing and knowledge of a number of Kyrgyz folk and art songs, she plays the Kyrgyz national instrument, the *komuz* lute, coordinates the choice of repertoire and discusses organizational events at which *Jagalmay* performs. Kazakh Elvira and Kyrgyz Gulsara, in addition to singing and dancing, play the Jew's harp. Besides Janyl's collection of songs, there are various sources of the repertoire, most often videos or other materials available on the Internet or in the memory of other members of the group. With the arrival of the two Uzbek players in 2009, the repertoire grew with songs sung in Uzbek with instrumental accompaniment by Farhod Tashev and Ulugbek Samandarev on the *doyra* and *rebab*. According to Janyl Chytyrbaeva, their influence represents a contrast to the music of the Kyrgyzes and Kazakhs. Janyl Chytyrbaeva, however, in return taught the Uzbek musicians how to master the Jew's harp, which had previously been foreign to them and they jointly sing in Kyrgyz and Kazakh. The group meets irregularly for rehearsals, the most frequent meetings in roughly weekly intervals for about a month before scheduled concerts. Despite the closeness of Central Asian languages, in case of misunderstandings they use Russian, which most of the members speak.

On the basis of observation and informal interviews during rehearsals, it is clear that each of the musicians comes to the band with different skills and knowledge of music specific to the region of his/her own origin. Some, in the framework of a program, can perform solo, e.g. when at all concerts the Uzbek drummer Farhod Tashev performs with his solo playing on the frame drum *doyra* or to the accompaniment of a small harmonium and *tabla* drums Afghan Asadullah Saifi sings songs in Pashto and Dari[87] on texts of Jalaleddin Rumi or other classical Persian poets. Elsewhere, specific regional elements are joined and used together in the form of arrangements created through the process of bricolage, i.e. the "do-it-yourself" combining of musical elements that are "at hand." Thus it does not always hold true that, for example, an Uzbek or Kyrgyz song is sung in the Uzbek language or in Kyrgyz costumes. On the contrary, it happens that on stage we see Kazakh and Kyrgyz musicians in Uzbek costumes playing the Jew's harp, the Uzbek Farhod in a Kyrgyz hat with an Arab *darbuka*, or the Kyrgyz dancer Gulsara dancing in her "own" fashion to Afghan music. We can thus observe a certain inconsistency or variability in the use of musical instruments, languages of the songs, style of dancing, momentary wearing of clothing and head coverings, or some sort of symbolic indicator of identification of the musicians

87   I.e. in Afghan Persian.

with this or that region. Everything is mixed together into one presentation of "folk music and dance of Central Asia," in which the unfamiliarity of the great majority of the audience understandably does not permit them to differentiate and identify individual elements.

According to Janyl Chytyrbaeva, the love of music common to all the musicians is primarily realized as a free-time activity. Not only concerts, but mainly house rehearsals provide an opportunity for meeting together and they are a means of recalling cultural customs of Central Asia which they miss in the Czech Republic, which are diverse, but close to the hearts of all the members. . Eating together, for example, is very important: after a rehearsal, some member of the group treats the others to food from his/her own country. The sense of the common performance of music is also expressed in the motto written in the Facebook profile of *Jagalmay* which is at the present the only Internet presentation of the group: "We play in order to ease our longing for our home and brighten the gray Czech sky". A similar attempt to remember their own ethno-cultural "roots" is also evident among other music groups I have researched, mainly the Arab *Ziriab*[88] and the Ukrainian band *Ignis*. I learned that *Jagalmay* actually does not perform in independent concerts that would be organized on their own initiative. Apart from playing in closed meetings of the Central Asian communities, these musicians' performance is part of a broader program of cultural events connected to various "folk", "national", and/or "folkloric" "traditions" and cultural-educational projects connected with the themes of migration, multiculturalism and the lives of ethnic minorities in the Czech Republic.

88   Skořepová Honzlová, 2010.

WHAT DOES IT MEAN?

Zuzana Jurková

Zita's "snapshots" differ in the musics that are heard, the listeners who listen to them attentively in an environment where an event takes place... and in many other ways. But at least they have one thing in common: foreigners, that is, those who came to Prague not very long ago from foreign cultures and languages, play and sing music which, at least to a certain extent, refers to their place of origin.

Let us look at their music-making through the optical lenses that we tried to create in the introduction of this chapter, that is, as "identity performances" in which the musicians demonstrate who they feel they are, where they feel they belong and where they do not feel they belong.

If we were to hold fast to Goffman's concept, then during those concerts or performances we follow primarily the area of the "stage" and "front region," that is, the musical event itself; at the same time it is useful not to neglect the backstage and the "back region," where it is possible to localize activities connected with *means, preparations and planning of performances, choice of repertoire and its arrangement, appearance of musicians (the visual expression of the musicians' intentions such as clothes, posture and gestures) and ways of behaving in front of an audience, place and form of promotion.*[89]

The first and basic factor determining the shape of a musical presentation is the audience, concretely if they are primarily listeners from the same foreign community as the musicians or if they are mainly Czechs. To a certain extent, this fact reveals the basic tendency of musicians in the field of acculturation, that is, adopting the culture of the host nation.[90] It is useful to pay attention on the one hand to what we mentioned in the introductory text in connection with Erik Erikson's concept of identity: i.e. the basis of identity is *a feeling enabling the individual to experience his own self as something that defines continuity and unity.* Thus if people or a group should accept their own identity, they must

---

89 Skořepová Honzlová, 2012: 371.

90 The basis for the structure of the following acculturation strategies is Zita's thesis; a summary of it is published in the article "Acculturation Strategies...," Skořepová Honzlová 2012.

experience (which also means, to a certain extent, present) the continuity of what they were prior to their migration, and of what they are now.

On the other hand, however, in the new environment they constantly come into contact with others with whom they must cope. There are several types[91] of this reconciliation of continuity (including references to their origin) and coming to grips with the new. If we wanted to create a scale of these strategies of interactions with the majority environment, then "impressive musical fusion" would be at the highest point and "music of invisible enclaves" at the lowest. Between them there would be ethnic music for entertainment and "exotic music" as a proof of multiculturality.

The strategic category of "impressive musical fusion" would include the performances of the Chinese singer Feng-yün Song as well as of the Iranian guitarist Shahab Tolouie. These two performers are aware of both their own musical potential as well as the potential of their home musical traditions, but, at the same time, they know that these traditions are not enough to attract Czech listeners. That is why they decided to join elements of their own musical traditions with the demands or expectations of Czech audiences and so create something new and exotic and, at the same time, acceptable to the local listeners. *The result of this is the experimental and esoteric playing of musical instruments with the dominant singing of Feng-yün Song or with Persian elements of the fusing "ethnoflamenco" of Shahab Tolouie.*[92]

It goes without saying that the important precondition of success is, on the one hand, distinctive musical talent and, on the other, the ability to guess how attractive this style is to Czech listeners. While the impressiveness of musical performances of Shahab Tolouie is obvious because of his technical virtuosity, in Feng-yün Song's case, her ability to communicate empathetically via language and especially via music is impressive.

As the last and perhaps strongest argument for the assumption that this strategy is an example of integration, we can mention the addressee of musical performances: despite the fact that the musicians refer to their Chinese or Persian origin, promotion is clearly targeted to the Czech audience, who clearly dominate the events.

---

91   We do not, of course, describe all the events of this type that took place in Prague. However, according to Zita's research, which included many others and also according to the available literature (see above-mentioned article), it seems that these are basic types which one can also find elsewhere. But at the same time, it is also apparent from the literature that in other cities there are also other strategies that we didn't find in Prague, e.g., segregation – when the members of the immigrant groups do not have opportunities, are not allowed to present their culture. This is exactly the choice of these strategies showing the specificity of a concrete city as it is discussed in the first chapter.

92   Honzlová Skořepová 2012: 373.

On the opposite end of the acculturation scale is **music of invisible enclaves**. This is apparent from the snapshots of the Nowruz celebration in the Prague Central Asian community or from the Ukrainian Malanka ball: one cannot learn about any of these functions in newspapers or on posters and thus the audience is dominated by those who heard about it by word of mouth. It is clear that besides music, this social dimension which determines its more-or-less informal character is important for the event. This influences musical performance in at least two directions. First, musicians do not need to accommodate the "foreign" taste of the Czech audience. They do not have to try to attract or keep the audience's attention or make music more acceptable with verbal clarification. At the same time they do not have to search for features which would possibly be considered the most typical by Czechs. Thus they do not have to look for the Czech image of Ukrainian or Central Asian musics. Second, the musicians are not under such great pressure in contrast to those who perform for a demanding Czech audience. S/he is here not primarily to demonstrate her/his technical or other artistic perfection but to create, with other participants, an illusion - however ephemeral -of the distant home.

As in the case of **"impressive musical fusion"**, in the category of **"ethnic music for entertainment"**, the emphasis on differentness has the function of a kind of promoter for a Czech (or broader Western) audience. If it is performed in a bar or restaurant, the music helps to create a "relaxed" Caribbean atmosphere (or better: the Czech image of such an atmosphere); at the same time it should not bother the listeners by its volume, length or complicatedness, and, generally, disturb the primary purpose of the place. That is why the same popular compositions are performed and constantly repeated (moreover in undemanding arrangements) which could be familiar to the listeners or easy for them to remember. If, however, it is club dance music, that is another matter: musicians play the way they are used to playing dance music at home. The sounds are thus not merely an accompaniment of the dance but an integral part of it. Here, however, the trouble begins because the Czech public is much shyer concerning dance, as is apparent from the snapshot of the "Africa Music Bar" as well as confirmed by the manager of Cuban musicians. [93]

And so the musicians have to decide between playing "their own way and for their own" - and belonging, to a certain degree, to invisible enclaves - or becoming a rather marginal part of the atmosphere of a luxurious bar. This provides them with a regular income at the price of abandoning their own musical ambitions. It is possible, however, to understand this as the common situation of craftsmen, as musicians in many world cultures are considered.

---

93   Skořepová Honzlová 2012: 378.

The title of the last strategic category, **exotic music as a proof of multi-culturality**, should be explained here. We are convinced that, during events like Refufest, music is used as a label, as proof of something which in reality is not completely so, as proof of a desired multicultural coexistence, thus integration, rather than a real one. First, musicians do not organize the events by themselves, but perform in frameworks of larger multicultural happenings, the organizers of which are multicultural NGOs. Musicians here attract the attention of relatively large audiences. Many musicians, however, do not perform elsewhere and thus there is no occasion for real integration, for denser and more common contact between musicians and their public. By the way, this is confirmed by the fact that the performances of the same musicians are composed of the same musical numbers on different occasions: it is not expected that the same people will be in the audience.

The choice of repertoire and the manner of its performance are determined by two key words: exoticism and tradition. The former should show the Czech viewer the attractiveness of the (of course, rather stereotypical) otherness: in the visual sphere, the roses in the hair of Romani girls, in the sound sphere, e.g., a "shamanic" Jew's harp, a rather curious instrument but without substantial musical possibilities. Some instruments of Vietnamese classical music, e.g., a monochord đàn bầu[94] or the đàn đày lute with a long neck and trapezoid body, can be considered exotic. If these instruments appear on stage, moderators don't forget to mention that they belong to the UNESCO World Heritage list. However, these instruments do not appear at events targeted to Vietnamese audiences. The second key word is "tradition", the very word which is recommended by the American ethnomusicologist Mark Slobin for a well-deserve rest.[95] In many of us, however, it evokes romantic ideas about the unspoiled "spirit of a folk" in distant pre-globalized times and folk treasures which have to be "safeguarded" (an expression frequently used in this context) and sometimes also "sorted", which means chosen as the most original and most characteristic for the given region.

Musical exoticism, which again has a promotional function here, tells the listeners something like "Don't be afraid of foreigners!" They are different, but you see how beautiful/remarkable they are and, moreover, they safeguard their beautiful old traditions!

---

94 An instrument with a wood box resonator to which a short, flexible, wooden or bamboo rod and a small coconut or gourd shell is attached. The only string attached to the rod goes through the shell and is fixed at the other end of the resonator. The player vibrates the string with one hand while regulating the pitch by bending the rod. The sound is characterized by glissandi. In the past, the instrument was often played by blind musicians.

95 Slobin 2000: Foreword.

The nature of light entertainment prevents broader resonance of the music performances in Czech audiences (to do so, musicians should go in the direction of musical fusion). For the same reason, musicians cannot identify themselves with their performances as a means of their own expression and communication with understanding listeners. These are found at the meetings of invisible enclaves.

ANTONÍN DVOŘÁK: RUSALKA
NATIONAL THEATER
SATURDAY, MAY 1, 2010, AT 7 P.M.
Zuzana Jurková

WHERE TO GO IN PRAGUE FOR OPERA?

It isn't a great problem to go to an opera in Prague: opera is the basic component of the repertoire of at least three "stone" theaters. The **State Opera**, whose
classical building is curiously surrounded by an arterial road, plays a primarily
international repertoire and, newly this past season, a musical – *Kudykam*. The
Estates Theater, historically the oldest opera house, in contrast to the others,
a filigree building in the very center of the city, is famous as the place where
Mozart's *Don Giovanni* had its premiere; here Mozart's operas still prevail in the
repertoire. Until a few years ago, in addition to these operas and a few plays,
they presented contemporary operas (for which, understandably, they did not
expect many viewers). This has changed in recent years: the only contemporary,
very experimental, opera with a strong political accent – *Zítra se bude (Tomorrow Will Be)* – is performed on the chamber stage of the nearby Kolovrat Theater.

Undoubtedly the dominant position belongs to the **National Theater.** Its
neo-Renaissance building, erected 1868–81 at the intersection of the Vltava's
bank and National Avenue, attracts the eye from afar with its golden balustrade
lining the crown of the roof, at closer glance with its dazzling majesty. One
must have a similar majestic feeling inside: a combination of the red velvet seat
covers and the gilt accessories (railings, massive chandelier...) and the richly
designed decorations (allegorical paintings on the ceiling, the curtain, the decorations in the adjacent spaces outside of the auditorium) evoke a celebratory
and even illusory impression, at least the first few times one goes there.

PERFORMANCE

Performances usually begin at the National Theater at 7 p.m. The building opens
three-quarters of an hour before the beginning – and people already stream
in at that time after having dinner across the street at the *Café Slavia* with its
spectacular view of the Prague Castle. Right behind the entrance doors, ushers
in cloaks with the theater's logo check our tickets. At seven, the thousand seats

National Theater

in the theater are more or less filled. At first glance, the audience is unusually varied: middle-aged and older men and women in formal clothing, young people (most of whom, judging by their language, are foreigners), and on the other hand, school-aged children with their parents or teachers, often informally in pants and sweaters. Looking down at the distribution in the audience, however, one can notice that in the lower part – the orchestra section and the first balcony – the formality of dark suits and evening dresses increases, as does the age of the opera-goers. Looking up, on the other hand, one can see a concentration of young people in jeans and sweaters and occasionally in batik dresses. The explanation is simple: tickets for seats in the orchestra cost roughly ten times as much as those in the second gallery: 600–800 Czech crowns as compared to 80 crowns; in addition, student discounts also apply here. (Perhaps, however, there is another reason: tickets to the National Theater are sold several months in advance, so that the best tickets are bought primarily by regular opera-goers, predominantly from the middle and older generations, while foreign visitors to Prague, who usually don't come dressed appropriately, are left with the last tickets in the galleries.)

The orchestra pit
in the National Theater

Statistical research on Czech musicality[1] carried out toward the end of 2013 gives the following picture of opera fans: there are three times as many women as men at the opera and the "core of opera-goers is situated in upper age categories." (The average opera-goer is 46 years old.)

Furthermore: there are twice as many university graduates as high-school graduates and three times as many as those with an elementary-school education. And quite understandably, those who have some musical education and/or play an instrument markedly outweigh those who don't.

What is, however, the most surprising is this: most operagoers come from cities with over 100,000 inhabitants – excluding Prague (in such cities, more than 20% of the inhabitants go to the opera while there are only half as many in Prague, which is a little over the average for the whole country). This surprising fact is explained by

---

1   See Bek 2003. By the word "musicality" the author understands *the musical preferences and the musical activities* of the Czech population (p. 34).

Mikuláš Bek (the author of the research) by two perhaps parallel factors: on the one hand, the extensive cultural offering in Prague, the only Czech metropolis, and thus the greater diversification of supply here, and secondly, by what we describe in the section about performers: that opera presents certain traditional cultural patterns which are slowly disappearing from the metropolis.

A few minutes before seven o'clock, 80 musicians, almost all of whom are men, enter the orchestra pit, which is two meters lower than the stage and juts out toward the audience. Almost half of the orchestra is made up of string instruments. (The first violinist, who sits closest to the conductor, shakes hands with him before the performance.) The other instruments come in twos or threes: flutes, oboes, clarinets and bassoons and, behind them, the brass section – trumpets, French horns, trombones and tubas. In the right hand corner from the point of view of the audience is percussion; on the left are two harps. Everyone is wearing black or black-and-white clothing: the men in suits, the women in black dresses. In the remaining minutes they tune up and rehearse difficult passages. At seven o'clock – after we are reminded in Czech and English to turn off our cell phones and also that we may not use any recording devices during the performance – the lights go out in the auditorium; only the music stands of the players are weakly lit. The conductor enters and we hear the first applause of the evening. The orchestra begins to play: first low strings and percussion in a rather quiet, short, rhythmic motif. Then suddenly – first still toned down and only in the strings, in the second repetition fully, with an addition of the wind instruments –a continuous and, at the same time, fluttering melody arises. It is quite easy to remember its first half (for that matter, it will return with several variations all evening), but the tones of the second half interweave in various instruments until it is difficult to distinguish them from the accompaniment. Besides, the melody constantly obeys with changing harmonies and tempi so that I seem to be in the middle of a colorful, continually changing sound surface. From it, a simple and distinctive melodic motif, which is played by French horns, the clear chords of which are interwoven with the clarinets, suddenly emerges. (The same melody is again heard in the second half of the first act: through it a male voice backstage will announce the arrival of the prince-hunter.) However, the calm, almost idyllic mood lasts only a few seconds; the melody disappears – what actually disappears is the tune one would like to sing – and nervous, rhythmic figures in the low strings and bassoons and at the same time frenzied runs in the flutes and other high-pitched instruments are heard – motifs that will accompany the figure of the Water Goblin during the whole performance. From this whirlwind, a hint of the main melody occasionally surfaces, at one time sort of mournfully, in solitude in the French horn and then the English horn. The overture ends in quiet chords. We have just heard a sort

This is the place.
Speak, oh you woods!

Closing scene from Rusalka

of soundtrack to the whole opera in which Dvořák guided us through the main motifs and instrumental colors of this evening for scarcely four or five minutes.

Then the red velvet curtain draws apart. In previous productions (in conformity with the instructions in the libretto) the audience saw "a meadow on the edge of a lake; woods all around…" This is where the touching story begins of the love of the water nymph Rusalka and the emotionally fickle prince whose infidelity destroys both of them in the end.

This time the stage director (the artistic director of the opera, Jiří Heřman) stages the opera untraditionally, symbolically. The water element is clear (its projection is helped by the lights); white and black prevail; some of the accents are ruby-red; there isn't a trace of details of the woods or the castle. Sexual symbols permeate everything. The text in the accompanying program characterizes Heřman's directorial language as "referring to a certain ritual of a soul."[2] My American colleague notes that the audience probably must know what it is about from earlier productions because the action on the stage has little to do with the words sung.

Rusalka, like other operas, is divided into three acts separated by twenty-minute intermissions. During these intermissions, the members of the

2   Program, p. 21.

audience buy something to eat at the snack bars or view the exhibitions about the history of the National Theater installed on the balconies. Mostly, though, they chat: those who came to the theater together or those who happened to meet there. Besides personal subjects, you most often hear appraisals of the performance: agreement or, on the contrary, denunciation of the "shocking" production and critiques of the singing.

Each act lasts about 50 minutes; the first and the third (according to the program) take place in a forest glade near a lake; the second in a castle garden. On the stage, soloists (the program lists eleven of them) alternate with the chorus and dancers. The most "populous" is the second act, where there is an extensive ballet scene representing a castle ball. The dancers –just like the singers – are very ostentatiously dressed. They apparently have no problem with the complicated choreography when the vocal chorus or soloists mix in.

The singers sing with trained voices; they are always turned toward the audience. Even so, sometimes their voices are drowned out by the sound of the orchestra, which practically never stops playing during the whole opera. The orchestra plays alone for the overture and the dance scenes; it accompanies the singers and, primarily, it creates the atmosphere, partly with its colorful sound combinations and partly with the transformations of the symbolic musical motifs. After the last note dies away, applause bursts forth. The curtain opens again and the singers and dancers arrive on stage and take their bows in skillful formations – from the least important roles to the main roles. The applause increases and once in a while you hear appreciative cheers. Finally, the conductor appears. The curtain definitively closes and, in front of it, the performers of the three main roles – Rusalka, the Prince and Vodník (Water Goblin) bow. At the end the orchestra leaves and the applause dies down. The performance is over.

WHAT ACTUALLY IS OPERA?

Opera is a musical genre which arose during the Renaissance in the Italian city of Florence as an (unrealistic) attempt at revival of ancient drama. Enthusiasts – associates of the group called *Camerata* – knew even less about ancient music at the end of the 16th century than we do today, but the ancient connection of the spoken word, action on stage, visual arts in the form of decorations and costumes and, primarily, music, was known to them, and they probably also knew about the extraordinary effectiveness of this connection. (By the way, the effectiveness of such a connection is confirmed by comparative material from the whole world: The Far East did not know any theater except musical theater until the arrival of Europeans; Indian epics were commonly performed in dance and song, as is also the case in Southeast Asia...)

Over the course of the next two centuries, opera took different shapes, but it remained the same in many aspects: alternation of solo singing (which either "propelled" the action forward or in which the characters expressed their emotions), choral pieces, and orchestral numbers (which were highly formalized primarily at the beginning of the opera, and/or they accompanied dance on the stage). The 18th century brought the so-called "ensembles" to opera – the simultaneous singing of several soloists. In any case, however, opera at the beginning of the 19th century was made up of individual numbers which were more or less independent. Only Romantic opera from the second third of the 19th century is interconnected with a constantly flowing stream of music and returning musical motifs which are always connected with one character, situation, feeling, and the like.

The 19th century belongs primarily to Italy and Germany in opera despite the fact that one of the most frequently performed operas – Bizet's *Carmen* – is French according to the nationality of its composer and Spanish according to the setting and the majority of musical stylizations.

In Italy opera was, for the whole of the 19th century, the dominating musical genre which enabled composers and librettists to express themselves about the most important events of their time, in the case of need, even metaphorically. (A lovely illustration of such metaphoric political involvement is the name of the most important opera colossus: VERDI, which is an acronym for the Italian "Victor Emanuel, king of Italy".) And operatic composers thus – like Czech song writers during the time of "normalization" – did this: not only the above-mentioned Giuseppe Verdi (1813–1901), but also the second Italian genius Giacomo Puccini (1858–1924). If today, however, Italian operas are the pillars of the repertoires of most opera houses, it surely isn't because of their political involvement, but mainly because of the emphasis on the beauty of singing. This is not identified with technical demands, but rather with the ability to convey an emotional message. Specific demands on the voice necessitated the rise of new (and today commonly accepted and used) singing techniques which are called bel canto (which means "beautiful song" in Italian).

German opera is mainly connected with the names of Carl Maria von Weber (1786–1826, the author of the romantic opera par excellence *Der Freischütz*) and the musical, mainly opera pioneer Richard Wagner (1813–1883) who in his concept of operas as *Gesamtkunstwerks* (= complex artistic works) again recalled the antique ideal of the close connection between music, text and visual elements. Precisely for Wagner's musical language there is, in addition to what was until then unprecedented harmonic complexity, a characteristic flow of orchestral sound and the use of so-called *Leitmotifs* (leading motifs). The method of composition using *Leitmotifs* often appears in the operas of Smetana – and also, as is apparent, in Dvořák's *Rusalka*.

It is certainly not surprising that opera had a special function in Czech society of the second half of the 19th century, in which intensive self-awareness of the Czechs and Czechness culminated. Assuming the highest place in the artistic hierarchy, it could turn to famous mythological or historical subjects (Smetana's *The Branden-burgers in Bohemia, Dalibor* and *Libuše*, Dvořák's "Slavonic operas" *Vanda, Dimitri* and *Armida* or Fibich's *Šárka* preceded a number of operas by Chmelenský, Škroup, Kott and others which are not played today but were important patriotic works in their time).

Opera could be sung in Czech on the stage, which, by the way, was in no way self-evident. František Škroup, the still-glorified author of the first Czech singspiel *Dráteník* and the composer of the music of the national anthem, also wrote a few operas in German. Incidentally, the librettos of Smetana's operas *Dalibor* and *Libuše* were originally written in German as well.

In addition, opera could also use melodies of folk songs or rather "folk-like" music; folk music was considered the keeper of the spiritual quality of the nation and the proof of its uniqueness. Another question was, however, its musical language itself: in the last third of the 19th century, the term "Czech music" had a rather vague meaning.

At the turn of the 20th century, when Antonín Dvořák (1841–1904) composed *Rusal-ka*, the Czech libretto was taken for granted. It corresponds to Dvořák's political conservatism that does not seek out nationally or politically confrontational topics: he uses the fairy-tale libretto of the young Jaroslav Kvapil (1868–1950), at that time literary advisor to the head of the National Theater. Kvapil, an utter romantic, famous in the 1890s for the dramatization of the fairy tale about Princess Dandelion, elaborated, for Dvořák's *Rusalka*, motifs by Hans Christian Andersen about the little water nymph, ballads by Karel Jaromír Erben and primarily a tale by the Prussian novelist F.H.K. de la Motte-Fouqué, *Udine*. This subject was treated more or less freely by opera composers of various nationalities.

The supremely romantic character of the libretto suited Dvořák very well: he composed the opera, the score of which had more than 500 pages, from spring to November 1900.

AND WHY IS IT THE WAY IT IS?

While trying for an interpretation of what we experienced during the performance of *Rusalka* at the National Theater, we were offered the concept proposed and researched by the American ethnomusicologist Alan Lomax: the concept of music as a reflection of social organization (see the box). According to this concept, Romantic opera is a reflection of the highly specialized, formalized and stratified society of the second half of the 19th and beginning of the 20th centuries.

Specialization is evident right from the entrance into the theater: the ushers have precisely assigned places where they check tickets; the cloakroom

The hierarchically structured stands of the National Theater

attendants serve not only the people going to certain parts of the auditorium, but even – because in every cloakroom there are generally several attendants – they put coats only on a few of "their" rows of hooks. Specialization is very evident when one glances at the program in which not only the performers of solo roles, but also the stage director, conductor, scene and costume designers and also the assistant director, assistant choreographer, are precisely written about, but also the vocal coaches and the prompter are written up.

The singers are also specialized, mainly in their own role of opera singer: they must completely master a special singing technique which allows them to "sing over" an 80-member orchestra and be heard as far as the second gallery. In addition, they represent a certain vocal type (e.g., a lyric soprano is capable of singing the same notes as a dramatic soprano, but her color assigns her to a relevant specialization).

The most obvious, however, is the specialization in the orchestra: the first-violin player (who understandably plays the same instrument as the sec-

The National Theater's dominant building

ond-violin player and whose parts are very similar) never sits in the second violinist's position; it is not even a question whether any player, except for the percussionists, plays more than one instrument (as is common, for example, in Chinese opera).

Specialization, however, to a certain extent, is also presumed among the members of the audience: understanding a sung text demands long-term practice.[3] To a certain extent they are aided by the program, which usually contains the whole libretto, that is, the text of the opera. However, during the performance it is impossible to follow it because the auditorium is darkened. In addition to the libretto, the program contains further information intended for the knowledgeable public: the history of the creation of the opera and a review of individual productions from the premiere to the current one.

Viewers, however, are not usually interested in the historical context alone: they intensely await the performance of the best known numbers and express their appreciation through applause. (In our environment it rarely

3   Today, however, the supertitles over the stage help; thanks to them, the viewers can read Czech and English titles.

happens that the public reacts negatively by whistling, stamping, or similar behavior.) Complicated ballet choreography can also be appreciated only by knowledgeable – and thus specialized – viewers. It is not surprising, then, that the majority of the viewers have higher formal unspecialized education or specialized musical education.

By the way, the building itself is very specialized. It was built in an exceptionally expert manner (e.g., specialists worked on the problematics of the acoustics) for a single purpose – theatrical performances.

Formalization is also obvious at every step. The above-mentioned ushers have the same uniform (those at the entrance even have the same cloaks); the orchestra players wear black suits, the conductor always wears tails. Neither on stage nor in the orchestra is there the slightest room for improvisation: every note is precisely determined; every step of the singer (including each member of the chorus) or dancer around the stage is prescribed by the stage director. Formalization is also to be expected to a certain extent by the behavior of the audience; applause after the curtain goes down or passing through the row facing those who are seated; the program also announces that "After the beginning, entrance into the auditorium is not permitted." Fittingly, the formalization of the entire event corresponds to rather formal dress.

The third social feature projected onto the operatic performance is high social **stratification**.[4] The viewers are stratified according to their place in the auditorium (and thus clearly according to the price of their tickets). Clearest again is the hierarchization in the orchestra pit: in the string section, the better the player, the closer s/he sits to the conductor. The latter, like the stage director, is at the very top of the pyramid (this also shows in the program) while he himself produces no sound (as would be expected in opera). His contribution is his special "know-how." (The clear parallel with industrial management is surely not a coincidence.)

Romantic opera, embedded in Lomax's comparative material (in which he used samples from 233 cultures from the whole world), corresponds nearly perfectly to his conclusion: the complex stratified society of the second half of the 19th century and the beginning of the following century corresponds to the dominant role of the solo singers and the complexity of their texts. This is also confirmed by the large accompanying instrumental ensemble. And also Lomax's incisive remark about social rigidity, which is expressed by the pop-

---

4   In connection with social stratification, anthropologists will miss terms like status and cultural capital, especially from the writings of the French sociologist Pierre Bourdieu. Because we do not identify with Bourdieu's theory related to art as formulated in particular in the book La Distinction (1979), and also because it is not connected to Lomax's theory, we do not discuss it here.

ularity of large instrumental ensembles, is entirely pertinent at least for the second half of the 19th century.

The prophecies about the "end of opera" as too sophisticated, as too "un-natural" a musical genre, from the musically-anthropological perspective, moreover as a genre reflecting "pre-enlightened" values, are as old as opera itself. Operatic performances nevertheless continually speak to further generations of listeners. Perhaps this genre resonates with very resistant structures of societies of Western civilization of the past centuries, perhaps with something more permanent in the structure of the human personality. From the full opera houses in Prague and elsewhere, one can judge that the twilight of opera has still not appeared.

ALAN LOMAX ON MUSIC AS AN INDICATOR OF SOCIAL COMPLEXITY[5]

Zuzana Jurková

The American ethnomusicologist and folklorist Alan Lomax (1915–2002) is perhaps known to us from the film *Songhunter Alan Lomax* and perhaps also as a collector of old Anglo-American ballads from the Appalachian Mountains in the southeastern USA. He is also, however, the author of a remarkable ethnomusicological book *Folk song Style and Culture* (1968). In it are published the results of the *cantometrics* research project. It is one of the most extensive and expensive projects in the history of ethnomusicology, the theoretical premises of which – comparisons of cultural phenomena without regard to their context – were, however, rather old fashioned at that time.

HISTORY OF THE CANTOMETRICS PROJECT

In 1953 Alan Lomax noticed that the way people sing in Spain differs according to the severity of the ban on premarital sex. In the south, where culture was influenced by the Arab world and its austerity, the music had a narrow ambitus[6] and people sang with "piercing, high-pitched, squeezed, narrow vocal delivery"; choral singing was almost impossible.

In the north (in Asturias, in areas influenced by the Basques and Gallics) penalties relating to inappropriate sexual behavior were more lenient, relations between the sexes simpler and more relaxed, and people preferred blended voices in choral singing with relaxed and deep voices.

Lomax observed the same north-south division two years later during further research in Italy and here, also, there was a clear correlation between sexual behavior and vocal tension (and the possibilities of choral singing connected to it).

At the beginning of the 1960s Lomax and his colleagues (linguists, statisticians, ethnographers and, in view of the inclusion of dance material, an

---

5   This text is based on my lecture at the *Hlasohled* conference in Prague in November 2009.
6   Melodic range.

ethnochoreologist) formulated the first hypotheses and mainly the basic research methods (see below).

More than 3500 musical samples were used for the research – field recordings (part of which had already existed before the beginning of the project and part of which were done specially for the cantometrics project), out of which an archive arose that was called "Folk music of world peoples." Some were later published on CDs. The archive contains samples from the Baltics to the Bering Strait. Only two large areas are not represented: China and Gran Chaco.

The second set of data was taken from the distinguished Murdock Ethnographic Atlas of the 1960s.[7] The team accumulated a sufficient amount of musical and ethnographic data for 233 cultures. These were submitted to cantometrics research and its results to a certain extent confirm the original hypotheses that are the subject of the book.

In the cantometrics project, Lomax emphasized two things: first, the testing of hypotheses concerning the relation of singing and culture and, second, the confirmation of the cantometrics method itself. This method was relatively exact (the book is full of tables and graphs) and could thus represent "real science" (mainly in the 1960s) for some critics of the humanities.

BASIC PREMISES AND FINDINGS

The starting hypothesis of the project is that folk song style[8] – just like many others – is a pattern of learned behavior which is common to people in a given culture. Singing, like speaking, is a special kind of communication, but much more formally organized and redundant, that is, its features multiply in various aspects (melodics, text, form, vocal technique, etc., testifying to the same). Whether it is choral or solo singing, the chief function of singing is the expression of communal feelings (or – according to some anthropologists – values). Therefore, folk song style is communal rather than individual, normative rather than special.

The intention of the experiment was to prove that singing style is an outstanding indicator of a cultural pattern.[9]

The authors wished to compare the folk song style and character of the cultures they researched. They therefore created two types of data: musical

---

7   Murdock, George (1962–67)

8   *folk song style*, this term includes both the manner of interpretation and also the interpretive form, including textual components

9   *Cultural pattern*, a common term used in anthropology denoting the characteristic choice of cultural elements in a given culture

and ethnographic. They characterized the folk song style with the help of seven aspects: (1) socially organized vocal and (2) instrumental groups; (3) extent of cohesion; (4) extent of explicitness – text and consonant load; (5) rhythmic organization; (6) extent and style of ornamentation; (7) degree of melodic complexity. They then further classified these aspects into 37 categories. In each category, they created scales upon which the given phenomenon can exist. In the field of ornamentation, for example, they differentiate among glissando, tremolo and melodic ornamentation; in each of these three categories there are, at one end, degrees of interpretation without ornamentation (non-use of glissando...), at the other, highly ornamented (sliding to the majority of melodic tones). These criteria and scales within them create a kind of grid upon which it is possible to classify any vocal expression.

The second type of data is ethnographic data. The authors characterized lifestyle by means of six aspects in which they ascertained that the following are consistently related to vocal expression: (1) production range; (2) political level[10]; (3) social stratification; (4) severity of sexual mores; (5) gender balance; (6) level of social cohesiveness, so-called complementarity. As with musical data, they created a kind of grid with which they gradually compared the musical grid.

This comparison brought two main findings:
(1) The geography of folk song styles follows the main route of human migration and maps the known historical distribution of culture.
(2) Some features of folk song style embody a strong relation with features of social structure which regulate interaction in all cultures; some – on the contrary – do not.

The basic synthesis of the entire cantometrics project is a statistically clear confirmation that folk song style compactly reflects the extent of behavior relevant to a given cultural context. It is an immediate reflection of a cultural pattern.

SINGING AND SOCIETY

If we consider singing primarily as a community occasion, the singing situation is reflected from this standpoint at two ends:

---

10   Here Lomax accepts Murdock's categorization which takes into consideration a number of levels of control, starting from the simplest one-level community, where the decision making is in the hands of the nuclear family, to the complex society with four levels of decision making and control.

(1) as highly individualized/solo singing, where the solo markedly dominates over the group. The solo voice is relatively vibrant and the sophisticated melodic line and precise enunciation show that the text itself plays an important role. It is possible to find this singing style on the main civilization roads from the Far East to Europe;[11]

(2) as cohesive, group singing, where individual voices do not "stand out" and are not too piercing: The texture may be polyphonic or monophonic, the melodics simple (even if often with greater intervals), without melodic ornamentation. Words are often repeated or alternate with meaningless syllables. Such expression prevails among the Central-African Pygmies and the South-African Sans and other very primitive cultures.[12]

Lomax and his colleagues ascertained that the dichotomy between groups and individual styles and their other accompanying attributes persists. Simplicity of melodic structure, absence of ornamentation, quiet sound and low specificity of individual voices are connected to the high cohesiveness of the singing group. Also the opposite characteristic, that is, melodically rich timbre with distinctive or piercing singing, is usually solo singing.

On the contrary, tempo, volume, rhythm and register are clearly independent of an individually collective dichotomy and, thus, their relationship both to the previous musical characteristics and cultural characteristics is somewhat arbitrary.

SCALE OF SOCIAL COMPLEXITY

One of the first, early findings of the cantometrics project was that many style elements thoroughly change in connection with the extent of the complexity of the society. The folk song style of simple cultures consistently differs from that of technically developed cultures. Lomax (with respect to Murdock's atlas) divides culture into five scales according to the type of subsistence: at one end are the gatherers, and at the other end is a complex husbandry system connected with extensive irrigation. It is important that the size of the community grows with each further degree: the more complex, the greater. And

---

11 See, e.g., an example from Iran: http://www.wwnorton.com/college/music/soundscapes/ch_assets/player.asp?chno=159.

12 In Lomax's understanding, technologically undeveloped cultures. See, e.g., example of singing of Central African Pygmies: http://www.wwnorton.com/college/music/soundscapes/ch_assets/player.asp?chno=31, or North American Chippewa Indians: http://www.wwnorton.com/college/music/soundscapes/ch_assets/player.asp?chno=179. In the basic features of folk-song style both are the same; they differ only in polyphonic/monophonic texture.

with that growth, the amount of social control also grows; while in small local communities the behavior of an individual is regulated only by the extended family, in larger societies this happens on higher (extra-local) levels. (A ruler can live relatively far away and still basically influence the people's lives from there). Other features characterizing the complexity of a society are, besides the size of the community, the duration of settlement, governmental control, stratification, exploitation of the individual and job complexity, that is, specialization.

COMPLEXITY IN SONG AND IN SOCIETY

The variables of the above-mentioned characteristics of culture in the realm of folk song style are mainly the pithiness of the text, the preciseness of the enunciation, the size of the intervals and the number of instrumental types in the accompanying instrumental group. It is possible to observe a direct connection: the singing styles of complex cultures have a high density of information, while songs of simple economies do not have much. The more complex a society is and the more exclusive the role of the ruler is, the more room the soloist (as a representative of the ruler) takes up on "center stage". He loses his piercing voice – a certain modesty, which corresponds to the fact that the role of rulers is no longer primarily physical, is valued. Emphasis is placed on extensive and rich texts.[13] According to some ethnomusicologists the understandability of singing in complex societies corresponds to the communication demands of those societies.

Besides the quality of the text and the clarity of the enunciation, a third characteristic feature is the size of the melodic intervals. The frequent appearance of intervals larger than thirds is striking mainly in gatherer communities. Scientists explain this by a more relaxed, freer approach to social and ecological space: a man living in a simpler society has a freer approach not only to the earth, but also, for example, to social statuses.[14] Equally distinctive, on the contrary, is the appearance of small intervals in very closed cultures.

---

13   See the above-mentioned example from Iran.
14   An example can be the singing of North American Indians (state of Iowa):
http://www.wwnorton.com/college/music/soundscapes/ch_assets/player.asp?chno=172,
or Pygmies from the Ituri Rainforest of Central Africa:
http://www.wwnorton.com/college/music/soundscapes/ch_assets/player.asp?chno=107.

SINGING AND SOCIAL STRATIFICATION

In connection with social stratification, two attributes attract our attention: melodic ornamentation and irregular rhythm. Both add a certain complexity to the sung melody. It is remarkable that it is possible to come across them mainly in the most complex societies. Representative of this folk song style is an oriental bard, a singing ruler, a courtly lover, and the like.[15]

The last note, related to the complexity of society and the corresponding singing style, has to do with an anthropological interpretation of **musical instruments accompanying singing**: According to Lomax, the accompanying instrument is primarily a sign of a certain formality (it is "outside of the body;" that is, less spontaneous than vocal expression) and it is possible to follow the clear connection between complex cultures and the size of accompanying instrumental groups. As far as types of instruments are concerned, it was impossible to prove any clear connection. He asserts, though, that formal, thus, instrumental musical performance is a sign of rising social rigidity, caustically adding that this is obviously the reason for the rising popularity of symphonic orchestras in the United States.

SOCIAL COMPLEMENTARITY

Relations between members of an instrumental group, it seems, reflect formal social structure. On the other hand, relations among members of a choral group have more to do with personal relations within society – face-to-face relations. This mainly has to do with the organization of male-female choirs (and this is also the case in the most primitive communities where a sung text has nothing in common with love or sex). If we wish to guess what the participation of women in the performance of music will be like, the best indicator of their participation is subsistence activity. Wherever they do not participate, they stand to the side during the singing. This is also true both in hunting communities and in Muslim societies where women are hidden within the family. Lomax designated six types according to Murdock's atlas of culture: in two of them, women participated decidedly less than men in procuring food, while in the remaining four, their participation was equal or greater. In the musical expression of the first two groups, men decidedly prevailed. The anthropological interpretation of this fact is this: in places where women participate in at least 50% of the procurement of food, they are also active in other areas –

---

15   See the example from Iran.

and men accept this. Music again copies the contours of society: mixed and/or polyphonic singing style in complementary societies compared to monophonic male styles in non-complementary ones.

A clear illustration is vocal polyphony, that is, concurrent singing of independent musical lines. The appearance of polyphony rises in direct proportion to the complementarity of a society. Lomax's research statistically proved the prevalence of polyphony in primitive and complementary societies (among gatherers and early farmers). However, it does not have to do with mixed polyphonies; polyphonies (more often two-voiced) can be also sung by women. A pair of different voices is understood to be like a picture of male-female distinction, even if members of the same sex sing the two voices.[16]

SUMMARY

When a human community sings, at the same time it declares much about the level of its complexity, which very strongly influences every aspect of life: the way of living, stratification, government, distribution of the main tasks, etc. When an individual sings, it reminds him or her of the type of community from which he or she comes. One of the functions of singing, then, is clearly to strengthen various levels of complexity which are the basis of all social behavior.

---

16   An example of female polyphony from Northern Russia might serve as an example here:
http://www.wwnorton.com/college/music/soundscapes/ch_assets/player.asp?chno=42,
or male polyphony from Georgia:
http://www.wwnorton.com/college/music/soundscapes/ch_assets/player.asp?chno=63.

THE MAKROPULOS CASE
AS A SEMIOTIC EXPERIENCE
Zuzana Jurková, Pavla Jónssonová

For more than a century of its existence, almost every aspect of ethnomusicology has been transformed: its name (from comparative musicology to ethnomusicology and musical anthropology or anthropology of music), subject of study (from the search for general laws of "musically beautiful"[17] to "music of those others"[18] to the study of all kinds of music) and understandably also methods. Despite all of the changeability,[19] though, one feature seems constant: the attempt to more than just describe (possibly in musically analytical categories) musical sound itself; an attempt to arrive at why a certain musical structure has the particular shape that it has. Authors look for the answer to this "Why?" in different directions, understandably most frequently in the area of a music-producing culture (therefore ETHNOmusicology or anthropology of music). Sometimes the answer is a whole configuration of culture. Sometimes the function of that concrete musical genre... What seems to be almost indubitable in the ethnomusicology of the last decades is the postulate about listeners as the main creators of musical production. In that case, then, the above-mentioned question of why a concrete musical structure has a certain shape could be: What does that music mean to the listeners? What does it bring them and how does it satisfy them? Why do they need it just the way it is?

Some ethnomusicological schools, emphasizing the undoubtedly communicative nature of music, utilize processes which are close to linguistics, inspired by linguistics or dealing with the relation between music and language or the reflection of music in language.[20] One of those schools is semiotics, mainly in the concept of Charles Sanders Peirce. The application of his complicated system was proposed for use in the study of music by Thomas Turino.

---

17 Hornbostel 1905.

18 Jaap Kunst 1950.

19 Because the discipline has been gradually and more or less continually transformed, and also because the scientific community more or less concurs on the continuity of the field, we consider German-Austrian comparative musicology to be the beginning of the broad field which today we most often call ethnomusicology.

20 E.g. Stone 2008, Feld and Fox 1994.

MUSIC AS LANGUAGE[21]

The Peirce-Turino concept of semiotics enables a more detailed analysis of our perception of music. We can thus approach the understanding of WHY music actually affects us. It thus opens up the possibility of understanding what is usually veiled by expressions such as "indescribable in words". In the semiotic analysis of music, though, emphasis on the *difference* between intentionality and the semantic-referential character of language on the one hand and the predominant unintentionality of music on the other hand is of basic importance; different ways of functioning come from this difference.

While one school of semiotics represented, for example, by the well-known Swiss linguist Ferdinand de Saussure, considered the sign-object dichotomy (as did Saussure's followers, e.g. Noam Chomsky), the other, called triadic and most often represented by Charles K. Ogden and I. A. Richards (and their most famous work *The Meaning of the Meaning*, 1923) think about a three-part scheme: object, sign and image of this sign in our consciousness. Charles Sanders Peirce (1839–1914) also belongs to this triadic tradition. Peirce described the relation among a designating/sign, a designated/object, and a perceiver/listener as trichotomic: it is (1) a *sign* that represents in human thought (2) *an object* which the sign points out (Peirce used the word "object": whether it is a material thing, an idea or, for example, a natural phenomenon). As a 3rd component, Peirce introduced the word *interpretant*; this word expresses the relation between an object and a sign, and mainly the effect of this relationship. Therefore: a concrete object is, as we perceive it, represented by a concrete sign whose relation to the object and importance are determined by the interpretant.

TYPES OF SIGNS AND SIGN-OBJECT-INTERPRETANT RELATIONS

Based on the complicated and comprehensive system and the less intelligible formulations of Peirce, Turino used the terms which he considered relevant to music in his application. For this text we used only some of them. We avoided the explanation and use of three basic abstract categories – Firstness, Secondness, and Thirdness, which are certainly useful for a more detailed understanding of which types of stimuli they evoke as responses, but for our text seem to be dispensable.

---

[21] Let it be said that we do not advocate Peirce's view of human spiritual life as stimulated solely by signs, nor do we share the concept of music as only a collection of signs; in this text we draw attention to the semiotic point of view.

1. TYPES OF SIGNS

According to his trichotomic concept, Peirce spoke about three types of signs. He called the first the *qualisign*: pure quality, embedded in a sign[22] (redness, magnificence...). The second type of sign – the *sinsign* – is the actual, specific realization of that quality (red color, perception via concrete red things...). The third type of sign – the *legisign* – classifies a concrete sign into a wider context (the color red belongs among other colors...). However close the first and third categories may seem, there is a different intellectual understanding of reality: thanks to the first category (the qualisign) we are capable of understanding/ realizing reality (the sinsign), while the third (the legisign) reflects our perception of the world (e.g. the formation of the general "color" category).

2. TYPES OF RELATIONSHIPS BETWEEN SIGN AND OBJECT

The first type of connection between sign and object is the relation of resemblance: a photograph means a concrete person to us, while looking at a picture of an unknown château we imagine a noble residence, and perhaps we perceive it as a reference to a concrete historical period or area. Peirce calls this type of sign an *icon*. The basis of the iconic process, that is, the connecting of similar objects and signs, is a classification of phenomena on the basis of resemblance of some aspects: physical appearance and also perhaps a style of clothing or a way of using one's voice: as soon as we hear high, characteristically cultivated female singing accompanied by an orchestra on the radio, we evidently classify it according to color, singing technique and accompaniment as opera, although we do not understand a word and we do not see the stage.

An iconic type of connection can partly be used intentionally by a composer or a creator of music: in many places in Smetana's *My Country* – two flutes imitating the sound of flowing water at the beginning of the *Moldau*, or the harp imitating some sort of mythical accompanying instrument of a mythical bard in *Vyšehrad* – are based on it. Secondly, however, the iconic process also provides space for the listener's own imagination, mainly in music with its free connection to physical objects.

The second type of connection between sign and object is based on co-occurrence, most often causality: smoke accompanies fire; the wind enables the unfurling of a flag... and both smoke and the flag are signs of those "objects" for us, which are intimately bound to our experience. Peirce calls this type of sign an *index*. An important quality for the use of indices mainly in music is the fact that we can encounter that very sign in various situations and thus – according to momentary circumstances – evoke various associations (this feature is

---

22   Turino 1999: 224.

usually called semantic snowballing). For example, the majority of listeners to western classical music connect three eighth "G" notes followed by one "E flat" (and, perhaps, followed by a descending transposition of the same motif) with the beginning of Beethoven's Fifth (Destiny) Symphony and thus emotionally with the image of a genius pursued by destiny or, more generally, with fatality. Those in the Czech lands who experienced anguish during the war and, at the same time, hope through the broadcasts of forbidden London radio, broadcasts which used as their theme tune the first notes of Beethoven's Fifth, clearly recall the more common feeling of fatefulness and, more concretely, their own war memories.

Like signs of the iconic type, indices also provide space for the listeners to interject their own connotations. In contrast with previous icons which lead people more toward the field of imagination, indices aim toward experiences.

The third type of relation between sign and object is, according to Peirce, the *symbol*. It is the type of relation that arises on the basis of an agreement, e.g. between the author and the listeners (Peirce speaks about "language limitation"). The most typical and widespread symbol is the word, in the musical context, national anthems, theme songs of sport clubs, etc., but also so-called leitmotifs, used in classical music of the 19th century: melodies with which the composer denotes (accompanies) a certain character or situation. Leitmotifs do, to a certain extent, affect the listener with their own musical quality (the listener can project his own experience or ideas into their color or individual melodic phrase, but their prevailing intentionality limits just what is typical and valuable: the connection with personal experience or ideas. Therefore, symbols are used less in music than both of the preceding types.

3. TYPES OF SIGN-INTERPRETANT RELATIONS
(THAT IS, HOW A SIGN IS PERCEIVED)

Of the three possibilities of relations between sign and the resulting interpretant, introduced by Turino in concordance with Peirce, let us discuss two or, precisely, two quantities of such a relationship in more detail. The first of these qualities – *rheme* – denotes the perception of the sign as representing an object on the plane possibilities: a melody imitating a shepherd's song, that is, representing "some sort of shepherd's song," should evoke a bucolic mood. Similarly, we perceive the abovementioned picture of a château as "possible" or a reference to the time when similar châteaux were "possible" as common.

The quality of a *dicent*, on the contrary, is understood as "real": if a weather vane turns in a certain direction, we are convinced that we know the direction of the wind (and we do not admit that the weather vane could get rusty). The first quality, that is, allows for our own (at least inner) creativity; the second, on the other hand, the understanding of sense and importance. The third quality – argument – has a symbolic character and is based on language premises; Turino considers it irrelevant for the analysis of musical signs.[23]

HOW DOES MUSIC ACTUALLY WORK?

Every musical event, be it listening to songs on the radio or the complex experience of attending an opera (and, even more, performing in a musical event) offers an enormously rich palette of stimuli. Any note at all, any fragment of a melody, a rhythm or tone color, any word or movement of a performer, and also the place where we hear music and people who listen to it or perform with us can become a sign – a catalyst of psychological response. If we encounter that same phenomenon repeatedly, various meanings snowball in our consciousness (= semantic snowballing) according to the new situation, and the sign resonates in us on multiple levels.

The second type of reaction is – besides semantic snowballing – the chaining of our inner reactions: the interpretant itself, caused by a stimulus, immediately becomes a sign and leads our response further – in a similar or in a rather different direction.

In regard to the number of stimuli/signs of various qualities, memories and ideas, emotions and rational echoes resonate in me simultaneously; my past (in memories) connects with my present (in an immediate experience) and my future (in ideas). And not only that. The social experience of listening, but even more, the social performance of music, create a strong feeling of belonging: while we can speak in words ABOUT belonging to each other, social music making produces the reality OF belonging to each other.

---

23   Turino 1999: 230.

THE MAKROPULOS CASE AS A SEMIOTIC EXPERIENCE

After long discussions about semiotics, we wanted to test its application as an analytical tool at a concrete musical event. A performance of Janáček's opera The Makropulos Case at the National Theater seemed opportune: Pavla saw it a few days ago – March 23, 2010; I had seen the same production somewhat earlier, at its premiere. It affected both of us strongly. At the same time, our personal histories are as different as they could possibly be.

An operatic performance evokes an enormous number of emotional and intellectual reactions (besides, is there such a great difference between them?) from the general framing of the performance to feelings we experience during individual musical phrases, colors of sound or gestures – the number of which exceeds the possibility of dealing with them within the frame of an article. In addition, we reflected on the performance only ex post. For both of these reasons, we limited ourselves to three basic fields, or, as we are presenting it here, layers, here described from the most ordinary – opera at the National Theater – to a concrete performance of The Makropulos Case.

First, we each wrote our texts individually, and only after the first versions were written did we discuss them. Our primary attempt was to capture the perception of/reactions to the performance. In order for our communication to be understandable, it was necessary to place it in the context of our personal histories, our thinking, etc.; we definitely did not intend to write an exhaustive commentary on the topic. Therefore, for the purposes of this text we did not study any new facts concerning Janáček, The Makropulos Case or any other topics mentioned below; we only looked for texts which readers could clearly understand. Once again, we did not write primarily about Janáček, his opera, or the production of this opera at the National Theater; our main purpose was to test the suitability of semiotics as an analytical tool.

ZJ: While attempting to capture how the performance of Janáček's *The Makropulos Case* in the National Theater affected me, I become aware of several layers. The deepest, most general is a feeling of **opera in the National Theater** that runs through me slightly at every mention of it, but I am generally aware of it at the moment I find myself in that enormous velvet auditorium with its golden chandelier which, it always occurs to me, would deprive Prague of a fourth of its opera fans if it fell. I actually came to music when I was about thirteen through opera; I mainly came to the National Theater, where, at that time, standing room tickets cost a few crowns. I became totally enchanted with that illusionary genre – and world. I knew the whole repertoire of the time and who would be singing in every performance; I knew the librettos of some of the operas by heart and the fate of their heroes touched me personally. Of course, I had my favorite singers...

Janáček's The Makropulos Case (photo: Hana Smejkalová)

A few years later, however, I was bewitched by Janáček; I discovered that there were other musical genres one could listen to, and that way I came to music of the 20th century. When I began to study the history and theory of music at the age of 19, I already perceived the world of opera as something difficult to take: cheap and full of pretending, somehow connected to my naive beginnings. In the following decades I went to the opera occasionally (with my husband, an opera buff, and my children...), but mostly without much enthusiasm and experience. Only a few years ago did I begin to go to the opera (and to the National Theater) more often... I can stand it pretty well; I'm a bit more indulgent. I no longer consider it as something "real," but rather as a momentary game of illusion, a game I can accept.

And all of this resonates within me in various ways in the auditorium of the National Theater.

PJ: Opera in the National Theater? During my high school years in the late 1970s, a lethal combination of coloratura "falsehood" in the "devil's den", as the National became the place where the best Czech artists were forced to condemn Charter 77. (This stain was elegantly wiped out when *The Plastic People of the Universe* accepted the invitation of director Ivan Rajmont to perform there in Tom Stoppard's *Rock'n'Roll* in 2008.) Moreover, there was a bit of a specific type of commodity fetishism connected with Trade Union opera tickets, extended to both the working class and the working class intelligentsia. Thank God for the solace of "another" music, authentic and true: Etc., Švehlík, Merta, Janota, Třešňák and so on. That music was played in smoky pubs, flats and on river boats for long-haired boys and girls with shining eyes. That was genuine free culture, reacting to the situation of an occupied country. In the 1970s, that type of music was the most important expression of all, an amplified protest Zeitgeist of guitars and drums.

I eventually got mine with the opera in the National, though. I am 45 years old, taking my students to see Smetana's *Kiss* – and suddenly the whole National Theater opera thing hits me. The libretto, the relationship of Smetana and Krásnohorská, the unpretentiousness of the piece, the smugglers, as well as the intensity of the sound (eighth row) penetrating into my bloodstream through my skin, pressing me down into my red velvet seat. Shortly after my *Kiss* initiation, I took the plunge and started to frequent the National. I took a liking to each and every piece, from the *Bartered Bride* to the *Grey Mouse Opera*. So far the deepest impact has been felt in *Jenůfa*.

My reality has been radically extended by opera dimensions, both historical and contemporary, as the penultimate music form. Even if I have never witnessed anything close to the sparkling eyes conspiracy and barriers dissolving, as often happens at a genuine rock concert, I was forced to admit that the sold-out screenings of world opera live transmissions in the Světozor and Aero do not necessarily testify to the fact that that Czechs are incurable snobs.

The seats and the whole theater, including the muse-guarded terrace towards the Prague Castle, have become a part of my world, something that belongs to me, a luxury we all need and deserve. This is the right mythical space to celebrate rituals with champagne after surviving in music battlefields of festival mud, defunct factory halls and stinking rock-club cellars. I pity the Parisians in their burnt out Bouffes du nord. Long live the Czech National!

ZJ: The second layer is **Janáček**. Opera pulled me into the **world of music**, that is, to that whole complex of events and relations surrounding musical occurrences on the stage. Janáček, specifically his opera *Jenůfa* (understandably at the National Theater), showed me the **experience of listening**: to how music can pierce the soul – like a shard in a bare heel. I could never get enough of the intensity of that experience. I think I saw *Katya Kabanova* thirty-six times, the *Glagolitic Mass* at almost every reprise in Prague (and, of course, I have several recordings of it); I wore out vinyl records of his string quartets... By the way, the oddly intensive, stabbing experience of *Jenůfa* is one of my arguments against Peirce's concept of a spiritual life as a continuous chain of references. I knew nothing of Janáček or his music and also, during my first hearing, nothing earlier came to my mind. The music simply affected me in itself. That moment was the starting point. From it, endless chaining begins. My permanent enchantment is very understandable in the frame of the Peirce-Turino concept. The basic role is played on the one hand by my age at the time – when my individual personality was forming – and on the other hand by Janáček's specific musical language. Starting approximately from *Jenůfa*, Janáček's musical language was based on so-called real motifs,[24] melodic-rhythmic figures, closely and admittedly coming from "speech melodies." Janáček was engaged in collecting speech melodies, that is, musical notations of people's speech, for decades and he attributed great weight to them because he considered them to be the maximally true picture of man's internal state of mind.[25] Real motifs are not exact quotations of speech melodies, but they are easily distinguishable within them. In vocal-instrumental works, the motifs are also heard in instrumental renditions, but primarily they are sung – and thus work as some sort of excitation – "the way someone really spoke, but even more strongly". In Peirce-Turino terminology, they are thus motifs with typical examples of *dicent indices:* this refers to a phenomenon (a word as it would usually be said in a certain emotional situation) on the basis of resemblance, and we perceive it (at least I perceived it that way) as real: yes, this is really true.

Janáček, his music and all available information – I soaked it up from approximately my fifteenth to my nineteenth year, at a time that is usually considered essential for the formation of (not only musical) identity. I do not know about teenagers today, but for me at that time the question of "truth" or maximum authenticity was crucial. That is why Janáček's music so easily became one of the cornerstones of my musical identity.

Then for a long time I wandered everywhere possible with music – and in a certain sense I am still wandering to this day. But as soon as I hear a piece of this special, excited, and at the same time somehow broken Janáček melody, so different from the lucid musical phrases of the classics and the unending Wagner melodies, and so close to how I would say those same words myself, I realize: I am finally home again.

PJ: When I think of Janáček, I see a unique and uncompromising man with a lust for life. Strolling through his morphogenetic field I hear sčasovkas, tensions between tonality and atonality, I perceive the psychology of the speech

---

24   Janáček himself speaks of them in the article "Váha reálních motivů" (The weight of real motifs) (Janáček 2007: 429–433). About their use, see Štědroň 1986: 90.

25   Most famous and truly heartbreaking are his notations of the last words of his dying daughter Olga; in an emotional article he again introduces and analyzes a few musical motifs of the speech of Jaroslav Vrchlický in Brno in 1898. He also discusses them in other texts (Janáček 2003).

melodies, and devotion to Kamila Štösslová. I see a man who transcended borders of his genre as inspiration for the rock super group Emerson, Lake and Palmer on their first album in 1970. As a "sampling" pioneer, he started to capture bird singing, doors closing, the melody of the dying words of his daughter, thus enlarging the concept of music before John Cage and "all that noise."

In the early 1990s, Czech TV screened a Swedish production of *Cunning Little Vixen*, in Lachian dialect with English and Swedish subtitles, which made me realize that this opera was loved by the whole world. What was behind it? What is that frog that jumps into the Forester's lap at the beginning and at the end a symbol of? Milan Kundera, in his essay *My Janáček* (2004), protests against any apotheosis in the last "quack". The Cunning Vixen herself is *dicentic* Kamila as well as *rheme* of all free spirited women. This is the same as when Marcel Duchamp renamed himself Rose Sélavy: Eros is life.

I mentioned *Jenůfa* as the strongest impression. I felt the pain shared with friends who were left as babies in orphanages, the cruelty of stigma of some single mothers – even if today's adoption possibilities would have made the situation of Kostelnička Buryjovka and Jenůfa simpler. Psychoanalytically speaking, I read the phantasm of the loss of a child, represented through the social topic of Gabriela Preissová. Their collaboration brings to mind the creative union of Czech composers with women librettists. On another level, behind the curtain, I saw Kostelnička Eva Urbanová and her parallel story of a diva, the most powerful among women, who is getting old and losing her power. So much to be amazed about.

Another peculiar issue about Janáček is his perseverance, the delayed acknowledgement, even worldwide. How many people I have met abroad with whom I have struck up an instantaneous friendship just by uttering his name? In San Francisco, Paris, London, he made people love Czech culture, as if he were a key to its door. Some of them just happened to see a screening of the *Unbearable Lightness of Being*, and Janáček's music reached them, forced them to come to the Czech Lands and discover what it was about us Bohemians.

ZJ: And now concretely to *The Makropulos Case*. In my mind I feel special tension connected to Čapek's philosophical theme (on the whole, coolly rational, as I feel it), the theme of the loss of happiness for the price of immortality, with Janáček's strongly emotional elaboration. In the music I hear exactly what Janáček once wrote, that he "felt sorry for that three-hundred-year-old beauty." My first reaction is primarily rational (how curiously it fits together), but at the same time I feel an empathy toward Elina similar to that of Janáček's.

For this particular performance, that central theme had further special significance. I was there with my closest friend or, more precisely, closest in many ways, including the amount of time we spend together and how harmonious that time is. But at the same time, my friend is painfully distant in our basic feeling about the world. I move about in my world more or less confidently and thus (or, on the contrary, because?) I consider the transient nature of things, even the most beautiful of them, as the other side of the coin of their beauty. In a world where I feel safe, I can rely on the fact that the next event will again be – uniquely – beautiful. The world of my friend is unfathomable and unreliable and therefore, every beautiful event is not only a source of pleasure, but also of a certain sadness, as something disappearing, never to return. And now from the stage, my world speaks with its authoritative essence, with the authority now reinforced by the distinguished Čapek and my adored Janáček. The Makropulos Case brings us together (my friend loves this opera) – and argues to my advantage. Janáček is on my side.

PJ: The immediate reading of *The Makropulos Case* led to the topic of immortality as a homage to Kamila Stösslová, a way to be with a beloved person when one cannot live with her. It seems that, when Janáček saw Čapek's play, he must have rejoiced at the iconicity of the femme fatale aspect of Elina. The Zeitgeist of immortalizing the beloved was there: in 1928, Virginia Woolf published her love letter to Vita Sackville-West in the form of a novel about Orlando, who receives the gift of eternal youth from Queen Elisabeth and then travels through centuries changed into a woman, Vita. The semiosis continues with the film version of the story by Sally Potter from 1991, which ends in a contemporary London park. Orlando is sitting under a tree with a book she has written with a hovering angel consoling her, while her daughter is filming it all on a camera. The message is a positive one – "I am the same as I was in Elizabethan times, noble and compassionate". The chain of immortality takes me then to Kundera's novel of the same name, which presents the relationship of Goethe and young Bettina with the sinister tone of the greed of a parasitical eternal life. Max Brod stopped Janáček from public declaration of his passion for Kamila, thus keeping their relationship on the subliminal level. Through Janáček, Kamila gained the best kind of immortality –hidden, iconic. True, Janáček had no mercy for the "lethal feminine" aspect, surpassing Čapek by killing Elina right on the stage in front of us, as if saying "I live my passion here and now". The theater program mentions Čapek fearing what the senior Maestro would do with his topic,[26] but he was not in a position to protest. Judging from today's view, it is as if Janáček produced a magnificent music video of Čapek's piece, which served them both well.

---

26 Blachut 2008: 40.

The second thing that hit me with *The Makropulos Case* was the presentation of Bohemia as a spiritual battlefield of world history. This is in connection with the alchemy project as a philosophical quest that ended in 1621 (in spite of Comenius' attempts to revive it). Ripellino hints at the project, but it took the US psychedelic researcher, ethno-botanist Terence McKenna, to arrive in Prague in 1996 and shoot a documentary on the visit of John Dee, the English alchemist, known for communication with angels,[27] to present it fully. The same acknowledgement was provided by the Czech surrealists, who, by their participation in the monumental exhibition Rudolphine Prague in 1997, embraced alchemy as their own in the psychoanalytical transmutation of the inner self into "gold".

The question of immortality has acquired a new face today since computer alchemists arrived with their formula named the Internet. Kamila Stösslová multiplied her immortality in the form of a Wikipedia entry.

Both Čapek and Janáček react to alchemy's attempts to approach God negatively. Čapek introduces his play with a polemic with the work of G. B. Shaw's *Back to Methuselah*, also published in 1922, saying the "thesis of Shaw will be used as a classical case of optimism and the thesis of this book as a hopeless case of pessimism..."[28] Thus, following the semiotic reaction of the archetype of the immortal femme fatale in English and Czech modernists, EM (by these letters I do not mean ethnomusicology, but Elina Makropulos) is a cold zombie, unable to utilize the experience of alchemic transmutation for any purpose, remaining without agency in the same way as when her father used her as a laboratory rat for Rudolph II. The power, which in a feminine form is necessarily represented in the form of an opera diva, follows only her narcissistic goals. That is unusual for modernism, which, as a project, aimed at social change. This points out the specific position of both Čapek and Janáček. Čapek's play, however, includes a scene where the men around Elina try to get hold of the longevity recipe for the "good of humanity", only to reveal the greedy interests of all present. That power-drive part of the plot was obliterated by Janáček as superfluous. It is worth noting, though, that Čapek saw his "pessimism" as public responsibility, as a celebration of the small relative goodness in life, otherwise full of diseases, poverty and drudgery.[29] This might sound like a step down from the "world spiritual battlefield", but still ranks the opera as a contribution to the never-ending immortality debate.

27   DVD, The Alchemical Dream, San Francisco: Mystic Fire Production, 2008.
28   Blachut 2008: 34.
29   Ibid.

CONCLUSION

The attempt at this semiotic analysis was started by our amazement at how it was possible that two distinctively different personalities – with different temperaments, experience and preferences – were powerfully affected by the same event.

At first, we became aware of the *qualisign*: the quality of "opera in the National Theatre" with its pertinent attributes – red velvet, grandeur of the building and illusiveness of the setting. Even that abstract sign evoked a rich layer of response.

The particular event – a production of Janáček's opera *The Makropulos Case* directed by American Christopher Allen and conducted by Tomáš Hanus[30] (*sinsign*) made Pavla realize the "obvious (in the sense of Kundera – 1967 and Bělohradský – 2010) world repute" (Zuzana experienced it earlier); international production, Prague and its stories, in this instance the alchemy story of longevity, as well as Janáček's music, have become a part of global culture (*legisign*), which is edifying for those of us who were born in this place.

In the areas where we both have extensive experience (opera in the National Theater), both of us experience snowballing (though, understandably, with a different content: with Zuzana, for instance, the change of perception of the sign from quality *dicent* to *rheme*). In places where our lengths of experience differ (especially in relation to Janáček's music), in the case of Zuzana it is snowballing again (understandably: there are things to snowball), whereas with Pavla it is predominantly chaining; moreover, in the case of Pavla, it is rather chaining of signs, understood in the quality *rheme* (how she imagines what), whereas Zuzana perceives more the quality *dicent* (especially in relation to Janáček). This would seem obvious to everyone who knows us: Pavla might be marked as more imaginative and Zuzana as more precise. In the resonance of the topic of immortality, we differ even more in regard to our temperaments and views.

There is no doubt that music, resonating on a thousand levels, stimulates a powerful emotional arch. This becomes a catalyst of reactions to what we have experienced as well as what we "only" imagine, a reaction proportionate to who we are. This integrates in us emotion and reason, the possible and the actual, the past and present, as well as the imaginative future. Moreover, we are connected (at least to a certain degree) with other opera fans: Pavla with her fear of commodity fetishism, Zuzana with the inhabitants of that "cheap world full

---

30   The production was a co-production with the English National Opera in London, premiering December 18 and 19, 2008.

of pretense." And, more loosely of course, with all lovers of Janáček as well as with those who deal with (im)mortality in some way.

The analysis, with the help of the Peirce-Turino semiotic tools, has also shown us our own perception of music. However, we do not doubt that, even if we had used finer instruments, there would still remain a lot that is unknown and unexpressed. Possibly unknowable and inexpressible.

LUCID DREAMS OF MR. WILLIAM HEERLEIN LINDLEY
SITE-SPECIFIC PERFORMANCE
AND LIVE EBU SATELLITE BROADCAST
ECOTECHNICAL MUSEUM IN BUBENEČ
OCTOBER 10, 2009, 6 P.M.

Zuzana Jurková

In the Saturday *Lidové noviny* I read Pavel Klusák's article "Only the rich will know silence". It is about the project "The most beautiful sounds of Prague" and also about a Bubeneč sewage treatment plant concert, which is supposed to be the culmination of this two-year project.

> "The most beautiful sounds of Prague" deals basically with creating an archive of sounds that Praguers like. There have already been similar projects in London (where actually today's "master of ceremonies", Peter Cusack, began with this concept), Chicago and Beijing. The resultant sound archive was and is open to anyone, whether a listener or a contributor. Thousands of sound reflections of the Czech metropolis were gathered on Internet page http://panto-graph.net/favouritesounds. It is possible to "leaf through" the archive according to categories (transportation, interiors, people, the outskirts, nature...), according to the localities or chronology. On a page of the archive is the logo Creative Commons, which tells us that the recordings are not protected by copyrights but, on the contrary, they are available for further digital copying and/or use, whether in musical compositions or, for example, in acoustic research.

Like most of Mr. Klusák's articles, this one also evokes the impression that not participating in a concert means making one's life unforgivably and irreparably poorer. My brother-in-law is a volunteer in the sewage treatment plant (which the whole family considers quite tolerable, but still with only one aberration: Who, in his free time and without pay, wades... hmm... in dirty water?)

Since no concert is advertised in the cultural magazine and I am incapable of finding out where to get tickets, I call my brother-in-law to make sure that, in case of emergency, he can ask the usher to provide me with a chair somewhere in the hall. He thinks it won't be necessary. ("Nobody comes to these performances".)

From the next-to-the-last subway station, there are two bus stops to the sewage treatment plant. We ride past gardens of luxurious pre-war villas until we stop in front of the small Bubeneč train station. After the underpass, under the tracks, the background changes dramatically into a street between old and

Sewage treatment plant in Bubeneč

new industrial buildings as if no pedestrians were expected. Besides, none are there. In predominantly anonymous architectonic expediency, one building complex attracts attention: on the sides, two tall slim red-brick chimneys, between which an odd conglomerate of constructions, of which two-story central buildings with light plaster and a little tower have the more or less typical appearance of houses from the beginning of the 20th century, while the two brick wings are definitely unusual. High wire windows refer back to some industrial purpose, but an arched gable strangely situated on the side and white brickwork around the windows add a sort of severe charm to the building.

I arrive at six, the announced beginning time. The main entrance to the building is open; nobody is taking tickets. In the entrance right behind the door there is a little table with CDs (free; I take three different ones) with yellow newspapers of non-standard format in German. The CDs were published by Czech Radio. They are called *RadioAcustica*. Their subtitle is *Acoustic Projects of "premedition" of a radio atelier.* (I would be curious to know what "premedition"[31] is.) There are four compositions on each CD. Among the composers are

---

31   Later I discover that PremEdition is the name of a broadcast of the program series Radio Atelier.

Floating bowls as an acoustic instrument

included two of today's participants, Michal Rataj (*African Beauty in Berlin*) and Miloš Vojtěchovský (*Stalker*).

Moving around the large and mainly high Central Hall are some fifteen people, mostly of younger middle age. The majority are men. Most are wearing sweaters or jackets. Some have caps on. I'm not surprised because it's cool in here. (Over the course of the evening, the number of spectators/participants just about doubles.) Six spotlights shine and during the evening in the semi-dark hall they sharply silhouette people and objects. Later, six large amplifiers resound. One of the "living" acoustic objects is a large bowl of water in various smaller metal bowls which are swimming, tinkling when they bump into each other. At the entrance there is a table on which a sign stands: Hot ginger with honey – free. Meanwhile, though, the table is empty. In addition to this, three counters have been placed around the room: one mixer and two tables with microphones. A man is sitting at each of them. The man with a ski cap is Peter Cusack.

After a while, steam begins to drift out from some kind of source and it impedes the view a little. Around 6:20, the men at the counters begin to read the names of streets, here and there with a number, sometimes with data about the quarter or some other text that I find incomprehensible. Various recorded sounds are added to this – in some places concrete, possibly the jingling of a tram or people's voices, in some places artificially generated. There does not seem to be a close connection between the location information and the loud noises. This "overture" ends after a quarter of an hour and is followed by some sort of formal entrée. The main speaker is Bohemian-looking Miloš Vojtěchovský, who, along with Cusack, is one of the two listed authors of today's event.

The cathedral of the sand-catcher (photo: Jiří Müller)

Michal Rataj speaks for Czech Radio and, after that, a few foreigners speak; English alternates with Czech. They all comment on and clarify the organization of the event, thanks to which a satellite broadcast is possible. I wait in vain for an explanation of what it is actually about. Probably everyone knows.

Then it is time for that hot ginger with honey. I meet a graphic artist colleague whose son works with Miloš Vojtěchovský. We sit on a bench against the wall of the majestic dark hall and quietly chat. After a while, we are aware that the amplifiers are emitting sounds, the sources of which are probably in the areas behind us. There are a couple of entrances to the basement and the people wander at their own tempo in their own direction.

We walk down a narrow winding staircase to the Cathedral of the Sand-Catcher – an almost majestic underground space with a brick vault. We walk along the walkways on the edge and on the bridges between them. Water flows very slowly and noiselessly under our feet. No sounds come from any of the unknown old machines which are spread around here (even though, in this complicated space with cathedral reverberations, I'm not sure of this). There is a clear connection between a pole that someone is splashing in the flowing water and the sounds gushing out here and resounding somewhere above in the roof vents or in the back in the shafts, to which sewage originally flowed from all of Prague. On top of this, women's shoes clatter as they descend the stairs and a white laptop lying here on the ground attached by a cable to the upper room seems to be another source. As I move around this strange space, something is heard from all around: I am not sure when it was I, when it was someone else, when it was a natural sound, an amplified sound, a canned sound or a sound transmitted from elsewhere, perhaps childish babble in a sand box in the Franciscan garden, or the sounds of a swallow – and when merely an echo. We all resound together in this huge brick resonator: today's sound producers with those who recorded their sounds earlier and transmitted them farther and farther; participants along with those listening on satellite. An astonishing and confusing experience.

WHY?

The evening in the old sewage treatment plant was certainly very different from the typical classical music concert. In fact, the organizers did not label the event a "concert"; nevertheless, they did use the English word "performance," that is a show, and the fact that the dominant element was sounds justifies our understanding of this as a certain kind of concert.

The make-up of the participants of the evening showed that the event was for a **specific public**; here the specificity lies, among other things, in the fact that the participants are willing, from time to time, to take part in the event without excessive hesitation, which is hardly imaginable at a concert of a string quartet or at an opera. In this sense, the evening in the Bubeneč sewage treatment plant is close to folk entertainment. Despite the lack of technical demands on the players, such events do not become part of folk culture (or entertainment, which would be rather easy).

This so-called New Music[32] separated itself from the main stream of existing classical music because of the basic ideas which – though many decades old – always seem unacceptable to listeners of classical music. The first main idea which applied during the Bubeneč concert, is **a change of understanding of music** from "opus factum," that is, a completed work, a product which was petrified in musical compositions of the Western tradition in the last centuries preceding that of the 20th **century** to **music as a process or concept**. The second is a certain **defocusing of the borders** both among various kinds of art and also, for example, between art and science.

---

32   Here, in the broader sense, for music of the 20th century, even though some composers still use more or less traditional approaches and concepts.

Conceptual music is most easily characterized by the expression "the idea/ concept of music is music itself" or "the idea is in itself the execution". [33] To go from this slightly vague clarification is, however, much more arduous. The designer Milan Knížák, who dealt with conceptual music in the 1970s, writes:

> We can think about anything as if it were music. In the same sense, we could, however, think about anything as if it were painting, literature, clothing, an idea, a house, etc.) As notation it would be possible to use an old shoe, a picture, a thought, a rainbow, the movement of a hand, the shimmering of stars, etc. This is nothing new or revolutionary. What is interesting about it is only that this understanding of reality uncovers some new possibilities that would be difficult to find in the usual way. It is possible to create a variant at random or to find new approaches. Everyone can try to do it and consider himself a co-creator in this case. He is welcome. [34]

I am not sure, however, if Knížák's words help us to understand the principle of conceptual musical creation.

A composer in whose work it is possible to track a continual development of thinking about music to crystalline conceptual art is **John Cage** (see box): from the first steps (inspired by his teacher, Arnold Schönberg) leading from conventional tonality to fractal structuring of the metro-rhythmic aspect of composition, he came to the rigorous application of extra-musical principles, e.g. the principle of equality of all sounds as a musical realization of the principle of the equality of all living beings – principles which form musical performance whose course the composer cannot influence later.

This was also the case in the Bubeneč sewage treatment plant. The authors write about intention/concept:

> Sound composition is conceived as an imaginary stethoscope placed on the material of an industrial construction which leads through a spacious labyrinth into an underground second city below Prague... Sounds reminiscent of inner voices resonate in the mind of the architect William Heerlein Lindley, napping in the room of the hotel U modré hvězdy. [35] They fill this concept of a stethoscope with collected, ready-made "Prague sounds," which are mixed with unprepared sounds caused by visitors at unexpected moments.

The expression "site specific" in the title of the program means "created for a concrete site" and refers to the second influence. It is easy to trace the con-

---

33   See http://www.nonalignmentpact.com/2008/04/week-75-conceptual-music.html (March 22, 2010)

34   Milan Knížák: Hudba tušená, myšlená.[Music intuited, imagined] 1978. See http://artlist. cz/?id=3057 (January 14, 2010).

35   From the concert program, see http://pantograph.net/favouritesounds/page.php?page=18.

nection to the Canadian school of sound ecology which first used the term "soundscape" in its title: **World Soundscape Project (WSP)**. It was founded in 1970 by the composer, musician and scholar Raymond Murray Schafer at Simon Fraser University in Vancouver. He was inspired by the German Bauhaus movement, which connected the concept of visual arts and crafts in a new way from which arose industrial design combining aesthetic qualities – beauty – with practicality. Schafer was driven by a similar vision of the combination of scientific and artistic disciplines concerned with sound when he newly formulated his approach to the sounds that surround us.

Schafer's key ideas were, first, to accept a positive attitude toward sounds (they are no longer "dirt" polluting our auditory organs), but stimuli to which we react according to our relationship to them. The second key idea was fieldwork: laboratory research cannot find anything substantial about how sound really functions in a human environment. [36]

So far, sound ecology looks like one of the scientific disciplines combining aspects of natural sciences with humanities and social sciences. Not coincidentally, Schafer was, however, also a musician and composer; this is why he saw – and particularly heard – in the sound environment not only a subject of scientific interest, but also a source of beauty:

The soundscape is no accidental by-product of society; rather it is a deliberate construction by its creators, a composition which may be as much distinguished for its beauty as for its ugliness. [37]

The expression "site specific" refers to one more feature of contemporary culture, a feature related to WSP: while its members blurred, by their approach, the borders between science and art (Is it science – is it a description of which sounds exist and where and how damaging they are for man – or is it art – a beautiful sound construction?) in the Bubeneč sewage treatment plant we register the emphasis on the combinations of different kinds of art (or different kinds of sensual perception). The truth is that, in the whole history of opera, we can repeatedly hear voices calling for a return to the antique ideal of art which has an effect not only through a musical component, but also through visual and textual ones calling for Gesamtkunstwerk, a complex artistic creation which affects all the senses. But in other genres, in the last centuries, it would be difficult to imagine that, for example, Beethoven would determine

36   These thoughts are obviously in a discipline which in its name points to ecology, that is, a science about the relations between living organisms and their environment; thus sound ecology is interested in the acoustic relations of living organisms to their environment.
37   Schafer 1994: 7, quoted by Griger 2007.

the place where his symphonies should be played or Janáček where his string quartets should be played. "Objectified" music, music as a product, is not bound to a certain place.

And here in this sewage treatment plant, it is possible to trace the influence of John Cage. He – succeeding the French Dadaist painter Marcel Duchamp (1887–1968) – speculates about the penetration of the dimensions of time and space; music does not resound just in time, but different sounds also come from different directions, meet and create a "musical sculpture".[38]

In the second half of the 20th century, then, the term "intermediality" appears on the scene; at first it denoted happenings in the environment of the New York Fluxus group.[39] In it, there was not only a combination of various media, that is, kinds of art, but mainly of traversing borders: borders between media and borders between art and life. This new concept of art/life returns us not only to conceptual art (and again, possibly, to Cage, who used the Chinese I-Ching both to search for the answers to personal questions and also as a modus operandi in his compositions), but also to the whole Bubeneč experience of a resonating Prague basement.

What was played out in the old Bubeneč sewage treatment plant, along with probes into thoughts and approaches in the background, almost perfectly corresponds to the picture of culture in today's world as is often imagined by the above-mentioned Arjun Appadurai (1996). Imagination, as a usual way through which not only individuals, but whole groups, are used to grasping the world, made it possible to create through the most varied technical means – by picking up and recording sound from its generation to the creation of space-sonic formations – a new world, a world of the "lucid dreams" of a more or less imaginary person (shielded by the name of the designer of the sewage treatment plant, whose historical context was more than suitable for such an imagination). And not only that. Technology also enabled the sharing of the "world according to (one's own) ideas"[40] with its "inhabitants" who are geographically distant from each other. It is difficult to imagine a more eloquent hallmark of this world than direct satellite broadcasting: despite everything that occurs in the surroundings, everybody can be wherever they are, can be its citizens at that moment.

---

38 French: sculpture musicale. From an interview, part of which is quoted in the box about John Cage.

39 The term intermediality is taken from "Intermedia," an essay by Dick Higgins from 1966. Higgins himself was a member of the Fluxus group.

40 Appadurai uses the expression "imagined world" in contrast to "imaginary", thus non-existent in reality, this "imagined" world is formed with images of its inhabitant.

JOHN CAGE, PILLAR (AND MOVER) OF MUSIC
OF THE 20ᵀᴴ CENTURY

In an interview one year before his death, the American composer John Cage (1912–1992) said:

When I hear what we call music, it seems to me that someone is talking and talking about his feelings or about his ideas of relationships, but when I hear traffic, the sound of traffic here on Sixth Avenue, I don't have the feeling that anyone is talking. I have the feeling that sound is acting, and I love the activity of sound. What it does is it gets louder and quieter and it gets higher and lower and it gets longer and shorter. It does all those things, and I'm completely satisfied with that. I don't need sound to talk to me. We don't see much difference between time and space. We don't know where one begins and the other stops, so that most of the arts we think of as being in time and most of the arts we think of as being in space. Marcel Duchamp, for instance, began thinking of time, I mean thinking of music, as being not a time art but a space art and he made it a piece called "Sculpture musicale," which means different sounds coming from different places and lasting, producing a sculpture which is sonorous and which remains. People expect listening to be more than listening and so sometimes they speak of "inner-listening" or the meaning of sound. When I talk about music, it finally comes to people's minds that I'm talking about sound that doesn't mean anything, that is not inner, but is just outer. And they say, these people who finally understand, they finally say, "You mean it's just sound?" thinking that for something to just be a sound is to be useless... whereas I love sounds, just as they are and I have no need for them to be anything more than what they are. I don't want them to be psychological. I don't want a sound to pretend that it's a bucket... or that it's a president... or that it's in love with another sound (he laughs). I just want it to be a sound. And I'm not so stupid either. There was a German philosopher who's very well known, Immanuel Kant, and he said there are two things that don't have to mean anything. One is music and the other is laughter (he laughs). Don't have to mean anything, that is, in order to give us deep pleasure. (to his cat) "You know that, don't you?"

The sound experience which I prefer to all others is the experience of silence. And the silence almost everywhere in the world now is traffic. If you listen to Beethoven or to Mozart, you see that they're always the same.[41]

In this interview that lasted only a few minutes Cage captured a great deal of the earthquake that "art" music has gone through in the twentieth century. Even at the beginning of the 1990s when Cage, this mover of avant-garde music, summarized his thoughts about the independent activity of sounds, his ideas seemed rather bizarre to most people. We are too used to the concept of music as closed, prepared "things" – compositions. But Cage only repeated what he had already expressed forty

---

41 http://www.youtube.com/watch?v=pcHnL7aS64Y (August 8, 2010).

years earlier in his homage to the composer Morton Feldman (1926–1987): "...changed the responsibility of the composer from making to accepting..."[42]

What kind of accepting – and of what, actually? Who else besides a composer should be considered as a c(C)reator par excellence!

The way John Cage contemplated music and the world in general, but also how he composed and created graphic works and wrote was considerably conditioned by his relation to Eastern philosophy, and mainly Zen Buddhism. When, at the end of his 30s, he came to it, it gradually became for him what for most Americans would be psychoanalysis.[43]

I was disturbed both in my private life and in my public life as a composer. I could not accept the academic idea that the purpose of music was communication because I noticed that when I conscientiously wrote something sad, people and critics were often apt to laugh. I determined to give up the composition unless I could find a better reason for doing it than communication. I found this answer with Gira Sarabhai, an Indian singer and tabla player. The purpose of music is to sober and quiet the mind, thus making it susceptible to divine influences. I also find in the writings of Ananda K. Coomaraswammy that the responsibility of the artist is to imitate nature in her manner of operation. I became less disturbed and went back to work.[44]

After Cage realizes the meaning of music, he creates (determined by Zen Buddhism) a concept of its ethos. *The taste of Zen for me comes from the admixture of humor, intransigence, and detachment.*[45] Despite the fact that he is well oriented in many non-Western musical traditions,[46] he makes no effort to imitate the sound component of Japanese or other exotic music. Gradually he creates/discovers compositional methods that resonate with his ideas. The first of them has to do with a rhythmic arrangement. Cage called it micro-macrocosmic rhythmic structure. In it, he discovers two very new elements – one sound, the other organizational.

This rhythmic structure could be expressed with any sounds, including noises, or it could be expressed not as sound and silence but as stillness and movement in dance.[47]

Most listeners know the name John Cage (if they have heard of him at all) as the name of an eccentric who enjoys bizarre sounds with damaged strings of the prepared piano, recordings of sirens and automobiles and the thrashing of a carp.[48]

---

42 Cage 1961: 128.
43 See his autobiography: http://johncage.org/autobiographical_statement.html (June 18, 2013).
44 Ibid.
45 An Autobiographical Statement.
46 Meanwhile, it is clear that he has an accepting view of many cultures: in his famous *Lecture on Nothing* he lists sources that he enjoys listening to: ceremonial singing of the Navajos, the Japanese Buddhist flute, the shakuhachi, Chinese bronzes...
47 An Autobiographical Statement.
48 When, in 1992, the National Slovak Gallery in Bratislava organized an exhibition in honor

What could perhaps be seen as an attention-getting gesture of an intellectual was, for Cage, the exact opposite: a return to ordinary sounds. On the contrary, he considered tonality over-intellectualized: You know what you are supposed to hear, but what if you don't hear it?[49]

The introduction of non-musical sounds, including noises, into musical language was not, by far, only an esthetic matter: at the moment when sound loses its exact pitch, it completely changes both melody and the possibility of accords (including tonality), thus harmony, the development of which was, in the past four centuries, a substantial element of music of the West. It is also necessary to change the way of listening.

It is difficult to compare, but at least as important as the equalization of all sounds in musical language is the new principle by which sounds are arranged. Like the way the known Buddhist metaphor enables one to see the whole world in a dewdrop, Cage creates a rhythmic page of composition on the principle of a fractal: large parts of a composition (movements) are ruled by the same rhythmic relations as their smaller units (phrases). Much more important than the number of measures or the fact of exponentiality of rhythmic units is, however, the basis of this compositional principle: the composer – after he has chosen his modus operandi – no longer has the rhythmic development of the composition under his control. Back to the homage to Feldman: the composer gives up creation and accepts only the result.

When, in his late interview, Cage talks about the experience of deep joy (and calls for his cat's agreement) he refers to the world outside of human culture (as it is understood by anthropology, which means mainly as a net of interpersonal relationships and meanings). Regarding music, it sounds foolish indeed: what else is more essential to culture than music? And still. Not only classical Chinese musical esthetic, however, (like Greek Pythagorean harmonics) considered music to be a reflection of the cosmic order... Besides, the Czech composer Petr Eben (1929–2007) sometimes spoke about his feeling that music already existed somewhere and he just wrote it down. And even not only composers as much as, to a certain extent, intuitive artists, but also more exactly oriented people, can perceive the world similarly. The famous French cultural anthropologist Claude Lévi-Strauss (1908–2009) said in a radio interview: *I don't have the feeling that I wrote my books myself, but rather that books write themselves through me, and, when they have gone through me, I feel empty and nothing is left inside of me. I have never had, and still don't have, a clear feeling of my personal identity. It occurs to me that I am a place where something is happening, but where there is no*

of Cage's 80th birthday, its catalogue quoted Cage's Credo (formulated in 1937), whose main theme is – besides the use of electronic instruments – the very introduction of non-musical sounds to music. See Adamčiak 1992.

49 Lecture on Nothing, In *Silence* p. 116.

Petr Kotík conducts Cage's Piano Concerto

"I". Everybody is a sort of crossroad through which something passes, and the crossroad is completely passive. Something is happening there and something else, not less important, is happening somewhere else.[50]

Still, there remains the question of what pleasure one can derive from music whose source is non-human. Insofar as it is possible to attempt to capture the effect of music – at least approximately – in words (which many people doubt, above all Zen masters) and if the feelings of those experiencing pleasure from the de-emotionalized music are similar, then perhaps Milan Kundera can speak for them: ... *as if the weeping of the soul could be comforted by the unemotionality of nature... because in unemotionality there is comfort. The world of unemotionality is the world beyond human life; it is the sea setting beyond the sun (Rimbaud). I remember sad years that I spent in the Czech lands at the beginning of the Russian occupation. At that time I fell in love with the compositions of Varese and Xenakis: the pictures of sound worlds – objective but non-existent – spoke to me about being liberated from aggressive and depressing human subjectivity; they spoke to me about the tender inhuman beauty of the earth in the time before or after people crossed it.*[51] Perhaps it is just such a world that Cage is seeking in his music: a world which comes up in deep sleep when the ego doesn't complicate the action.[52]

---

50   Wiseman, B. – Groves, J. 2009: 175.
51   Kundera, Milan, 2006: "Improvisation in homage to Stravinsky". *Host* 3/2006, pp. 14–23.
52   Composition as Process, In *Silence*, p. 37.

This basic thought about the source of music[53] remains the same in Cage's work, although the methods of composition (that is, of "acceptance", referring to Feldman's way of composing) change. In *Music of Changes*, 1951, he uses techniques of chance, including in the Chinese canonic Book of Changes (I Ching). A few years later, in the second half of the 1950s, his idea of music shifts from "objectness" (a composition until then is still an "object" – sound structure that has a beginning, a middle and an end) to the idea of process.[54] In an "object" defined in advance (by any means), there is not enough space for Zen nothingness – and a composition is to be a bridge from one nothingness to another – a bridge over which anyone can pass.[55] It is therefore necessary, on the one hand, to provide space for any action, to anyone who wants to cross the bridge but, at the same time, makes it impossible for the ego (of the composer as well as the performer) to prevent the nothingness.[56]

However the techniques[57] in later individual Cage compositions change, some guiding ideas remain. First, there is the obstinate insistence on equality: people, ideas and sounds. Therefore, he refuses to let a conductor function in his usual way when the players are subordinate to his "arbitrariness".

The second "ostinato figure" of Cage's works is uniqueness: the uniqueness of every person, phenomenon – and performance of music. No further repetition is the same; a recording is nothing more than a mere picture postcard from a vacation.[58]

When on November 5, 2010, the *Ostravská banda*, an ensemble specializing in the interpretation of contemporary music, played Cage's *Concerto for Piano and Orchestra* in Prague much of the still unusual principles was obvious at first glance. For example, the founder and conductor of the ensemble, Peter Kotík, himself a distinguished avant-garde composer who, in addition, rather disagrees with Cage's concept of a conductor,[59] accepted the role here of living watches: by movement first of the left arm, then of the right one, he imitated the course of the second hand. According to its position, individual instruments began to play; the course of their playing is, however, in the absolute jurisdiction of the players.

---

53 Anyone to whom it seems Cage's understanding of music is the direct opposite of what contemporary mainstream ethnomusicology is right. For the majority of ethnomusicologists, music is not understandable outside of human culture; outside of it, music has no meaning. But they also cannot deny Cage his right to a voice.

54 An Autobiographical Statement: I was to move from structure to process, from music as an object having parts, to music without beginning, middle, or end, music as weather.

55 "Lecture on Nothing".

56 Cage deals with this in the second part of his cycle "Composition as Process," in the part "Indeterminacy." See *Silence*, pp. 35–40.

57 In Cage's terminology, "methods" of choice of different parameters of composition.

58 Indeterminacy, p. 37.

59 In an interview for Lidové noviny on June 5, 2010, e.g., Kotík says: *Cage was simply wrong in his attitude toward the orchestra. He didn't understand at all how to work with them. An orchestra has to obey. Otherwise there will be a slaughter.*

aph

Both the pianist and the other musicians (who totaled 13 in Prague, but there could have been another number) produce the ordinary tones, but also very extraordinary tones; on the trumpet mouthpiece alone, or on a tuba muted in an unusual way; the pianist plays not only with his whole forearms and he not only prepares the strings of the instrument with slips of paper, but he also rattles a grager (rattle). His part, besides this, is written on 64 independent pages whose order is not determined.

The players were scattered not only in a strange, asymmetric manner on the stage, but also on the sides of the auditorium. The resulting sound impression was uniquely three-dimensional – the shape was determined by this concrete, specific and understandably unique space with its combinations of sounds and tones. Nobody had ever heard the piano concert in that shape before – and nobody ever will.

It seems understandable, even banal, that silence is a sound realization of nothingness. Cage, however, often repeats that his favorite silence is not, above all, the absence of sound; it is a change of mind, a basic reversal.[60] A kind of condensation of his ideas about music is the composition 4'33" for any instrument: a composition in three parts (their length is precisely determined) is filled with the silence of the musician and random sounds produced by the audience or the surroundings. Nothingness always different.

---

60   An Autobiographical Statement.

BENEFEST VOL. 1
MODRÁ VOPICE (BLUE MONKEY) CLUB
MARCH 26, 2010
Jakub Jonáš

Slightly after 7 p.m. I step out of bus number 177 at the "K Žižkovu" stop in Prague's Vysočany. Right after getting out I notice that a bus with the same number is also coming from the opposite direction. Through a window I see that inside there is a man in jeans and a torn jacket on which metal ornaments are glittering. He can't find his way to the door to get out. He is continually pulled away from the exit by some unknown force until one of the other passengers gets up and literally throws him out. The man stands up; it is clear that stability is causing him great problems. With a lopsided expression, he tries to orient himself and finally he decides to set off uphill. It has been a long time since I last saw someone struggle so hard to climb up the hardly two-hundred-meters long hill. After watching him for a little while, I, too, resolve to set off in the same direction, that is, to the club whose name is mentioned almost every time there is talk of the Prague punk scene. Yes, I go to *Modrá vopice.*

As I approach the club I slowly begin to hear music; from this distance it sounds like a mere rumble. I walk the along the club's outer wall, which faces the street. On it is painted the logo of the club and an ad for Pilsner Urquell and Gambrinus beers. A few meters farther, on the sidewalk in front of the entrance to the property, a group of about ten customers are sitting – men and women from 18 to 25 years old – and drinking wine out of plastic bottles. From the exterior, the club looks like a wooden shack. I go through a blue metal gate and, at the moment I enter the club's courtyard, whose dominant feature is a stage made of tree trunks built about a year ago, a ticket-taker of about the same age as the group I just saw drinking in front of the entrance grabs my arm. He asks me to pay the 100–crown entrance fee. It flashes through my mind that until 7 p.m., entrance costs 70 crowns and so I try to convince him that it is just a little after seven and ask if I couldn't pay the lower price. He looks at me with a dog-like look and answers, "Today it is for children. The whole concert is a benefit for the children's home in Dolní Počernice." I smile, give him the hundred crowns and add that I was just trying. When I go out into the courtyard, I have, on my right side, the club and, on the left, a wooden fence near which are ash trays; the fence is completely covered with graffiti. Over the fence, auto wrecks prepared to be scrapped and a mechanical crane arm

In front of the Modrá vopice (Blue Monkey) club (photo: Jakub Jonáš)

that manipulates them are visible. The club is in an industrial quarter where loud music and shouting can't bother anyone. The inside of the club is painted light blue. In winter, the interior space is warmed with a heater. When you go through the door, the sound engineer's mixer and a bar are on your left. On your right there's a stage about 40 centimeters high. The indoor space is divided into two parts. One is in front of the stage and is used for dancing. The other, separated from the stage, is full of tables and is used for sitting.

On the stage right now there is the five-member formation *Děti v lihu (Children in Alcohol)* whose singer, as I later learn, devised the whole benefit. I follow half of the concert from outside because the side wall of the club facing the courtyard is open. They finish playing the first song that I hear that evening and, having added "We really fucked up this one", they begin the second song. Standing next to the singer on the platform is the trumpeter who, it seems to me, doesn't play a single exact note during the whole concert. The playing technique of the guitarist consists of sliding a power chord, that is, in accord with two tones (it is mostly a basic tone to which a fifth was added) along the neck of the guitar, while there are three or four chords in the song. There are also the bass guitarist and the drummer, who plays the same four-beat rhythmic pattern, in which the regular pulse of hi-hat is heard, on the first beat the bass

In the Modrá vopice (Blue Monkey) club (photo: Jakub Jonáš)

drum is heard, and, on the third, the small drum; the whole thing is spiced with sparse sounds of the cymbals. Their style is quick, energetic and aggressive; short songs with an important provocative visual aspect are clear musical expressions of rage and indignation.

The band members refresh themselves with beer and a few times there is haggling over which song will follow, upon which the band members proclaim: "We don't keep to a playlist". They are not the only band to use this sentence during the evening.

The people below the stage, regardless of gender, prance around, kick and strike out at each other, in short, do the dance that's called the pogo. Most are wearing punk clothing, which is mainly black and red; there are also plaids, jean vests and leather jackets. The leather coat called a "jackknife" is very popular. It is desirable for the clothing to be shabby, even full of holes, and decorated with all sorts of metal studs, spikes and pinned-on badges with the names of bands and punk slogans. The women also wear torn black or red stockings. They have to have high leather laced boots, although classic tennis shoes are also very popular.

After some thirty-five minutes, the band says good-bye to the public and thanks them all for coming to support this event. You can hear words like Facebook, through which the event was partly organized. I ask the sound engineer when the next band is going to play. He answers that when the sound check is done, that something like the schedule broke down during the performance of the first band. The only thing that holds is the order of the bands.

I decide to take a little rest. I order a beer, which here means a Gambrinus. If I wanted the more expensive kind – Pilsner – I would have to specify it. Beer and wine, which the audience brought along and drink outside, flow in streams; it's the same with cigarettes and marijuana. About a hundred guests have gathered in the club while, thanks to their ever increasingly staggering walk, I am beginning to take notice of how almost everyone is becoming more and more under the influence of alcohol. I sit down at a table where a forlorn hairy man of about my age, that is, about 25, is sitting. We chat for a while until suddenly, out of the blue, he grunts that he doesn't understand why setting up the sound is taking so long because real punk shouldn't do the sound, that it's completely pointless. As if telepathy works, from the stage where the next band is doing the sound, we hear, "Sorry that it is taking us so long. We know that punk shouldn't do the sound."

After the sound check, a band with the name of *A Crash* begins to play. They are three men, about 20 years old, in dark, shabby clothing; one has a Mohawk or rooster hairdo, which means that his head is shaved on the sides and on top he has long, stiff hair that reminds one of a cockscomb. The instruments of the band are a guitar, a bass guitar, and percussion. The bass guitarist sings.

The guitarist sometimes joins in. The texts of their songs have typical subjects: alcohol (*I'll have another beer / I like it with my friends / We all drink beer / And that's exactly why we live. / Beer is flowing / From our wonderful tap / We just look at it / And it is already drunk.*), "Nazi idiots" (*Metal muscles and empty heads / You beat up people, I ask you what for? / Fucking opinions about one race / I say you Nazis are pigs. / The Nazi idiot admits to murders / The Nazi idiot waves his right hand...*), anarchy (*What are we going to do / The system fell / Lord Jesus / What are we going to do / We are not going to pay taxes. / It is already here, the news has already come / Anarchy is here / So call out in jubilation / We are going to live like an organic-pastured cow / No duties no laws*).

There are also songs about grandpa, whose pontification still hangs around a person's neck or about "David's former neighbor lady who was a real swine". The more vulgarisms that appear between and in the songs,, the greater the applause that follows them.

After their act, the director of the Dolní Počernice Children's Home goes on stage and thanks for the money that was collected. It is clear that he is rather confused when looking at the tipsy young people, but he tries to keep face and, at the same time, express partial sympathy to all the participants. He constantly repeats that he and his friends basically did the same thing at the age of the audience. Each thanks to the audience is followed by a noisy roar, by which the audience members express their sympathy. The director finally adds that everyone who is there curses his or her parents, but there are people who are much worse off. He thanks them for the four thousand crowns that were collected – and on the program is another band, this time not from Prague like all the previous ones, but from Kladno.

The band calls itself *Wajgl (Cigarette Butt)*; from first glance we can see that all their members are older than the members of the previous bands. The group consists of two guitars, a bass, percussion, and singing, and their compositions are technically more demanding and very precisely performed. Listening to them, therefore, I have a momentary feeling that this is no longer punk but metal music. The music is recognizably more solid, full of relatively elaborate guitar solos, and the singing is somewhat more sophisticated. The listeners accept them, but not as enthusiastically as the previous bands. It is hard to say why; it could be the style; it could be that they don't know them as well. As for the texts, their subjects are the same as their predecessors'.

After this band, the *Thunderbirds* take the stage. They introduce themselves as punk rock'n'rollers. For the first time this evening, English is heard in the room; the audience listens. Applause follows the songs, but the pogo, that is, the main confirmation of acceptance of the audience, is not danced.

My attendance at the Modrá Vopice ends at 11:40. In the courtyard, customers are standing around or sitting on the wooden stage as well as on benches;

they are drinking beer and wine and smoking cigarettes or marijuana. Everything looks just as it did when I arrived, the only difference being that nobody is taking tickets any more.

RIOTOUS MUSIC[1]

Punk, in the true sense a riotous musical style (the word *punk* means a troublemaker or a rioter), arose in the middle of the 1970s in the USA as a return to the ideas of beginning rock'n'roll, which at that time seemed a bit stale in mega rock concerts. The main idea is resistance to mainstream society (from which it is just a short distance to punk anarchy and to one of the later basic slogans of the punks: the *fuck off system*) and the frequent practice of **provocation**. Among the punks, this is an especially striking visual component (as Jakub described).

One of the anthropologists of the so-called Chicago School (see box Michel Mafesoli), Albert K. Cohen (born 1918), calls various elements visual provocation *exploratory gestures*. According to Cohen, their use is part of the subcultural strategy: those who don't want to or cannot meet accepted norms and values of the majority society experience feelings of frustration which, on one hand, distance them from the majority but, at the same time, bring them close to those who feel similarly. Exploratory gestures become marks, standards or even symbols of the group. Cohen brings in one more function – the function of so-called protective provocation. Negative or even outraged reactions of the environment, on the one hand, confirm the negative relationship to the majority and, on the other hand, eliminate the hesitation regarding one's own attitudes and behavior.

The American *Ramones*, founded in 1974, are considered the first punk-rock band. In their music, in which they follow, in some aspects, the *New York Dolls* or the far left-leaning *MC5*, what was appealing from the beginnings of rebel rock returns: simplicity and energy. With the transition of the new style to Europe, concretely to Britain, punk acquires real roughness – and subsequent appreciation. Groups like the *Sex Pistols* or *The Clash* (both founded in 1976) immediately gained – and, for that matter, still have today – crowds of loyal fans. On the whole, they decidedly differ from each other in their original ideology:

---

1   After the formulation of this text, the Czech book *Revolta stylem: Hudební subkultury mládeže v České republice* (*Revolt through Style: Musical Subcultures of Youth in the Czech Republic*) (Kolářová 2011) was published. One chapter of it is dedicated to today's punks. For people interested in an in-depth discussion we recommend the chapters by Michaela Pixová (2011).

on the one hand, it is the nihilism of the *Sex Pistols*, including alcohol and hard drugs and, by this, stimulating another famous slogan *No future* and, on the other hand, the political left orientation of *The Clash*. What attracted listeners, bored by the gentility of jazz a few decades ago, to nascent rock'n'roll, is the same thing that now attracts them to punk: they don't need anything to listen to it and almost nothing is needed to perform it. The basic methodological principle is **Do it yourself! (DIY)** This instruction is far from applying only to music created by musical groups and to energetic, but in no way refined, playing and singing, but to the whole concept of culture. In the musical context, that means a refusal of more than basic specialization, the organization of concerts and recordings and distribution of recordings on one's own, that is, "personally" taking charge of the whole cycle connected with musical production. Like every musical wave, punk also spread far out and it is thus easy nowadays to find pop (that is, commercial) versions of these most special punk attributes that are disseminated by global commercial networks.

The Czech or, concretely, the then Czechoslovak, scene began to appear as early as at the end of the 1970s, which is surprising in light of the Iron Curtain -. Beginning in 1978, the *Jazz Section* first laid the foundation for this with listening evenings. The first live production of punk music was provided in 1979 by the alternative *Extempore* (founded in 1974), but the real punk groups at the end of the 1970s were *Zikkurat* and *Energie G*; somewhat later, in 1984, came *Plexis* playing compositions of the American *Ramones*. Like members of other branches of music alternatives, the lives of punks – who differed most strikingly from the others – were constantly complicated by the state police (this pertains mainly to the Teplice group FPB). From 1982 until today, the *Visací zámek* band, the most famous Czech punk (rock – their musical style changed in various ways) band, has been playing.

Today's punk movement is already thoroughly diversified in the world and in our country. After the merger of the punk movement with the recreated anarchistic movement in the 1990s, references to "Nazi idiots," as Jakub mentions, appeared in the texts of affected young bands. For such bands, internal **solidarity**, which often spreads to other weak and marginalized people seen as victims of that system, is necessary.

Two of today's punks discuss the connection of the above-mentioned values with Karel Veselý:

K.V.: That connecting idea is "do it yourself" – DIY. Is the accent on the word "do" or on "yourself"?

Šroub: *Nowadays only the word "do" is fantastic because most people don't do anything. For me, DIY is an attitude. When someone talks about freedom, he must begin with himself and he ought to be independent – of the state; of social benefits –*

and be able to take care of himself. *Another phase is to create work places, help the people around him, and create his own structures independent of the establishment.*

Kanár: *DIY isn't about individualism, but about doing things in a collective. When you see these eternal complainers who say that there are no concerts and that these things aren't worth shit, then I say: If you give a shit, then take it and do it. But that doesn't mean to pretend to do it. I know lots of festivals that these people create with their own money and without sponsors and that have their own great charm... For me it is important to do something for this thing.*[2]

One more feature from Jakub's text shouldn't disappear: that the absolute majority of the bands sing in Czech; English can be heard only in connection with rock'n'roll – and the band doesn't have such a response as the others. It is clear that communication of the text is primary. This is the case with any of today's famous punk bands – *Totální nasazení, Znouzectnost, Zóna A or TV Marvin.*

---

2   Kmeny, p. 67

FACE TIGERS AND STILLKNOX
PARUKÁŘKA, HILL OF THE HOLY CROSS, ŽIŽKOV
AUGUST 12, 2010
Pavla Jónssonová

I am rushing through Žižkov from the bus stop at Konëvova, past a statue of Jaroslav Hašek sitting on a horse made of beer pipes, past the John Huss church hall, where the band *Žižkovský dezert* rehearse. A tall tattooed boy in a skirt strides right in front of me, a girl with dreadlocks and a huge dog behind me. We turn left on the steps at the Riaps crisis center and ascend along the graffiti-covered music/rock climbing bunker club in the rocks in the middle of the hill. Up on the top, dogs fight gleefully; they belong to the beer-drinking clubbers who are lounging along the wall on the edge of the slope. It is mid-August, but the grass and trees still glow emerald green. In the rays of the sun setting behind Prague Castle I spot the music anthropologist from Columbia University, Daphne Carr. She introduces me to the boys from Silver Rocket, a community of independent musicians, and to the DJ from Radio Wave, Craig Duncan, who also organizes concerts of Nigerian musicians on the roof of the Kotva department store.

I go to fetch my beer at the stall next to the venue, a wooden shack with huge windows, where the opening band, *Face Tigers*, is already playing.

The Parukářka club was set up during the chaos after 1989, when enthusiasts illegally erected a cabin next to the park toilets and started to organize occasional concerts there. Prague 3 City Hall released a decree in 2007 to tear it down because of its poor hygienic conditions, but a petition of five-and-a-half-thousand signatures has postponed its demolition.

Beer is tapped both inside the venue and in the outdoor stall, which is adorned by car license plates, an invitation to Sunday open mikes beginning at 4 p.m. (guitar and a microphone available) and instructions on how to obtain beer (either a fifty-crown deposit for a glass or in a plastic cup for two crowns). Two elderly ladies in out-of-place T-shirts and 1970s hairstyles cut in front of me in the line. The alternative bartender pours their beers with the utmost respect. They seat themselves at a table, kick off the dogs, light their cigs, and enjoy the view of the Žižkov Tower and Hradčany. I pick up my plastic cup of Pilsner and go inside to check out *Face Tigers*.

The mixing sound panel is operated by Jarda Švec Umělec/The Artist, notorious for performing with the dada band *Ženy* and from the lyrics of the *Visací*

Zámek song "Známka punku"/"Sign of Punk". Face Tiger is the new group of Eliška Kohoutová of Stillknox. Other members are Jana Zuzjaková (known from various bands, e.g. *Ricksha*) on drums, Ron RaBob of *Dead Souls* and *Black Mummy* on bass, and Thor Garcia, author of a controversial literary work, is holding the mike and singing. The audience is roaring and the sound technician has to fight off wild dancers who are trying to get at his equipment with screams: "Volume to the right, dude!" In the ensuing chaos of the battle I run out to my buddies still enjoying the sunset outside. Daph is emptying a cup of dark liquid, laughing: *I've been drinking Kofola like there's no tomorrow!* We discuss yesterday's creative commons Kundolab event, consisting of recording cover versions of favorite songs on used tapes and subsequent free distribution in distros[3] like Polí pět.

Through the windows we can see *Stillknox* getting ready and so we dash inside so as not to miss the opening hit of the band, a tender, a cappella three-voice rendition of a children's poem by J. V. Sládek: *I know a crystal spring/ where forest is the deepest,/ where dark fern grows with red heather all around/ birds and doe come to drink/ under the maple trunk/ the birds during the white day, the doe only at night.* That gets the audience boiling and the consequent grunge explosion with guitars and drums resonates with a blissed-out roar.

Eliška Kohoutová, a student at Charles University, Faculty of Humanities, has worked her way up to becoming the best electric guitarist this country has ever had. Her style is not based on long solos, but on precision, density and color. She is the conceptual mother of the Stillknox project.

Her English and Czech lyrics range from philosophical topics ("Brighter the Light") to the activist riot grrrl platform (e.g."Stillknox," explaining the Dadaistic title of the band (*When the air is still-knox down the pill*) with the lyrics: *we are sisters thrown in space, / moon shines above within our grace:*

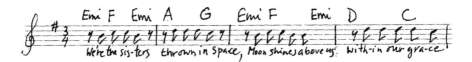

and a pseudo folk song "Kebych mala"/"If I had". Its lyrics, set to an original Czech Christmas carol, were composed by the singer of the band, Zuzana.

Elda's cousin, bass-guitarist Hana Blažíková, is a professional vocalist and instrumentalist in the Philharmonic Orchestra, which is both a blessing and a curse, as her classical music engagements practically prohibit regular concert activities. Fronting the show is the riveting singer Zuzana Beránková, a nurse

---

3   Literature and music distribution points.

at the Bohnice mental hospital: her expressive manifestations of a sex-goddess bring the audience to one orgasm after another. The band is completed by drummer MSc. Jiří Hladík, a.k.a. Athlet Fucker.

Stillknox manages to build a ship of sound at Parukářka, taking the crew of the club off to an energy dimension on it. These beautiful wild girls become avatars of freedom and rebellion.

The concert climaxes with "Memories," producing a final catharsis. We leave the concert as if after a therapy session. We re-enter the emerald park, and the shining Prague Castle and the Žižkov tower are the backdrop for feeling these are the ultimate moments in an ultimate place.

RIOT GRRRL

This radical reaction to the meager influence of women within the framework of alternative music started in 1991 at the International Pop Underground (IPU) Convention in the university town of Olympia, Washington, USA.[4] The "girl day" featured Jean Smith of Mecca Normal and a number of other musicians and poets, and a chapter of "girl rock revolution" started. It consisted of launching music groups (*Bikini Kill, Bratmobile, Babes in Toyland, Lunachicks, Le Tigre, Huggy Bear, L7, Sleater Kinney*), self-published zines, magazines (e.g. *Revolution Girl Style Now, Girl Germs, Malefice*), festivals, poetry evenings, and writing manifestos calling for sisterhood and getting rid of jealousy as a "killer of girl love".[5] These were often girls who experienced sexual violence in the family, ran away, struggled through life, surviving thanks to prostitution (*Sister Spit*). The solidarity meant salvation for them. Open debates on incest, rape and sexuality helped to break through the isolation and alienation.

The movement suffered from media trivialization, but it was clear it questioned traditional ideas of femininity and refused technical virtuosity as a necessity for being creative. This basic punk DIY ethos had a feminist color of slogans like "Girls of the world, take guitars and play." Among other goals was fighting for space where girls could express themselves freely, also including the creation of a "girl mosh-pit" under the stage without being crushed by raging male punks, and a connection to the gay/lesbian punk homocore/queercore movement.

Czech anarcho-feminists started the riot-grrrl zines *Bloody Mary* (2000) and *G Bod* in 2011. The most important riot-grrrl band in the country is *Stillknox*.

---

4   O'Dair 1997: 457.
5   Manifest Bikini Kill 1991: Kathleen Hanna, as the most erudite, functioned as the spokesperson of the movement. She called the establishment of riot grrrl groups around the world until a systemic change occurred which would enable them to participate in musical life.

ROCK'N'ROLL[6] REBEL

Zuzana Jurková

Outside of society – that's where I want to be,
Outside of society – that's where you're gonna find me!
Patti Smith, Rock'n'Roll Nigger

Two features of music join and strengthen each other in the phenomenon of the rock'n'roll rebel. The first is its ability to strengthen – and sometimes even to generate – collective identity (as we write about it in the second chapter): the group I belong to defines itself first of all through music which it listens to and/or performs.

The second component is some sort of social alternativeness that accompanies the performance of music – in contrast to, e.g., tax consulting or tailoring. Across history and culture we can see that professional musicians or people otherwise closely connected to music stand on the edge of society; they are tolerated, or, in fact, even non-standard behavior is expected of them. This is true for West African *džali*, musicians of the Mande group, allegedly inclined to have supernatural strength,[7] as well as for professional musicians and the production of instruments in the Near East[8]; incidentally, the view of European Romanticism of the icons of the time, e.g. Nicoló Paganini or Franz Liszt and many a Romani musician, was similar...[9]

Thus, music, that strange and somewhat suspicious activity, often stands in the core of groups which are, in different ways, radically delimited in relation to the majority of the society.

If it is possible to say that many musical styles symbolized alternative or rebel positions (and to a certain extent one can say this about the majority of them because new phenomena come most often as an alternative to or protest against what already exists and new generations often want to delimit what has preceded them), but afterwards their protest edges have worn away, then *rock* and *punk*, which one can find in today's Prague, often and in many respects have kept up their original musical and non-musical "rebel" features. This is

---

6   In this text we use the expressions "rock" and "rock'n'roll" as synonyms.
7   Turino 2001: 177ff.
8   Nettl 2001: 52ff.
9   We certainly do not wish to state here that performing music is an alternative matter always and everywhere; it is also a part of social representation, etc. Despite this, the above-mentioned feature seems rather striking.

undoubtedly because here music is not only a sign of alternative/rebel identity, but is its constitutive element – and also because the musical language is directly formed by the idea of rebellion.

The rock rebel is an archetypal figure with many shapes: brothers in arms (*The Clash*). Missionary (*U2*), the cruel dandy (Brian Jones), the Dionysian androgyne and transvestite – basically a Dionysian character has all the rock and punk looks of rebels, see box – (*Rolling Stones, New York Dolls*), delinquent (*Sex Pistols*), aristocratic playboy and potential savage in royal robes (Jimi Hendrix, Prince), latent homosexual (David Bowie, *Boys Keep Swinging*), anarchistic drunkard (*The Pogues*); among the oldest Czech rock groups, poetic revivalist UJD (*We will stay clean just the same, only when we want to – and we are not going to sob*), the mystic children of the god Pan (*DG 307*), the grossly direct (*Hever a vazelína*) or folkloric *Umělá hmota*.

The German philosopher Friedrich Nietzsche (1844–1900), in his classic work *The Birth of Tragedy from the Spirit of Music* (1872), used the names of two Greek gods, the god of art and leader of the muses, Apollo, and the noisy and lively god of wine, Dionysus, as a mark of opposite ways to reach basic life truths, to take a look at the essence of the world. His categorization was taken over by the American anthropologist Ruth Benedict and her influential book *Patterns of Culture* (1934), in which she applied it to entire cultures. As she understood it, the Dionysian type approaches the world by demolishing the usual borders and the acquirement of limits of existence; at the moment when it is most appreciated, he endeavors an escape over the border delimited by the five senses, an opening to other levels of experiences. The yearning of a Dionysian-type of person is to reach via his personal experiences and rituals a certain psychic state, to reach an extreme. The closest parallel to states which he is looking out for is drunkenness and, above other things, he values and appreciates inspiration originating in madness... Just like Blake, he believes that "the road to the extreme leads to the palace of wisdom."

The Apollonian type of person approaches all of this with mistrust and often has a rather foggy idea of such experiences. He manages to banish it from his mind. "He knows only one law – self-control in the Hellenistic spirit." He keeps to the central path; he does not abandon the known map, and he does not play with upsetting psychic states. As Nietzsche so beautifully expressed it, the individual of the Apollonian type in the whirl of dance "stays the way he is and keeps his civic name."[10]

Benedict then uses her categorization for the explanation of the character of three very different cultures: two North American Indian tribes (the Zuni and the Kwakiutl), who are as antithetical as possible, and the Pacific Dobuans.

---

10 Benedict 1934:78–79.

It is hardly possible to imagine a more apt characteristic of the rock rebel than the one from Benedict's pen relating to the Dionysian type. Everything about the traversing of borders, the break into other levels of experiences and the ways of reaching them holds perfectly. Nor is it an accident that here she quotes the English mystic poet William Blake (1757–1827), who was not only considered by *The Plastic People of the Universe*, but also by the American beatniks such as Allen Ginsberg, both a visionary example and – in the case of the musicians – a favorite author of texts.[11] A rock concert is some sort of liberating and, at the same time, unifying ritual, a little Bachtin carnival, that is, a ball of perverted values,[12] in which it is possible to experience purification and the opening of new possibilities. The sound character of music itself plays a basic role: the volume and physicality quicken the metabolism, free the adrenalin, and thus the intensity of a common experience is compared to shamanistic rituals and also to some sort of hallmark of genuineness connected with mutual trust.

ARCHETYPAL REBELS: *THE PLASTIC PEOPLE OF THE UNIVERSE*

Only those artists who understand that the gift of art was sent down to them so that they would address those close to them through this gift, and not so that they would be better off, they will bear this name henceforth.

Ivan "Magor" (Bird-brain) Jirous, artistic director of the Plastic People of the Universe: *Report of the third Czech musical revival*

In the Czech environment, the band *The Plastic People of the Universe* was an exemplary rebel archetype. If we find it difficult to chase away the inner image of a rebel as a lone individual opposing the whole world, thus rebelling against everyone and everything, we can make it easier for ourselves to accept group rebellion in different ways. One of these is the specific situation in socialist Czechoslovakia at the end of the 1960s, a situation urgently demanding collective resistance to the system. Another explanation is the medium of music itself requiring at least a musician and a few listeners. Through music, it is possible to resist only collectively. Anyone who would not be satisfied with concrete, more or less practical reasons, finds an almost perfect theoretical explanation, an optical lens through which it is possible to see in *The Plastics* events around them and their place in what was then Czechoslovakia after the Soviet invasion, in Turner's concept of *communitas/community* (see box).

---

11 For example, the group *The Doors* took their name from the book by Aldous Huxley, "The Doors of Perception", which was inspired by Blake's poem, "The Marriage of Heaven and Hell".

12 Actually, the reversal of values (ritual, "the power of the powerless") is, according to Turner – see box – one of the characteristic features of liminal stages, and thus communitas as well.

Vratislav Brabenec

The bass guitarist Milan "Mejla" Hlavsa founded the band *The Plastic People of the Universe* in 1968 with guitarist Jiří Števich, singer Michal Jernek, and drummer Josef Brabec (drummers continuously changed). At the time of the meeting with poet, philosopher and guru of the underground Egon Bondy and the setting of his poems to music (1974–75) the core of the group was established: besides Mejla Hlavsa, there were the saxophonist Vratislav Brabenec (who was forced to emigrate in 1982), Josef Janíček on the guitar and keyboard and Jiří Kabeš on the violin and viola. A side project of Mejla Hlavsa was his cooperation with poet Pavel Zajíček in DG 307, where resistance against the establishment was realized by the Dadaistic avant-garde. In 1988 the group split up; after the change of the political situation and the return of Brabenec from exile, the group began playing again in 1997.

In 1973, the group was denied professional status for political reasons; the following year the police broke up their concert in České Budějovice. In 1976, some of the members were imprisoned – Jirous for 18 months. The trial of the group became the basic stimulus for the unification of the Czech dissidents; at that time the initiative Charta 77 (Charter 77) [13] arose.

---

13   I am quoting data relating to the history of the group both from their official Web pages.

Besides the compositions that the group adopted and played during their beginnings (*The Velvet Underground*, Frank Zappa, *Captain Beefheart*), Milan (Mejla) Hlavsa was almost the exclusive author until his death in 2001. Thanks to him, the band had a distinctive musical style from the beginning. The texts came from a broad spectrum of foreign (Blake, Shakespeare…) and Czech authors; of these, in the first half of the 1970s, the most important were Egon Bondy and, later, Ladislav Klíma and Vratislav Brabenec. For concerts of *The PPU*, the visual effects, in the beginning mainly fires, were important. Later, the concept of theatrical performances became stronger.

In 2001, their first studio CD, *Líně s tebou spím* (Lazily I Sleep with You) came out; in 1997-2006, remastered old recordings [*Muž bez uší* (Man without Ears) - 1969–72, *Egon Bondy's Happy Hearts Club Banned* - 1975, *100 bodů* (100 Points)- 1978, *Jak bude po smrti* (What It Will Be Like after Death) - 1979, *Co znamená vésti koně* (Leading Horses) - 1981, *Hovězí porážka* (Beef Slaughter) - 1984, *Půlnoční myš* (Midnight Mouse) - 1985], and in 2004 the newly instrumentalized *Pašijové hry velikonoční* (Easter Passion Plays) (originally 1978).

The ideas *The Plastics* as well as their music, create a peculiar solid crystal which corresponds perfectly to Merriam's analytic model: it both illustrates the interconnection of the individual aspects of music and mirrors the essence of rock rebellion. In addition, we are lucky that *The Plastics* - like their beloved *The Velvet Underground*, whom they adored in the beginning - had their artistic leader who did not take part in shaping the sound of the band, yet did have decidedly artistic and cultural as well as broad philosophical-political opinions. In contrast to Andy Warhol, Ivan "Magor" Jirous was powerful with words. Through clear, fresh, poetic and convincing language he managed continuously, as well as from a distance, to describe the rise and development of the group and also the changes in their basic thoughts and positions.

The Plastics were connected with their American models, not only through the figure of their non-playing artistic leader, but also with the term **underground**. The Americans had it built into the name of the band and for *The Plastics*, the idea of *their own special world existing apart from established society with a different internal charge, a different esthetic and consequently also a different ethic*,[14] was key - opening the understanding of the entire related culture. And the effort to build such a community - *let us perhaps call it underground* (which is actually that "special world" because here it is primarily a question of people

---

www.plasticpeople.eu, and from texts of their members, mainly Jirous (1997, 2008) and Kalenská (2010).

14 Jirous 2008: 7.

and their relationships) – *cleaner and different people*[15] was the main content of this "rebel" culture of the Czech underground. There is no doubt that through *The PPU* the underground became one of the main concepts of political-cultural reality of its time.

The Plastics, by using this term, follow the broad Western intellectual stream (to which another of their heroes and musical models, Frank Zappa, belonged); they refer mainly to the thinking of the French painter Marcel Duchamp (1887–1968). *The great artist of tomorrow will come into the underground.* As Jirous explains: *By this formulation, he thought of the underground as the new spiritual approach of an honest artist reacting to dehumanization and the fucking up of values in the world of a consumerist society.*[16] *The underground is the spiritual position of intellectuals and artists who consciously define themselves critically toward the world in which they live. It is a declaration of a battle with the establishment, the entrenched system...* (2008: 11).

If the artists represent the pillars of such a pure community of the underground – and this would not be surprising because *The Plastics* themselves, at least since 1976, have been aware that they have been leading a solitary fight with power through their purely artistic means [17] – then extraordinary demands are understandably placed on them: *Only those artists who understand that the gift of art was sent to them to reach their neighbors and not to be better off will carry that designation hereafter... It is better not to play at all than to play music that does not spring up from one's own musical conviction. It is better not to play at all than to play what the establishment wants.* [18] Thus the artists were the first to realize the basic demands of the underground, the demands of sincerity and separateness.

The starting idea of the underground as a separate and special world first strengthened by the inspiration of the Jewish Cabala and Celtic mythology, later markedly by Christian spirituality, so different from the shallow and profaned Marxist materialism which at that time penetrated every sphere of life in society. It was expressed both in song texts[19] and in the ideas around them. Jirous' famous utterance *The moment the devil (who today speaks through the mouth of the establishment) sets the first condition...* certainly is not connected only with Karásek's favorite song *Tell the Devil No*; it is a good illustration of the

---

15 Jirous 2008: 173.
16 Jirous 2008:11.
17 Jirous 2008: 172.
18 Jirous 2008: 11.
19 V. Jirousová – e.g., *The Song of the Fafejta Bird About Two Unearthly Worlds*, M. Jernek – *The Sun*, V. Brabenec – *Easter Passion Plays*.

spiritual vocabulary not only of the author. The frequently used word pictures of the first Hussites going to the mountains, which *The Plastics* and their friends used[20] for their meetings/concerts, also show that spiritual dimension.

The social and spiritual concepts of *The Plastics* were reflected (unsurprisingly for those who had already come to like the ethnomusicological point of view) in their musical language. In it are interwoven their own original approaches with stimuli of world rock as *The Plastics* and their listeners encountered them on recordings which were very difficult to obtain. Separateness and genuineness, those qualities of *the special world*, are embodied in music by ecstasy, that is, Dionysianism, psychedelia and complexity.

The orientation toward **psychedelic sound** was typical of Hlavsa's musical language from the beginning. Jirous writes about *The Plastics* in the first half of the 1970s: *they attempt to induce in their listeners a special state of mind which, at least for a while, liberates one from everything and strips one of the basis of one's being. Apart from music, a series of other means serve this end – the use of the immediate effect of elements – water, air and, above all, fire, techniques taken from graphic art or relating to the happenings movement...*

That "series of other means", bringing a special state of mind, as he mentions it, is really long. It is possible to find visual and broader conceptual media in it (*fire burns on the stage, attended by costumed fire makers, the members of the band play with painted faces... during the performance that same evening when the first humans landed on the Moon they burned flying saucers...*).[21] Alcohol and drugs (certainly causing a radically special state of mind) belong in this sphere; for that matter, they are an essential component of any Dionysian festivities.

There is another important feature of the music of *The Plastics* composed and performed until the middle of the 1970s, music in the broad anthropological concept: orientation toward **human corporality**, including sexuality. After the first period, when they put texts by Blake, Jirousová and Kolář to music, and most often sang them in English (apart from the songs based on Jiří Kolář's texts) they found the true underground poet and philosopher in Egon Bondy (1930–2007), their later famous text writer. In Bondy, who *dealt with topics of the deepest concerns of man, from his social dimension to his wounded and imperfect biological being ... and ... in his poetry inadvertently fulfills one of the points of the program which the representatives of the underground formulated in 1964: "To exterminate entirely and forever the lie of St. Paul, silently presuming in Christian convention that people don't shit, don't piss and don't fuck."* (Here, however, is the right place to recall that, after working with Bondy, *The PPU* recorded, in 1979,

20 Jirous 2008: 5.
21 Jirous 2008: 9.

Pašijové hry velikonoční (Easter Passion Plays); they generally do not stop shocking interested foreigners, including those professionals, with their Christian orientation. Bondy's texts appear in a number of *TPP's* albums, especially in the famous album *Egon Bondy's Happy Hearts Club Banned* (1975). It is obvious that it was necessary to understand such texts, and thus, after meeting Bondy, *The Plastics* definitely decide to sing in Czech.

VICTOR TURNER ON *COMMUNITAS* AS SEPARATE FROM THE SOCIETY OF THE PURE

The English anthropologist Victor Turner (1920–1983) dealt with communitas/communities in some of his works.[22] His starting point is the concept of rituals, as they were set forth by Arnold van Gennep (1873–1957) in his famous work *The Rites of Passage* (1909). According to him, all rites of passage have the same phases: pre-liminal (separation), liminal (transition) and post-liminal (reincorporation).

Turner followed the concept of van Gennep's characteristic liminal phase as van Gennep described it on the basis of the similarities in many cultures of the whole world. Turner applied them to greater social units. In Turner's concept, there exist two modes of social existence or two kinds of relationships which can be encountered across history and cultures. He calls the one that is stable *structure*: structural, hierarchized society in which individuals have ordinary attributes of their position (homes, clothing...). Basic features of the other, liminal, are primarily humility, sacredness, homogeneity and camaraderie.[23] A more detailed list contains 26 characteristics, of which at least 16 are valid for *The Plastic People*.) Turner calls this mode *communitas*.

A characteristic feature of communitas, besides others, is the presence of prophets and artists, "people on the edge" who, with passionate candor, struggle to rid themselves of the clichés connected with the maintenance of some position and with the playing of some role, and attempt in reality or in fantasy to connect with other people in live relationships.[24]

As one of the modern examples of *communitas*, Turner mentions the generation of beatniks and their followers who voluntarily defy society, accept the stigma of a lower status, dress like bums, lead a nomadic existence... and support themselves with occasional manual labor... They place emphasis on personal relations... and regard sexuality (which is usually limited in the communitas movement) as a flexible instrument of immediate communitas, not as a basis for permanent structured social ties. The poet Allen

22 Here I use mainly the Czech translation of *The Ritual Process: Structure and Anti-Structure* (1969).

23 Turner 2004: 97.

24 Turner 2004: 124.

Ginsberg particularly apologetically expresses himself on the function of sexual freedom. The "sacred" attribute often connected with communitas is not missing here[25]*... with the help of eclectic and syncretic use of symbols and liturgical acts chosen from a repertoire of many religions and "mind expanding" drugs, "rock" music and blinking lights, they attempt to link among each other an "absolute" connection... They look for a changing experience that goes to the roots of the being of everyone and in those roots they find something deeply common and shared.*

The frequent identification of the basic words "existence" and "ecstasy" on the basis of their etymology is, in this case, fitting; to exist means "to stand outside," i.e., to stand outside of the total of structural positions... To exist means to be in ecstasy. [26]

The Hippie emphasis on spontaneity, immediacy and "being" shows one of the ways communitas stands in contrast to structure. Communitas is concerned with what is now, right now, while structure, by means of language, laws and habits originates in the past and reaches toward the future.[27]

Turner continues to emphasize that both modes, *communitas* and structure, are parts of the dialectic process in society. *Communitas* exists only in relation to structure; it exists as its liminal, ephemeral face, as its opposite.

25   Turner 2004: 111.
26   Turner 2004: 135.
27   Turner 2004: 111.

MICHEL MAFFESOLI
ON URBAN NOMADS
Zuzana Jurková

In 1950, the American sociologist David Riesman (1909–2002), in his book *The Lonely Crowd*, presented his concept of the polarity of the "majority" and the "subculture". He used the term "subculture" to designate the research topic which, at that time, pushed the thus-far exclusive world of anthropological research – exotic, so-called primitive cultures – into the background. Neither the topic itself nor the concept of the passive and homogenized majority – homogenized by the media and lifestyle – and the subversive minority was anything new. The so-called Chicago School had been engaged in the understanding of the subculture as a deviant or even pathological element of the cultural whole since the 1920s. Contributions in this stream which are famous, and important for musical anthropology, are (much later) the book by Dick Hebdig *Subculture: The Meaning of Style* (1979) and Sarah Thornton's *Club Culture: Music, Media, and Subcultural Capital* (1996). But I have to add that the term subculture has almost never had that "subversive" meaning which it is easy to attribute to it when researching urban youth. In the cultural perspective, and often also in musical anthropology, subculture simply means a lower socio-cultural unit than a whole culture. The fact that musical subcultures are frequent subjects of research only confirms that music – its style and way of performance – either generates a subculture itself or at least distinguishes it markedly.

In 1985, the French sociologist Michel Maffesoli (b. 1944) came up with a new term whose contents were not basically different from what was called a "subculture", but which was more attractive, the term **urban tribes**. He then elaborated it more thoroughly in the book (1988) *Le temps des tribus: le déclin de l'individualisme dans les sociétés postmodernes* (The Time of the Tribes: the Decline of Individualism in Mass Society). According to him, urban tribes are "microgroups of people in the urban environment who have common interests," incline to the same view of the world, ways of dressing and behavior... Their social interactions are mainly informal and emotional, that is, different from the urban culture of late capitalism, which, according to Maffesoli, is based on "dispassionate logic". He mentions the punkers as the most obvious example of an urban tribe.

The Time of Tribes is followed by an extensive essay, *Du Nomadisme* (On Nomadism) (1997), in which Maffesoli attempts to understand today's tribalism.
With a light pen but in a philosophical manner, he considers the paradox of the
interior of a person and of the whole society, the paradox of "dynamic root-
edness," the paradox of the simultaneous longing for rest and an instinct to
wander. The point of view is that "wandering and nomadism in their different
nuances become more and more evident reality". What is basic about this is
that "before our eyes there repeatedly surface motionless, constantly renewed
structures of ancient, archetypal things..." – and Maffesoli thus, in his careful
exploration of the character of contemporary nomadism and today's tribes,
reveals eternal, "timeless structures". The key to understanding is the concept of **wandering** – wandering as a phenomenon on the one hand relevant to
"the plurality of a person and the dualism of existence", and, at the same time,
the fundament of every social unit. And by the fact that it "expresses fierce or
restrained revolt against the established order", wandering is a gate to understanding the latent rebelliousness of the young generations."

First: wandering is an integral part of **each of us**; by wandering we are
penetrated through and through. Like that archetypal structure, nomadism
consists, according to Maffesoli, of the pluralistic character of our personality
which gropes around among several identities and, in doing so, acquires the
wisdom of uncertainty. At the same time, nomadism is an initiatory approach,
a modern "quest for the grail", an ancient yearning for the abolishment of the
reclusiveness and permanent residences that are so typical for modern times.
This yearning gives birth to an aim simply to exist, to resist social functionality
which makes us into mere wheels in the industrial mechanism of the world;
an "aim that does not define a purpose", that is, however, "in its strongest sense
a real cultural synthesis determining every form of cohabitation". And one of
the basic characteristics of this new, and yet archetypal, mode of existence is
Dionysianism, a wildly ecstatic experience of reality, the Dionysianism which
voluntarily renounces control over oneself – for an unexpected, strong, real
experience of life (see the box in the text Rock 'n' Roll Rebel).

Even more crucial is the **social dimension** of modern nomadism. Maffesoli considers wandering the direct opposite of the settled society of modern
times, which, by way of specialization, has almost frozen social circulation –
and what can seem like an expression of individual or social progress, about
which we repeatedly speak and dream, is in reality a symptom of a certain
closeness and gradually has a deadening effect on society and the individual.
Wandering comes like a shaking in this modern sleep of death. The myth of
eternal progress, which – as we were being convinced – is reachable via specialized institutions, is getting weak. From this also arises the eternal mistrust
of every official policy toward nomads wandering on the periphery, no matter
what form they take – tramps, hippies, homeless or damned poets.

The idea that a nomad is lonely is erroneous. On the contrary: the consequence of a tramp's spirit of freedom is "care about the other, without regard for his race, ideology or convictions". "A tramp's freedom, then, is not the freedom of an individual, a financial manager of his own life as well as of the world, but freedom of his person, striving for mystical experience with existence. This experience is primarily communal, and that is exactly why it is possible to speak about mysticism. It always demands help from the other, whereas this other may be someone belonging to a small tribe which we have joined or a Big other in the form of nature or some deities." "A certain insularity... strengthens integration into a community. For example, the insularity of a monk who understands himself only in relation to the mystic body of the church... What it is about is not such an empirical 'I', an ego belonging to the western tradition generally and to Cartesianism in particular, but rather – through some sort of contagious expansion – something that Buddhism calls 'the original I'. We are confronted with some sort of orientalization of the world."

Maffesoli opens with a comprehensive passage about nomadism across history and cultures, with metaphors of a bridge as a joining motif and a gateway as a closing and limiting one. He applies this dichotomy to the civilization of ancient Greece, Jewish culture, medieval Paris with its goliards, tied in with intellectuals like Villon, or Japan, penetrated with wandering. For Maffesoli, looking for and finding elements of nomadism thus confirm its archetypality.

For us, two motifs are especially important. On one hand, the repeated (thus, in Maffesoli's understanding "wandering") reminder of how the thought of the "rolling stone" is an obsession in rock music. "The remembrance that man is on the road – *I'm a rollin' stone* (Muddy Waters, 1950) – taken from the myth of black slaves torn away from their native Africa reappears in Bob Dylan – *like a rolling stone* – and, of course, also as the name of the famous rock group. This "spiritual nomadism" – *I'm a wandering spirit* (Mick Jagger) – can be considered, for more than one reason, as an emblem of the forming of the world.

The second motif, taken from Maffesoli by many other anthropologists, sociologists and journalists, is a motif of the city as a jungle and its inhabitants as tribal nomads. It is usual to call the contemporary city a concrete jungle. Just like a jungle in the strict sense, the city is also, from many points of view, unfriendly, enigmatic and impenetrable. Well, the characteristic of the labyrinth is that it does not respect the dichotomy of "outside/inside", or rather, it holds this bipolarity together: it is simultaneously and unreservedly both. Urban space plays this double role as well. Perhaps all of this is the cause of nomadism, or better, the nomadism of the wanderer, but also the nomadism of the loafer, of friendly groups and various tribes wandering from one place to another... All of this gives rise to the broad stream, unascertainable in its extent which appears to be endless, at least in large cities.

TOM STOPPARD: ROCK 'N' ROLL
NEW SCENE OF THE NATIONAL THEATER
JANUARY 27, 2011, 7 P.M.
Zuzana Jurková

The New Scene is a curious double building on National Avenue, neighboring the historical building of the National Theater, to which it belongs administratively. I remember well how much most of my friends disliked it when it was completed in 1983. At that time, it seemed to me that the massive glass isolation panels on its right side corresponded well to the stone massiveness of the National Theater.

In the glassed-in entrance hall, from which a green winding stone staircase takes you upstairs, and twenty minutes before the beginning of the performance, music can be heard. I pass people and a little dog at the café tables on the second floor. On the third, I drop into the auditorium. The people have not yet taken their seats; on the stage in front of the curtain the band is already playing. *The Plastic People of the Universe*. The keyboard player, Janíček, and the drummer, Kvasnička (the youngest of them all), in the rear; on the right in front, two hairy old men: Brabenec with a saxophone and Kabeš with an amplified viola; sitting on the left, the guitarist Karafiát and the bass-guitarist, Turnová. The music sounds quite loud to me; it's hard for me to find my bearings, but the sound and visual impressions evoke various associations and interferences. I like the way sometimes wild saxophone ornamentation is heard against the current rock background. Short tunes on the viola among ecstatic half-sung, half-recited lines of poetry explain a bit to me why the *Plastics'* music has been called mystic. This is how the texts of the songs also affect me: *We live in Prague that is where / A Spirit will appear / We live in Prague that is where,*[28] / *Apocalyptic bird / Hides wings of clouds / Apocalyptic bird, drops the iron curtain...*[29] The last song in the show is the new "In God's garden."

The various degrees of decrepitude of the musicians seems very remarkable to me (and I am sure that it is not only the grinding away of the wheels of time, and perhaps not the quantity of alcohol consumed: I remember a certain nihilism that breathed on me from the book interview *Evangelium podle Brabence* [The Gospel according to Brabenec]).[30]

---

28   E. Bondy: Magic Nights. Quoted from PPU – Texts, p. 52.
29   Pavel Zajíček: Apokalyptickej pták (Apocalyptic Bird). Quoted from PPU – Texts, p. 64.
30   Kalenská 2010.

The Plastic People of the Universe at the New Stage of the National Theater

Then the play begins. Of the few plot lines, I am most interested in the one that happens in dialogues of Jan and Ferdinand. Jan, a doctoral student at Oxford in 1968, then a journalist, later a baker and, after the revolution, a professor at Prague University, a character close to the play's author, including his passion for rock'n'roll, usually meets Ferdinand, whose name corresponds to the dissident pseudonym of Václav Havel, generally over some political petition. The author can thus (true, somewhat too didactically, but in a play intended for the international stage, it seems to me to be easily forgivable) on the one hand explain exactly what was going on in Czechoslovakia (house searches, imprisonment of dissidents, the police breaking up a *Plastic People* concert in Rudolfov, the emergence of Charter 77...), and also hint at the search for understanding among an originally apolitical underground and political opposition.

Individual scenes are separated from one another by parts of recordings of rock legends; their texts correspond to the play.

There is an intermission at 8:30. The audience: some 250 people filling perhaps two-thirds of the auditorium with gray-green leather seats. I have rarely seen such a varied society: a few children, teenagers in colorful tennis shoes, youths in suits, girls in formal and very informal clothing, a few alternative people with pony tails or in batik, and also a few couples who seem to have wandered in from the National Theater.

Vratislav Brabenec, Jiří Kabeš, Josef Janíček

The last scene is a short video from the *Rolling Stones* concert in the Prague Strahov Stadium in 1990; the concert Ferdinand spoke of earlier, as if about something unimaginable in socialist times, about the real proof of freedom. Shortly before this fulfilled dream, the second half of the motif that began at the very beginning of the play is heard. The motif has to roam around my head for some time before it falls into the right place.

Right after the last scene, the *Plastics* play another song: *Tygr* with lyrics based on the text by William Blake, the very Blake who has been connected with their career since the very beginning[31] and whose mystique is wrought with the poetics of all rock 'n' roll. (See the text Rock 'n' roll rebel) Brabenec staggers during the first bows so that the others have to hold him up and then he does not come out from backstage. On the whole, I have a rather good and somewhat confused impression: I like Czech "worldliness" that Pavla mentions in connection with *The Makropulos Case*. At the same time, however, I somehow feel that the *Plastics* do not go with this stone mass (and I can imagine that in the National Theater, where *Rock 'n' Roll* had its premiere and was performed until last year, the coupling was even more inappropriate. As if they do not walk through time, which means that they were not at the tip of the minute hand of a clock but, on the contrary, as if they were in the middle of a clock's face and time ran around them. People and things changed... and the musicians now stand and play in front of an internationally presented play which is about

---

31   *Tygr* is in the very first album *Muž bez uší* (Man without Ears), see PPU – Texts, p. 43.

The National Theater's New Stage

them – and at the same time, they do not belong here. At this moment, the Shem fits in and it seem to me that I understand what Stoppard thought with this Pan.

The play opens with a scene at night in a garden. A whistler is sitting on a wall. A song is heard. It is *Golden Hair*, sung by Syd Barrett (1946–2006), co-founder of the band Pink Floyd, a mystic figure of British psychedelic rock, a genius, narcomaniac, and schizophrenic. Barrett sings for Esme, a sixteen-year-old "flower child." Esme identifies the singer as "the great god Pan". Only these few minutes in the whole play have any sort of breath of romance or fantasy (which could very well point to drugs or psychedelics in general).

And shortly before the end, before that apparently triumphant *Rolling Stones* concert in Strahov, in the last live scene we hear an excerpt of a Plutarch text: "*... announce that the great god Pan is dead ...and a loud lament was heard, not from one person's lips, but from many.*"[32]

To me, reared on Debussy's flute solo *Syrinx* (referring to one of the tales of the Greek god Pan), it took a while to get rid of the association with that most fragile possible sound, with filigrees created by breath. Of course! The Pan of a Dionysian procession is much closer than an impressionist solo flute to ecstatic rock 'n' roll, which truly lives only in rebellion.

---

32   Text quoted from the Rock 'n' Roll program brochure, Prague, National Theater 2007: 169.

FILM *MŇÁGA – HAPPY END*
SCREENPLAY AND DIRECTION: PETR ZELENKA
1996
Filip Schneider

It all began when John Heather became the director of the Czech branch of the international musical concern BGM. This originally unsuccessful actor noticed that there was missing on the Czech scene a sort of "generational presentation of those most ordinary boys, those somewhat slow, not very good-looking dumbbells, nice, trustworthy..." in the words of the journalist Jiří Černý. There were only two possibilities: to wait until such a band appeared or simply to create one. The film is called *Mňága – Happy End* and it tells the story of this band.

The repertoire was not a great problem: the texts of the songs were already done; the screenwriter Martin Daniel wrote a few depressive poems during his therapy in a psychiatric institution after a bad LSD trip. The internationally known Ivan Král was called in to set the poems to music. Originality was not a condition; they were to be like the *Madness* band's style. There was a contest for the role of frontman which, despite a great deal of competition among well-known names, was surprisingly won by Petr Fiala, a cattle feeder in the JZD (an agricultural cooperative) whose voice had a tritone range. The computer program Band-maker was used for the composition of the rest of the band; this program suggested the faces of all of the musicians to which it was then necessary to find similar people. (The *Sex Pistols* and *ABBA,* e.g., allegedly originally began in the same way.) It was actually such a band of indistinctive exotics who visually blended and couldn't play at all; but if you have the international concern BGM behind you with enough means, such an objection is irrelevant.

Step by step, then, we follow how a bunch of timid Moravian boys became the group *Mňága and Žďorp,* the flagship of the publishing house. Hired specialists like Boris Hybner and Martin Schulz teach the members of the band how to move or how to memorize standard replies to predictable questions of journalists about how to become stars. Awareness of the band quickly rises as well as the number of enthusiastic concert-goers. The first record (which actually, apart from the vocals, was recorded by Ivan Král all by himself) sold over 300,000.

Their first tour comes, 60 concerts in three months with an ever increasing number of concert-goers. BGM doesn't keep secret that it is a completely artificial band, but that doesn't seem to bother anyone. The turning point, then, happens during a concert in the Prague club Na Chmelici, when there's an electrical outage and in the darkness the band plays some of its own songs by candlelight. Surprisingly they are a success and the most beautiful period of the band dawns, though it won't last long...

At the beginning of 1996, BGM with all of its property – including Mňága – is bought up by the international grocery conglomerate *Fruit International.* Their directors do not grasp the musical enthusiasm and idealism of John Heather and they decide to use the band for marketing purposes. From now on we can hear their sad songs mainly in ads for fruit and, when the curtain falls, the band is ordered to live exclusively on apples and Budvar beer, a business partner of Fruit International. Finally, their trademark sailor suits are also exchanged for fruit costumes, in which they can't exactly play their best. Yet Richard I. Brown, business director of the firm, "doesn't give a shit": according to the contract that the boys once signed with BGM (without reading it) the band belongs to the company and must eat, drink and wear what the company asks. To raise the profits from the band they even hire the director Zdeněk Troška to make the film "Sun, Hay and Mňága," the "true" story about the first meeting of the musicians – with Marek Brodský and Marek Vašut in the main rolls. The high point of everything was when the musicians ascertained that Fruit International had bugged their instruments. Then they decided to forget everything and completely hide from the world and from the lawsuits by Fruit International for breaking their contract.

The contract finally elapsed and it seemed that the Mňága and Žďorp band was a thing of the past when Petr Fiala learned that they had a concert in Pardubice. Arriving there, they found other people in their clothing and playing their songs with the hall filled with enthusiastic fans. The show must go on. *In England they talk about whether artists are conscientious, but in my opinion it is hard to be conscientious when your public can be bought. Mňága was indeed an "artificial" band, but I think that its public was even more "artificial,"* as the producer of the band, John Heather, evaluates the situation.

"Nothing in this film is true. Everything really happened." The white letters explain the real meaning of this. It is the middle film of his mystifying documentaries (in the Anglophone world captured by the play-on-words *mockumentary*). The first was the TV *Hanging Lock 1982–2007* (filmed in 1993, half of the film thus documents a fictitious future); the third, then, the award-winning *Year of the Devil (2002),* a film documenting eight years in the life of the songwriters Jaromír Nohavica and Karel Plíhal, the group Čechomor and the American music experimenter Jaz Coleman. Although these three films are very different from each other, they have in common their close connection of reality with fiction, real concert shots with shots made according to screenplays and implementation of true stories and figures reinterpreted so that they

become illustrations of the directors' ideas... The story of the Mňága and Žďorp band is mostly fictitious, but Zelenka reveals to the audience the real practice of the so-called "music industry." The German pop band Milli Vanilli can serve in good stead as a more than appropriate example of the fabrication of bands for the purpose of profit. This band was founded in 1988 by composer and producer Frank Farian and it contained two handsome, young Blacks whose main task was to look good on posters in girls' rooms and, at concerts, to open their mouths synchronized with music sung by other singers – people whose existence was kept secret at any cost because they lacked a marketable image. Farian was convinced that this plan would work mainly thanks to his experience with the band Boney M, which began in exactly the same way. When Charles Shaw revealed to the media that he was actually one of the singers of Milli Vanilli, Farian allegedly sent him $150,000 so that he wouldn't exaggerate with this candor. Under the pressure of questions which this testimony elicited but also because of an incident when at a concert carried by MTV television, during the song "Girl You Know It's True," the tape got stuck and chaos broke out at the endless loop "Girl you know it's..." and both performers were so frightened that they ran off the stage, a year later Farian publicly confessed to the whole deception. Before that, however, the record of "Girl You Know It's True" went platinum six times; all five singles put out by them climbed to among the top four on the sales chart. The band earned three American Music awards and one Grammy as the discovery of the year (but, after the revelation of the whole scandal, it was taken away from them). Nothing about this group was real except the million dollars for the sales of their records, and that's what mainly counts.[1] I don't know if it was exactly this story that Petr Zelenka had in mind when writing his screenplay, but it is only the tip of the iceberg in the world of false music for false listening. In a world where "unmarketable" means the same thing as "useless."

Filip's text about Zelenka's film opened the topic of music commodification, that is, the understanding of music predominantly as goods intended for generating profit. This is a subject inspired to a certain extent by Appadurai's *financescape* – and our texts, mainly in the "Radio Case," really do partially corroborate Appadurai's characterization of the difficult traceability of the flow and influence of money. One of the consequences is some sort of amorphousness of this "-scape": its mechanisms grasp various musical styles and treat them in their own ways. This is partially reflected by our treatment. Precisely because we surrounded commodified music from all sides and because it

---

1   http://www.allmusic.com/artist/milli-vanilli-mn0000412710 (March 18, 2013).

has various shapes, we had to supply more substantial theoretical lenses. We first describe intellectual approaches leading to the concept of music as (some other sort of) goods and, in connection with them, the basic concept of commodification – copyright. In the text about Theodor Adorno we approach his characteristics of the consequences of commodification on musical language and on the listeners, and in the half-century more recent "continuation" – *KLF Manual* – the connection of music with business.

We intentionally chose snapshots from three different fields: radio broadcasting, a Czech musical and a concert for foreign tourists at the Prague Castle. Cleaned lenses show how much these have in common.

MUSIC AS GOODS/BUSINESS
Zuzana Jurková

If you open the Czech webpages of the Copyright Protection Association (OSA in Czech), you may be bewildered by the menu options. There you will find "gastronomic appliances," "services and business," "accommodation facilities and spas," "Instruction and sport" ... Confusedly you will begin to click around to see if you haven't made a mistake and are really on the pages of the organization representing "composers and authors of musical texts, musical publishers..."[2] When you have more or less calmed down (at least you didn't get lost in the Internet) you will learn that here you will find mainly numbers, that is, numbers relating to money. This menu bar referring to gastronomic and other apparatuses deals with how much one has to pay here and there, for example, in "bars, restaurants and refreshment stands" (you will pay, perhaps, 157 CZK [US $8.00] per month if you have one radio or audio player and sales over 150,000 CZK [$7,800], while if your sales are lower, music will cost you only 152 CZK [$8] or 143 CZK [$7]). The only thing that seems to you to be relevant in relation to music is money. And, by the way, it is not a negligible amount: a year's OSA budget is about eight hundred million CZK ($41,300,000)[3]; the costs of this "non-profit organization,"[4] mostly for running its own business, are about one hundred and fifty million Czech crowns ($7,800,000).

This may seem strange to us: why not be concerned with money, specifically in the case of music? First let it be said that in the chapter about commodification the main topic is not the question of whether the musician or the composer receives money for the production or creation of the music, and even less whether the listener (whether at a concert or at home by the radio or audio player) pays for the music. The subject is what happens when music becomes primarily (!) goods, that is, a commodity destined for generating money and, more concretely, what happens when it is involved in the "music business." Let us take Timothy Rice, who is quoted in the introduction, and his formulation

---

2   OSA statutes § 1, 1.2.

3   The annual report of OSA for 2011, according to which the income in 2011 was CZK 884 million.

4   OSA statutes § 2, 2.1.

"Music is X," i.e., music can mean different things to different people. Its variety, however, basically determines its shape.

Music created primarily as goods has been a certain peculiarity of Western civilization for scarcely two centuries. In many cultures – e.g., in classical Chinese Confucian music, among North American Indians or in the music of India as we write about it in connection with a Prague *harinam* in the seventh chapter, and also medieval Gregorian chant of Europe – music is a sort of realization of heavenly laws and/or a means of influencing them. Although this does not exclude a financial reward for whoever is performing for my benefit, it basically prevents viewing it primarily as a commodity.

Elsewhere the performance of music is a basis for a more or less intimate community which is perhaps even constituted by musicking: this is when male Arab musicians gather, most often with relatives or friends, in one of their homes and (drinking coffee or strong tea) they play their favorite instrumental compositions. And despite such a great decibel difference (and also the drinking of different drinks) *Modrá vopice* is, in this respect, close to this concept.

In connection with commodification and copyright, in the professional literature written in English, the participants are the three Cs: creators, consumers (the public/listeners), and commerce, by which is meant the whole complex including both production and related advertisements, etc. Here we will first deal with intellectual presumptions of the creation of a copyright; then we talk about its basic features in our environment, including those connected to digitalization and the Internet, and, finally, with alternative concepts, especially *Creative Commons*.

Two boxes support this topic: In the first we point out the main ideas of Theodor Adorno on the influence of the concept of music as goods in the shape of this music and also about the thoroughly devastating effect on listeners. The second text – *KFL – The Manual, or How to a number one the easy way...* is fifty years more recent and at the same time as if it were another work in the same series. While the first work was about "human participation" in copyright, *KFL – The Manual* is mainly about the third segment – business.

How did we in the West come to the situation when our most influential and richest musicians' organization is not some artistic council overseeing esthetic criteria or a professional union attending to the welfare of the musicians, but the one whose Web pages are full of numbers – for example, about how much is paid by stallholders turning on the radio while selling hot dogs in rolls. The basic step was some kind of double freeing of man. The first freeing has to do with his unbinding from the vertical dimension. We are not going to get into the moral consequences of the loss of consciousness of a higher authority. What is important to us is only one aspect: the idea that man is the absolute owner of his time. This is generally divided into time needed for making a living and leisure, time for entertainment. It didn't take long until the new industrial branch, the entertainment industry, arose which had to fill free time. In economic discourse: "The entertainment industry is a monetized function of leisure."[5]

The second freeing, leading to the commodification of music, is the unbinding of man from the collective, that is, emphasis on the person, the individual as the great French Revolution elevated him. The idea of ourselves as "independent" is so strong in us that we scarcely doubt it. Hardly anybody – at least publicly – is as capable of reflecting upon his connection with the human environment as Judith Becker, a seventy-year-old American ethnomusicologist (whose research we will discuss in detail in the sixth chapter):

By the time one reaches my age, there is no pretending that one has original ideas, that my words have sprung virgin from my mind, or that I can lay proprietary claim to whatever thoughts and ideas appear in this book. As the Australian historian Greg Dening has said, we cannot plumb the depth of our own plagiarism. We live in a milieu of ideas that surround us, that permeate us, and that lay claim to us in ways that we never fully comprehend. My words are only partially mine, my thoughts are probably even less my own.[6]

If we could think as rigidly as Judith Becker, music and other intellectual products would hardly be able to become goods because it would not be possible to create a copyright, a cornerstone concept (and also instrument) of musical commodification.

One of the concrete musical consequences of emphasis on individuality is the preference for originality, primarily originality of the melodic idea; this exact succession of tones is, on one hand, the emblem of the composition and, on the other, it belongs only to me. Until Baroque times, a heavy emphasis was place on technical performance and thus a change of motifs (= melodies), for example, between Vivaldi and Bach, was not considered anything suspicious – after all, mastery was proved by the "artisanal" treatment.

One more – broader – musical feature is related to our topic: for the West, the typical concept of music as an *opus factum*, a completed work – what can be called the concept of "music as a thing." If instead we understood "music" more as "musicking," that is, an activity, it would be much harder (though, as later demonstrated, not entirely impossible) to relate the idea of individual marketable property to it.

5   Hull – Hutchinson – Strasser 2004: 1.
6   Becker 2004: 1.

COPYRIGHT LAWS

are an aggregate of laws which regulate the relations between the creators of "works of authorship," their users and the works themselves.

In contrast to the American concept which understands copyright as an instrument encouraging authors to create for the good of society,[7] the European one was conceived as a means of equalizing powers and interests in the environment where art becomes goods.

The beginning of copyright in Europe is generally connected to the so-called Statute of Queen Anne (1709); on the international level, that is, in the field of mutual recognition of rights, with the Bern Convention (1886). In today's concept, mainly at the beginning, it was about protecting authors from publishers and/or producers and sellers: it is logically much simpler to earn money for copies sold, e.g., of printed songs or later phonograph records or CDs – all the trump cards would be in the hands of the publishers. That began to be clear in the first decade of the 20th century, when the production and sale of sound recordings developed so much that it was possible to earn a good amount of money from them. At that time it became apparent that there was a need for the legislative transfer of part of the profit of the producers to the authors.

As we have already indicated, copyright can relate only to something fixed. Such a concrete, unique expression of a creator's (author's) thoughts is called a **work of authorship**. It can have a tangible character (a picture, a sculpture...) or an intangible one (which touches, among other things, on music). Besides musical compositions, artistic performance also belongs here. This means that a work of authorship, protected by copyright, is on one hand a composition and on the other – actually another work of authorship – its recording, the artistic performance.[8] As shown, this is a very important moment for the music business.

In the group of copyrights concerning composers, there are two types of rights: personal and property. Nontransferable personal rights have to assure the author of the use of his name in connection with the work; he has the right to decide on the publication of the work or the right of the inviolability of the work. Personal rights expire with the death of the author.[9]

---

7   Hull – Hutchinson – Strasser 2004: 52.
8   It should again be emphasized that the copyright does not apply to the plastic on which compositions and performances are recorded.
9   They expire for the author, but partly pass over to an heir – see section 11, articles 4 and 5:
     (4) The author cannot give up personal rights; these laws are not transferrable and they expire with the death of the author. The provision of paragraph 5 is thereby unaffected.
     (5) After the death of the author no one may claim his authorship of the work; the work may be used only in a way that does not reduce its value and, if it is usual, the author of the

The aim of so-called property rights is (or, at least, was so originally – see below) to enable the author to decide on the use of the work and thus to influence his economic welfare. Property rights expire in the Czech Republic – as in many other countries – 70 years after the death of the author.

As previously stated, a song/composition is not, however, a recording: it is considered to be another work of authorship and is connected with other rights. That the rights to the recording usually belong to the recording company (less often to the performers) is not particularly surprising because the company often has considerable expenses for their acquisition. Yet one might be surprised to learn that most of the payment connected with an author's song/composition ends up with the publisher; in the Czech Republic the author generally receives about 10% of the earnings.

CUI BONO?/TO WHOSE BENEFIT?

In this legal frame there also exists in the Czech Republic the OSA (Protective Authors' Union); if we call it a part of the music business, then a much greater emphasis will be on the word "business" than on "music." Firstly: the position of the OSA is not "ordinary" (and anyone who is perhaps even slightly aware of how business works, including all the global chains and business tendencies to accumulate influence, will in no way be surprised): since 2001 the OSA has held the legal status of a "collective manager." That means that it collects commissions for all music played in the Czech Republic. Usually such a position denotes a monopoly.

Moreover, the OSA represents almost 4,500 Czech authors, but only about 500 have the status of a "member," while the others are only "represented."[10] Only members, however, set the rules according to which the collected money is distributed. The status is, at the same time, determined by how much the author earns.[11] It is easy to imagine that the members who earn more might

work must be mentioned if the work is not anonymous. Any persons close to the author can demand protection. 1a) they have this authorization even if the time of the duration of the author's property rights has elapsed. The trustee or collective administrator may also demand this protection (§ 97).

10 According to the annual report of OSA for 2011, this organization represented 7,198 clients, of whom about 4,500 were authors; the rest were heirs and publishers. Of the 580 members, 324 were composers of popular music, 85 were composers of art music, and 99 were lyricists. The rest were publishers and heirs.

11 According to OSA statute section 4, 4.1. the candidate for membership "after four consecutive years must earn at least 80,000 CZK (US $4,000) per year; or in the period of the last five years collectively 1,000,000 CZK (US $51,000). For authors active in the field of art music and their heirs the required minimum commission is reduced by ½."

have different interests from the others. Economists know this model well and call it the problem of the minority owner: despite the fact that he can be in the numerical majority, he has only limited influence.

And third: The OSA submits the contract to those who are represented by OSA for signature. In it, OSA stipulates the "right to provide an exclusive agreement for the use of all publishable compositions..." Such a strong partner can certainly allow himself to do this, but the question necessarily arises regarding one of the original important intentions that would allow the author to decide on the fate of his music himself.

YOU STOLE MY COMPOSITION!

Concerning the work of authorship and the right to its protection, the question necessarily arises as to what exactly is "unique" and a "creation," that is, original. In the Czech environment such a case was solved in court for the first time in 2008, when Jan Kalousek sued a member of the *Support Lesbians* group Jaromír Helešic because in the chorus of his song "In da Yard" he used a theme from "Chodím ulicí," an old song of Kalousek's. The expert report of a musicologist specified that both compositions were "ordinary, not innovative and using elements known for a long time and from elsewhere. In two measures they are melodically identical; in some other measures they are only slightly different." Helešic replied that he was not at all familiar with Kalousek's composition. The judge agreed that there could have been an unintentional use of elements of Kalousek's song (Helešic might have considered them his own after he had remembered them earlier); nevertheless he awarded 200,000 CZK ($10,000) to Kalousek.[12] However the judge refused his suggestion to ban the song because it contained his own original elements.

The problem of allegedly unintentional use of not-too-original musical ideas can be looked at from various angles. One of them is the angle of Adorno (see box). Or it is possible to agree with the point of view of the court, which decided in the case of the *Chiffons* group versus George Harrison. Harrison's song "My Sweet Lord" (recorded in 1970) was in its structure, the greatest part of the melody (including some melodic embellishments), and excerpts of the text, similar to the song "He's So Fine" by the *Chiffons* (from 1962). According to the court Harrison, *in seeking musical material to clothe his thoughts, was working with various possibilities... There came to the surface of his mind a particular com-*

---

12   See e.g., http://www.lidovky.cz/kalousek-vyhral-spor-o-ukradenou-pisen-helesic-zaplati-200-tisic-psf-/kultura.aspx?c=A100907_121729_ln_kultura_pks (June 20, 2012)

bination that pleased him as being one he felt would be appealing to a prospective listener... His subconscious knew it already had worked in a song; his conscious mind did not remember.[13]

Yet the court's 1981 decision was in its intention similar to that of the Czech court: Harrison had to pay over a million and a half dollars.

COPYRIGHT IN DIGITAL TIMES

Even if much in the field of copyrights can seem rather bizarre, the situation until the beginning of the '90s was relatively transparent: the whole "music-in-dustrial" complex incited the author to create such (perhaps not very original) "works" that the greatest number of people would want to "consume," and, at the same time, would be willing to pay for; this was also protected legislatively.

The situation basically changed with the prevalence of two inventions: digital technologies and the Internet.

The use of digital technologies has a whole list of interwoven consequences that can be understood as various facets of the same thing. The basis is **easy copying without a loss of quality**.

Copying, understandably, does not begin with digitalization. The invention of the 8-track tape recorder at the beginning of the '60s and the immense boom of tape recorders in ordinary life ten years later were substantial for the creation of illegal copies. While, until then, lovers of (recorded) music were reliant on records that could not be copied privately, now anybody could get hold of his own recording – or perhaps a copy of a recording that was protected by a copyright. In the USA they guess that at the beginning of the '70s up to a third of all sold recordings (primarily cassettes) were illegal copies. The first half of the mid-'70s saw the beginning of legal protection of recordings themselves.

In contrast to earlier analogue copies, the digital ones are of incomparable quality or, more precisely, they are identical to the originals. As if an unlimited number of the originals arose at the same time.

In the digital era it is a philosophical rather than a technical question whether more than one original can be created. A similar discussion developed in the field of the visual arts. The photographer William Egglestone became famous in the '70s when prints of his (non-digital) photographs were sold for hundreds of thousands of dollars. Not long ago, however, he digitalized some of his photographs from that time and again sold them as enlargements – for similarly large or larger amounts of money. One of the collectors, Jonathan Sobel (who owns

---

13 Hull – Hutchinson – Strasser 2004: 85–6.

almost two hundred Egglestone photographs) feels damaged because, according to him, the market value of art is its scarcity. The photographer's attorney defends Eggleston in that there is no law forbidding enlargement/reproduction from the same negative.

Apart from the easy purchasing of perfect copies and their consequent sale outside of a frame defined by existing laws, digitalization has opened doors to further secret chambers. The closest is the **concept of an art work**. As we have seen in the example of Kalousek's dispute with Helešic and *Chiffons'* with Harrison (and if we admit from the court's angle that there was no conscious plagiarism), it is sometimes impossible to decide unequivocally what is whose – and only his – work. Or the ideas of Judith Becker return here about the bringing to light of material which until now arises somewhere in the subconscious or exists in collective memory. In any case, today new works are built from such subconscious/collective material. Those methods which use already existing works or parts of them in a new context (while the context gives meaning to the used elements) are considered legitimate. As shown in the 6th chapter, **sampling**, that is, using already existing "samples" is a basic creative technique of, for instance, electronic dance music, among other things. Such an approach is more broadly denoted as appropriation: the creator appropriates existing material in order give it a new meaning by putting it into a new context. Many a classical musicologist is properly contemptuous of similar techniques (not long ago I overheard something scornful about second-hand music); nevertheless the musical world is permeated with them. And so it is necessary to remember that while the dogs bark the camel will continue its way...

INTERNET

The second basic invention that influences the shape of today's music is the Internet. Surprisingly or not, the majority of the flood of articles dealing with music on the Internet refers to the copyright question. It presents virtual and non-virtual reality as trench warfare: on one side there are those who open the "floodgates to the road of culture for people" (an example can be the Ubu-Web portal which its initiator Kenneth Goldsmith conceived of as an archive of the inaccessible avant-garde of the early 20th century).[14] These individuals are deemed (at best) pirates by the other side. The latter are those who consider – like, e.g., Petra Žikovská, head of the Czech branch of the IFPI (International Federation of the Phonographic Industry) – *the situation on the Internet to be*

---

14   www.ubu.com

indefensible – at least from the point of view of the copyright holders[15]; therefore, according to them, it is necessary to control the Internet.

The positions of musicians are not only on both extremes, but also anywhere between them. Many complain in the sense that, when they pay one hundred thousand crowns for a studio, it is strange when a listener downloads their work free of charge. On the contrary, the rapper Bonus says: *When my music is spread around, that is a greater boon for me than what earns me money... For music it is better when someone listens to it. Today success is hard to measure by the sale of records and downloading contributes to people going to concerts.*[16]

In any case a significant change has occurred: while earlier the publication of a work (whether written or in the form of sound) was a condition and more or less guarantee of its protection, now, with regard to the Internet, it is the opposite: nothing protects a work from either illegal copying or from ripping it into the smallest pieces and anyone can treat these smallest pieces anyway he wants. As Pavel Turek writes: *the Internet doesn't wait 70 years (for the expiration of a copyright) and takes everything and immediately.*[17]

Various musical opuses pieced together from alien shreds of sound which, in addition, are deformed, plus purely computer-generated sounds, aimlessly, as it were – often with many clones – wander in the real sense of the word "passively" around the Internet. Perhaps it is the consequence of technologies that outdistanced us. But perhaps we can listen to them like a journey (back) to the time when the main place of music was not in business.

15   Reflex 7/2012: 50.
16   Respekt 18/2012: 61.
17   Respekt 18/2012: 60.

CREATIVE COMMONS
Zuzana Jurková

As we tried to explain in the preceding text, copyrights, as they are applied in the Czech Republic (in harmony with EU laws), originally arose as an instrument that enabled creators to earn assets for their work. As conditions changed (thanks to the Internet, among other things), however, other approaches appeared. While copyrights, enforced by the OSA, represent to a certain extent one extreme (only slightly exaggerated: "nobody may play or listen to anything free and/or without authorization"), closer to the opposite end of the spectrum of authorization freedom is the license group *Creative Commons* - CC, formulated in 2001 by lawyer Lawrence Lissig. The idea is indicated by the word *Commons*, which, in British tradition, designates public property, whether material (park), or non-material (folk song). The basic idea of CC refutes the concept of a work primarily as a commodity; that is: gain is not everyone's interest for a creation. Take, for example, amateurs who want primarily to share their work. (During intellectual browsing in this field it is good to get rid of the classic Western combination of amateurism and incompetence and, instead, to remind oneself that in many places - including Europe a few short centuries ago - a professional musician was understood to be an able craftsman without his own free will.) CC or similar approaches, however, are used by many top professionals who - materially secure - want to make their work more or less available. And it is exactly in this "more or less" that there is one of the advantages of CC: the author must determine - and with the help of simple pictograms signify - how he wishes his work to be treated. It is understood that it will be disseminated. Is it enough if he is listed as the original author? Is anyone else permitted to adapt this work? And sell it?

Clearly we are not alone in our understanding of the classic approach to a copyright and its enforcement by the OSA on one hand and Creative Commons on the other hand like two distant conceptual poles between which there is a wide, foggy land for which not even one legal system is suitable. Petr Jansa, J.D., who has long dealt with copyrights, writes:

Only later did I begin to understand the broader context. I started to ask myself and publicly in various debates if a CC license and other instruments that simplify distribution in the digital world are enough to compensate restrictive and, for many, overly complicated copyrights. And I began to be aware that they do not suffice. Gratis licenses are excellent for an amateur work, study materials, scientific articles or products of public institutes (perhaps they would be very suitable for Czech Radio broadcasts and Czech Television!). For the majority of authors who need payment for their work to be assured of existence and future work, gratis licenses are as extreme as overpriced commercial distribution. To find the possibility of balance between these two extremes is in itself an artistic feat. I keep my fingers crossed for all who succeed.[18]

---

18   Petr Jansa: From the introduction to the prepared anthology *The Power of Open*, which introduces Creative Commons licenses based on examples from experience.

PUBLIC SEMINAR OF THE CZECH RADIO COUNCIL ON MUSIC PROGRAM DIRECTION OF CZECH RADIO 1[19]
KARLÍN STUDIO "A" OF CZECH RADIO
1 DECEMBER 2011, 2 P.M.
Zuzana Jurková

At the beginning of October, Pavla forwarded an e-mail to me from a Dr. R., a member of the Czech Radio Council. Due to frequent criticism of the musical component of the broadcasts, the Council is organizing a seminar at which independent professionals are to meet Radio employees and try to come to some innovative conclusions. I did my best excuse myself from this by pleading incompetent, but the joint insistence of Pavla and Dr. R. finally coaxed me into agreeing. In my mind I sorted out a few thoughts in advance about the use of music, to which I'm on the whole allergic. Apart from what generally bothers me about the midstream of popular music, that is, mostly some kind of kitschy sound, what angers me more about this station is, for one thing, that I never find out who is singing or playing and, for another, it seems to me that the music is in no way related to what was said a couple of seconds before or what will be said. The allergy crystallized into one of household rituals: Whenever I walk into the bedroom where my husband is listening to the radio, I say ironically: "Lovely music!" upon which, with a faint sigh, he counters: "I don't care for it either, but I'm waiting for the news." Naturally, my invitation to the Radio's seminar is then a source of entertainment in our household.

Roughly a week before the seminar, the newspaper *Lidové noviny* reported on the event; I received from Dr. R. a compilation of emails from listeners; some were very concrete; in others, writers asked if they could come without notice. It was beginning to look as if I would meet more people than just the six panelists, members of the Council and a few Radio employees, as I had originally expected.

A quarter hour before the start, there is quite a large gathering in front of the entrance to the Karlín radio studio. Following the less than rigorous registration at reception, we overflow into the studio; there are over a hundred people here. In the first four or five rows there are tags on the chairs. I greet a

---

19   The seminar was devoted to the music program directing of the two main stations of Czech Radio, Czech Radio 1 – Radiožurnál and Czech Radio 2 – Praha. This text is only about the first part, which dealt with music program directing. That is because, in it, music and its use are criticized much more.

few musicologist acquaintances (some, like me, are here "from outside," some as employees of the Radio). Among the some dozens of mainly young people in the audience is my former student, Bára.

A table with six microphones rests on a slightly raised podium. To the right is a large screen on which will be projected what the camera films in the studio. (I presume that the same picture will be seen by those who are watching the broadcast on-line.) To the left is the projection screen on which those in the studio will watch the presentation. However, those of us now sitting at the table don't see much of it. *(The event is more public and more formal than I had expected.)*

It begins, as stated in the program, exactly at 2 pm.[20] The first speaker is the president of the Council, Mrs. I., who conveys two things: The first is that she is pleased at how many people came, from which she presumes the "musicness" of the Czechs *(I perceive this rather as appeasement of a potentially unfriendly crowd).* Secondly, she tells how, in the '90s, she was irritated by the music on this station, though this does not happen to her any more even if, of course, not all of the songs are exactly to her liking. *(I can't believe that she listens to music on Radio Journal carefully; or does her affiliation with the institution affect her taste so strongly?)* But everyone likes something different – and has the right to, don't you think? Besides, satisfying all of the listeners – this station has seven hundred thousand of them and is the fourth most-listened to – isn't possible.

After Mrs. I. comes the newly elected general director of the Radio. The directors of the Radio allegedly want to listen to the voice of the public, but not to obey it. He believes that today is the beginning of a dialogue between the Radio and the professional and lay public.

Then we the panelists sit at the table. In addition to the commentator, there is the well-known music journalist O., two people from the Radio – the music program director of the station that will be discussed, X. (occasionally he makes allusion to his status as an outside worker. Only later do I learn from the newspaper that he is a Metro driver), and Mr. G., a specialist in research. Apart from the moderator, there are three of us "radio outsiders": a well-known writer and musician A., a bohemian-looking music journalist J., and myself.

The first to speak are the people from the Radio. Mr. G. explains that compositions are chosen according to the known picture of the listener. The listener of this station is an older person who tunes in for the news. He marginally mentions that potential listeners are from two other related stations and therefore "we must be especially careful to keep them listening." According to the research, listeners apparently change the station from this setting because

20 Video clip of the seminar: www.rozhlas.cz/rada/seminare/-zprava/videozaznam-seminare-rady-cro-k-hudbe-na-stanicich-radiozurnal-a-dvojka-984175 (Dec. 12, 2011).

they do not wish to listen to bad political news, not because of the music. Later, however, he says that listeners change the station most often when they don't like the song that is being played at the moment.

The music program director opens his report with the announcement that "tests govern a music program director; the programmer doesn't govern the tests. The listeners determine what they want to hear and we are subject to the choice of the listeners." (For that matter, G. formulated it similarly; the station is primarily informational, and therefore music has the function of holding the listeners to the news. At the same time he sort of accidentally revealed that the proportion of music to words is 60:40. X. further explains the functions and role of the frequently criticized software Selector (*On one hand I have a feeling that one could say this in a fragment of the time taken; at the same time I am surprised by which criteria – for example that it is a male voice – the program selects a succession of songs.*) The task of the music program director is supposedly to choose songs so that the "mix of songs has the strength to keep the listener at the station." And he ends resolutely: "There is no other way."

The moderator turns to us "non-radio panelists" with the question of how the public service aspect should be reflected in the choice of music. The eruptive A. says that he did not expect such a pithy formulation with which he completely disagrees. He considers the dictate of ratings a total error which tends toward tabloidization. He offers to prepare a broadcast which anyone who reads *Blesk* or *Aha!* will listen to. As a composer he is horrified at what is done with a musical work which is here degraded to noise – noise that is supposed to fill in the spaces between news bulletins. "What you are doing here looks like some suspicious business." He proposes either completely discontinuing the music on this station or returning to quality music program direction. "If you assure us that you are doing your best, then I tell you that you are doing your worst. You should resign and there should be a competition for your position." (Repeated applause in the hall.) Mrs. J. adds that the absence of the younger generation among listeners is perhaps not so much the result of the station's broadcasting of news so much as the fact "that they can no longer listen to it." Another slight gunfight takes place between A. and the music program director, who asserts that the quality of his work is a question of opinion. A. counters that X. does the program directing of a robot that obeys imaginary tests while behind him are "other people and other interests."

The audience demands more and more vehemently to be heard. While the moderator refers them to the last twenty-minutes of this block, one free microphone is grabbed by a man in the audience who introduces himself as the former head music program director of the station. He recalls an on-line article written not long ago by the music editor P., who emphasized that anyone who does not have the responsibility should not give advice about a program and also, for that matter, why should the idea of uplifting the musical taste of the nation by means of one public service station "belong in the category of delirious dreams." And when the speaker himself tried to push through better program directing, the station lost tens of thousands of listeners in half a year. We should supposedly leave the program directing to professionals.

I timidly remark that we should perhaps talk about what music actually is and what its function on the station is that takes up more than half of the time. We non-radio panelists apparently think that it is a special phenomenon and not just a sagging kind of advertisement. A. agrees with this and asks about the musical education of music program director X. He does not respond.

Mrs. N., who is sitting in the audience, takes the floor. She is "responsible for those hated statistics," as she herself says. According to her, today only 2% of the station's listeners are dissatisfied. (*I am surprised that the most obvious argument does not occur to her: those who are dissatisfied with the station simply don't listen to it.*) The musical element, according to her, is not the reason for listening to this station, while, however, 24% are satisfied with it. She comments on the ironic or disagreeing commotion in the studio, saying that we possibly number 100 here and that this is negligible compared to seven hundred thousand listeners. To make a strategy, according to her, does not mean to orientate oneself toward those who have the strongest voice, but to respect everyone (by the way, how could one force people to listen to what they don't want?) and to try to get what they expect from the station.

A. gets angry that the same thing is constantly repeated. (*I remember the methodic instruction about data saturation: if the same arguments or the same data are constantly repeated, it is possible to terminate the research.*) A public service institution should show diversity, protect minorities, develop the education and the cultural feelings of the people. It is not, of course, possible to force anyone to do anything, but it is necessary to try to captivate people and not to be satisfied with merely not annoying them.

The moderator quotes from an announcement of the editor of BBC: In Britain the conviction prevails that, if the public pay a charge for BBC, it is connected with a certain responsibility... We have already traditionally aimed at achieving the best results both with information and in integrating music into the broadcasts... Part of such work is sensitivity and attentiveness... to new thoughts, streams... to watch the genesis of new forms of culture and entertainment, this is the role of public service media. Who else would do it? We have to be the first, not to follow others..." O. asks if the radio would join in this concept. According to Mr. G., every station has its own purpose and developing the public's taste is the responsibility of another station.

The promised discussion part that the public was clearly looking forward to then followed. First, Dr. R. reads the questions listeners are sending in (or have already sent in via e-mail). The most frequent ones are about the number of compositions in the Selector: the listeners evidently perceive their current number as insufficient. Music program director X. dodges the question, saying that Selector has a large capacity; he does not give the concrete number of compositions. *(I don't understand why.)* Someone else asks in an e-mail if the Radio could express a greater interest in Czech musicians (at the same time he refers to the initiative "Czechia for Czech Air."[21] A. is of the opinion that diversity should be supported "so that we can know that there are many possibilities in life."

Then it is the turn of the public in the studio. A young woman who has been calling out for a long time identifies herself as a member of the Facebook page entitled "the Music director of Radio Journal is an idiot" (laughter in the studio). She complains about the small choice that she connects with the declining musicality of the Czechs; she is not surprised at the apparently similar choice of music on the radio. The president of the Council Mrs. I. answers by explaining her concept of public service: because it is paid for by the taxpayers, a radio license is actually an indirect tax. Therefore anyone who pays these fees has the right to get what s/he wants. *(Data saturation is pounding in my head; moreover, I wonder why someone doesn't say something about that number of songs.)*

The next discussant says that he worked for twenty years for foreign radio stations. He praises the news service, but perceives a monopoly of one in the musical component. "Not even in the times of totalitarianism did one person decide on the music repertoire." He sees the other total non-correspondence between the music and the spoken word as another problem – mainly in situations where the listener would expect such correspondence. He names four examples of broadcasts in the recent past.

He then again asks about the concrete number of compositions in the Selector – and insists on an answer (applause in the studio). The music program director X. asserts that one title cannot be heard several times a day. One song can be repeated in three and a half days, the average being in four or five days. Since listeners do not have to like all songs by the same performer equally, he includes only the favorites. "Absolute favorites remain for keeps because why should we take away from people what they like?"

The audience protests that it IS possible to hear the same song several times a day. Finally the director of the station takes the microphone. She utters that magic number: today there are 891 active titles in the Selector. It is possible to hear new ones several times daily; compositions that are played during the day may be repeated at night. Ordinarily compositions "return" in four or five days.

---

21   http://petice.05.cz/

O. calls for a break, which somewhat calms down the relatively explosive mood in the studio.

I walk out with the feeling that we have spoken in skew lines and therefore did not understand each other's idea of what actually music is and what it is for and that most likely not much would change. The people from the Radio keep repeating (a) that we cannot lose listeners, (b) the high number of listeners proves that they like it and, since they pay a radio license fee, they have the right to get what they like. Anyways, everyone has the right to his/her taste. (*Zimbardo's assertion that systems – and, evidently, institutions – have a tendency toward self confirmation comes back to me.*)

The non-radio "professional public" demand that music be considered autonomous and not only as "glue for the news." They think that a public-service institution does not only have to satisfy the licensees, but also should take part in shaping the public soundscape (and with it the musical taste of the people). Perhaps at least the basic demands of the correspondence of music to the spoken word and the basic expansion of the repertoire (which in itself demands a qualified music program director or, ideally, several music program directors) were formulated.

The next day I read in *Lidové noviny* "From the discussion there gradually developed a barricaded fight between two sides." The editor cites specific innovative suggestions by the general director to enlarge the number of music program directors and also of songs in the program, but his ending is as pessimistic as my feelings: "His subordinates, however, feel differently. The current state most likely suits them."[22]

CODA[23] IN THE VIRTUAL WORLD

My impression that the discussion has ended thus proves to be false: it continues intensively in the virtual world. One of the panelists of the second session sends a link to his on-line article on how it pays to have culture, as is generally known. I agree, but I point out that I find it rather irksome to speak constantly in economic categories:

> It seems to me important to emphasize something else; namely, that the economic payoff is neither the only one, nor the highest goal. Do we really want to accept the argument that the GNP is the main indicator of the quality of life?

---

22   *Lidové noviny*, 2 December 2011, p. 4.
23   In Italian music terminology, the concluding part of a composition.

It is also possible to add in that sense a couple of more sophisticated arguments by Levitin (This is Your Brain on Music) on the importance of music from the neuropsychological point of view or perhaps of Csikszentmihalyi or Turino (Music as Social Life) from the (psycho)social point of view. This, however, does not change the basis of it in the long run: music does not exist in order to keep a listener at the radio or in a shopping center. Without it, we would not be people.

Then, however, a bright light comes from another side. Dr. R., the *spiritus agens* of the whole event, points out to us that the Universal Company, allegedly the main producer of music played on Czech radio stations, published a letter to the general director of the Radio concerning the discussion about the choice of music.[24] In it the company expresses the view that the discussion, including the seminar, is "to a great extent unconstructive"; it supports the music program director and his erudition (the discussion collapsed into a public lynching) and the company sees the "absence of tasks" as the only problem of the music program directing. It recommends not being guided only by the results of tests and "their simple application to a select target group." The relatively great disagreement of the professional public apparently casts a negative light on the station and can influence the listener who has been satisfied until now.

Dr. R. is surprised by some of the contradictions in the letter, but the experienced journalist C. writes:

"I agree that the letter is" odd, but I also think it is easily decipherable."
    If Universal is a 50% provider of the music, then it is right to worry that any discussion or change will disrupt this hegemony.
    If one could theoretically manage to lower the contents of the musical trash in the playlist, it is in the interest of Universal that the eliminated titles be replaced by others from its catalogue. Therefore it also chooses rather understandable arguments: "On the other hand, the relatively high disagreement of the professional public, who cast a negative light on the whole affair..."
    ... in the same breath it defends "its man" (the music program director) and, by that, also (I suppose) it reveals its cards.

Further comments sound similar. Z., the director of a famous institution focusing on popular music:

---

24 http://www.mediar.cz/gramofirma-universal-vycita-sefovi-ceskeho-rozhlasu-absolutni-absenci-zadani-hudby-na-radiozurnalu/ (Dec. 12, 2011)

It is possible, in my opinion to translate transparently: we end with the sale of the media and we unconditionally need earnings of identifiable, but mainly non-identifiable payments (here what is understood by earnings is what for us, UNIVERSAL, the Czech Copyright Protection Association provides. The Copyright Protection Association will advise you upon request that 95% of the income which it will "get" is directed abroad. Czech Radio perhaps contributes only one or two percent to the original/home-made product itself... As for me, this is only quick speculation; I would like to be wrong. And a marginal parallel also occurs to me, e.g., with Janáček: publication rights are sold abroad, too. Would such a commercial and public-service sector have the same goal? A logical key question: have we at home at our own disposal *de facto* 0.5% in the air? Is it possible to refute this speculation of mine? If so, how? The question of contemporary public service constantly acquires only sharper and sharper commercial contours...

Moderator O. summarizes:

It is really touching that Universal itself proclaims to be the arbiter of music in the public space. Universal, which through its long-term marketing and reluctance to think about the dimension of the Czech cultural market drove away all the best musicians it used to have in its catalogue... It also fails as a distributor of the world cultural heritage: for a long time it has not done anything sound for Deutsche Grammophon and other brands that it owns exclusively. It is simply a Czech branch of a German firm, not a cultural institution...

Adorno's scheme (see box), it seems, is completed. First of all: music loses its autonomy that Western tradition of the last centuries attributed to it. It is therefore not possible to measure, e.g., its quality (under the slogan "Let everyone listen to what he likes"). The value of this "sound" – music that can in any way be modified, shortened or bent – is only in the number of licensees kept listening to the news. And the agreement of the majority of "listeners" (rather in the sense of the emic term from the milieu of the media because the listening of the "sound background" possesses qualities different than the purposeful listening, which we are used to when we say "listener") is apparently confirmed by research.

The symbiosis of the medium (radio) and the production company (Universal) is evident and apparently creates the famous circular model: a song is repeated – therefore it is popular and people want to listen to it – therefore it is repeated. And the smaller the sample is, the simpler the choice, the more easily the song can be remembered. It is hard to imagine a better example of the manipulation of popularity – and later also of taste. Such strengthening of popularity (and by it also – mainly – salability) of course satisfies the concerned companies. After all, the main goal of companies is profit.

DĚTI RÁJE (CHILDREN OF PARADISE) –
COLLECTIVE MEMORY AS BUSINESS
GOJA MUSIC HALL, FAIRGROUND, PRAGUE-BUBENEČ
SATURDAY, APRIL 13, 2011
Filip Schneider

The musical *Children of Paradise* (*Děti ráje*) had its premier on November 14, 2009. It is played four times a week: Friday evenings, Saturday afternoons and evenings and Sunday afternoons. The number of reprises is approaching 400, including the performances in Slovakia. The theater is still always pretty full. Sometimes it's even sold out. People come to see it from all over the Czech Republic and also from neighboring Slovakia, and there are also people who receive a discount because they have already seen it thirty or forty times and they can't imagine a weekend without it. Rumor has it that people have gone into debt for tickets. The best seats, which are always sold out, cost 699 CZK (US $35). The total attendance figure has already exceeded 300,000. On April 8, 2011, the two hundred thousandth person attended a performance. It is clear from this data that *Children of Paradise* is a unique venture and an example of maximum commodification that fell on fertile soil and after a year and a half of uninterrupted performances it is still bearing golden fruit. And it is still going on.

The space of the Goja Music Hall, where the performance takes place, is interesting in itself. It is a pyramidal building on the Prague exhibition grounds, right in the fenced-in area of the St. Matthew's Fair. The closeness of the attractions has, on one hand, a negative affect in the form of a rather disturbing grunting that has nothing to do with the performance. On the other hand, a less numerous group of theatergoers are recruited from the fair visitors (on the day I attended the ticket seller said that 30 of them bought tickets). The auditorium holds 864 seats, which gives a picture of the size of the whole theater. It is interesting, however, that the auditorium is constantly being adapted so that it looks packed. Indeed, as my friend pointed out to me, the theater was half empty (or half full, if you are an optimist). The cheapest seats on the sides were completely closed off and a black curtain hid the unoccupied seats in the center of the auditorium. Then the people were moved as necessary, often even to the most expensive seats without having to pay a surcharge. The true meaning of this artificial illusion of a mass of people didn't come to me until the end of the performance, but we're getting ahead of ourselves.

GoJa Music Hall

The performance of *Children of Paradise* is proud of the title "First Czech hit musical."[25] It is a Czech variant of the English term "jukebox musical." The principle of these musicals is the creation of a new story with the use of popular songs that have already been published and originally with no musical connection (The term began to be used in the 1940s; the first work to use this principle, however, was John Gay's *Beggar's Opera* (of 1728). In *Children of Paradise* the discotheque hits of Michal David, František Janeček, Zdeněk Barták and the Kroky band played the main role; around them the producer, scene writer and performer Sagvan Tofi constructed a romantic story of love lost and again found. The distributor's official text describes it in this way:

> At the end of the '80s a bunch of graduates spend their free time in discotheques. Big dudes – "DJs" Tom and Stanley – reign over them. Only the dreamer Michal, who writes poetry and composes songs, is unique and the target of their ridicule. Michal's love for his classmate Eva is thwarted by the intrigues of her girlfriend Kájina. Twenty years later Eva (Míša Nosková, Šárka Marková) again meets her first great love Michal and the never-ending love story returns in the form of her daughter Bára and Michal's son Mickey getting together.

The stage design consists of some sort of a slightly shabby square of a small Czech town. In the first half of the performance, which takes place in the '80s,

---

25   http://www.detiraje.cz/

Dancing children of paradise (photo: Tomáš Martínek for Children of Paradise)

the Ráj (Paradise) discotheque, the Pramen (Source) grocery and the police station dominate it. In the second half, already in our millennium, the Rock Club discotheque, the Magic Planet Casino grocery and walls decorated with graffiti replace them. Suitable lighting then transforms the stage into various interiors. In both parts there is a scene with a scaffold which enables vertical movement of the performers. Dance choreography considerably draws from authentic discotheque bouncing and the song "Buds," which was played during the Spartakiad.[26]

Besides regular doses of emotions, the musical attempts to offer the viewers some laughter. Humor is mainly the domain of Čusbus and the two DJs. Čusbus is a child hero who, as Michal's best friend, comments on the whole relationship with a classical childish way of understanding. In the second half, as a more serious figure, he unravels the whole story. Idols of the '80s, Lukáš Vaculík and Sagvan Tofi, as the simple-minded and conceited DJs Tom and Stanley, make people laugh. In the first half they parody the archetype of a discotheque show-off. In the second part, they become soaked alcoholic losers in track suits whose dream to make a living through music was realized when they led a dance band of plump cleaning women. The whole performance is

---

26 An international sport event of the Eastern Bloc countries during Communism. The song "Buds" was the musical accompaniment of one of the mass exercises.

Sagvan Tofi alias Stanley (photo: Tomáš
Martínek for Children of Paradise)

also larded with allusions to things typical of the pre-revolutionary era, such
as *Antiperle* candies, *Pedro* chewing gum, the *Vitacit* beverage and *Partyzan* cigarettes. One scene incorporates a cancan dance number from the program *Ein
Kessel Buntes*, which follows a "comrade" teacher on television. The audience
had already reacted with laughter at the very mention of them, occasionally
and gaily whooping.

The songs of the Kroky band are used here in several ways, sometimes
only as an accompaniment to the story (e.g., in snapshots in the discotheque
scenes), sometimes to move the story forward (some dialogues are realized in
the form of slightly altered songs) and, in some cases, in the framework of the
story there are songs composed by specific people. Some of the hits in the musical are repeated several times.

After the three-hour performance I thought that I would go home disappointed. The happy ending had already taken place and that whole time I didn't
notice anything special about the public. Most of the people were between 30
and 50 years old. There were more women than men, sometimes in couples.
There were few older people and the obligatory children weren't too numerous. The majority wore light, comfortable shirts and T-shirts and rather bland
"leisure" clothing. They sat and laughed through the whole performance; some
quietly and merrily sang their favorite songs. Applause followed practically
every musical number. But then it began. In the aisles between the theatergo-

ers, Luka and Sagi appeared in the Rájovanka brass band playing and singing the well-parodied Buds; this started the final approximately half-hour section of the musical in which they repeated only the best known songs. Some of the actors remained on the stage; others ran through the aisles. Unbelievingly I watched the whole theater gradually stand up and begin to sing and dance. A giant disco ball appeared over our heads and the theater changed into a gigantic disco. This was topped off by a long standing ovation and musical encores. By then there was hardly anybody who wasn't singing and only five of us remained in our seats. When there are many people, it allegedly sometimes happens at the end that the dancing mass creates an unbreathable atmosphere and someone collapses. Fortunately, that didn't happen this time so that the buoyant gaiety was in no way disturbed.

On the whole I had the feeling that the musical was a very professionally executed work, precisely made to order for its target group, adults with families who, after a week of work, want to enjoy an undemanding weekend and cast their minds back to how, in *tesil*[27] pants or gaudy leggings and sipping a Coke, they met their first love. It is a musical for children of normalization "paradise" who want to live nonstop,[28] technically a very well made performance – and, from a purely commercial point of view, a blockbuster.

---

27 Synthetic fabric typical for clothing in Czechoslovakia in the '70s and '80s.
28 Words from Michal David's most famous song.

THEODOR ADORNO ON POPULAR MUSIC[30] AND ITS FETISHIST CHARACTER

Zuzana Jurková

The listening to popular music is manipulated not only by its promoters but, as it were, by the inherent nature of this music itself, into a system of response mechanisms wholly antagonistic to the idea of individuality in a free, liberal society.

This key sentence from the essay *On popular music*[30] summarizes the main thoughts of the German philosopher, sociologist and musicologist Theodor Adorno (1903–1969), a musicologically oriented member of the famous Frankfurt School.[31] At the end of the '30s, in the USA, where he emigrated because of racial persecution, he wrote a number of essays in which he tried, through music, to understand the society that was heading toward a world war. He views music through a prism of the Marxist concept of commodification.[32] Music – namely the popular kind that he strictly separates from "serious" music – is in his view becoming in the 20th century (due to technical possibilities, especially the possibility of mass reproduction) a commodity which, however, should not happen.[33] Moreover, it is connected to the music industry, which fundamentally influences the listener.

---

29   Here we use the same expression as Adorno, who speaks about *popular music*. In other connections, however, we consider the term "popular music" as an umbrella term for the most varied music genres except that of classical music; that is, also jazz, rock, folk, crossover, world music, etc., for which, however, many Adorno characteristics do not hold. These are concentrated in the genre that we call pop music.

30   "On popular music," in *Studies in Philosophy and Social Sciences*, New York: Institute of Social Research, 1941, pp. 17–48.

31   The Frankfurt School is the name of a group of German left-oriented theoreticians in the Institute for Social Research, which was founded in 1923 at Frankfurt University. Theodor Adorno, Max Horkheimer, Herbert Marcuse, Walter Benjamin and others analyzed culture in conditions of mass reproduction and they are considered the founders of "critical thinking," systematic sociological theory, which substantially influenced the following generations.

32   The process through which objects become commodities whose value is given not only as a utility value, but also (often primarily) as an exchange value.

33   A reader familiar with various musical concepts of music around the world knows that the understanding of music as a sort of craft is common in many a culture and such a craft has no pejorative connotations. Adorno was trapped in the usual Western usage formed by Romanticism.

The basic feature of the musical language of popular music is, according to Adorno, **standardization**. This is expressed on all levels: in the field of form (for example, equally long basic structural parts of a song), harmony, rhythm, and even in details, the essence of which should make every composition special, but which are repeated so often that they have earned special terms (*blue notes, break…*). Such standardization constantly leads the listener to the same listening experiences until he stops expecting something new. His nod to the heard (or even still unheard) song is not especially a nod to one concrete composition, but to a pre-existing whole – a previously given agreement to a previously given composition. A standardized sound product obviously evokes a standard reaction: the listener, deprived of the spontaneity of surprising experiences, does not have to bother to follow the concrete course of the music. This is already "pre-digested." But because listeners have vague ideas about what they want to hear – ideas having to do with fields where music is supposed to belong rather than primarily its sound (these ideas will be discussed later) – the reality of standardization must remain hidden. It remains hidden behind what Adorno calls *pseudo-individualization*: making special the details (which, however, may not disturb the basic structure to which they are subordinated so that the listener always feels secure within the framework of well-known schemes), a certain "specialness," individuality of the interpreters, an individuality that is emphasized, but is not too distinctive. It is necessary to place such an emphasis on this very interpretation because it can make an otherwise non-individualized and almost indistinguishable type of music distinguishable.

As an illustration Adorno introduces two contradictory examples: from Wagner's opera *Parsifal* the Kundry motif, which the listener (as Adorno writes rather ironically: "the listener with normal musical intelligence") remembers right away – in contrast to melodies of popular music which require great effort to remember.

If the musical language of popular music is of the utmost simplicity, the same applies to the social demands, which popular music requires for life. The first and foremost one is **advertisement**. However, only products that fulfill, on one hand, standard needs and, on the other hand, are distinguishable from other, very similar products are advertisable. Therefore the "hit" must have at least one memorable element – melodic, harmonic or, perhaps, rhythmic or instrumental. Its "individuality," that is, its distinguishability, however, must always be in the framework of those standard schemes. Constant repetition of a potential hit is necessary, not only for the above-mentioned reasons, but also because of the creation of the idea that the already accepted, i.e., successful, song is played.

Adorno pays rather exhaustive attention to the process of recognition and acceptance of a song hit. On one hand he points out the basic difference between a way of "recognition" of a composition in the fields of "serious" and popular music. In art music, recognition does not consist of discerning motifs of, say, a Beethoven sonata, but of recognition, that is, understanding of the mutual relations of individual elements and thus the sense of the whole composition. If I identify with the entire meaning, I accept the composition as mine. Because a similar process is not necessary in popular music (after all, mutual relations of individual elements have been clear for a long time), the acceptance of a composition proceeds on another level: identification with the opinions of the others. So many people appreciate this particular song, which I am also capable of recognizing, that by it they confirm its value.

For Adorno, the basic question is how is it possible that all of this type of music/the whole field of popular music is so appealing to the masses (because a description of the functioning of its own mechanisms is not yet the whole answer). According to him, the main reason is the insertion of popular music into the framework of free time, that is, the sphere of leisure and fun without any need for concentration.

Here is an expression of Adorno's Marxism: *Distraction is bound to the present mode of production, to the rationalized and mechanized process of labor to which, directly or indirectly, masses are subject. This mode of production, which engenders fears and anxiety about unemployment, loss of income, war, has its "non-productive" correlate in entertainment; that is, relaxation which does not involve the effort of concentration at all.*

It is exactly this character of undemanding fun that enables the direction of advertisement toward the field of luxury (Adorno uses the term "glamour") as it is otherwise commonly used for advertisement of any kind of product. Meanwhile it is clear at the same time that it is about the independent play of ideas.

The last important feature of an advertisement is that it does not relate only to music, but to the whole field of popular music, mainly its performers; the media also perceive them in situations that have no connection with music.

In an analysis of the essay *On popular music* Adorno ties in another article – *On the Fetish-character in music and the Regression of Listening*. In it he describes social mechanisms that function in an environment of popular music in the same way as in other branches of the market – mechanisms of production (primarily the production of sound media), distribution and advertisements. The listener, deprived of his own spontaneous interest in music and pleasure from it, becomes defenseless against these mechanisms. The most curious part of the whole process is that the question of an exchange value, that is, "how much the product costs," receives on the spot a question about the experience of the pleasure.

The price of popular songs, not the songs themselves, becomes a subject of worship – a fetish, voodoo. The listener adores a concert conducted by Toscanini (and even more a Madonna concert) not for the experience of their musical achievements, but for the price s/he pays for the ticket.

Louis Althusser, Jurgen Habermas, Jean Baudrillard, Roland Barthes, Jacques Derrida, Michel Foucault, Jacques Lacan, Jacques Attali and Julia Kristeva, for example, followed up on Adorno's analysis of culture and society and, with various modifications, continued an important trend of contemporary cultural studies. A very famous thematic continuation of an analysis of the mechanisms of pop music took place at the end of the '80s in a book by the pair of British musicians Bill Drummond and Jimmy Cauty *KLF - The Manual: How to Have a Number One the Easy Way.* In it the authors describe tongue-in-cheek how, without money, talent and experience, to make a number one hit.

HOW TO HAVE A NUMBER ONE THE EASY WAY
Zuzana Jurková

In 1988 Bill Drummond and Jimmy Cauty were already among the inhabitants of the British pop-music world; nevertheless the sale of a million singles with their song "Doctorin' the Tardis," which made the top of the hit parade, caught them by surprise. Maybe at that moment they fully perceived the character of the pop-music business (when the expressions they used for it, such as cliché and superficial, were the most gentle and decent). Or – as some journalists speculate – they already knew it and all of this was only one of their happenings? In any case, they immediately wrote KLF – *The Manual: How to Have a Number One the Easy Way.*

WHO ARE KLF?

When the talent seeker Drummond got together with the guitarist Cauty in 1986, it was primarily because of his interest in electronic music and also in the novel trilogy *The Illuminatus!*, which later became an inspiration for their projects. As pioneers in the sampling of other people's recordings (in "All You Need is Love," e.g., KLF combined the Beatles with Samantha Fox). Their group, The Timelords, released "Doctorin' the Tardis" (1988), the creation of which – and the road to the top of the hit parade – are discussed in *The Manual*. Then they shifted from rap to dance music and with the change in style they also changed the name of the group to *KLF*; this abbreviation was most often explained in the spirit of the philosophy of the members of the group as the Kopyright Liberation Front. It was actually under that name that they were the most famous: as creators of the new (sub)genre "chill-out" (see chapter 6), and mainly as the authors of house music; in 1991, they were the best-selling singles act of this genre in the world.

The popularity they earned was apparently not right for them: they reacted with provocations in the music, and then art world. It was actually because of their reputation as troublemakers that nobody believed that they really withdrew from the artistic world. Their most famous action convinced the majority of their fans of this: the burning of a million pounds sterling in a fireplace in 1994.

One can approach the thin *Manual* in various ways: as entertaining reading by the fireplace, as news about the *modus operandi* of the (obviously not only British) pop-industry of the '80s – and possibly as instructions on how to get to the top of the hit parade with the help of the Golden Rules. By the way, the Austrian group *Edelweiss* allegedly followed these instructions for the production of the hit "Bring Me the Edelweiss," which then sold five million copies.

The second way of reading is the most interesting for us. Cauty and Drummond gave a report in the form of some sort of five-day timetable for potential winners of the hit parade. Wedged in them are partly the golden hit rules, but mainly they explain in individual steps how the pop-music business functions.

The basic assumption: *you must be skint and on the dole. Anybody with a proper job or tied up with full time education will not have the time to devote to see it through. … If you are already a musician stop playing your instrument. Even better, sell the junk… If in a band, quit. Get out…*

THE FIRST WEEK, SUNDAY EVENING
Watch Top of the Pops religiously every week and learn from it… (Taking the angst-ridden, "I'm above all this!" outsider stance only gets you so far.)

You are going to have to come up with a name for your record company. Nothing too clever or inspired. Something that sounds solid.

MONDAY MORNING
Get:

a record player (the crappier the better); the expensive set-up is only for judging coffee table records.); the latest in the series of "Now That's What I Call Music" and "Hits" LPs.; all the 7" singles in your house that ever made the Top 5; a copy of the Music Week Directory; a hard back note book and a fine point, black ball Pentel.

You are going to need to book five consecutive days lock out in a manually operated (non SSL) desk, twenty four track studio hopefully starting from the following Monday.

MONDAY AFTERNOON
Do whatever you want and think about two things: money and the name of your group or project.

Open a current account and make that appointment (with the bank manager).

THE GOLDEN RULES

JUST AFTER 1 P.M. TUESDAY
Have a spot of lunch and read the following chapter. It will allay any doubts you might have in your talents as a hit song writer and explains the Golden Rules. Between now

and next Monday morning you are going to have to come up with the goods. Those goods are out there waiting for you to find before the others get there.

All the important British producers who got to the top of the hit parade – Lieber & Stoller, Goffin & King, Berry Gordy or Peter Waterman – *have all understood the Golden Rules thoroughly. The reason why Waterman will not continue churning out Number Ones from now until the end of the century... is because after you have had a run of success and your coffers are full, keeping strictly to the G.R.s is boring. An aspirant for the top of the hit parade must meanwhile beat into his head that there is no undiscovered road, there is no point in searching for originality;*

The first of the component parts you are going to need to find is the irresistible dance floor groove.[34]

Secondly, it must be no longer than three minutes and thirty seconds (just under 3'20 is preferable).

*Thirdly, (a composition) must consist of an **intro** (This is simple. The classic thing to do is have an instrumental version of the chorus.) **verse** (The text of the verse can be completely ridiculous; it only depends on the chorus); **chorus** (The chorus is the bit in the song that you can't help but sing along with. It is the most important element in a hit single because it is the part that most people carry around with them in their head. It's the part that finally convinces the punters to make that trip down to the record shop and buy it.); second verse; second chorus; breakdown section; back to a double length chorus and finally the **outro** (Yet again your mix engineer is going to come up with the answer for you.)....*

Fourthly, lyrics. You will need some, but not many.

Because this isn't the place to try for originality, an excellent solution is a rehash of "correct kernels of the past" *(the result will undoubtedly have 100% success). Or there is an alternative: To put together hidden, slightly changed and im-proved parts of old kernels.*

FRIDAY

By Friday night you will have to have got yourself a title, a groove, a bass line, lyrics and melody for a chorus that you can sing at the top of your voice in the bath on Sunday evening. By this, everything on your part is done which could be, with a certain approximation, called a creation. The rest is business.

Take it easy over the weekend. Enjoy it because the following week is going to feel like the most dreadful few days in your life.

---

34   Pattern made up of a rhythmic section.

THE SECOND WEEK: IN THE RECORDING STUDIO

On Monday at eleven you sit with a cup of tea with the soundman and the programmer. *Play them the groove track you want to rip off and sing them your chorus lines. Let the experts work.* Meanwhile you are going to have to get yourself a plugger, an accountant, a solicitor, a manufacturer and a distributor. *Be ready for vast depression on Tuesday. What stuff you have got down is sounding like total crap. It's not just your paranoia that's telling you its crap. It is crap.* Nevertheless, don't despair; instead of that, follow the birth of the phoenix as it rises from the ashes of despair because soon *everyone will begin to realize that the recording is a potential hit.*

A basic concern: dance around (insufficient) money. It appears at the latest when you have to pay the studio owner. Three traps are waiting here for the beginner: the owner proposes assignation of the copyright to his publishing company, the publishing of the track on their indie label or negotiating the publication of the song by some major company. *On the first one, publishing, this is the one area that you might be able to make some real money from the whole venture. To give that away now for nothing when your hand is at its weakest is at the very least a shame.* The other two possibilities would reduce your chances of being in first place to zero – whether because of a bad memory connected with that label or non-interest of the representatives of big companies whose interest is in international megastars.

On Friday night you will carry home a half dozen cassettes with crudely mixed songs. A great feeling.

THIRD WEEK: LONDON

Find an older experienced solicitor. From now on you will not sign anything before your solicitor reads it through. *The trouble is, solicitors become addictive. He will be the one person in London who will always be on your side and see your point of view. Talking to him will give you a sense of warmth and comfort – just like heroin. But remember, his services will cost you at least £50 per hour...*

Get yourself a distributor who isn't going to want more than a 30% commission and convince him to deal with the production of disks. The graphics on the sleeve must be professional, but you don't have to pay more attention to it than it's worth. *Just make sure that it's bright and colorful and that the name of the song and the act jumps out of the front cover.*

The most important person in the jigsaw is the plugger – *the man responsible for getting the nation to hear your record.* He must know perfectly everything that shapes the personality of the producer of the hit parade radio. In his team the plugger usually has a publicist whose task is to provide the greatest coverage in the printed media. However, in your case his role is secondary because *for overnight success which is in your interest, the music press is small-time. Use the publicist* to stick photos, gossip and some of your half-baked quotations into tabloids and teen magazines at the moment the record rises.

FOURTH WEEK: MIXING

Decide which of the material you have recorded on the multi-track tapes you will use. *Don't stop the beat... Worship at the feet of the primeval goddess of Groove.* But basically leave everything to the mixing engineer. And don't forget that the whole thing must fit into three and a half minutes.

THE FIFTH WEEK

The fifth week will be action packed. You have to cut the master disk, then get the records to clubs (many records become hits thanks to clubs) and then – mainly – to chart return shops according to whose sales (at least those alleged sales) the GALLUP charts are assembled. A salesperson ensures that your record is in a chart return shop. Without such a team of men no *record stands a chance of charting.* For this they will ask for bonuses and gifts. *Bonus or no bonus – that is the question.*

And then begins the final countdown. *The right clubs play your single; the plugger had a meeting with a good friend from radio.* You break down approaching the deadlines for paying your invoices. You break down even more over the sleeve. *"Nobody will buy a record with such a crummy sleeve!"* You turn on the radio. *You almost explode. They're playing it!* Your plugger calls to say your song is on a play list. The clubs announce that sales are good, but you are still going to have to undertake the recording of something awful: a video (*the disease of our time; adverts pretending to be art, made by arseholes pretending to be artists*); nevertheless the main thing is already here: Sunday night, five to seven. You're in first place. *This moment is going to last forever. Now you can get anything you want.*

A WALK ALONG THE ROYAL ROAD
JANUARY 4, 2012
Hana Černáková

The Royal Road is the traditional route where the coronation processions of the Czech rulers walked before the actual coronation took place. The royal coronation route **begins at Republic Square**, where earlier stood the Royal Court, the second seat of the Czech kings, and continues along **Celetná Street** to **Old Town Square**. From that square the route leads along **Karlova Street** to the **Charles Bridge** and then farther to the **Lesser Quarter.** From the **Lesser Quarter Square** the route continues up Nerudova Street to the **Prague Castle**.[35]

Today the Royal Road belongs not to the rulers, but to the tourists – and to those who make a living off them. That isn't surprising because it connects the main dominant architectonic highlights of Prague and because it is featured in foreign tour guides like *Lonely Planet.* This time I decided to walk in the opposite direction of one of the coronation processions. The main advantage is that I won't have to claw my way from Lesser Town to the top of the hill.

I get off at the Pohořelec tram stop before three o'clock and head for the Castle. My main goal is to scout around for musical events. Twenty minutes later I leave the Castle without success. Among the many tourists, I didn't meet anyone who looked as if he had flyers with an invitation to a concert.

I set out for Ke Hradu Street, leading to Nerudova, which I intend to descend toward Lesser Town Square. A large concentration of tourists grasping flyers suggests to me that I will be more successful here than in the Castle area itself.

On Nerudova Street I acquire my first invitation to a concert at number 22, which is the Church of Our Lady of Perpetual Help and St. Kajetán. Above the entrance door there is a large banner (it doesn't appear to be very professional) on which there is, in large letters, "CONCERT." A woman is standing behind the ticket table at the entrance. Her colleague is giving out flyers on the street and luring people. I approach the woman and want to take a flyer off the table to find out what the concert is about when she begins talking to me. She speaks

---

35   See: http://www.praguecityline.cz/trasa-kralovska-cesta (May 1, 2013).

quite fluent Czech with a Russian accent. She invites me to the concert, which begins in about three-quarters of an hour. It is called "Organ Gala Concert" and, according to the flyer, it is repeated every afternoon from January first to eighth at four o'clock. The only exception is the sixth, when they will play the Czech Christmas Mass by Jakub Jan Ryba at six o'clock. Today you apparently have to pay, but admission is free on the sixth. I come across blurbs for this concert all along the route to Lesser Town Square.

On Mostecká Street a little pack of flyers is attached to a street lamp and I pull one off. It invites me to a "Guitar Concert" today at seven. The Czech guitar duo of Jana and Petr Bierhanzl will be playing compositions from Vivaldi to flamenco style. I will again come across these ads on lamps in Old Town Square and Celetná Street.

I walk over the Charles Bridge without harm to my health, nor am I robbed, which in this throng and madness wouldn't have surprised me, however without a flyer or any other invitation to a concert. But this will change as soon as I walk through the passage from the bridge and stand in front of the Church of the Holy Savior. I am invited to a concert starting at five; a gentleman literally "pushes" me toward the box office and asks where I'm from. I beg off, saying I don't want to go to a concert now, and continue along Karlova Street.

Karlova Street is most probably a paradise for concerts and cultural events in general. Right at the beginning you are lured to the Ta Fantastika Black Theater. Although I don't see anyone handing out flyers, the posters in the theater building are emphatic enough. That they play the same show twice a day, once at five and then at eight-thirty is very reminiscent of the "Best of" tourist concerts. The advertisements attract the viewer to the special effects of the Black Theater and the music of Bedřich Smetana and Antonín Dvořák. However, I wouldn't have learned of this if I hadn't understood English or other foreign languages. This is the only performance that offers tickets on-line, but the choice is already limited a month in advance. Every day only about thirty tickets – always for the same seats – are available for 720 crowns.

A few meters farther on, a man hands me a flyer for a performance of *Don Giovanni*, which you can see on Karlova Street 12. They play it daily at five and at eight. The "distributor" points out the nearby box office where I can also obtain a flyer for a performance of the famous musical *Cats*, which is given daily at seven-thirty on Na Můstku Street 3.

I stopped for a while at the underpass near the box office so I could organize my papers and all the detailed notes I've taken. I say this because when, after that, I went a little farther, an older man invited me to a performance in the Church of St. Clement. Before he could finish telling me something about the concert in bad English his younger colleague rushed over and roughly informed him that he could relax and speak Czech to me, that I was surely Czech

Best of in the St. Nicholas Church

and that he saw that I was writing something. I gave this younger man a quizzical look and he immediately, in his Russian accent, added that if I were Czech I wouldn't like music and wouldn't go to the concert – and he began to take the flyers away from me. I didn't allow that and protested that I did like music and that it wasn't his business what I was writing. Then I quickly disappeared because he seemed quite angry.

I continue along Karlova Street. In front of the Klementinum I receive a flyer from a completely charming man, but when I thank him in Czech he turns his back as if I don't interest him any more. Here they are also in a pair: while one distributes flyers on the street, the other sells tickets at the portal. The concert should begin in a while and so he is trying to attract the greatest number of tourists immediately.

I come to the last part of Karlova Street. Near the front of Little Square I see a small, older woman who is angrily shouting at a young pair walking away from her. I wait to be sure she has calmed down and again begun to give out flyers. I take a colored paper from her and, in English, ask what it is. She looks at me mistrustfully and checks if I'm really a foreigner. After a while it seems that she does trust me – fortunately her English is worse than mine. I steer away from the question of where I'm from and ask her about the price.

Ticket sellers on Malá strana Square

Tickets are supposedly 400 crowns. I ask her if it's only today or if I can also go another day. Today it starts at six. On the back side of the flyer there is another concert today, only later, but this doesn't interest the woman and she takes out a block of tickets which appears more like an ordinary, badly printed pub pad. On it the price is 490 crowns. The woman explains to me that I am a student and therefore can have it for 400 crowns. She asks if that is very expensive and so I explain to her that I would rather go on January sixth and that I have to discuss it with friends, that I won't buy a ticket now. The woman asks me how many we would be and suggests a group discount and prepares the tickets – for six people it would be even cheaper. I spoil her mood by refusing to buy the tickets and the woman begins to be unpleasant and so I prefer to say goodbye and continue to Old Town Square. I would be interested to know to whom she offers the tickets for 790 crowns which I see she has hidden under the cheaper ones.

At Old Town Square nobody is giving anything out anywhere (or I don't notice anyone because of the crowd of tourists), and so I prefer to walk toward to the equally bustling Celetná Street. Right after its beginning I obtain from two young men the same flyer the previous woman offered me. When I take it, one of the men thanks me in Russian. After my English answer, he adds, "Thank you." I have an impulse to try "thanks" in other languages, but instead I continue on.

Ticket sellers on Karlova Street

I come across the last flyers in front of the Municipal House; apart from the "distributor" I can also take them from little stands at the entrance. There are really many concerts here, even in the large Smetana Hall. Today, for example, I could go to an eight o'clock concert called *The Best of Mozart and Dvořák,* but then I wouldn't make the performance at eight-thirty which is called *Pop and Classical Music: from W. A. Mozart to Freddie Mercury*. On other days the Municipal House offers me jazz or music from musicals, which, however, compete with Antonio Vivaldi and The Four Seasons and other pieces, e.g., *The Best of Classics with Soprano.* All the concerts are repeated several times. I obtained five flyers. It will be four thirty. In an hour and a half on the streets of Prague I have received invitations to almost fifteen concerts. All are *The Best of,* in those "best spaces" with "the longest traditions."

PRAGUE CASTLE CONCERT *PEARLS OF CZECH AND WORLD CLASSICAL MUSIC*
LOBKOWICZ PALACE IN THE PRAGUE CASTLE
MARCH 4, 2013, 1 P.M.
Zuzana Jurková

After many overcast winter months, today for the first time the sky is really bright and sunny and the eternal tourists are enjoying it. Although still warmly dressed, they are already streaming through the Lesser Quarter, from where I climb to the Castle (in the little park in their midst I come across a poster for "my" daily castle concert); somewhat higher, then, they enthusiastically blink over the Lesser Quarter roofs and the Vltava (Moldau) River or again up to the Castle's silhouette. The Old Castle stairs are still quite empty; a couple of weeks later it will be almost impossible to walk this way. Even so, two guitarists are already playing "Latin" music here and collecting money in a guitar case. Immediately behind the gates guarded by two members of the Castle Guard is the Lobkowicz Palace on the left side. This is the only private building in the Castle complex. Next to the monumental Baroque portal giant posters hang inviting you to the palace's museum to view Canaletto's pictures of London and also Beethoven and Mozart manuscripts.

The young woman at the box office gives me the choice between the first tier for 490 CZK ($25) (the first two rows) and the second tier for one hundred crowns less. Along with the ticket I receive a leaflet with the program and other foreign-language advertising materials full of sunny photographs. In the brochure for the whole Lobkowicz Palace I learn that I can buy a "Combo Ticket" in which I save money on a ticket to the concert and to the museum and I will have an additional 10% discount in the Lobkowicz café.

I walk along a red carpet to the second floor and to an antique door in front of which Beethoven on a poster admonishes me, "Quiet Please!" I don't have to obey yet though, since there is still a quarter of an hour till the beginning of the concert. I have time to examine both the room with its ceiling frescos, chandeliers on the walls and ruffled curtain and also the audience. So far there are only five people, but in the next quarter of an hour 18 people, mostly middle-aged couples, two bohemian-looking young men and a threesome of women join us. I am evidently the only Czech. Nobody runs in at the last minute, to say nothing of arriving late.

On a desk at the entrance one can read the names of the performers, though it doesn't seem that anyone is interested. At three minutes after one a pianist

The posters show the way like trail markers – up to the castle

in a black shirt and black pants arrives. He will play some compositions solo; in others he will accompany a violist. The first piece is a piano solo, *Invention*,[36] by J. S. Bach. For this – or for any of the other compositions – the program does not mention the key or the origin; I guess that it belongs to the collection Two-Voice Inventions. The pianist plays for hardly two minutes. When he finishes, the audience applauds briefly. The player bows – and the violist has already arrived. Without much ado, the two play together the slow *Adagio* by Albinoni and immediately afterwards Gluck's *Pizzicato*. The first piece to attract the audience's attention much is Mozart's *Turkish March*; the Italian woman in front of me shakes her head to the rhythm of the repeating main motif and even one "Brrravo" is heard with a raucous German rrr. A similar response is evoked by Chopin's *Piece for Piano Solo*, which the pianist plays in an upper dynamic register, thoroughly fogged by the pedal.

In the second half the pianist plays several solo numbers one after the other: Beethoven's *Moonlight Sonata* (actually only its first movement) and *For Elise*, a piano adaptation of Smetana's *Vltava* and Dvořák's *Humoresque*. At the

---

36   For the titles of the compositions I use the versions written in the program.

The quieted Beethoven

very end the violist appears and thanks the audience in English for coming and wishes them a nice day, upon which he launches into Khachaturian's *Saber Dance* (yes, this is the same composition that was played by the Budapest Gypsy Symphony Orchestra as well as by the trio of Roma in the 7 Angels Restaurant). At the end the audience applauds more enthusiastically than before, and so both musicians return again, shake hands and again bow. Evidently, however, they don't intend to play another encore – nor does the audience seem to be expecting one. A few minutes after a quarter to two we leave.

I ponder over this rather unusual experience. Thirteen pieces in fifty minutes: this isn't usually managed even in pop music, to say nothing of "classical." There were only several-minute compositions, during which it is not possible to apply what Adorno characterizes as listening to classical music: following internal relations between individual elements and the understanding of them. One group of numbers in today's repertoire was composed of classical hits. The popularity of *Humoresque*, the *Turkish March*. the *Saber Dance* and *For Elise* is assured by the beginnings of distinctive, easily remembered melodies (not, for example, by sophisticated structure) – exactly that "pseudo-individualizing" moment which, according to Adorno, "makes" pop music a hit – and, as one can see, also in the case of a "classic." The word "popularity" is, by the way, appropriate not only as a reference to a style of popular music, but also because of the extremely widespread social life of those "pearls" which today we hear more frequently in advertisements or on cell phones than on the concert stage.

The second group was compositions somehow typical of a given style: Albinoni's *Adagio* or Eccles' *Sonata* in Baroque style, Haydn's *Adagio* in Classical style and Chopin's composition in Romantic style. The compositions to which you can apply the idea of Adorno's standardization – a thousand times agreed-on scheme and sound of generally agreed-on musical style. While listening to them the public is not distracted by the mood of the Castle and, at the same time, it is not "troubled" by a too-long composition: apart from Eccles' short Baroque sonata, whose four movements do not last more than five minutes, all of the other numbers are played as one-movement pieces, although many of them originally belong to longer cycles.

Apart from complete compositions, there is also a lack of other components common to classical music concerts, such as more information about the compositions which more demanding – specialized – listeners look for.

Apparently, however, here there are no more demanding listeners who would evaluate the concert after the performance – those listeners who sometimes rush in at the last minute because they are so busy, but they can't miss THIS ONE!

Instead, aside from standardization and pseudo-individualization I also find other main Adorno characteristics of popular music. Above all, the importance of advertisements is undeniable: in the Castle complex (and below it) the omnipresent colored fliers on chalky paper, their electronic version on travel agency pages, a discount on admission to the museum as another form of incentive... And here the appeal of non-binding entertainment embedded in the sphere of almost dreamlike glamour makes itself felt.

The concert at the Lobkowicz Palace, as though at first glance, disproved one of the most basic ethnomusicological theories, that musical language (which we sometimes call "style") is formed by social values surrounding the performance of music. How come the style of classical music, that musical expression of stratified and specialized society, is inserted here in the context of commodification, a context into which we are used to placing pop music? A second and third glance, however, confirms our theory: the environment, which, in the first place, concerns the generation of profit, chooses from almost any styles those "products" that are most suitable to its needs for standardization and, at the same time, alleged individualization. In the Lobkowicz Palace these are the most typical or the best known, in short, the simplest "pearls" of the classics. These are grasped – in Adorno's words – by "a whole system of interconnected mechanisms." By means of advertisement and a glamorous environment it is able to attract such a number of musically undemanding tourists that their (relatively high) entrance fee covers several times the relatively low payment to two or three regularly performing musicians. A small, castle, tourist-oriented commodification.

ELECTRONIC DANCE MUSIC
Zuzana Jurková

The variable that basically determines the shape of music in this chapter is *technology*, concretely, the technological inventions of the second half of the 20th century. Various technological improvements understandably accompanied music throughout its whole history and had an influence on it, but – at least from our point of view – it seems that only **electronically generated sound** and other technological innovations of the past few decades have made an essential change in music.[1]

The term **electronic** is used to designate **music** that is created by electronic instruments; these either create new sounds or they edit existing sounds. Synthesizers and samplers are used for the generation of a sound and its editing; the sounds are then processed in computer music programs – so-called DAW[2] like, e.g. Cubase SX, Pro Tools, Logic, Nuendo, Sonar, Reason, Ableton Live, Fruity Loops, etc.

It is possible to divide the genres[3] of electronic music very roughly into **fully** electronic (e.g., techno, psytrance) and **semi-electronic** (hip-hop, r'n'b or some other popular musical style combining electronic sounds and the live performances of instrumentalists or singers). Another possible aspect of division is function: apart from prevailing dance genres, there are also non-dance (music for listening) genres (chillout, downtempo...).

Another sphere of non-dance music, whether fully electronic or electro-acoustic, is art music. Among the first to introduce the new sounds was the famous visionary John Cage: already in his *Imaginary Landscapes Nos. 1–3* from the end of the 1930s and

---

1   One of these technologies is sequencing – automatization of the control of an electronic musical instrument by means of a program (most frequently MIDI or CV/Gate) which enables the instrument to play back compositions which are otherwise physically unrealizable by a human interpreter. In the rendering, the instrument has become more precise, faster and more tireless than a person.

2   Digital Audio Workstation.

3   In regard to the variously understood terms of style, genre and subgenre, we use the word "category" in this chapter for the whole field of electronic dance music (EDM). We further divide this into genres (techno, psytrance...) and within their frames into subgenres (e.g., morning psytrance...).

beginning of the 1940s, the basic element is electronic processing of sound of various rhythmic instruments.

NEW SOUND

For this chapter we have chosen, from the whole "electronic" spectrum, only two dance genres: freetekno (the form heard in clubs and outdoors) and psy-trance. We will deal with their formation and basic features later; first it is important to briefly describe the most important **changes** that **electronically generated** or edited **sound** brings to music. They have affected the behavior of people around music, musical sound itself and the idea of what music actually is and why it sounds the way it sounds.

What seems most striking to a music anthropologist is that the basic twosome constituting performed music, the musician and the listener, [4] has basically changed (and in some cases it has almost disappeared). For whole millennia, there were those who played music - Egyptian court musicians, Israeli temple priests, medieval minnesingers, opera singers and folk musicians - and those who listened to it and sometimes also danced to it. Their interactions were and still are obvious in various ways because they are formalized in various ways; nevertheless that basic communication situation remains: the musician plays in order to be heard and the person who listens reacts to this.

And suddenly, the situation - at least apparently - changes: people dance face to face to loudspeakers, that is, to machines which are totally non-tangential to their reactions, or they sit in a concert hall where unusual, non-human sounds flow to them from the stage - from machines. Incidentally, it was similar in the old Bubeneč sewage treatment plant which we write about in the third chapter: when we walked through the underground space, apart from the sounds that we ourselves were making, only laptops were "playing".

Actually, the formulation about the disappearance of the musician isn't quite true: at least in the case of dance music, behind the "boxes" there is a disk jockey[5] (DJ), and from under his hand comes sound which is, however, usually at least prepared in advance.[6] The importance attributed to this DJ by

---

4　Let us leave aside the other possible mode of performance, as Thomas Turino calls it, for now. We will mention, namely, the situation when everyone takes part in the musical production, it in the next chapter - because electronic music did not wend its way in this direction.

5　This is the name for the person who puts on the music from all different sources, not only from phonograph records.

6　The second way of "sound production," the so-called LIVEACT, when the "producer", the creator of the music, also puts it on, will be discussed later in this chapter.

the dancers is different, however, in various genres and contexts, as is clear in our snapshots. In any case, it is possible to ask if the disk jockey is a musician. The very fact that DJs are not called musicians reflects a certain hesitation in this question. And the massive share of technology further changes this basic social situation in a striking manner.

For the listener who is mainly interested in the sound of music itself, nearly everything has changed. Until now, it has generally been quite easy to judge what music is and what it isn't: in the first place, according to the sounds used which have a clear pitch (sounds with a regular sinusoid called "musical sounds" or tones are also not in vain) and mostly well-known timbre. None of this is guaranteed in their synthetic generation; on the contrary, in EDM a regular sinusoid is considered uninteresting or even boring. Apart from the "material" used, the listener of Western music was, in the past centuries, used to the fact that the main component of musical language was melody (this definitely first and foremost) and its harmonic accompaniment, and then rhythm. With new sounds, however, creators handle their work in a new way: suddenly the melody (more or less) and the harmony (completely) disappear. In the foreground, pulsating rhythm – at least in dance music – remains.

The character of the sound material and structure of the components of the musical language are not the only thing new in electronic music. What is most essential is the course of the music which is closely connected with expectations that the participants have. The form of the musical language of electronic dance music, so different from that which existed until now, will be discussed in more detail in the interpretation part. A new expectation – or the consideration of a new one – also relates to art music using electronic material.

Adelaida Reyes mentions a few examples from the field that is most often called "sound art". One of these is the composition by Russell Pinkstone *Song for the Living/Dance for the Dead*, from the year 2000. It is dependent on a MIDI touch-sensitive dance floor. Thus dance is transformed into sound and visual signals which form a video creation and real-time sound.[7]

In the chapter about musical commodification, we deal in detail with two more phenomena from the field of the social existence of music which are connected with modern technologies and mutually connected, and now it is time to recall them again. The first is the field of authorship[8]; here – especially in electronic music – the technique of *appropriation*[9] emphatically applies;

---

7   Reyes 2005: 96.

8   In EDM connected to the word "production," whose connotations in other fields of popular music attribute it rather to the supervision of studio recording, see note 5.

9   Here this has the form of a sampling.

without it, electronic dance music would be unthinkable. This, however, often comes into conflict with the concept of copyrights.

In digital and internet time, music is susceptible to drifting – perhaps only in fragments – through virtual space; all the more if its basis is exactly digital sound. However, the authors/producers attempt to prevent its uncontrolled spread as attentively as in other genres.[10]

WHY?

Technological preconditions, which were just discussed, were and are, however, only possibilities, material for use. They became the cornerstones of our musical style – of electronic dance music – only in connection with the broad stream of a philosophical and cultural **alternative**.[11] The alternative, whose quest Petrusek considers as a ubiquitous phenomenon of history[12] (thereby more or less agreeing with Claude Lévi-Strauss and his concept of binary intellectual opposites). From this concrete alternative line whose continuity could be followed from the 1960s: in the academic field, perhaps, from the famous book by Roszak, *The Making of a Counter Culture* (1968), or the more recent *The Greening of America* by Charles Reich, and in the academic realm, Allen Ginsberg and his camp followers. They all reflect on the contemporary social state as binding[13] and they see the liberation of the individual from this bondage as the main task of the alternative.

Ginsberg suggests

> that everyone, including the president and all of his generals, office workers, judges and cooks, find himself a good teacher in the shape of an Indian spiritual leader and subjugate his consciousness with LSD. Afterward, I presume and predict a new consciousness will enlighten us and we will enter an infinite space, rip ourselves away from our everyday habits and clothing, from the subjugation of our government… and join the global society.[14]

---

10   Therefore, they publish either their author's albums or they sell individual tracks to labels which assemble compilations from them. Nevertheless, there also exist, music labels or internet communities that distribute music freely in the framework of Creative Commons, e.g. ektoplazm.com.

11   Another offshoot of this same intellectual plant is the rock'n'roll rebel of the 4th chapter.

12   Petrusek 2006: 58.

13   Reich speaks about the "corporate state," in which democracy also faded because "it does not express individual interests, but organized ones". (Petrusek 2006:60)

14   Quoted from Petrusek 2006: 60–61

If we disregard the idealistic ideas of the new consciousness and global society, then it is worth considering here – mainly in connection with our topic of electronic dance music – both the confidence in the wisdom of India (we will come to its inspiration in connection with psytrance) and the mention of LSD. Drugs play a relatively important role here, because they strengthen the experience of one's self and, at the same time, break down its borders. It is from this very point that all sorts of "liberation" allegedly begins.

In this spreading alternative stream, there are two more accents which have already been mentioned – one more emphatically, one less so – in connection with rebellion, which are important for our topic.

The first is the emphasis on one's own artistic realization: mainstream culture, according to alternative people, is distorted by the mass entertainment industry (also see the text about Theodor Adorno in the chapter about commodification) and thus it transforms consumers into passive, pitiful people. The basic method of extraction from that binding state is one's own individual and group creativity. Its expression is the DIY (Do It Yourself) culture which we mentioned in connection with rock'n'roll rebels and it also applies here.

The other accent which we have already mentioned, is on physicality, related to, but not necessarily connected to, the new "free" approach to sexuality. The task of experienced physicality is, from some point of view, to reveal the "forgotten self," the same longing-for-freedom self, whose experience is strengthened and altered by LSD or some other drug. In the case of free techno dancers and their unisex clothing, one can hardly speak about emphasized sexuality. However, here physicality is apparent, above all in the truly physical perception of sound.

LOSS TEKENOS IN THE CROSS CLUB
A MONDAY IN THE SPRING OF 2010
Jan Stehlík

On Monday evening I set out to do my research in the Cross Club. The club's producer, K., whom I have known for many years thanks to chance and to the fact that we live in the same housing development, recommended the regular Monday evening *Loss Tekenos*. It is apparently interesting how many customers are there even though it is a Monday and a techno night. On the club's website I found the program and who is to be playing there. Then I found further information about the DJs by looking up their pseudonyms on myspace.com: tonight someone from the NSK free techno soundsystem should be playing here.

Cross is a well-known music club in Prague's Holešovice, which used to be a port and industrial quarter, the main part of it lying on the left bank of the meandering Vltava (Moldau). The tall apartment house in which Cross has its asylum is located at a frequented intersection of three roads with tram and bus transportation, approximately three hundred meters from the Holešovice railroad station. Across the street is the Prague Gas Company building and, behind it, a second-hand auto lot. On the way from the metro I see young people in baseball caps and sweatshirts streaming by.

Not long ago, when I was standing at the traffic light of the above-mentioned intersection (from which the club evidently takes its name), I noticed monumental objects/sculptures of welded metal that whirled colors and glitter and moved and turned... Now some of them were phosphorescent in the dark. Recently, a *Cross* sign with opening hours appeared on the façade of the house; until that time, the sculptures had been the only outdoor sign of the club's presence.

To get into the club I have to go past a horizontal bar separating the street from a parking lot for taxis, cars of the inhabitants of the house, the staff of the local police station and buses or delivery vans of travelers and techies on their way through Europe. Today there is only one delivery van covered in graffiti; it has French license plates. This probably isn't yet the season for travelers. Right behind the parking lot begins the two-story garden of the club, the construction of which is welded from pieces of old iron and iron rods added to reinforced concrete. The tables are also made of iron rods, as are most of the benches. As protection against injuries, smooth iron balls are welded on

Cross Club entrance

to the end of the iron rods jutting out. In the garden, there is a very small well of welded iron, and a staircase to the second floor is also made of iron rods. On the second floor, there is a round opening through which a magnificently spreading linden tree is growing. It provides shade during the day and at least a pleasant scent at night. Three doors lead from the garden to the club: one to each floor of the club. The garden then rises to the second floor of the house (its third floor is the balcony of the second floor of the house). Groups of the club's customers, some of whom I recognize and greet, are sitting all around. They are drinking beer and smoking – in the whole garden there is a mixture of the scent of the linden tree and the smell of marihuana, which is as popular here as in most of the Prague clubs. In the garden, club music emanates from record players situated in the middle of the garden on a balcony. I meet a group of punks I know in leather jackets; I ask them if they came for techno, but they raise their plastic cups of beer and indicate that they don't care what kind of music is being played just now in the Cross.

I go in through the middle door and at a stand I meet a bunch of laughing clubbers who are consuming French fries and toasted sandwiches with a large vegetable garnish.[15] I slowly continue to the middle floor where techno is already pounding and lots of people are standing at the bar, drinking a little and cheerfully chatting: although it is Monday, there is a party on the middle floor, where friends of the DJs and the soundsystem and fans of techno have come for entertainment and dance.

The club looks futuristic and industrial: each of its parts is made up of the connection of a few used parts found in a junkyard. I have the feeling of being in a spaceship or a U-boat and, at the same time, in a squat full of young people.

Opposite the bar, there is a double-decker construction of iron rods; seats are made from discarded bus seats, the tables from thick iron pipes, the ashtrays from washing machine doors, the small lamps from iron the parts of automobile wheels. Everything is decorated and lit up with colored lights. The walls are adorned with transparent objects filled with oil and rising air bubbles.

From the next room the beats of a bass drum resound in regular, quick tempo with other rhythmic sounds and noises complementing the industrial electronic bases of techno dance music. These are not the sounds of ordinary acoustic instruments, but synthetically generated noises that create rhythmic patterns. Everything is amplified with strong loudspeakers. The rhythmic sounds are repeated, but they also vary – always in very quick tempo. The music and the interior create a whole which is practically unbelievable – industrial music composed of technical sounds fills the whole free space in the industrial environment of the club full of people with dreadlocks that look like cables, body piercing and other accessories and decorations. The club reminds me a huge machine, of an industrial environment that grew out of an old cellar of an inhabited house in the middle of an industrial quarter.

I walk through a narrow path between the people at the bar. A short young woman in cargo pants with red and black dreadlocks asks me for some "joint" paper and at the same time sways back and forth and nods her head to the rhythm of the music. The place is almost full and everywhere there are darkly clothed people in cargo pants, sweatshirts or T-shirts with spirals and other futuristic pictures, which are in fashion in the techno community. They drink beer and other beverages from plastic cups and chat; it is tremendously noisy here because they all have to shout over the booming of the music in order to

---

15   This club snack bar is a rather rare phenomenon, not at all typical for music clubs. It corresponds, on the one hand, with the fact that people spend all night here but, on the other hand, with a certain hedonism of the techies.

make themselves understood. But nobody minds; on the contrary, they even nod in agreement and the quality of the music is very often the subject of the conversation.

I walk through the club to the cellar. There is a long line at the bar. The people form a cluster pushing toward the bar. Narrow hallways lead in various directions; at the end of each is a space for bus seats and iron chairs. They are all one of a kind and actually made for this concrete place in the club. Every free space on the walls is filled with some sort of interesting artistic object, as in a gallery. Objects originally used for something else become art here – the whole club is one giant art work of postmodern design which takes one's breath away with its sophistication and emphasis on details. I walk around bar chairs made of rotary saws and look into a room in which there are three soccer tables – two on the floor and one on the ceiling. I walk into a room with a DJ stand of exceptional design – the front of the platform is full of round lights and the whole thing reminds me of the front of a car or a flying saucer. In the glow of the lights, about thirty techies are dancing.

On the second floor of the club, there is a pleasant, quiet café divided into three rooms. The decorations on the walls are made up of reeds. Tables and chairs are wooden. The walls are decorated with oil paintings. Here there is even a room where smoking is forbidden. The smell of pizza puts the finishing touches on this pleasant environment where everyone is quietly chatting to the sounds of melodic music.

There is free internet here and the window facing the street, non-existent in the rest of the club, brings in daylight. A projection screen has been placed in the last room. However, they aren't showing anything today, so the customers of the club are sitting at the tables and chatting. Before I went through the whole café I was startled by the screams of two masked figures: "Theater! Who wants to go to the theater?!"

In the evening in the theater under the roof of the house, they are playing *Pustina (The Waste Land)*, a multimedia dramatization of T.S. Eliot's famous poem. On the flyer they have underlined that the performance is DIY[16] (like probably everything in this club). I meet my drummer friend who is rehearsing in one of the many practice rooms and workshops over the café. Now he is sitting here and passionately debating about music with players in his funk band. At another table, two men in ties are sitting over papers with numbers and a group of deaf people are conversing with their hands. When they instinctively laugh out loud, I become aware of what connects us all here (later, I meet two of them dancing to the beats of the loudspeaker system).

---

16   Do It Yourself!

On the middle floor, there is the main stage of this evening's program. At 11 p.m., the dance floor is quite full of techies. Most are young people between eighteen and thirty years old wearing cargo pants and hoodies and some have on baseball caps with the peaks bent upward. The room, however, is full not only of people; it is also filled with the noisy booming of a bass drum. I even feel its beating in my skin. After a while, my heartbeat adjusts to the rhythm of the quick quarter beat and I feel a bit as if I were running.

There must be about sixty people in the room: the number of men slightly exceeds the number of women. Every one of them is swaying back and forth and, at the same time, from side to side. They all bend their knees with every beat of the bass drum. The stroboscope flickers quickly so that everything looks like short sparks; colored lasers are moving around above the dancing techies. Everyone is dancing alone; nobody touches anyone else; they are all dancing in rows facing the disk jockeys. There is no interaction among the techies except for a couple of them in the first row, who occasionally shout or raise their hands. In the front, above the dancing crowd, stands a disk jockey who puts records on the record players. He has headphones on and he presents us with variations on the main theme - four loud beats of the bass drum in one "measure." Every once in a while he changes one of the two disks, but the music stream never stops. The music changes constantly; when I listen attentively it seems to me that rarely is any part repeated even though there are always different rhythmic patterns.

Above the heads of the dancers, a futuristic, about two-meter-long chandelier on which orange and blue lights rotate, turns around and around. The wall on the left is all decorated with printed circuits. The basic computer boards are placed in small wooden frames - here they are changed into pictures. Everything is lit up in green and blue. Behind the disk jockey there is a screen on which animations and pictures alternate and intermingle in quick sequence. The music is really loud; it is not segmented into individual songs (and, in fact, nobody sings); it never ends and constantly flows over into new figures and rhythms dominated by synthetic, hard, regular beats. The stream of noise is a continuum into which one can completely immerse oneself and rely on the fact that after a while one is completely engulfed. I find something comical, playful and entertaining in it - it is elaborate, but at the same time, technical and aggressive and its beats attack so close to the bone. The people move similarly monotonously, but also in a relaxed and natural way; on accented beats, they transfer their weight from side to side and fling their arms about. "Technicity" is everywhere here: on the walls; it fills the air with the strength of the sound and it fills the heads of people who come here to forget the cares of everyday life - to turn off everything and abandon themselves to artistic expression created purely for dance and movement.

HISTORY OF ELECTRONIC DANCE MUSIC
Zuzana Jurková

Various genres belong in the wide stream of EDM, differing in rhythm, tempo, structure and other musical features, and also in the behavior of their members and the values they profess. A common characteristic is the use of electronic technologies mentioned earlier (even though it is also sometimes possible to hear an acoustic instrument or a vocal). At the same time, however, it is a basic "live" performance: playing by which the DJ chooses and combines various parts of previously recorded material and manipulates it so that a sound product arises which is distinctly different from pre-existing materials; and mainly "live" dance. This is an inseparable part of the music – its attribute incarnate – and the response of the dancers to the musical stimulus is the hallmark of the quality of the musical event.

The very changes in social dance can be seen as one of the stimuli of the rise of EDM: until the 1960s, people danced in pairs; in addition, in the urban environment the dancing required sophisticated steps and choreography. Beginning with the twist, dancing was not necessarily in pairs (which was understandably much more than just a change in the field of movement; it mainly stepped into social reality!) and, in addition, it did not demand much kinetic competence.

The beginning of the 1970s saw the rise of New York clubs,[17] attended primarily by Afro-Americans, *disco* style. It was not a distinctive musical style – DJs put on funk and soul records, largely acoustic, vocal – while it anticipated EDM in other ways. Firstly, spending the whole night in a club dancing became an established custom. Secondly, this is where DJs began mixing records to create a continuous flow of music.

At the end of the 1970s it seemed that the *disco* era was slowly coming to an end. In some clubs, e.g. in the New York Paradise Garage or the Chicago Warehouse, however, DJs were trying to create a new sound by joining acoustic recordings to new technologies. Out of such connections, the electronic musical style, named for the New York club – Garage, arose.

---

17 Butler 2006: 36 lists the Sanctuary, Loft, Haven and Gallery clubs.

The parallel Chicago scene also comes with a phenomenon that will be fundamental for EDM: its main DJ Frankie Knuckles begins to add newly created bass lines and repetitive rhythmic passages to already existing recordings. The resulting sound is thus more industrial than *Garage*, but not so much as in later techno. Similar to the New York style, this one also takes its name from a house club – *house*:[18] a name which, for a while, became the general label for EDM.

In the formative years of *house*, one more basic thing occurred: technology for the creation of electronic music became financially accessible.[19] In the environment of industrial metropolises, "unnatural" sound esthetics spread which found resonance here and become attractive. This happened only a little later in other industrial large cities on the North American continent – in Michigan's Detroit, where the new musical style got the label *techno*.

The earliest EDM recordings were created in the first half of the 1980s; actually, "No UFOs" from 1985 is considered to be the first pureblooded one, that is, with complete electronic instrumentation. Its creator (producer) was Juan Atkins, who decided to publish his recording himself on his own label, "Metroplex."

A year later, EDM flowed over to England. There, however, it collided with a barrier in the shape of required closing of clubs at the latest at 2 a.m. Dance-loving English people invented a new form – the so-called rave parties (*raves*) in the countryside or in abandoned buildings. Thanks to them, EDM became unusually popular in Britain over the next few years. The golden era of *rave parties* in Britain was ended by the *Criminal Justice and Public /Order Act* of 1994,[20] directed against the hosting of similar events. According to it, no more than 20 people may gather to listen to repetitive music. Mobile soundsystems thus began to travel around Europe (France, the Netherlands, and Italy). One of the stops of the *Spiral Tribe* and *Mutoid Waste Company* soundsystem was the Czech Republic.

A cornerstone was thus placed by the already legendary CzechTek event in the summer of 1994.

---

18   Another variant of the name of the style refers to "home" production thanks to the financial accessibility of the necessary technologies.

19   The first to be mentioned were the units of the Japanese company Roland – "drum machines" TR 808 and 909 and bass synthesizer TB 303 (Butler 2006:40). Some authors derive the name *house* from "house" accessibility of technology.

20   http://www.legislation.gov.uk/ukpga/1994/33/part/V/crossheading/powers-in-relation-to-raves.

PSYTRANCE

The *psytrance* genre is intellectually much closer to the alternatives of the 1960s than to urban techno. It is related to the wandering tendencies of the hippies and their longing to find places appropriate for a free lifestyle. One such destination appeared in the mid- 1970s in the Indian state of Goa; going to India is in no way surprising when we consider, perhaps, the Indian inspiration of the Beatles or the above-mentioned quote by Ginsberg.

At the beginning of the 1980s phonograph recordings of groups such as the Doors, Pink Floyd or the Grateful Dead, along with other styles such as reggae and ska could be heard on the beaches of Goa. But DJs, familiar with the post-punk productions of Europe, slowly also began to play electronic dance music. With the growing concentration of influences in a relatively small area and, at the same time, with emphasis on the psychedelic aspect, a new genre called Goa trance formed during the 1980s. In the mid-1980s, all the beach parties were already purely electronic. At this time, they have about two hundred participants; the place is lit by a few colored and fluorescent lights; music plays for two or three days without interruption. When, however, in the course of a couple of years, the number of participants increased to 1,500 (in 1991)[21], the Indian government limited similar public musical production until – with the exception of a New Year's party –the government forbade it altogether in the mid- 1990s. As in the case of British techno, the answer was a spread of the genre throughout the whole world – beginning with Japan, then Israel, then Europe and the USA. In some places, large music festivals were organized[22]; elsewhere the genre – renamed psytrance in 1996 – became more or less a part of mainstream EDM[23] and in other places – e.g. in the Czech Republic – it remained in small communities hidden more or less in the underground.[24]

---

21   Cole – Hannan 1997: 1–14.

22   The best known are the Portuguese Boom, the German Full Moon and Ozora in Hungary.

23   http://www.etnomuzikologie.eu/index.php/studium/studentske-prace/80-psytrance-coby-zanr-paralelni-reality-bakalarska-prace

24   For the history of psytrance in the Czech Republic, see http://www.psytrance.cz/cs/history-psytrance-czech-republic.

ANDĚLKA FREE PARTY
JULY 25–26, 2008
Peter Balog

OVERTURE: CZEKTEK 2006

In the summer of 2005, I was in Spain. I learned on the Internet that members of the *Czektek* festival were brutally attacked by the police. Various questions occurred to me, but as I had never been to such a festival I couldn't imagine what was happening there and why the police would attack the participants. I told myself that I would have to go to Czektek the following year.

The next summer I set out with a friend for Czektek, which was to take place in a military field near Mašťov. Since that day was very hot, we hitchhiked in shorts, sandals and T-shirts, with only a little money because we knew that there was no entrance fee. We decided that we would not spend much money. In the early evening we were only a few kilometers from the place, which we could tell by the high concentration of tattooed people with dreadlocks, police and variously decorated delivery trucks; they were all rolling along in one direction.

We stopped for refreshments in a small village where people with large backpacks, sleeping bags and tents sat down with us. We began to ask them if we were going in the same direction, and they answered affirmatively. In return, they began to question us about whether we wanted to go there the way were dressed – in shorts and sandals – as this was new to them. Then they began to mention names of the *soundsystems*[25] who would be playing there and we had no idea what they were talking about. With a feeling of bewilderment and awareness that we didn't know what we were going to, we set out with them.

It was already night when we were about five kilometers from the location of the Czektek 2006 performance. The roads were blocked by cars and delivery trucks and in the distance I saw something that looked like a blinking slot-machine the size of a small village from which were emanating sounds that I cannot describe in words. The closer we got, the larger the crowd of people became and the decibels coming from the "slot-machine" also increased.

---

25   The word *soundsystem* is used for the group of people in charge of the operation of the musical equipment on the technical and music side. It is also used for the sound equipment, as I will describe later.

In an hour we were at the venue. Unusual sounds came from every corner; blinking stroboscopes, but the stroboscopes didn't allow us to make out the exact source of these sounds. People everywhere were wearing a variety of clothing. They were everything except sober. After some time I began to register that they were gathered in front of large walls composed of loudspeakers. Under the onslaught of those outsized loud sounds, lights and the behavior of the people whom I couldn't manage to understand, we literally escaped. This experience, nevertheless, drew me to a further event. I wanted to know more; I wanted to see more.

ANDĚLKA 2008

On July 24, 2008, Alena called me to say there would be a *free party* at Andělka.[26] Alena suggested that I go with her and that she would introduce me to people from the PESS soundsystem with whom she used to go to free parties and to *technivals*[27] and also with whom she occasionally worked as a VJ.[28] This offer enabled me to ascertain what it was like at a technival after I had made my cowardly escape from the last one.

A photographer friend and I decided to take the bus from Prague to Liberec, then a train to the nearest village and then we'd walk to our destination. We had gathered information about the event for about two weeks, most of it from the Internet site tekway.cz, where there was a black and white flyer with a listing of soundsystems that would play, parking information, the date of the event, the region of the venue (north Bohemia, no precise place) and two telephone numbers through which it was possible to get further information about the location. On the other side of the flyer, it said how people shouldn't behave and what they should avoid. It also discussed who could take someone in his car, etc.

When on July 25 we arrived at the Liberec train station, groups of techies were walking around us. Most of them were wearing camouflage pants or shorts and black-and-white T-shirts with motifs about freetechno culture, e.g., pictures of loudspeakers, spirals or people who had implanted in their bodies technological elements like perhaps printed circuits (they looked like robots with human features). The people at the station had visible piercings, *tunnels*,[29]

---

26 Free party is an event where, in most concentrated form, the concept of freetechno counter-culture are represented. Andělka is the name of a meadow in north Bohemia.

27 Festivals of people identifying with freetechno culture.

28 Term for a person who does video projections – see below.

29 Earrings shaped like circles poked through earlobes .

dreadlocks,[30] *Mohawks*,[31] gaudily colored hair, tattoos; they were wearing hoodies; accessories were backpacks or knapsacks. The smell of marihuana wafted through the station.

We got into a train: about twenty techies were seated in our car. They were sipping beer and wine. One couple asked the conductor if they were going the right way for the free party at Andělka. He advised them to pay a surcharge for the tickets to go the next stop, which we also did. Besides us, about a hundred techies got off at the Višňová – Filipovka station and, because Alena didn't remember the exact way, we set out behind the others.

When we were on the road for about half an hour we heard a booming noise and twenty minutes later we saw delivery vans, trucks and cars in the distance. We heard various sounds coming from this place that we were unable to identify as music. It was a tangle of sounds from several soundsystems. Alena kept telling me how great it was six years ago when she was here and that she was very much looking forward to it. After a while, we encountered a fork in the road where a police car and four policemen were standing. We greeted them and then moved on.

The extensive area of Andělka was one and a half kilometers from the Polish border and it was possible to enter it from various sides because it wasn't enclosed by a fence or anything else. There was just one access road for cars and residents of the adjacent village collected one hundred crowns for the entrance of a car to the area. We walked along a forest path that extended about another three hundred meters toward a large meadow. Cars with Czech, German, Dutch, British and French license plates were parked along this road. I didn't see any system in the parking: wherever a car stopped, that's where it stayed. In addition to cars, the access road was lined with sleeping techies who were not lying on mats or in sleeping bags, but rather, on the ground. Often they covered themselves with some straw that was at hand. The event had begun on Friday – and on Saturday afternoon, when we arrived, there was a whole "city" built in the meadow.

A little tent city had been created at one end of the meadow. However, it did not keep within this space and flowed into the forest. The little tent city was composed of commonly sold tents, canvases and camouflage nets thrown over cords tied to trees, cars, delivery vans, trucks, and buses. The vehicles were often adapted in various ways and painted as if people wanted to domesticate them. On one side of the tent city there was a preponderance of Czech license plates whereas on the other side there were European plates, most of which

---

30 Hairdo in which the hair is shaped like cables.
31 Hair arranged in the shape of saws.

Decorated soundsystem (photo: Peter Balog)

were French. The tent city was in no way separated from the space holding the soundsystems; on the contrary, both spaces were interwoven and it was not exceptional to see tents or vehicles next to soundsystems. The smell of marihuana and diesel was everywhere.

The entire meadow was intersected by the "main artery" which had been beaten down by cars and people in one day. Little paths branched out from it which, after three days, merged in an undifferentiated earth-covered straw substance. When we arrived there in the afternoon, the soundsystems were already playing very loud music. I felt the pressure of the sounds over the whole surface of my body, even from a great distance. Diverse EDM genres spilled out from the soundsystems: techno, jungle, drum and bass, hardcore, breakbeat and psytrance. The music had a fast tempo that, as I ascertained later, quickened toward the evening. At first it was apparent that the sounds that were used in the individual music genres were not created with the help of acoustic instruments, instead, they sounded like ten-year-old mobile telephones or pinball machines. They sounded electronic.

We began to look for the PESS soundsystem so that we could greet its members. The trip across the meadow took about fifteen minutes, during which I counted more than twenty soundsystems. They were made up of between four and forty loudspeakers, trucks, projection screens, lighting equipment and a bar. Farther along, I saw large tents that looked like a circus big top. People took shelter from the burning sun; again there were cars all around, with large canvases and military nets thrown over them. We found "our" soundsystem on the edge of the meadow. It was a wall made up of loudspeakers of various sizes, functions, brand names and decorations that measured about ten meters wide by five meters high. Alenka recognized it from the patterns and decorations. About twenty people standing in front of the soundsystem, rocking about to the rhythm, smoking and sipping beer.

They were just a few centimeters away from it. Some of them even touched it and put their cups of beer on the loudspeakers. On the left side was a bar that belonged to the soundsystem, on the right side stood a delivery van and, behind it, loudspeakers, turntables and many cables. A DJ was also standing there, hidden under a small canvas shelter.

Alena led us behind the delivery van where two approximately twenty-year-old boys were standing. We greeted each other, after which they offered us vodka and a joint. They were "boys from the system," however, not original members: "around the system" people allegedly change frequently. While Alena went to a friend of hers, the photographer and I chatted with the boys mostly using gestures. They offered to let us leave our backpacks in the delivery van and assured us that we had nothing to fear, that nobody would steal them. Alena returned without her friend, but with drinks. We continued in a partly pantomimed conversation about who liked which music, who liked what kind of decorations, what they did at night and what we did in our everyday lives.

The sun began to set and Alena suggested that we go for a walk and buy "something good" on the way. As I discovered, "something good" meant hallucinatory drugs. I was surprised that the area we had entered in the afternoon changed toward the evening. Empty places on the meadow filled with newly arriving soundsystems, people, dogs and trash. The smell was always the same, marihuana and diesel from the electrical units; the lighting changed. The systems began to switch on stroboscopes, lasers and scanners and video projections. At one soundsystem I noticed that sculptures made of metal parts that looked like beetles, or rather "techno-beetles," had been placed near it. We found our way to an area with a high concentration of French people and Alena announced that this was what she was looking for. She went from car to car and asked in English if they had any "crystal" - MDMA or "trips" - LSD. The first guy offered us cetamin, but she refused it. But she was immediately successful with the second guy. As she bought several "trips", she haggled over the price. He explained to her that they were not extremely strong, and I also joined in the conversation. After a while it surfaced that he was here with a French soundsystem and, beginning in June, he would travel around Europe and mainly around the Czech Republic. because in other countries such as Germany, France, England and Holland, there were major problems with arrangements for free parties and the traveling way of life. Allegedly, the police

often raid such events, whereas here this wasn't such a problem. After the end of the free party at Andělka he was taking the system to Portugal, to the Boom Off festival, which was the antithesis of the commercial psytrance Boom party, where ticket prices can climb as high as two hundred Euros. Entrance to Boom Off is free – like the free party at Andělka.

About half an hour after the application, Alenka's pupils were unbelievably dilated and she began to communicate non-verbally rather than verbally. She kept stopping at soundsystems until I lost sight of her. I remained only with the photographer. On the way we found an approximately twenty-meter row of mobile toilets, but the participants were not shy and took care of their needs right where people promenaded, so by the second day we registered another smell.

Until morning when it began to be light out, I stood in front of soundsystems and followed the video projections. On them people move or dance and, by shouting, stimulate the music. Groups of people were standing in front of most of the systems, most of them dancing individually in place. Farther on, people were gathered in front of bars; otherwise they streamed all night from place to place. The greatest concentration of people was in front of the largest soundsystems, and in the framework of each system, as near as possible to the loudspeakers. While observing them, I had a problem with my concentration because the stroboscope caused me to see everything chopped into pieces. Furthermore, there was a stroboscope in practically every system and their effects

Dancing in front of the soundsystem (photo: Peter Balog)

mingled, which elicited the feeling that everything, including the ground, was moving. In addition, the whole area was lit up in every color by the scanners and lasers. There was even a fire show to be viewed on one of the systems. A girl and a guy were twisting chains whose ends were wrapped in fabric dipped in oil and ignited. The twisting to the rhythm next to a soundsystem created various figures and shapes which constantly changed. Many bystanders were gathered around them. The loudspeaker boxes of the soundsystems and mainly "snails" – baffle boards of bass and sub-bass loudspeakers – were painted periodically with neat black and white stripes like crosswalks. Old televisions were incorporated on some system walls. These televisions were either non-functional or were running the same picture as the projection on the screen. In addition to the TVs in the soundsystems, there were objects like a free-hanging chandelier from a living room or a doll with its hair pulled out. Not every soundsystem had such objects; these were, rather, each system's attempt at being individual. The loudspeakers were also used as places to put personal things, e.g., small backpacks, drinking water or beer. Next to the systems, directly on them or as protective roofs of bars that offered food and drink, there were canvas sails painted with motifs like the ones on the T-shirts of the participants. Apart from the loudspeakers, there were frequent varied graphic forms of the number 23 and mainly black-and-white spirals, most frequently incorporated into the pictures of a man with an "improved" mechanical arm or some technology or only black-and-white stripes. These were painted on soundsystems, canvases and T-shirts, and were repeated in the video projections or were painted black on a white circle base coat and turned with the help of a small motor. I had never seen any of these things in a shop: the people had made them themselves and, as they showed me during the evening, they were quite proud of them. The age of the participants, who I guessed numbered about a thousand, ranged between fifteen and fifty and neither sex dominated significantly.

During the evening I met Alena. She began to tell me that never in her life had she seen a more beautiful night sky. It really was beautiful, but it seemed to me that Alena was radically somewhere else. I wondered if we were in the same place. When I spoke to a passer-by, a guy who asked me for a cigarette and who confided in me that he had "polished off paper," that is, that he had consumed LSD, I realized he was telling the truth because he took me to a canvas on which there was a black-and-white curved stripe and said that that canvas pulled him in and that it felt as if he were on a merry-go-round. Besides that, he said that everything was wavy as if it were alive and that everything was changing colors. Then, when day began to break, he swore and said that the sun rose too early and that the light disturbed his state after he had "polished off paper."

Around six in the morning, I looked for the soundsystem where we had left our things, but because the delivery van was locked, I lay down under it like some of the other people. When I awoke in the afternoon, the soundsystems were still playing. The photographer, Alena and people from the PESS soundsystem were lying next to me. We began to eat breakfast. People we didn't know offered us food and drink, made fun of a guy who "was very.... at night". It was Sunday and I noticed that in the late afternoon the majority of the soundsystems had turned off the sound. When I asked why, I received the answer that there was a mass in the nearby village and the organizers who rented the meadow had promised the mayor that they would turn off the sound for the hour of the mass. Although the soundsystems were turned off, I heard repetitive beats kept going round in my head and the others said that they did, too.

In the afternoon, people lounged around or stood in front of soundsystems. Some juggled or twisted chains without burning fires. They chatted, smoked joints and drank alcohol. Stroboscopes and other lighting equipment were switched off. Children were chasing each other and splashing water on each other in front of the French system. I even met a group of tourists dressed à la Bushman – on their chests they had tags with their names and the name of the tourist organization that provided them a "safari" tour.

On Monday morning I packed my things and left with the photographer. Alena went to Liberec and we took the train to Prague. Every motion of the train evoked sound images in me, images of the periodic repetitious beats that I had shaken off the evening of the second day.

SYLLABUS – PSYCHEDELIC TRANCE AND BROKEN BEATZ
CROSS CLUB
SATURDAY, DECEMBER 3, 2011 (9 P.M.) – SUNDAY,
DECEMBER 4, 2011 (6 P.M.)
Tickets: until 10 p.m. – 70 CZK, after 10 p.m. – 110 CZK.
http://www.psytrance.cz/cs/party/syllabus
Veronika Svobodová (Avellaneda)

LINE-UP:

Psychedelic stage:
9 p.m. – 10:30 Tranceformer + VJ Perplex
10:30 – midnight Plech + VJ 000333
Midnight – 1:30 a.m. LAB (LIVE set) + VJ 000333
1:30 a.m. – 3 a.m. MiM + VJs Kashmir & Alisa
3 a.m. – 4:30 a.m. LAB (DJ set) VJs Kashmir & Alisa
4:30 a.m. – 6 a.m. Ejczka + VJs Kashmir & Alisa

Broken Beatz stage:
9 p.m. – 11 p.m. Jarin
11 p.m. – 1 a.m. Stantha
1 a.m. – 4:30 a.m. Rudeboy & M4Y4

Trailer of the event in original version www.nyx.cz:
First Saturday of December: outstanding Portuguese dark psychedelic trance
project LAB is coming to the Prague Cross Club to play live and DJ set.

SYLLABUS

Course format: lectures and seminars
Educators:

Lecture hall/Psychedelic stage:
Prof. LAB (No Comment Records, PORTUGAL) LIVE + DJ set
Prof. MiM (Biocore)
Asst. Prof. Tranceformer (Yupisashi)
Dr. of Natural Sciences. Plech Ph.D. (Polyhedra, Tuesday Night)
Ejczka, Ph.D. (Polyhedra)

VJs
Prof. 000333 (Mimo-TV)
Prof. Perplex
Kashmir, M.A., Ph.D. (HedoniX)
Alisa, B.A. (Tuesday Night)

Seminar rooms/Broken Beatz stage:
Prof. Rudeboy (Shadowbox)
Prof. M4Y4 (Shadowbox)
Asst. Prof. Stantha (DNB Fever)
Asst. Prof. Jarin (Yupisashi)

Time and Venue: Cross Club, Prague, December 3, 2011, 9 p.m. – 6 a.m.
Requirements: Attendance of at least one of the lectures or seminars.
Entrance requirements: Recommended for all levels. Interest in the most varied forms of electronic music an advantage. Tickets: until 10 p.m. – 70 CZK, and after that 110 CZK.

BRIEF ANNOTATION OF LECTURES AND SEMINARS

At the beginning of December, teachers Plech and Ejczka of the Polyhedron Institute prepared a series of lectures for you in the spaces of the Prague ghettollege, the Cross Club. In the lecture hall, the Psychedelic Stage, the main guest will be Portuguese Prof. LAB of the Institute of No Comment Records, in which, Prof. CPC and Prof. Necropsycho work. Renato Moreira, a.k.a. Prof. LB. came across electronic music at the end of the 1990s and quickly got into his own musical production. From breakbeat, downtempo and house music, he reached hard night psytrance. His production is based on quick groovy beats and strong futuristic industrial themes supplemented with conspicuous metal sounds. He began to perform as a live act in 2005. On Saturday, December 3, he will perform first with a 1½ hour live set and also at a more advanced night hour there will be a 1½ hour DJ set.

In the lecture hall, Prof. MiM, Asst. Prof. Tranceformer, Dr. of Natural Sciences Plech, and Dr. Ejczka will appear on stage with their musical contributions. The interior of the Psychedelic Stage will get a professional assistant from the German Cosmic Walkers Institute. For a more complex understanding of the discussed topics of the lecturers, there will be a supplement of visual contributions to their musical presentation by Prof. 000333 of Mimo-TV, Prof. Perplex, M.A., Kashmir, M.A., Ph.D., of the HedoniX Institute and Alisa, B.A., of the Tuesday Night Institute.

The seminar room Broken Beatz stage will be filled in the spirit of broken beats. The contributions of individual DJs will rotate from psybreaks to autonomic sound. To deep d'n'b to hard techstep and, as morning approaches, more dancing forms of drum and bass. Profs. Rudeboy and M4Y4 of the Shadowbox Institute, Asst. Profs. Stantha and Jarin of the DNB Fever and Yupisashi Institutes will present their musical contributions. The German specialists from Cosmic Walkers will, in this case, also take care of the interior of the Broken Beatz stage.

We hope to succeed in creating an extraordinary musical and visual experience when both stages correspond to each other not only visually, but musically.

Required educational materials:
http://www.myspace.com/lablabs
Further recommended educational sources:
http://www.nocomment-records.com
http://www.discogs.com/artist/LAB+%284%29
http://djmim.net
http://www.yupisashi.com
http://www.shadowbox.cz/booking.php?djById=92
http://www.shadowbox.cz/booking.php?djById=95
http://cs-cz.facebook.com/pages/DNB-FEVER/146877345243
http://www.crossclub.cz

A SNAPSHOT OF A PSYTRANCE SYLLABUS EVENT

I learn of the event from the communal server nyx.cz, where the virtual "event" containing all necessary information (see above) was created. People not registered on nyx probably learned of the event from the web site psytrance.cz or via other web pages concerned with electronic-music or from their social networks.

On the day of the event, 80 users registered at nyx, a number which indicates a rather exceptional psytrance event. In various Prague clubs, there are one or two psytrance events a week between autumn and summer, and the number of people registered on nyx is usually around 20. Club psytrance events often offer free entry. Admission is charged only in the case of greater expenses (e.g., the participation of foreign guests, etc.). In the summer, these genres are performed mostly at several-day outdoor festivals, where it is possible to experience psytrance in all of its manifestations, while in clubs these genres are often reduced to only the basic ones. For many people, such club psy-

µGen

Psytrance syllabus in Cross (photo: Mjugen)

trance evenings are hence a sort of psytrance hibernation, which is indicated by the number of participants.

The SYLLABUS event is thematically conceived of as a cycle of lectures, and therefore the organizers attribute academic titles to all of the performers, with the most experienced receiving the more pretentious titles. The greatest attractions are unquestionably the Portuguese music producer LAB, decorations from the workshop of the German Cosmic Walkers and also the deputies of the VJs – 000333, who is generally the maker of the video projections which he projects at the same time (so-called video-live act), and Perplex. The latter is one of the last VJs in the Czech Republic who create their psychedelic video mixes of VHS cassettes, which are already anachronic today, and, at the same time, he is also the main organizer of the biggest and longest-lasting Czech BIO psytrance festival.

The beginning of the event is announced for 9 p.m. That is when I come to the Cross Club, in front of which there is a group of three techies and one psytrancer. They can be recognized at first glance from their clothing: all the techies are wearing typical camouflage pants, sweatshirts with black and white industrial motifs and "Palestinian" scarves are wrapped around their necks. In contrast, this psytrancer's clothing colorfully shines from a distance and on the back of his sweatshirt there is an elf surrounded by colored mushrooms.

We enter the club through the industrial garden. I help Perplex carry his heavy, bulky suitcase full of VHS cassettes and video players and I think aloud about how convenient it is for the other VJs with their notebooks and data recorded in them. I have learned that it is a question of taste and nostalgia (some contemporary DJs still also play vinyls instead of CDs) and also the time they need to transfer material from VHS to another format.

At the entrance we receive an illegible UV-active[32] stamp and we head toward the stage.[33] In the area containing the main bar there are, at this time, about ten people (as a rule, the club doesn't fill up on weekends until around eleven in the evening) and there are five people standing on the main stage. In the middle of the stage there is a stepladder on which, within a few minutes, some technicians finish hanging one of the five decorations which, thanks to the installation of UV lights, phosphoresce colorfully and very intensively. The concept of decoration of the space this time is in minimalistic floral spirit and design which, according to some participants, correspond excellently to the otherwise entirely industrial furnishings of the Cross Club. Colored, climbing flower motifs frame the platform; others on are hung on the walls and in the middle of the stage. We can see typical psytrance static decorations in the form of draped canvas with various psyart motifs in the halls of the club.

PSYART

Specific decoration and video projections are component parts of every psytrance event and their aim is to add the final visual touches to the atmosphere of a given place. These visual environments are generally called "psychedelic art," for short, "psyart,"[34] which, as a rule, is colorful and fluorescent (UV active). What is very typical for psychedelic art is work with symbols and their incorporation into unusual multi-layered combinations in which their meanings are deformed and mutually interact. Emphasis in psyart is placed on a large gamut of colors, the density of which is furthermore highlighted by the use of UV lights which, to a certain extent, imitate the intensity of the flamboyance of the objects in psychedelic experience. The fractal motifs, which work with organically structured geometric shapes and often recall the morphology of natural objects, are also similarly multilayered and deformed.

---

32   Luminous under ultraviolet light (so-called black light) thanks to the fluorescence.

33   A commonly used word for the dance floor plus the platform on which the DJ generally plays.

34   Typical decorations are canvas usually painted with acrylic UV colors, various 3D decorations (e.g., mushrooms, flowers, animals, totems, thematic figures, UV fibers of interlaced geometric bodies, etc.) Frequent motifs are also mandalas, abstract natural elements (fractals), as well as motifs taken from fantasy literature (elves, fairies, magi) and sci-fi (aliens, space ships, extra-terrestrial flora and fauna).

The aim of psyart is the intensification of the esthetics and partly also the simulation of psychedelic experiences. An essential part of psyart, then, is emphasis on originality, multiple meaning and individual appreciation of the creativity of the participants themselves. The suggestion of the psytrance cradle is often apparent in the form of imagery of Indian patterns (mandalas, etc.) and Hindu deities. Also connected to this is a choice of "picturesque" localities and recalls ocean beaches and jungles, which, among other things, differentiates psytrance from techno and other rather industrial styles of EDM, where not too much demand is placed on the choice of venue (a techno party often takes place in old industrial buildings, plain cement halls, etc.).

A projection screen hangs behind DJ Transformer, who is playing right now. On it, a few minutes later Perplex begins the projection – for technical reasons, however, not with a prepared VHS, but from his notebook. He can't blend and interlace the prepared videos, so he starts a few pre-prepared video loops, which he doesn't interfere with too much. However, in his video projections the above-mentioned emphasis on the variety and gayness of colors intermingling with psyart motifs is always evident. Mandalas may mix with floral fractals until, finally, there is a flock of flamingos catching fish in a river. The VJ is sitting a few meters from the DJ – at the VJ's mixer, from which not only the screen, but also the DJ and dancing crowd, can be seen well. The choice of projected videos continuously conforms to the character of the music the DJ is playing.

The loud music has a tempo corresponding to approximately 130 bpm.[35] The motifs in it are, for now, less complicated than those that will be heard in the course of the evening; this is typical of so-called "progressive", which the DJ is playing right now. That is to say, it is possible to divide psytrance into a few specific sub-genres that copy the day's cycle: individual sub-genres are mostly played at the corresponding time.[36]

The arrangement of musical motifs is similar to the visual ones: they change relatively quickly and individual sounds are layered on each other (frequently to the point of being irritating) so that they can be disturbing to a person who isn't used to listening to psytrance. For psytrancers, however, the unpredictability of sound combinations is the desirable and expected variety of sound stimuli for which they have come here.

---

35 Beats per minute, which means the number of beats of the bass drum per minute.
36 This is also characteristic of the Indian understanding of music, because similar divisions also apply to Indian musical forms, so-called ragas, which are assigned to concrete three-hour phases of the 24-hour cycle.

Psytrance syllabus in Cross (photo: Mjugen)

PSYTRANCE – MUSIC

"Psytrance differs from other EDM genres, e.g. techno, mainly through a slower rhythm, supplemented by a wide range of psychedelic sounds, noises or adapted samples through which the compositions are interwoven. A characteristic sign is multi-layering, which means that these sounds and noises are organized into developing patterns, which are very coherently interlaced into a compact whole. Playing with space stereo effects is typical: percussive and melodic motifs taken from ethnic music, mainly Indian and Arabic, are often added to booming rhythm. The vocal part is reduced to occasional samples from films or suggestive announcements; classical sung texts are usually absent. On the other hand, the timbre of sounds is emphasized which evoke the noise track of some story or even some strange discussions of alien civilizations, including an emotive intonation" (*Ikarie* 2005: 14).

After a two-and-a-half-hour DJ set, the room begins to fill up. During the DJ change, the public mostly applauds the outgoing DJ and at the same time welcomes the new one. The new DJ is Plech, one of the organizers of today's event. At the same time the VJs rotate and 000333 (or Nulatrojka) sits down at the mixer. His projections are made up of various colored and complicated fractal figures, mandalas and other psychedelic motifs which interlace in several layers. Nulatrojka occasionally mixes these images in with real shots (e.g. Peruvian Indians, monkeys cleaning their coats, etc.).

µGen

The DJ takes the place of the musician in psytrance - the Portuguese LAB (photo: Mjugen)

The new arrivals mostly greet their friends on stage. Exceptions are a couple of foreigners who come here because – according to them – someone recommended Cross as one of the most interesting clubs in Prague. The ages of the guest ranges between 20 and 35 years, while the proportion of men to women is 2:1. At the bar I also meet "Little Spiral" – a girl with long red-and-yellow dreadlocks and face piercings who has been coming to psytrance events for several years. As she says, her favorite occasion is the Bio summer festival and she generally prefers outdoor events. However, she also came to this event with a friend from Pilsen because she wanted to hear the Portuguese LAB. Two local performers are standing at the bar. They are talking as if they were two "old professor friends" who had met. Evidently they are playing the roles assigned to them in the annotation of this event and they are having a great time. The stage is already crowded before midnight and it isn't possible to dance too much. The room is stuffy and the guests are just sort of swaying. Some have their eyes closed; others are staring at the video projection behind the DJ. Psychedelic motifs on the clothing of some of the participants shine intensively under the UV light so that the dancers become some sort of mobile decorations. I notice a group of three people studying in detail the motif on the back of the T-shirt of one of the participants and a couple of times they burst out laughing. On the stage, there are also a couple of classic "hippies" – e.g. a man with John

Lennon glasses, long hair, a striped sleeveless T-shirt and wide Indian pants. This reminds me how far contemporary psytrance is from the original Goa trance – the style from which the community of the local "Western" followers of the hippie movement originated on the beaches of Goa in India.

At exactly midnight, the long-awaited LAB makes his appearance at the DJ's mixer. During the first composition the public, which had not been too active up to that time, starts to heat up – both with his music and probably also because he dances alone at the mixer and makes active contact with the public; mainly the dancers in the first rows react to him immediately. The connection between the musician and the public is thus much warmer than what it was like in the case of the more-or-less stiffly standing Czech DJs, who mostly mixed the tracks and looked at the pubic only occasionally. The fact that the behavior of the DJ is as important as the music he plays is something I verified with the help of a small experiment I did with a few friends a couple of years ago at the open-air psytrance event at Milešovka.[37] At that time, Perplex was invited to perform not only as a VJ, but also as a DJ and, because according to his own words he hadn't mastered live track mixing, he prepared a whole set in advance. He planned to play it without doing anything else with it. Instead he planned to dance. At the beginning there were about 20 people on the stage. After a few minutes at the mixer, he stopped enjoying standing there and really walked away. The music played on; although it didn't change markedly, in a few minutes, most of the people stopped dancing or even left. I thus had the idea that it would be possible to alternate other "actors" at the DJ's mixer who would make contact with the public and only fake the DJ show. As soon as someone appeared at the mixer, the people returned and began to dance, whistle and actively react in other ways. The greatest success of the would-be DJs was reaped by a friend who eccentrically jumped around behind the mixer, pretending at the same time that he was perhaps producing every new sound on imaginary machines personally. Nobody minded that it was apparently only a parody of some sort of star live act (this will be explained below). And then, when the mixer was again orphaned for a while, the interest of the audience again ebbed away. (Only those with closed eyes and those who cared only about the music remained.)

Let's return to the Prague club. The first LAB performance of the evening was a so-called live act, which means that the man at the mixer was the author of all of the compositions played. In contrast to the DJ, then, he presents his own work and he further modulates it at the party "live." After an hour-and-a-half live performance, LAB returns to the mixer once more as a DJ and then

---

37 The highest mountain of the Czech Middle Mountains (České středohoří).

plays and mixes compositions (tracks) produced by other composers. During the evening I asked a few other participants in Czech psytrance why they had come to this party and their answers differed. In a conversation with former DJ Cymoon, who was one of the first Czech psytrance DJs (from 1998), I found out that he had come out not only because of his friends, but also to find out if psytrance had moved somewhere else since those years. He was allegedly disappointed with its development for a long time and so he shifted to other, unexplored (by him) EDM genres like, e.g. dubstep. For him, psytrance was the most attractive from the end of the 1990s until approximately 2005 when, thanks to newly developing technologies, always new and interesting sounds, noises and ways of composing appeared. Today, apparently hardly anything about psytrance surprises and captivates him; the genre is depleted. On the other hand, he is aware that, for many people who began to listen to psytrance later, there is always something to discover in it and his feeling can be very subjective.

In contrast to Cymoon's opinions are those of the Portuguese LAB, who is ten years younger and came to psytrance from metal and various EDM genres until around six years ago. He believes that psytrance "will even have something to say to listeners in the future". He allegedly enjoys playing in the Cross Club very much and he particularly likes people dancing in the crowded environment and noisily showing their satisfaction with the music.

Several times over the course of the evening I also went to look at the stage one floor lower. There the music was somewhat "calmer" and slower EDM genres – breakbeat, psybreaks, drum'n'bass, etc. The stage here was almost empty until 11 p.m. (as on the main psytrance stage upstairs), but it also filled up gradually with time. Among the participants there non-trancers – according to their clothing –prevailed. The occupants of this stage did not markedly change, even when the "star" of the evening was playing on the main stage.

The whole event ends at exactly 6 a.m., when the main stage is lit up. The people chant and don't intend to stop just like that and therefore the DJ adds two more tracks – now with bright lights. . After a few minutes, the music stops and most of the people sheepishly go to the bar for a last drink or to the buffet for something to eat on the way home. Gradually landing at the sunny end of the ongoing party with a stream of calming music is but a privilege of open-air festivals.

Zuzana Jurková

In her 2004 book with the slightly mysterious title of *Deep Listeners*[38], the American ethnomusicologist Judith Becker aims to come closer to an understanding of the relationships of "music, emotion and trance." She is, of course, not the first: she follows Gilbert Rouget and his *La musique et la transe* (1980, English 1985); in addition, she brings her own knowledge plus examples of music of South and Southeast Asia that she has researched over the past decades. Atypically for an ethnomusicologist, she is also concerned with findings from natural and neural sciences. All of this is interwoven with the experiences of people who have been in a trance.

In her initial assertion, Becker takes the same position as Rouget: because trance occurs across geographic and cultural axes, it could seem that it is a universal phenomenon. More extensive research, however, shows that there are **many kinds of trances**. They have quite a bit in common, however: their basis is strong emotion accompanied by physical reactions, e.g., crying, rhythmical swaying or horripilation. What is also universal is the loss of consciousness (some scientists speak of a different "self" in a trance from the normal "self" and an extraordinary ability to withstand fatigue. Sometimes types of knowledge and experience surface which are inaccessible in non-trance events.

Some types of trance are more connected to music than others. It is impossible to find an unambiguous connection between a certain type of music and a certain type of trance.

The bases of a trance, then, are strong **emotions.** Becker researches them as phenomena rooted in the body – and in more detail in cortical and subcortical structures of the brain. However, she does not adopt the opinion that this is a question of activation of the autonomic nervous system.[39] At the same time,

---

38   In it she was inspired by the American accordion player and composer Pauline Oliveros, who pursued "a heightened consciousness of the world of sound," see deeplistening.org. Becker uses the expression *deep listening* as a secular parallel to trance, which she connects with a spiritual context. In our text, the word "trance" refers to both environments.

39   "Autonomic" means independent of our consciousness or will. Our body temperature or breathing are influenced by similar processes.

however, emotions are phenomena "from the moment of birth ... continually being shaped by culture."

Of the whole scale of emotions, then, Becker focuses closely on "musical" ones, that is, those that evoke music in attentive listeners or musicians. These **musical emotions differ from emotions** connected to life experiences: they are rooted in basic physiological excitement and are therefore accompanied by the above-mentioned physical reactions. They generally take the shape of some form of happiness or sadness.

In contrast to predominantly "calm" musical emotions, they are **emotions connected to trance** (across cultures), **acute** and **strong (Becker uses the expression "emotions of high arousal")**; scientists classify them among the so-called primary emotions. Joy, fear and rage prevail here. After a trance, feelings such as peace and humility, and also the experience Becker calls pleasure, generally appear. Such a feeling is somehow a confirmation of the quality of the experience and, at the same time, it evokes a longing for its repetition.

In connection with musical emotions, their strength and physical rooting, it is appropriate here to focus on **music during trance.** As has already been said, it is not possible to connect individual types of trance with a concrete type of music; trance music can differ according to the instruments, the presence or absence of singing, or a concrete melody or rhythm. Despite this, it is possible to spot various things in common: loudness (dynamics) or at least shrillness and rhythmically vibrant, that is, sensuously stimulating features. This corresponds well to the physical rooting of the strong emotion that is the basis of a trance.

One more feature should be mentioned in connection with trance: transcendental experiences. A trance relatively frequently takes place in a religious context - as a component of ceremonies or confirmation of a religious experience. However, this does not apply exclusively as the snapshots in this book confirm. In a secular environment, participants also often proclaim **experiences** that are **close** to **spiritual** ones. *It was like in a dream...I was soaring and they played just for me.* (p. 54)

I find it very difficult to find words for this music that I have experienced so strongly at one occasion. The closest description I can come up with is that it was a cosmic wholeness-experience beyond time and space. The body and the music became a whole, where I knew that I was dead, but it was a death that also gave birth to something that was liberating. (p. 54)

Pleasure is the right answer to this experience. It is, on the one hand, a confirmation of the experience and, at the same time, a call for its repetition.

TRANCE AS A LEARNED ART OF THE UNLEARNABLE

While Judith Becker describes various forms of trance – from southern Italian *tarantismo* to Sufi rituals and various ceremonies of Indonesia to contemporary Pentecostal churches – one basic question constantly pops up: how is it that all participants fall into a trance more or less at once? In answering this question, Becker connects two only seemingly different realms: biological and cultural. A trance occurs where it is culturally admissible as an acceptable/appropriate/ desirable form of behavior. In such an environment, then, people learn (with the assistance of strong sensory stimuli, e.g., music) to control those parts of the brain that are usually considered uncontrollable. The result is a strong, psycho-physical experience, again reconfirmed by the subsequent pleasure.

UNLOCKING THE GROOVE OF HABIT[40]
Zuzana Jurková

The presented genres of EDM differ in many ways: the club form of free tekno is, after all, more adapted to a city, while its natural form brings out initial alternative values more obviously[41]; minority and elite psytrance best reveal a sophisticated complexity aiming at a parallel reality. Nevertheless, they have the basics in common: they aspire to "unlock the groove of habit," to create an alternative space disentangled from the dominant surveillance of limiting institutions and omnipotent commerce (understood as other forms of surveillance, that is, surveillance of finances), space for one's own creativity. And again, we emphasize that this attempt does not only reflect; these genres are its instrument.

If we understand ethnomusicology as a discipline combining musical and non-musical anthropological data in its argumentation, then EDM provides ideal material. The first turn is taken by an anthropologist and the data s/he collects in clubs and at parties.

In the club form of free tekno at the Cross Club, escape from institutions and surveillance does not seem as striking as its outdoor form at Andělka. A more-or-less accidental guest, however, is surprised by the atmosphere of freedom, disorganization (which can appear a bit like chaos), the way people freely flow and are not particularly interested in the existing schedule (a fan of classical music where everything begins with minute precision would probably be confused), by the way they chat during the music as if it were not being played even while simultaneously indicating that they like it...

This breaking free from surveillance and the resulting experience of freedom is, however, perfectly apparent at free parties. The conspiracy with which the venue is kept secret until the last minute seems necessary so that "Big Brother" and his institution – the police – won't prevent the event from taking

---

40 "Unlocking the Groove" is the title of Butler's 2006 book . The author explains it as a metaphor in which he uses the technical term EDM in the broader sense.

41 The book by Marta Kolářová et al. (2011) was published only after Peter had written his text. In this book, there is a chapter by Ondřej Slačálek dedicated to free tekno.

place.[42] This is, however, mainly a "game" – at a time when an owner offers his land – that is, permits some sort of official realization of a party – the whole event becomes almost uninteresting.[43] It might seem to many that such refusal of "free space" contradicts the real longing for freedom. But that is not the way it is: persecution is necessarily a part of experienced escape from the system. Viewers of the film *Matrix* by the Wachowski brothers, mentioned in the next chapter, know what we are talking about.

Total non-commerciality is clear in all of the described events. Taking place in a city, however, understandably sometimes collides with the practical necessity of some charges, perhaps for rent. Therefore, such "real" free tekno or psytrance events[44] often take place outside of Prague. However, it is necessary to add that at psytrance events, because of the characteristic emphasis on esthetics, the related need for decorations and above all, the selectiveness in choice of venues, an entrance fee is also typically charged outside of Prague.

The DIY ethos is also much more obvious at events outside of urban areas. It is possible to view it as versatile artistic creativity of the systems, but also in how literally every participant must guide him- or herself because there are no posters providing precise instructions: participants must be interested in the events, find out the venue (in a relatively complicated way), get there (again, not an entirely simple task), and do so with their own equipment... And even if they do not belong to any soundsystem, they can contribute to the atmosphere with what they can do (in Peter's text there is, for example, mention of a fire show). Particularly strong emphasis on creativity is evident in psytrance: the "BIO" psytrance festival decorations are produced several weeks in advance while the organizer tries to coordinate them visually with the space and theme of the event. The theme of the festival is announced in advance so that the guests can creatively prepare for it on their own; the guests then complete the harmony of the place by producing smaller decorations which they then place around the space or with which they thematically decorate their huts or tents... Basic emphasis is placed on the novelty and surprise of the decoration and mainly on its psychedelic character.

---

42 One of the informants mentions a further reason for the conspiracy: to keep information about the event secret from the "lizards" ("lizards" are, in free tekno vocabulary, snobs who show their external attributes and who, according to other tekno participants, don't understand the real values of EDM).

43 In 2007, that is, two years after the famous brutal repression of CzekTek by the police, the organizers declined an offer of a landowner. Today, however, rental of lands is quite frequent for free parties (Krásno near Karlsbad, Bratronice).

44 The expression "real" is in quotation marks because, for the anthropologist, every realized event is real. Here we use it to indicate the evaluation by the participants themselves.

In the context of the initial alternative philosophy, we also mentioned corporeality undergone through a bodily experience. This is provided by electronic **dance** music to the highest degree, more than by other genres to which one can **also dance,** because EDM is realized through dance. Only the fact that people dance means that it is real EDM.

As the final – last but not least – element referring to the American alternative 1960s, let us mention what Ginsberg states as one of two basic conditions for escape from everyday life[45]: drugs. And in the harmless club form its consummation is commonplace; experiences caused by drugs bring on – as their consumers[46] attest – in the ideal case the feeling of "infinite space" and oneness, some sort of local variant of the "global society" of which Ginsberg spoke.

The experiences of an anthropologist provide multidimensional proofs about EDM as an attempt at escape – or a sort of real, but temporary, escape – from unwelcome dominant social reality. Let us accept the biblical instruction that *"A matter must be established by the testimony of two or three witnesses."*[47],[48] The second witness will be a musicologist analyzing EDM **musical language.**

The material of this language is electronically generated (or unrecognizably adjusted) sound which does not refer to sounds from the ordinary world. The first, perhaps just short-lived, sound experience, already carries the listener over to non-ordinary reality. And in it, a process takes place totally differing from ordinary musical processes and, for that matter, also non-musical ones.

In connection with the new ideas of John Cage, we mention his concept of independent activity of sound in the third chapter: in the original, Cage uses the term "indeterminacy." It is exactly in this point that he was an innovator: the absolute superiority of Western music, classical as well as popular, not only before Cage, but also after him, is in the majority "determined." Determined in the sense that it is fixed in a written or another way. The reason for the visual fixing is, however, deeper than merely so that musicians don't forget what they are to play. The composer uses it primarily in order to guide the listener along some sort of musical path. Therefore, he acquaints him with material that develops (this is the determinacy of what follows by what has preceded, which Cage wanted to abolish); he uses forms that help him to develop this road, repetitions of different parts, the principle of contrast...

45 The second request is an Indian guru; we can find his traces in the family tree of psytrance.
46 These, however, immediately point out the possibility of the so-called bad trip caused either by a bad drug or by a bad internal "setting" of the consumer.
47 Deuteronomy 19:15b.
48 In the social sciences this approach is called *triangulation* and is understood as a method meant ensure the credibility of the findings.

The EDM language is built on other principles. Its basic unit is the **loop** – a rhythmic figure realized in several sound colors which repeatedly return[49]. The concept of repeated rhythmic cycles brings us close to the Indian (and Middle-Eastern) musical traditions which again are connected to the traditional cyclic understanding of time. Or it is possible to see the inspiration in an industrial environment with cyclically repeating sounds of factory production.

In any case, the basis of the musical language of EDM is the layering of repeated *loops* of various colors and various lengths.[50] In perceiving it, a participant falls into another experience of time: returning time without causes or consequences. What's more, the experience of repeating *loops* alone is personified/realized through dance: dance, which is not the road from A to B because it is "infinite."[51,52]

Such an infinite, cyclically returning experience, and thanks to one's own dance, a co-creation of other time, are strengthened by further factors: high tempo and high volume, which produce physical feedback. In the snapshot from Cross, Jan describes his feeling of a quick run which is provoked by the fast, booming beats of a bass drum. In front of a soundsystem at a free party (more than in the club, even it is also true there) the strength of a physical experience, the whole body overwhelmed by the sound, is crucial: according to Peter, at Andělka most of the people were crowded in front of the biggest, and thus the loudest, soundsystems. One of his informants says, *I could stand ten meters from those boxes and until they turned them off I couldn't move because it was a terribly strong sound and the pressure of the sound that I normally felt gave me knots in my stomach, my intestines, my heart...*

In the film *Česká RAPublika* (Czech RAPublic),[53] in a dialogue with distinguished classical musicians, a rapper explains the sense of loudness in the following way: *You get information about music; we are immersed in music. EDM dancers experience much more than just all-pervading and infinite music: they themselves are, by means of their bodies, a part of it.* Peter's informant explains: *...If I feel like it sometimes... I stick my head into a box, perhaps for a half-hour... I think constantly, but here I completely turn off. In short, some know how to meditate, to sit*

49 Other sounds are also arranged in loops: effects, synthesized melodies, etc.
50 Recent years have seen the prevalence of the approach that "the better the live act/track, the less detectible the loops." But this does not change much in that they still are the basis of the musical language.
51 Here let us recall that the ability of DJs to create an uninterrupted flow of music by mixing records is considered one of the basic conditions for the rise of EDM.
52 Peter suggested an interpretation focused on the dancer, whose habits and also technical and chemical means placed him in the center of a story (*trip*), the backstage of which is represented by *loops* and, at the same time, the unending growth of energy which is called *rise* by the EDM producers.
53 Film director Pavel Abrahám, 2008.

and turn off the flow of thoughts. And this is fast enough and a sort of easy way, if you have it in your nature, to stop the flow of thoughts.

The cornerstone of data from both realms is the **soundsystem**. It is primarily a technical device which reproduces the required sounds – with appropriate strength, which – as we have seen – is of essential importance. In addition – and, from the point of view of an anthropologist, first and foremost – the soundsystem is a group of people realizing their concept by means of the soundsystem as an instrument. DJs, VJs, their assistants... and because ethnomusicology recognizes the premise that "music is created by the listeners," which holds true in the case of dancing EDM listeners, dancers are undoubtedly also immediate members of a soundsystem. Here, in front of a wall of loud speakers, is – in Ginsberg's words – space for "escape from oppression of the government", space "to enter infinite space"... Space for escape here has at least two meanings. On the one hand, it is the society of those who profess the same values – and also behave according to them; those whose agreement I necessarily need for self-confirmation. Some sort of peculiar *communitas* of the technical age. And, secondly, it is space for even more radical escape: with the help of various hallucinogens, the unceasing booming music with physical and other sensorial stimulations, and also with the agreement of the others (see box: Judith Becker on music and trance) the dancers – this time each one separately – break into a totally different reality, where neither institutional surveillance nor the dictates of money worry them in the least.

HARE KRISHNA MANTRA IN PRAGUE STREETS: THE SACRED, MUSIC AND TRANCE

Zuzana Jurková and Veronika Seidlová

It's a warm sunny Wednesday afternoon in April, 2011. I'm standing on Republic Square (*Náměstí Republiky*) in Prague, a place crowded with tourists blocking my view and I'm getting a bit nervous. I've come across Czech Hare Krishnas singing and dancing in their orange and white robes in the Prague Old Town so many times before, but now, when I deliberately want to join their regular music procession, I simply cannot find them. From the official website of the Czech Hare Krishna movement I've learned that they start their Nagar-kirtans[1] (devotional singing in the town) every Wednesday and Friday at 4 p.m. from here. It's now 4.15 p.m.; I've been waiting here for half an hour and nothing…and this square is so large… Finally, I hear some drumming and see a few orange robes on the corner of the luxurious Art Nouveau Municipal House. The little group starts moving and turns the corner to Příkopy Street … I quickly join the end of the procession where there are two young ladies in colorful saris. I am walking with the procession for the first time. I don't know the devotees personally, nor do they know me. I did, however, talk to one of the representatives of the movement about my research and he encouraged me to go and see the harinam (another name for the Hare Krishna Nagar-kirtan) anytime unannounced.

The group is walking quite fast, close together, in twos and threes, playing instruments and dancing while clapping their hands, and, with or without instruments, nearly all of them chant the Hare Krishna mantra:

"*Hare Krishna Hare Krishna
Krishna Krishna Hare Hare
Hare Rama Hare Rama
Rama Rama Hare Hare.*"

They keep singing only these words, though in many different tunes. The tempo and melody are changed and set by the leader of the group in a call and response pattern, the leader singing one phrase, the group repeating the whole phrase after him. All the melodies are simple, generally in a regular four-beat meter, with a one voice

---

1   *Hare* is another name for the gods Vishnu and Krishna; the word *nam* means name.

line, easy for people to repeat and even memorize. The group also chants the most typical tune of this mantra commonly heard in India (though Indians usually chant the words in a different sequence: Hare Rama, Hare Rama, Rama Rama, Hare Hare, Hare Krishna, Hare Krishna, Krishna Krishna, Hare Hare). The tune goes as follows:

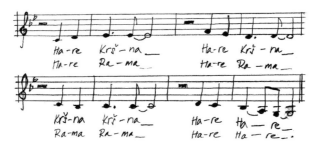

One of the famous versions of a Hare Krishna mantra tune; it was also heard in the musical Hair.[2] Transcription by Veronika Seidlová

I can count sixteen people altogether in the procession; men exceed women in numbers (twelve to four). Gradually, I also find out that the procession members are more or less lined up according to a certain ideal pattern which might reflect a certain hierarchy. Men and women walk separately; first men, women behind them.

Four men in their 40s and 50s lead the procession. They wear Indian shirts and dhotis,[3] both of orange color, which is a color traditionally worn by Hindu monks. This traditional Indian outfit is interestingly combined with modern sport shoes, trekking sandals and socks in many colors. All of these men have a particular white marking on their foreheads (tilak)[4] – a sign of the Vaishnavas.[5] In appearance, male Vaishnavas - especially the monks - are usually easily recognizable not only by the aforementioned tilak, but also by a specific hairstyle called shikha. This Sanskrit word refers to a long tuft or lock of hair left on top or on the back of the shaven head.[6] A quite extravagant hairstyle by European standards, this is also worn by the

2   This tune can be heard both in the stage version of the musical of 1967 (music by Galt MacDermot and text by James Rado and Gerome Ragni) and in the film version directed by Miloš Forman from 1979.

3   traditional Indian men's garments, rectangular pieces of unstitched cloth, usually around seven yards long, wrapped around the waist and the legs and knotted at the waist

4   Tilak(a) is colored clay with which devotees of various Hinduistic streams make marks on their bodies.

5   Vaishnavism is a tradition of Hinduism, distinguished from other schools by its worship of Vishnu or his associated Avatars, principally as Rama and Krishna, as the original and supreme God. Source: http://en.wikipedia.org/wiki/Sikha; The Hare Krishna movement was founded in 1966 in New York City by A. C. Bhaktivedanta Swami Prabhupada as part of the broader Gaudiya Vaishnava movement founded by Chaitanya Mahaprabhu (1486–1534) in India in the 16th century. Source: http://en.wikipedia.org/wiki/Gaudiya_Vaishnavism

6   Though traditionally all male Hindus were required to wear a shikha, today it is seen almost only among Hindu celibate monks and temple priests. However, Swami Prabhupada made

four men in orange. From close up, I also notice small wooden beads on their necks – a third compulsory feature of a Krishna devotee.

The procession of Hare Krishna devotees is one of very few more-or-less regular opportunities to hear live music in the Prague streets. This unusualness, further strengthened by the clear spirituality of the procession, is quite unexpected for those of us brought up with ideas of enlightenment stressing the importance of the separation of the church (sacral) and the civic (profane) and, thus, the exclusion of the sacred from civic space. Some people even seem wary of it. Orange robes, the partly-shaved heads of men and red marks on the foreheads of women, unusual melodies and musical instruments – all of this attracts attention and begs an explanation.

SACRED MUSIC?[7]

In listing the universals of music (which itself is a cultural universal) Bruno Nettl writes about second place (after singing):

> In all societies, music is found in religious ritual – it is almost everywhere a mainstay of sacred ceremonies – leading some scholars to suggest that perhaps music was actually invented for humans to have a special way of communicating with the supernatural. And, too, it seems that, in all cultures, music is used in some sense for transforming ordinary experience – such as producing anything from trance in ritual to edification in a concert.[8]

Leaving aside the argument about the origin of music for the time being, there is no doubt about the dense connection between music and the sacred. There are also ample reasons for stating its use in the transformation of ordinary

---

it a compulsory sign for all the male members of his Hare Krishna movement. He often referred to the *shikha* as a *"flag,"* a term which illustrates the idea that the body is a temple with a flag on top. Srila Prabhupada felt that the *shikha* hairstyle was an important facet of his Krishna Consciousness movement, indeed a vital facet: *"I have no objection if members of the Society dress like nice American gentlemen; but in all circumstances a devotee cannot avoid tilak, flag on head, and beads on neck. These are essential features of a Vaisnava.'"* Source: http://en.wikipedia.org/wiki/Sikha

7   In this text we use the expression "sacred" to designate music which is used for religious occasions in the broadest sense, which means when *existential experience of our relation to anything which transcends individual life* (Sokol 1998: 11) is discussed. Thus we do not accept Volek's distinction between sacred music and uses *which became part of liturgical rites* (1998: 24) and spiritual music in a broader sense. This distinction is difficult to apply in other than very petrified religious forms.

8   Nettl 2001: 9.

experience. It seems to us quite possible to connect both features stated separately by Nettl: the omnipresence of music in spiritual rituals and its ability to transform the experience of the time. This is an easy connection if we accept Sokol's idea that the roots of religions can be found in holidays and their (collective) celebrations.[9] First of all, it seems very probable that this could also include the origin of at least some kinds of music, perhaps merely for the almost exclusive collectivity of music, requiring performers as well as listeners. The ability to organize a collective (dances, liturgy, etc.) is also relevant. Secondly, continuing with Sokol's concept, a holiday and its celebration turn attention from the ordinary and temporary (of this time) toward the transcendental (thus, into different – even time – space). Such a transformation of time is in the very substance of music: its course brings the participant into a different time-space through tempo changes, the punctuation of time, etc. One more feature of music corresponds to the celebration of holidays: its impracticality, i.e. it is seemingly useless.[10]

All this – its collectivity, special organization of time and impracticality – lies in the anthropological fundaments entailing the symbiosis of the celebrations (primarily religious) of holidays and music.

THEORETICAL REFLECTIONS

Theoretical reflections upon this striking universal symbiosis of music and the sacred lead out in different directions. One of them – currently prevailing in Western musicology – is summarized by Tomislav Volek[11] who, however, mainly examines the material of European Christian churches. He considers sacral music to be that which is used for the liturgy of the Roman Catholic Church and Protestant services. The form of this music evidently differs depending on the confession as well as the time. Volek adopts the basic idea from the Greek musicologist Thrasybulos Georgiades (1961). Musical features do not, in his view, make music sacred. It is the sanctification, the function of music, that does this. Moreover, sanctifying is only "*das Weihende*," the sanctifying word. The sacredness of music is thus conditioned by the sacredness of the word.

Another direction in reflecting upon sacred music can be called *universalistic* explanations: music and the sacred coexist symbiotically since their natures

---

9   Sokol 2004.
10   Some musical styles certainly coordinate, e.g., work activity or movements, but it is not possible to explain the origin of all kinds of music through this function.
11   Volek 1998.

are necessarily joined, either because they are directed by the same rules or because they share a casual connection. Although today's Western musicology is dominated by the direction first described, this second direction should not be overlooked. Its roots are in ancient Pythagorean harmonics: Socrates (as quoted in Plato's *Republic*) believed that musical modes are the primary milieu where moderation in clear form rules and that they are thus basic models for virtues. The chief representative of this direction is the Florentine Renaissance humanist Marsilio Ficino (1433–99), whose thoughts resonate with the ideas of Plotinus (3rd century), as well as the Arab-Islamic theorists, above all Al-Kindi (9th century).

The framework of Ficino's thoughts is the idea of the "ensouled" world, where all subjects produce vibrations. They compose the music of the spheres, the general harmony of the universe which gives power (and, thus, also meaning) to the words/sounds of an individual. Ideally, music is the expression of this harmony accessible through the senses. Ficino, although a physician, considered the effects of music more powerful than medicine.

Ficino's work *De Divino Furore [Divine Furor]* (1959) is especially relevant for our text since he is concerned with songs performed in a state of "prophetic furor." According to Ficino, prophetic furor is a state in which heavenly beings rule over the soul, or the soul of a man wanders in ecstasy in supernatural space. The sources of singing in this state are *the similitudes linking heaven and earth.*[12] More concretely: *magical music allows humans to close, at various points and at will, the circle of similitude which constitutes the universe.*[13] To concretize Ficino's ideas we need to add that the soul should be molded by liturgy, the disciplined arts (including prayer as well as pictorial and musical practice),[14] and only then can the soul, in a state of possession, meet transfiguring images originating in different types of realities.

Ficino had, in the European tradition, many followers such as Johannes Kepler (1571–1630), who – in his summa of modern mathematics, *The Harmonies of the World* (James 1993) – measures the exact movement of the planets, compares the differences in their speeds, and deduces musical intervals.[15] Another of his followers, Isaac Newton (1643–1727), remained convinced his entire life that *the soul of the world, which propels into movement this body of the universe visible to us,*

---

being constructed of ratios which created from themselves a musical concord, must of necessity produce musical sounds...[16]

The last in the row of European thinkers mentioned here is the French anthropologist Claude Lévi-Strauss (1908–2009). He sees music as revealing basic laws (of mind, which are, however, at the same time absolute laws): *music and mythology bring man face to face with potential objects of which only the shadows are actualized, with conscious approximations...of inevitably unconscious truths which follow from them.*[17] How similar to the ideas of Ficino (whom Lévi-Strauss does not mention, but considers Plotinus, along with Ficino, as his muse). Music uncovers, through the visible heavenly order, the unconscious truth or *the similitudes linking heaven and earth.*

If this universalistic line of reflection of sacred music is marginal in the European tradition of past centuries, it is, on the contrary, common in non-European cultures. Surprisingly close to Plato's formulation is the discourse of some classical texts of Chinese Confucianism related to the mutual relation of music and social conditions: *music of an ordered empire is calm; music praises the harmony of its government. The music of a disordered empire is painful and thus expresses the suffering of its people.* (Yu Ti – Diary on Music).[18] Music is thus a sort of microcosm ruled by the same order – the Order of Heaven – as the whole universe.

On the contrary, the North American Blackfoot Indians (like many other North American tribes) understand the relation between the supernatural realm, music and human reality as causal:

In many Native American cultures, songs are thought to come into existence principally in dreams or visions... Music has supernatural power. In Blackfoot culture, it is the song that, as it were, holds the power. Thus, each act must have its appropriate song. In a ceremony in which a medicine man is trying to influence the weather, he will have a bundle of objects which he opens and displays, but their supernatural power is not activated until the appropriate song is sung.[19]

Both of the above-mentioned examples thus represent the universalistic connection of music and the supernatural realm, although, it is firstly understood as analogical and secondly as causal.

The undoubted representative of the universalistic line is also the Indian tradition, which is so strongly presented on the sidewalks of today's Prague

---

16 James 1993: 167.
17 Lévi-Strauss 1983: 17–18.
18 Quoted according to Dvorská 1990.
19 Nettl 2001b: 262.

Women in the procession (photo: Veronika Seidlová)

when the Hare Krishna procession walks and dances there. First, Veronika will accompany them on their regular route to the Góvinda restaurant, where their weekly production ends. We will then try to lay the fundaments for understanding what is actually happening in today's streets of Prague by giving a brief characterization of traditional Indian understanding of sound.

One of the four men in orange is undisputedly the main leader of the whole procession. Walking at a consistently fast pace, he plays an Indian harmonium hanging on a thick belt over his shoulder, the instrument positioned before him. For those who have never seen or played an Indian harmonium, it can be described as a massive wooden box, half a meter long, approximately 30 cm wide and almost as tall, where air is pumped inside with the left hand and keys are played with the right one. Although it was given the adjective "portable" when it was brought by Christian missionaries from France to India during the mid-19th century, the missionaries were obviously not expected to play this heavy instrument (around 10 kg, but can weigh up to 17). In India, where it was further and uniquely developed by Indians adjusting it to their musical needs and became an inherent part of the Indian sound environment (and especially of Hindu and Sikh devotional group singing), it is mostly played while seated on the floor. I have to admire the physical condition of the Hare Krishna group leader, who carries the harmonium for the next two full hours - and he is not only simultaneously play-

ing, pumping the air and walking at the same time, but is also the lead singer for the whole procession! He enthusiastically sings into the portable head-set microphone, and later he even adds little jumps and dance steps.

Another devotee in orange plays the double-headed clay drum mridangam, which hangs on his body in a hand-made cloth case with a belt – the case embroidered with a picture of the black head of the God Jagannath.[20] The third man in orange is playing kartals, the hand-held brass Indian cymbals about twenty centimeters in diameter, and the fourth man in orange next to him raises his hands above his head, singing and dancing. Behind them walks a younger member of the movement in a white dhoti and white Indian shirt, also with a shaven head and a shikha and with little Gandhi-like glasses. On a belt he carries a big speaker, wirelessly connected to the singing leader's microphone. He is followed by two bhaktas, disciples who are not yet full members of the movement. They can be identified by their locks of hair, as their heads are not yet shaved. One of them wears cargo pants with a plain shirt and plays the mridangam, the other one in ethnic-like cotton pants and shirt claps his hands and sings. Behind them I can see slightly older men who obviously are not members, but supporters of the movement – a man with long blond hair in shorts, who plays the mridangam, a man in cargo pants and an orange cap playing small kartals, a burly man in his fifties sporting a smile on his sweating face as he sings, and finally a long-haired man with a big backpack and resembling a homeless person. Bringing up the rear of the procession are three younger women and a lady in her fifties, obviously the mother of one of them. All the young ones have long braided hair and wear an Indian sari with an unusually long blouse and sneakers. The older lady wears a Panjabi dress (Indian woman's dress made from a longer tunic, trousers and shawl) but without the shawl. All of them chant, clap their hands and walk with special little dance steps in a zigzag manner, two steps to the left, two to the right.[21]

Various tourists follow the procession, for a while taking pictures, but apart from two curious Japanese girls nobody keeps walking as long as I do. There is actually one more member of the parade, although he is not part of it, nor is he singing or dancing. He is a young Krishna devotee in a cream-colored dress who rotates around offering fresh handmade coconut sweets[22] to the tourists, and to the Czechs he sometimes offers a book with Czech translations of the movement's theology. This offer is followed by a request for a donation.

Leaving the broad pedestrian zone of Příkopy Street, we soon arrive at Můstek and merge into the crowd on a narrow walkway that leads up the right side of Wenceslas Square (Václavské náměstí). On one side, shop window displays, sausage

---

20   Jagannath is considered an aspect of the god Vishnu or his avatar Krishna.
21   In his ethnographic study of the environment of the Czech ISKSON, Jaroslav Klepal calls this movement a *swami step* (Klepal 2005: 117).
22   During another harinam I met a devotee who offered biscuits labeled "karma free."

Dancing and singing the mantras in front of the astronomical clock in Old Town
(photo: Veronika Seidlová)

and tobacco stands; on the other, locals hastily on their way and tourists walking at
a leisurely pace. People naturally make way for us, waiting till the procession passes
while watching it curiously and continuously taking photos – if not with a camera or
camcorder then at least with a mobile phone. It is interesting to watch their smiling
faces and positive reactions as they observe the joyously singing and dancing Hare
Krishnas – not once have I seen an upset face, nor have I heard complaints about having to make space for the procession. We constantly pass by smiling people, and some
of the onlookers, usually youngsters, even start fooling around for a while, euphor-
ically screaming. Even a businessman in a suit smacks another one on the shoulder
and shouts: "The hell with everything, let's join them, what do you say?" None of them
really join though.

In reaching the top of Wenceslas Square, we walk around the statue of St.
Wenceslas mounted on his horse and descend the other side of the square. The Rus-
sian-speaking shopkeepers on Melantrichova Street come out of their shops with glass
and souvenirs, exchanging looks and greetings with the Hare Krishnas as if they were
old acquaintances.

The astronomical clock shows exactly 4:50 p.m. as we arrive at Old Town Square.
Crowds of tourists are already waiting here to take a snapshot of the famous moving clock as soon as it strikes five. Something unexpected happens here. The devotees
stop walking and start playing on the spot. Then they start moving in a circle while
dancing with both hands raised above their heads and singing the mantra with even

more energy than before. The tempo of the music is getting faster and faster, the sound louder and louder. The tourists, bored with waiting, watch them curiously. A group of maybe thirty young Italians are standing closest to the Hare Krishnas. A few of them, maybe a bit tipsy and showing off, immediately join the circle and start dancing too. Within a few minutes almost all of the thirty Italians form a disco-like "snake" and are joined by exultant Englishmen and a mix of other foreigners. Suddenly, a wild mass of maybe sixty people is whirling around! The drummers are crazily banging the drums and the leader of the harinam is now practically shouting the mantra in the microphone, bending backwards as if he didn't have a harmonium but an electric guitar in his hands. The dancing mass seems to go completely wild. The sound is so loud that you can't hear your own voice, not to mention the mechanical crowing of the cock on the clock which should perform any minute and which is actually the thing all the tourists are waiting for. The Hare Krishnas seem to be completely carried away. Yet their timing is perfect – exactly one minute before the clock strikes five, the drummers give a few last big slow strokes, the leader shouts the last "Hare Krishna!" and the dancers burst out laughing, catching their breath and wiping sweat off their foreheads. As soon as this spontaneous happening is over, the cock on the astronomical clock finally crows, Death starts moving her hand holding the hourglass and the apostles start appearing in the little windows. The crowd claps hands and the devotees of Krishna, quietly drumming, set off towards the Charles Bridge....

(I must leave them at this moment since I have a compulsory PhD. seminar at the University.)

I join the harinam again the following week. The leader of the procession is the same, though some of its members are different. However, the group is as big as last time with the same division of roles, instruments, etc. This week, the weather has turned unexpectedly chilly, so all the devotees are wrapped up in large woolen shawls and thick fleece sweatshirts. Nevertheless, they can still be seen from quite far away since they are now carrying a big dark red velvet banner with golden embroidered words of the Hare Krishna mantra.

They follow the same route and timing as last time and, on Old Town Square at 4:50 p.m., I surprisingly witness exactly the same scene with excited dancing in the circle together with another group of spontaneous young male tourists from southern Europe.[23] Today, the devotees somehow seem to be even more exultant than last week. One young man in orange, who carries a heavy wireless speaker on a shoulder strap, is dancing as if it weighed nothing, practically flying above the ground.

23 It seems that "dances with tourists" are influenced by the season, i.e., the tourist season. In the harinam in which I participated in January 2012, the devotees crossed the nearly empty Old Town Square without stopping. The only people who joined in their music and danced spontaneously were homeless men and women with plastic bottles of wine in front of the Municipal House. In winter, a punk who begged behind the procession also joined the harinam.

Later, while walking towards Charles Bridge, this devotee also distributes little leaflet-stickers advertising the oldest ISKCON vegetarian restaurant Góvinda at Palmovka. The leaflet is in Czech and invites us to the singing of mantras, readings from the Vedas and a degustation every Thursday at 6 p.m. Along with a personal invitation for Thursday, he also gives me a little 3 x 3 cm orange paper, printed in English on one side and in Czech on the other. It reads:

"Chant Hare Krishna [...]Rama Rama Hare Hare And be happy! This mantra meditation is an ancient method used to free the mind and soul from the miseries experienced in this material world. Its chanting purifies the heart and leads one to the self-realization and the perfection of human life. www.Harekrsna.cz."

This man would have liked to talk to me more, but he is carrying the speaker and cannot linger behind. The leaders are already calling for him to move forward. We are now passing through Karlova, perhaps the busiest medieval street in Prague, and are approaching a little square in front of the Charles Bridge. We have to wait here for the lights to change to cross a road with cars and trams, and this provides us with another opportunity to make a little happening with others waiting.

The next clearly ordinary stop is a place under the bridge tower. Here, the stone walls and ceiling amplify the drums so much that the volume becomes both great and almost unbearable. The devotees have evidently looked forward to this acoustic effect and clearly enjoy it, their eyes absently shining, faces smiling with even more joy (if this is possible). The tempo of the music gradually increases as they ecstatically bang on their instruments, jump in place or spin in a circle, fully immersed in the music. It seems as if they (and particularly the leader) are falling into something of a trance, or an altered state of mind, but the whole thing lasts very shortly, maybe a minute or less...or maybe it just feels short, because just watching them gives me goose bumps and makes my eyes water, and I feel a bit lost. The Hare Krishna girls are waving to me to join them dancing, but I just cannot take my eyes off the leader. Before I find myself "back," it is over and they have already started walking back, taking the same street to Old Town Square.

Interestingly, the second stop on the Square today does not cause the same effect as the first one. I suppose this is because it is 5:30 p.m. and there are not enough bored tourists waiting for the astronomical clock. Nevertheless, the Hare Krishnas seem to enjoy the harinam more and more, just playing for themselves. By now, they have been playing, singing and dancing intensively while walking for an hour and a half without so much as a little break, some of them carrying heavy instruments. They do not seem tired at all, but full of energy.

On Celetná Street, the procession attracts some young people who walk with us up to the Powder Tower and in front of the Municipal House, where the devotees stop and play for a few minutes. It is 5:45 p.m. and the harinam finishes with the last few strong beats of the drums and a wild improvisation on the harmonium, while shouting, "Hare Krishna!" Then they quickly and smoothly pack their things into a car,

obviously highly experienced in this task, and are ready to move to the nearby Góvinda restaurant (run by the Czech ISKCON) on Soukenická Street, where a program for
the public starts at 6 p.m. I am immediately approached by the girls, who warmly
invite me to the event. We chat as we walk there and I tell them about my fieldwork
on mantra singing in the Czech Lands and I am told that the Hare Krishna mantra
is the best because it purifies the heart of all who listen to it, and that is why this kirtan (public devotional chanting) is done. I also learn about the harinam leader: he is
59 years old (which I find hard to believe as he looks at least twenty years younger),
has a rock band and has been leading the Prague harinams for the last thirteen years.

By the time we reach the tearoom of the vegetarian restaurant, there are already
about ten people waiting for the program to start. Another ten people join later. The
harinam leader is already there, setting up a microphone on a low stage. Then, while
sitting crossed legs, he plays and sings together with a drummer and a kartal player
for one more hour with the public answering in a call and response pattern. The rep-
ertory contains not only the Hare Krishna mantras, but also devotional songs about
Krishna. The public consists of both the official devotees and friends of the movement.
People are sitting on low chairs, singing and clapping their hands. No dancing or going "wild"... The performance is followed by a lecture from the Bhagavad Gita and by a
Prasadam – a vegetarian Indian dinner free or paid for on a donation basis. The whole
event finishes slightly after 9 p.m. Some of the devotees go to their Temple in Lužce,
where they live.[24] Other occasions for meeting are the one-day Ratha-yatra festival,
the so-called Festival of Vehicles in mid-July, when the big music-dance procession of
devotees pull an eleven-meter-high chariot with deities,[25] or an August music festival
in Trutnov, where the Krishna devotees have for years had their own stage featuring
mantras in non-traditional arrangements.[26]

SACRED SOUNDS OF INDIA

For an understanding of what is actually happening during a Prague harinam,
let us turn our attention to the traditional Indian understanding of sound and
word. In Indian cosmology, the importance of sound is so fundamental that
some researchers resort to sonic theology.[27] To explain this concept, they usu-

---

24 The Temple Shri Shri Navadvipachandra and the Center for Vedic Studies are part of the
    international society ISKCON and have been located in Lužce since 2011, when the Prague
    devotees bought and reconstructed the edifice and built the temple space, the kitchen, and
    the bedrooms for men and women. For more details http://www.harekrsna-luzce.cz/kdo-
    jsme.php [April 29, 2013].
25 http://www.rathayatra.cz/index.htm [April 29, 2013].
26 http://www.festivaltrutnov.cz/ [April 29, 2013].
27 See Beck 1993, and, consequently, Burchett 2010.

ally go back to the oldest Vedic text – Rigveda – where the term *Vak* appears; two of its several meanings are relevant for us: (a) speech generally and (b) the goddess Vak as the revealing Word. In the Rigveda and the Atharva-Veda there is a hymn to the goddess Vak:

> I am the one who says, by myself, what gives joy to gods and men. Whom I love I make awesome; I make him a sage, a wise man, a Brahman. (8) I am the one who blows like the wind, embracing all creatures. Beyond the sky, beyond the earth, so much have I become in my greatness.[28]

The terminological merging of speech and its godly personification reveal much: among other things, the emphasis of aural and oral aspects of language, its ability to communicate with the sacred realm and also its understanding as a principle of productive energy. The goddess Vak was later identified with the developing concept of Brahman, the Absolute. This concept of language as a powerful sacred (active) sound also permeates other Brahman literature.

The basic term of sonic theology is the word *mantra*. Its nature is already clearly understandable from its etymology: the Sanskrit root *man* (= to think) is connected with the instrumental ending *tra*, expressing that mantras are instruments, bearers (in the sense of an agent) of ideas or – as Burchett suggests – *an instrument of producing (a special kind of) thought*.[29]

Beck's description of a mantra, one of the shortest there is, can be used: *A mantra is a chant formula of words and syllables in the Sanskrit language*[30] with Burchett's addition that *they may constitute a single syllable or an entire hymn; they may convey clear semantic meanings or they may appear completely nonsensical*.[31] Nevertheless, we will come closer to understanding the concept through the respected characteristics of Gonda, who tries not only to catch the emic conceptions, but also the later development from Vedas to Hinduism and Tantrism:

A Mantra is a word believed to be of "superhuman origin," received, fashioned and spoken by inspired "seers," poets and reciters in order to invoke divine power(s) and especially conceived as a means of creating, conveying, concentrating and realizing intentional and efficient thoughts, and of coming in touch with or identifying oneself with the essence of divinity which is present in the mantra.[32]

---

28 Beck 1993: 29.
29 2010: 813.
30 Beck 1993: 31.
31 2010: 813. Burchett writes about uses of mantras for several reasons: besides transcendental, also for very secular reasons.
32 Gonda 1965: 255.

It is also possible to approach mantras from a different angle: through an ancient Indian concept of language. Sanskrit words are not considered simple symbols of reality, i.e. arbitrary labels on reality (a concept common in Western linguistics), but as *sound forms of objects, actions and attributes, relating to the corresponding reality in the same way as the visual forms*,[33] and differing from them only by the medium of perception. This relation of word (signifier) and signified is the intrinsic relation of the word to reality and thus a powerful instrument of influence. Two influential means then merge in mantras: the sound itself of a pronounced word capable of invoking *divine powers* (which is why correct pronunciation is important) and the word as a manifestation of reality that can be manipulated.

We will later discuss several categories of mantras, for all of which it is true, as Jan Gonda writes, that they are perceived not as *products of discursive thoughts, human wisdom or poetic phantasy, but flash-lights of eternal truth, seen by those eminent men who have come into supersensuous contact with the Unseen.*[34]

One more note is appropriate here; it follows the concept of sound as an "objective" communicator with the sacred realm and is related to music. The sound of music is of the same music and, thus, of the same power. That is why in Indian musical theory (here it is difficult to distinguish music aesthetics and music psychology) the concept of *ragas* has developed as an objectified collection of rules of how to shape a musical performance. The concept of *ragas* has a universalistic nature similar to the ideas connected with the effects of words and sounds, meaning it did not take into consideration the individual and cultural biography of the listener. It is wedged into the broader (rasa) theory.[35] Keeping the rules of *ragas*, one of eight fundamental mental states or forms of consciousness (rasa) is supposed to be established, and also the harmonization of the spiritual and concrete physical environment. The *raga* rules determine in which mode (ladder) the music is performed as well as which tones are more important; the way of melodic ornamentation is prescribed, as is the time in which the musical performance should take place. Most often *ragas* are attributed to a three-hour interval in the 24-hour day cycle, but, in some cases to other periods, e.g., to the rainy season.

One might expect more attention to be paid to Indian music theory when discussing mantra singing in the streets of Prague, though this is not necessary since this complex theory mainly tartgets the style most likely described as art music; the simple melodies of mantras do not provide enough material for this.

---

33   Hopkins 1971: 20.
34   Gonda 1963: 247.
35   For more details, see Becker 2004.

The basis for our understanding of the Prague *harinam* is, thus, the Indian concept of mantras. This combines the power of sound (strengthened by singing) as sound invoking "divine powers," and the power of the word which has an immediate relation to reality and which can therefore manipulate it. A closer approach can be attempted by categorizing the mantras and understanding the context of these categories. In our opinion, we come closer not only to Indian and Prague reality, but also to two universal modes of sacred music.

In the following text we will discuss two different concepts of mantras in the sacred context[36]: as a part of the Vedic sacrificial ritual and as part of the Tantric Vaishnavism religious practice or, more specifically, the *Bhakti* movement.

In the Vedic sacrificial ritual *yajna*, mantras, together with sacrificial fire, are the constitutive elements of the ritual and their connection is fundamental for it: Howard even describes the correspondence of the arrangement of stones in the sacrificial altar and mantras which were sung during the placement of the stones.[37] Mantras are agents of sacrifice. Even before the beginning of any ritual event, sacred sounds, mantras, needed to be recited. *If ritual acts and ceremonies are to be performed successfully the consecratory word is an indispensable requirement.* In this sense, the ritual function of mantras is close to the functions of "songs" in the rituals of North American Indians. If the ritual is successful, the right song should be sung and, actually, it is the song which makes the ritual successful.[38]

It was, indeed, the objectivity of the effects of the sacred sounds which necessitated the best possible performance. This was done by the Brahmans, members of the highest Indian caste. They orally transmitted and transmit the way of a ritual's performance, either in families or in the schools/tradition to which they belong. Every school developed its own support system for memorizing long texts which would be recited and also for avoiding mistakes in performance.[39] The second security element for the proper functioning of a sacrificial ritual is a written version with markings indicating the way of performance. Each of the four Vedic texts uses different forms of markings.[40]

While performing mantras as part of the Vedic ritual, an individual's emotional involvement is not considered decisive (a ritual requires complicated

---

36 We are not discussing here the private use of mantras for secular needs, although even this use has a certain supernatural dimension.

37 Howard 2000: 238.

38 Nettl 1989: 128 ff.

39 For more details, see Howard 2000.

40 Marginally: various schools differ in their interpretation of the same performance markings.

rules to be effective); on the contrary, the *Bhakti* movement,[41] in which inner involvement and striking emotionality are fundamental features, takes the opposite approach. If the Czech Hare Krishna devotees call their mantra chanting during regular processions through Prague *kirtans*, they are referring exactly to the Bhakti movement, the egalitarian ideas of which were broadly attractive (understandably in India, strictly divided according to castes). They still seem to be attractive, not only in India, but in the West, too. The Hare Krishna movement is proof of this.

In the narrower sense, the term *kirtan* designates a form in which verse and chorus alternate. More often, however, *kirtan* has a broader meaning: it is devotional singing by which a soloist and a choir alternate in a responsorial way. The Bengali saint Chaitanya (1486–1534) is usually called the originator of *kirtan* singing. He is also considered the founder of the *Gaudiya Vaishnava* movement that Hare Krishna is part of. The above-mentioned emotionality and inner involvement are expressed in the way of singing. Contrary to many Hinduistic directions, modest in their singing of mantras, *Chaitanya and his followers proclaimed that the loud singing of God's name(s) was more effective in the requisition of salvation, since [it] is more expressive and thus conducive of the kind of Bhakti [devotion] sentiments required for the highest spiritual experience, namely, love of God.*[42]

We can consider two of the described modes of mantra use and their contexts as two different ways of approaching the sacred, as well as two different approaches to reality in general: one is through the utmost discipline and exactness, the other through intensive inner involvement, emotionality and spontaneity. Our main focus is on the Prague *harinam*, which we will confront with the above-mentioned Indian theoretical models. Let us first, however, introduce its other phase: a video available on the Internet that the Prague Hare Krishna group uses for presentation purposes and which can be considered an emic voice of Prague's Hare Krishna devotees.

HARINAM THROUGH ITS OWN EYES

Harinam in Prague[43] *is a 24-minute film about the Hare Krishna music procession in Prague, freely downloadable from Google in the Google video section.*

---

41   A Sanskrit term referring to religious devotion in Hinduism, understood as the active involvement of a devotee in divine worship. The term is used within the Vaishnava monotheistic branch of Hinduism, referring to the love felt by the worshipper towards the personal God. Source: http://en.wikipedia.org/wiki/Bhakti (July 26, 2011).

42   Beck 1993: 201.

43   http://video.google.com/videoplay?docid=-8096811527582997164# (March 18, 2012).

The subtitles say that the film was shot and directed in 2007 by a certain "bh. Eze-quiel." The mysterious shortcut "bh." obviously means "bhakta" – a Krishna devotee who has not yet been initiated and therefore has not received a full new name with a suffix – das (servant). After an extensive search I find out that the filmmaker comes from Spain, was 28 when he made the movie, and became a professional filmmaker with experience in advertisements. That all makes sense because Ezequiel made his film Harinam in Prague in such a way that it seems like an advertisement for the Hare Krishna movement. What is really interesting about the movie is the way he made it.

Ezequiel's short film resembles a computer action game. This is achieved by adept-ly made fast cuts, the camera, and mainly by unexpectedly different music. The film doesn't start with the obligatory Indian sound and chanting of the Hare Krishna mantra, but surprisingly with music from The Matrix – the iconic sci-fi action movie!

For those who haven't seen the movie yet: The Matrix is a science fiction action film written and directed by Larry and Andy Wachowski. It was first released in 1999 and became the first installment in the famous Matrix series of films, comic books, video games, and animation. The film depicts a future in which reality as perceived by most humans is actually a simulated reality created by sentient machines to pacify and subdue the human population, while their bodies' heat and electrical ac-tivity is used as an energy source. Upon learning this, computer programmer "Neo" is drawn into a rebellion against the machines, involving other people who have been freed from the "dream world" and into reality. The film contains many references to the cyberpunk and hacker subcultures and to philosophical and religious ideas such as Hinduism (the concept of Maya or "illusion" in Advaita Vedanta philosophy), Plato's Allegory of the Cave, Descartes' evil genius, the Judeo-Christian idea of Mes-sianism; Gnosticism, Buddhism, mystics of Kung-Fu and Occultism, etc. Specifically, it draws on Jean Baudrillard's book Simulacra and Simulation, which is even featured in the Matrix film, and was required reading for the actors. (However, Baudrillard commented that The Matrix misunderstands and distorts his work.) In Postmod-ern discourse, interpretations of The Matrix often reference Baudrillard's philosophy to demonstrate that the movie is an allegory for contemporary experience in a heav-ily commercialized, media-driven society, especially of the developed countries.[44]

Ezequiel clearly draws on the above-mentioned ideas. At the beginning, he in-troduces the streets of Prague – through a red camera filter, he shows an old homeless man on a street on a dark, cold night. The atmosphere of mystery, horror, tension

Source: http://en.wikipedia.org/wiki/The_Matrix and http://www.insidehighered.com/
    views/mclemee/mclemee135 and Meinhold, Roman (2009). *Being in The Matrix: An Example
    of Cinematic Education in Philosophy*. Prajna Vihara. Journal of Philosophy and Religion.
    Bangkok, Assumption University. Vol. 10., No. 1-2, pp. 235-252. ISSN 1513-6442, available
    at http://www.roman-meinhold.com/matrix.pdf

and a certain aggressive, hostile depression is evoked by film symphonic music - fast string and wind instruments quickly alternate and become even faster and louder in contrast to dramatically slow-motion shots of the walking people, "lost" and freezing, of blinding lights and neon signs of the metropolis, of fast foods and casinos. All this is followed by a short, blurred slow-motion shot of a few men with drums and a red banner with a Hare Krishna mantra. Then the camera turns back to the abandoned homeless beggar. We hear a creaking sound of electronics and the crazy cacophony grows stronger and stronger, but suddenly it breaks with the sound of a jet plane just taking off. A pure white quotation without any further comments appears on an empty black screen:

"In this age of quarrel and hypocrisy the only means of deliverance is chanting the holy name of the Lord. There is no other way. There is no other way. There is no other way." Chaitanya Caritamrta Adi 17.21.

While we read the quotation, we hear a few arrhythmic and confused dull strokes. A few seconds later there is the highly dramatic sound of a rising jet. As soon as this sound becomes unbearable, a fast cut suddenly occurs and we hear the rumbling rhythmic electronic music full of deep bass sounds, something that I would call tribal techno.

My colleagues Peter Balog and Veronika Svobodová found out that the music used in Ezequiel's film Harinam in Prague is actually a remix of the song Voodoo People[45] by the group The Prodigy that was used in the Matrix movie. The Prodigy is an English electronic dance music group that achieved mainstream popularity in the 1990s and 2000s (over 25 million records sold worldwide). They make use of various styles ranging from rave, hardcore techno, industrial and breakbeat in the early 1990s to electronic rock with punk vocal elements in later compositions. Similar electronic music can be found in one of the fight scenes of The Matrix where the warriors fly in the air in slow motion as in a computer game.

As in The Matrix, there is a slow-motion shot in Ezequiel's movie capturing the parade of energetic young men in white or orange Indian thin cloth dhotis ("skirts") drumming in the streets of Prague - they resemble fighters or action movie heroes. Bundled up in sweatshirts and caps, they proudly carry the Hare Krishna banner and dance. They jump in the same rhythm; some of them have their gloved hands raised above their heads. Farther behind them, we can see cheerful Hare Krishna women in long skirts as well as ordinary passers-by. Electronic music is complemented by the recurring shouts of men as a kind of tribal inspiration.

Then the pictures purposely start moving fast, in scattered shots. In a fast spinning sequence, we see a man waving from a car, the harinam leader with a portable microphone, another devotee with an amplifier on his back which looks like a little

---

45   The composition was also recognized by the software Shazam. March 19, 2012.

do-it-yourself mobile techno soundsystem, and a drunken young Rom yelling "Hare Krishna!"; then once again we see the leader, who is both the main vocalist and a harmonium player, with the instrument strapped to him – he is bending backwards in ecstasy, in a pose like a rock star with a harmonium instead of an electric guitar – and finally comes a shot of how the Hare Krishna boys jump together under "the horse" on Wenceslas Square; from a distance it seems like a Masai ritual. The aesthetics of *The Matrix* (or of some older computer graphics) are then once again recalled with a green flashing cursor writing the exact dates on the screen: "Prague, meeting time 4:30 p.m., temperature –10 degrees C." Electronic music also resounds in Ezequiel's film as young men prepare themselves for the harinam – as they iron their dhotis, as they store their portable amplifiers and megaphones in the boot of the car as if they were going to a techno march, and as they run together to the metro. The camera captures their joyous faces and their behavior as decisive and active.

For a little while, the film also shows short random interviews with people on the streets of Prague asking questions about the movement and showing people's positive reactions towards it. However, the camera soon returns to the Hare Krishna men. Instead of the electronic music, we now hear their own music with drums, harmonium, cymbals and exultant loud singing, which, as evening and the cold progress, is becoming more and more ecstatic. Their music, at least its rhythm, no longer seems so different from techno. With graduating tempo the ecstasy progresses, and for some short moments some of the men seem to be even passing into a trance. As Veronika Svobodová remarks, this is mainly visible at minutes 9' and 20' of the movie when the tempo of the kirtan (common public chanting) quickens and reaches a value of bpm (beats per minute) similar to genres of electronic music, e.g. techno or psytrance (120–150 bpm depending on the subgenre). In these moments, the devotees are evidently excited and collectively carried away – a feeling that fades after the song is over.

In the final part of Ezequiel's film where the line between reality and dream seems to be blurred… more and more rejoicing people from the street join the parade until it is one big orgasmic party celebrating Krishna. The film Harinam in Prague ends with exhalation and calming symbolized by the sound of air emitted from the harmonium, as when one shuts an accordion, and the camera finally shows the hazy, tired but happy and knowing smile of the lead singer saying good-bye with the Hare Krishna statement "Hari, Hari bol" (vaguely translated as "Lord, Lord, speak").

Veronika's excellent description of the video provides a lot of important observations. Most significant for us is the connection to the film *The Matrix* (and therefore to the Hinduistic image of the world as Maya, an illusion) and *techno* music. This style is clearly not here to be used in the film *The Matrix* merely due to the director's taste or in an attempt to attract *techno* fans. Instead, this connection seems to be much deeper.

MUSIC AND TRANCE

As stated in the previous chapter, one of the main values creating the *techno* subculture is the concept of otherness as differentiated from the surroundings. Above all, complex musical language is used for this purpose for which fast tempo, repetitiveness, electronic sound, continuousness and loudness with physical response are characteristic. Besides the stimuli of musical language, the feeling of otherness is also created by visual components, uninterrupted movement and also often chemical stimulants (drugs). In the most concentrated form, all of these elements are present in psytrance, musical (and subcultural) style, where otherness also has a more concentrated form, the form of general ecstasy,[46] escape and trance.[47] Escape from the place or its new experience (psytrance events usually happen in isolated and visually suitable places) and, of course, ecstasy from leaving the usually experienced sound and moving toward an altered experience of reality.

Blissfully smiling, dancing Krishna devotees certainly experience outside reality differently than the Praguers and tourists standing around.

Here let us summarize her conclusions: Only someone who faces a trance as culturally accepted (perhaps even appreciated) behavior, who is emotionally sufficiently excited, who longs for a transcendental experience and who is taught to listen to music to lead one into a trance could experience it.

This is exactly the case of Prague Krishna devotees: they long for transcendental experience (above all, they are God's devotees) and for joyful emotion (their broad smiles are striking during their Prague procession as well as in their video presentation) and for escape from this world of illusions (in the video, pictures of urban "misery," a beggar, a casino...keep returning). And the *techno* style is, for many of them, linked to the film *The Matrix* or, more likely, to the *techno* subculture that some of them may have recently belonged to and that is built on the feeling of otherness/ecstasy, escape.

In the Prague procession three lines merge. The first is the singing of Indian mantras, those *flash-lights of eternal truth* securing contact with the Unseen, not as sophisticated instruments of the Vedic ritual in the streets of Prague, but in the spirit of the Bengali saint Chaitanya, proclaiming obedience and *the loud singing of God's name(s)*. The second line is the concept of trance as escape

---

46　From the ancient Greek ekstasis (I displace). (1) intense pleasure. (2) state of emotion so intense that a person is carried beyond rational thought and self control. (3) a trance, frenzy, or rapture associated with mystic or prophetic exaltation. Source: http://en.wiktionary.org/wiki/ecstasy

47　In this text we use the expressions "trance" and "altered state of consciousness" as synonyms.

from this illusory, ephemeral world, with ecstasy bringing those emotional and transcendental experiences. The third one is today's Prague Krishna devotees; mantras are (as *techno* music could be for some of them) the right medium for bringing them through its sound shape and extra-musical context into the sought-after spiritual reality.

THE SAINT WENCESLAS FESTIVAL
THE 20TH INTERNATIONAL FESTIVAL OF SPIRITUAL ART
PRAGUE SEPTEMBER 3 – OCTOBER 2, 2011
Zuzana Jurková

A PILGRIMAGE FROM LITOVICE TO THE MONASTERY IN HÁJEK
A procession with singing on the historical pilgrimage road to the oldest Loreta north of the Alps to the Hájek monastery.[48]
As part of the 2011 Saint Wenceslas festival
Saturday, September 10, 2011, 8:30 a.m.
Hostivice – Staré Litovice

The Saint Wenceslas (Václav) Festival is proclaimed as an "international festival of spiritual art"[49]... It takes place (this year for the twentieth time) in September and is centered on Saints Ludmila and Wenceslas, important saints mainly in the Roman-Catholic tradition. The program consists of nine concerts, five events in the "Culture with Liturgy" section and a composition competition arranged by the main organizer of the festival, the Society for Spiritual Music, with the theme "Music for Liturgy." The concerts have a very broad thematic and stylistic range – from songs of old Persia rendered by Shahab Tolouie (about whom Zita writes in connection with the Persian New Year), to various Baroque masters, love songs of medieval Spain and "chapel and Fraucimor music" at the Jemniště castle, to a combination of Jaroslav Seifert's poetry and Mozart's music. The annual Spiritual Fest, a two-day festival of spirituals organized by the *Geshem* choir, was not held this year.

I noticed that the "Culture with liturgy" program included a pilgrimage from Litovice to the Hájek monastery and that the group *Ritornello* is mentioned as participants. I have some of their recordings of Czech semi-folk Baroque – Michna's *Loutna Česká – Czech Lute*, and *Jestličky a staré nové písničky – Christmas Cradle Songs*. The recordings made the same impression on me as the group explain on their Internet pages (which I read much later): that they aspire to a very knowledgeable interpretation (they therefore play only period instruments or copies of them and devote themselves to research and editori-

---

48 From the program notes.
49 2009 program.

al activities) while maintaining that specialization is not their exclusive goal; instead, "they try to return music from the category of 'art music' to the basic needs of man as a universal language of understanding through even the smallest musical forms... in their concurrent elegance and rawness..."[50] It seems to me that the "processions with singing on the historical pilgrimage road," are very close to the aim of *Ritornello*, and so I am looking forward to this event listed on the program.

As we leave the highway not far from Bílá Hora, we see on this sunny morning a nun briskly marching along the edge of the road: we take this as confirmation that we are driving in the right direction. At the meeting place, a small square near a medieval fortress that now lies in ruins in a village on the outskirts of Prague, it is 8 a.m. and there are barely ten people. A half hour after we have set out on our walk, we number nearly fifty: the smallest participant still being carried in a baby carrier on the bellies of his parents; a young husband and wife; a little boy with a bicycle; a few seniors... Some apparently came together; others are vaguely acquainted – perhaps they saw each other here last year; some most likely do not know each other.

Even before we start out, we are joined by our friend, Mr. Dvorský of Kladno, a sportily dressed new pensioner. Somewhat foolishly we ask him how he has heard of today's pilgrimage. Apparently from the website of his Roman-Catholic parish. This is the fourth time he has taken part in this pilgrimage. He also speaks appreciatively of today's lead singer, Michael Pospíšil, and praises him with the words: "He has a voice." This indeed proves to be a basic precondition.

On the grass beside the road four musicians take instruments out of their cases and start playing. Two are going to play oboes resembling dulcians (which differ from oboes mainly in that they do not have keys), one a shorter bassoon and one a trombone. The lead singer, a fifty-year-old with a black hat, gives us brief instructions: he will go to the rear so that we can hear him and can repeat after him. During the repetition, the musicians will accompany us. And "Don't worry. The songs are long: some have sixty verses, so you'll manage to learn them." Then the procession starts out – people walk in twos or threes. With a large open folder with the scores on his back, the singer walks at the rear with the musicians walking closely behind him so that they can read the music off his back. We proceed in accordance with the age and health spectrum of the participants, while trying to maintain a pace that would get us on time to Hájek, where the mass begins at 10:30: not quickly, but without stopping. (We eventually cover the four and a half kilometers in seventy minutes.) Most

---

50   http://web.quick.cz/ritornello/stranky/ritornel.html (September 27, 2011).

Singer and musicians at the end of the procession

of the pilgrims evidently are not here for the first time: not only do they know which of the small roads to take, but also where to turn off onto the field path and where to turn afterwards toward the monastery. Of the thirteen small chapels of the Stations of the Cross, which joined the Hájek Franciscan monastery with its Loreta to Prague's Loreta monastery in Pohořelec and thus lined the pilgrimage, there were originally only four on our route. One of them, lying in ruins, was pointed out to me by Mr. Dvorský. The last one is restored and it shines from afar in the field a short distance from the monastery.

After a few steps, Mr. Pospíšil begins to sing. He has a strong, flexible voice (it reminds me somewhat of the voice of his teacher, the National Theater's famous bass, Jaroslav Horáček) and he such clear pronunciation that we also enjoy various Baroque expressions such as "anjel," (an old Czech version of the word angel). The first song has a simple four-line form. The lead singer sings two lines and everyone repeats them after him with harmonic instrumental accompaniment. Then he finishes singing the verse and we do the same. The musicians do not appear overly concerned with the tuning, and it matters little as none of the pilgrims seems to be interested in the artistic side of the event. Only some of them sing, and even they sometimes stop at times to tell their neighbor something or eat a roll. At the very head of the procession the voice of the lead singer is surmised rather than clearly heard.

The song has about thirty verses. The first twelve or thirteen are related thematically – they describe the search for Jesus Christ: Nor can I satisfy my

The procession route is marked by stations of the cross

mind in any way if poor me doesn't find Jesus Christ (13th stanza). The following ones pile up various Biblical motifs and images:

Perhaps I will find you in the garden / Of beloved Jesus / I will ask the gardener... (14th stanza).

I can imagine that they are inserted differently according to the needs of the procession. We sing the song for more than a quarter of an hour - the lead singer concludes it with a sonorous Amen - and when we finish we have walked almost a quarter of the way.

When I later ask Mr. Pospíšil about the origin of the song, he explains: Its text was created by joining what were originally two songs that are sung to the same tune. We find different variations of the song in the hymnals of Holan (1694) and Božan (1719) ... The originals of all the songs are mostly written only for soprano and bass, and I supplemented a tenor and alto for instrumental accompaniment in my transcription the way we find it in sources of that period. But generally such accompaniments were improvised; the scores were rarely carried in the processions.

You can find the second "Song about St. Mary Magdalene" (27 stanzas) in Božan's hymnal (1719) (pp. 662-663). It is intended for St. Mary Magdalene's Day, but you will find the same song (sung only by soprano, without a bass) among the Marian

The destination of the pilgrimage is the celebratory mass in Hájek

songs in the fifth edition of Steyer's CZECH HYMNAL (1729). They felt a bit different, broader... Mary Magdalene and the Virgin Mary are two "banks" between which
beats every - sinful - human Soul... We will find the melody and texts related to this
song in many places; I found the oldest variant in a song collection of 1669 by Johann
Scheffler-Angelus Silesius in German.[51]

For a while we just walk and though earlier far from everyone joined in the
song, now the absence of music seems somewhat inappropriate. The next song
has an unsurprising Marian subject (after all, we are going to a monastery with
a chapel dedicated to the Visitation of the Virgin Mary), yet surprising with its
complicated, apparently Baroque rhythm. At the beginning, therefore, the pilgrims' singing is rather inhibited, but around the tenth verse they more or less
adjust to the rhythm. Then another Marian song[52] – and from the road the green
of the monastery garden can already be seen. The pilgrims and musicians min-
gle among the many other people sitting or standing around in the courtyard
of the slightly shabby monastery and waiting for the solemn Holy Mass, which
will be celebrated by the archbishop, to start in twenty minutes. This is clearly
the main goal of my fellow pilgrims.

51   e-mail correspondence from October 6, 2011.
52   As a second song, MP introduces the "Song of St. Kazimír," translated by A. V. Michna as
      "Every day worthy of praise" and, as the next one, the originally Polish O Gloriosa Domina –
      see e-mail from October 6, 2011.

ST. LUDMILA'S DAY VESPERS

Friday, September 16, 2011, 5 p.m.
St. George Basilica in Prague Castle
Schola Egidiana/Kateřina Bartošová
Choral vespers

The second event that I wanted to hear as part of the St. Wenceslas Festival was the choral vespers, i.e. early-evening services during which a chorale sings. There were two on the program (St. Ludmila vespers on September 16 and St. Wenceslas vespers on September 28) and because I have a friend, Jana, who has been singing and researching choral music for many years, I ask her if she takes part in any vespers.

Dear Zuzana,

As for me, I intend, as I do traditionally, to take part in the following vespers: http://www.svatovaclavske.cz/nespory_ze_svatku_sv_ludmily.php. We have been singing for years from the edition published by Dominique Patier, originally studied by Hanka Vlhová and in the past years conducted by Kateřina Bartošová, head of the Schola Egidiana (that is, the schola of St. Giles). It is almost exclusively a chant from manuscripts of the St. George Monastery, realized as real vespers, including all necessities.

Texts with translation into Czech are available to the public.

It is usually very lovely and most of the singers know it already, so come directly to the dress rehearsal. Usually there is quite an organizational chaos, but it always turns out well.

Come and see.

Jana

We are in front of the red façade of the St. George Basilica twenty minutes before the beginning. Tourists are still streaming through, eagerly inspecting the Roman interior of one of the oldest buildings in Prague castle. It was right here that, from the second half of the 10th century, an order of Benedictines, whose female members (that is, there was a convent here) sang a Gregorian chant – the chant that we have come to hear.

The Gregorian chant is the official Holy Mass singing of the Roman-Catholic Church. Although the name points to the authority of Pope Gregory VI (590–604), the style, which has been called Gregorian since the 9th century, arose with the unification of various liturgical traditions of the so-called Frankish-Roman synthesis in the second half of the 8th century.

Vespers in the Church of St. George

The young woman at the entrance says she will not let us in until 5 p.m. Short-ly before 5, both entrances really are opened for the concert audience. (A few tourists take advantage of this and avoid paying the entrance fee.) The hundred or so places on the benches are quickly filled; other listeners stand along the walls. Two hardly ten-year-old boys here with their grandmother are the only youngsters; middle and older generations prevail; women are slightly in the majority.

Five men in church vestments sit in front of the altar with four candles. During the vespers one of them will read from the Bible and, somewhat later, another one will pray. This will be the only occasion when the singing will be in Czech instead of Latin.

From the altar in the direction of the audience/benches there are two rows of women in black and white standing face to face. Some of them have veils covering their heads, typical of members of orders. Only the closest woman in the row on the left has a yellow scarf; she will sing the first note and also, with flowing gestures, conduct the singing of the choir and encourage the partici-pation of the "people," that is, of us, the audience. Jana says that the woman studied choral singing in Paris and art history at the Catholic Theological Fac-ulty in Prague. Apparently the other singers are mainly from two groups. One is a choir with a broader repertoire; the other is a rather limited choral group of Giles Church's Schola Egidiana conducted by Kateřina Bartošová and whose the members are "singing believers" rather than "artists."

The audience/the "people" receive brochures with the music and Latin text. The scores are a bit different from those known and used by the majority of musicians in the West: they have only a four-line staff at the beginning of which there is a different key, and the note heads have rectangular or rhomboid shapes. There are almost no note stems or hooks, and yet some of the music is written in some sort of clusters. As a classically trained musician, I am more or less able to follow the rising and falling melody, but I cannot imagine the rhythm.

A short *Introductio* is sung almost all in one tone; it thus recalls one of the functions of singing in liturgy, i.e. the function of some bearer of the text: a word that is sung is carried around a space much better than a word that is simply read or recited. Moreover, the entire liturgy, all of its sung parts, produces an impression of a compact style. (Yet I am not sure if that was exactly the intention of their creators or reformers, or if the unusual features of choral musical language affect me this way.)

During the next part, *Hymn*, my distant first impression of the Gregorian chant comes back: in the air, freely floating undulations of sound on which I am carried by an unintelligible and thus impersonal text. By occasionally resting long enough to breathe in and out, I solidified a rather unusual feeling of freedom.

This feeling is, I guess, created by two main features of the chant: almost perfect homophony and the absence of a regular rhythm or meter. The non-existence of a regular rhythm evokes an impression of the absence of a horizontal link in time; again the pure homophony of the non-existence of any sort of vertical link. The feeling of compactness of the sung melody is also so strong because mostly (except for the input of the "people") only women or only men sing – after all, the chant was originally sung mainly in monasteries. Moreover, the way of singing without any force on the vocal cords (therefore that lightness, though at the same time an absence of dynamic differences) eradicates individual differences. And so it is sometimes difficult to distinguish if only one soloist or the whole choir is singing. Surprisingly, I have a feeling of free, pure, unanchored lines even when the choir sings in two parts, as was just the case in some of the parts of the *Hymn*.

The *Hymn*, which I discern (even with my weak knowledge of Latin) celebrates St. Ludmila, is followed by five *antiphonies* with relevant Biblical psalms. Each of the songs begins with a short, ornate section sung by the choir, which is the antiphony; the same section is heard once again at the end. After the antiphony, the "psalm tone" is repeated many times, a melody in two parts on a few tones. As in the Introductio, here the singing is the bearer of the text and so the length of the melody differs according to the number of syllables of

Choral notation of the antiphone and the melismatic responsorium

the verses that are sung. The first part is first sung by a soloist; the choir then answers in the second part. The "people" join another repetition of the whole melody. (I would be curious to know if the older man next to me and the woman behind me can sing from the choral notation or if they know the melody. Jana later says that they most likely learned the vespers at a monastery church where the vespers are regularly performed.)

After the five antiphonies with psalms, one of the men seated in front of the altar reads a short text from the Bible. The *Responsorium* then follows. As elsewhere, here the soloist and choir alternate; this time, however, after much longer sections. The "people" do not join in – nor could they since the melody is exceptionally ornamented (in one place the notation shows 28 signs over the syllable "pa"). Because of the calm, as if dreamily floating in space, it definitely does not remind me of the vocal exhibition of most coloratura operatic arias.

I notice that the next part is again in antiphonic form, even if it is not indicated as such. Again it has a melodically rich introduction which is sung only by the women's choir and which comes again at the end. The text of the main section is the Marian prayer "Magnificat" and in it the "people" again alternate with the soloists. In the "un-peopled" parts, for special effects, three-part singing rings out.

After another of the men in front of the altar reads some prayers of intercession, once again everyone sings the last two songs: *Pater Noster* and *Salve Regina*. Their melodies are richer than those in the psalms, but much simpler than the songs that only soloists or the choir sang. With a few exceptions, most syllables are sung in only one tone; the neighboring tones are near enough each other for the melody not to pose a problem for the average participant of the religious services. Shortly before 6 p.m., the vespers end. Some of the singers and part of the audience leave; some stay for the following mass, during which the cathedral choir and orchestra will play Gounod's *Missa Breve*.

CHRISTIAN? MUSIC?

Even if we are perhaps initially taken by surprise by the variety of Christian music in today's Prague, it is possible to become aware of certain common features and tendencies leading in various directions.

First let us look briefly at the history of Christian music; looking around, we will allow ourselves to be led to the Canadian theologian and musicologist Gerald Hobbs. He considers Christian music, in the first place, as the heir to Biblical **psalms of ancient Israel,** psalms sung in the Jerusalem temple before its destruction in the year 70. The most obvious connection is that the texts of the psalms are today part of almost every sacral gathering, regardless of theological orientation. (the choral vespers in Prague in 2011 also confirm this.) Of greater essence is the fact that a wide range of devotional moods (both very intimate lamentations and expressions of devotion of the whole community; they contain joy and often also despair...) can be found in the psalms and various forms of expression of this devotion (from the very intimate to indicating a majestic collective performance with the accompaniment of instruments to a form showing the alternation of solo and choir or several groups). It is also the use of the songs on different occasions that correspond to various devotional moods: not only during religious services, but also on extra-liturgical occasions; for example, processions or pilgrimages, during home observances, etc. – just as it is with the music of today's Christians. The psalms are then a kind of model for a later – and today's – variety of spiritual music.

In the Book of Psalms, i.e. the collection of the 150 psalms contained in the Bible, there is also a rudiment of **polarity**, which later developed into the music of the Christians: a polarity in which, on one hand, it was the clergymen (whether they were members of orders or parish priests) and their helpers who performed the liturgy as professionals and, on the other hand, lay members of a church community. The specialization of church music was also supported by the use of special languages, incomprehensible to the layman (Latin in Western

Europe, Old Slavonic in the East), and also the more and more sophisticated liturgy in the Roman-Catholic Church, including changes in form for various occasions. The Gregorian chant – extraordinarily challenging from the point of view of coherence and therefore demanding constant practice; using special notation and Latin as a "non-laic" language – is a perfect example of such specialization.

Just as the participation of professional singers is obvious in the Biblical psalms, the participation of amateurs – the Church community/the "people" – is evident here. The extent of their involvement, however, both later and today in various churches fluctuates, which (unsurprisingly) is connected with different theological directions and different concepts of the church as an institution. In general we can say that the Roman-Catholic Church emphasizes objectivity (including objectivity of its effects) while the Reform Church, coming from Luther's basic thesis that salvation takes place "sola fide, sola gratia" (by faith alone, by grace alone) provides more space to each individual, including laymen, and therefore to subjectivity. (If what goes on between me and God is decisive, the church institution has no such power.) These different emphases also correspond to the musical situation: while in sophisticated Roman-Catholic choral vespers the clergy and/or "specialized" laymen bear the main share and the "people" participate only in the simplest songs, mainly psalms and a few common prayers (Pater Noster...), in reform churches the role of the "people" is fundamental. The key concept of reformation – the personal active relation of laymen to God and God's word – is also expressed in the music: "folk singing" in the national language is a basic component of the religious service. Anyone who sings a spiritual song joins with the whole congregation and thus connects his unique personal identity with the identity of the whole community. At the same time, singing is the realization of faith: I believe, therefore I sing. Thus, the tradition of liturgy in the vernacular; thus, the emphasis of Huss and Luther on the spiritual song in the vernacular. (For the 16th century alone about a thousand melodies and ten times as many texts of spiritual songs from Bohemia are known.) These were sung both during services and outside of them. In view of the low medieval literacy, the form of lead-singer/people was a relatively frequent form – such as we can still hear today on the pilgrimage to Hájek.

From the reform concept of singing (by singing I express who I am before God and in the world) it is possible to understand another feature of spiritual songs, especially those that were sung outside of the context of a religious service: their up-to-dateness. This referred both to songs of the Hussites (*Rise up, rise up, great city of Prague*) and, almost a half-millennium later, to Afro-American spirituals. When Afro-American Christians sang before the abolition of slavery (1865) the spiritual

When Israel was in Egypt's land
Let my people go
Oppress'd so hard they could not stand
Let my People go

it was clear that they were singing about themselves. And when they sang the same thing, a long time after they were slaves, in the 20th century, it was clear that they were singing about racial discrimination, which they felt similarly.

The association of music of old Israel is not the only dimension that can be considered in connection with Christian music of today's Prague. Another dimension is its **contemporary shape**; this is attested to by those who perform and listen to it. Since we stressed spirituality next to music in the title of the chapter, it is certainly interesting to ask how important the spirituality component is for the participant and how, on the contrary, our prevailing concept of music as "art" is shown. At the very beginning of the chapter we pointed out that the connection of music and spirituality is universal – and one of the few universals in music all together. At the same time one can easily perceive that the more spiritual music assumes – at least in our environment – the form of concerts, i.e. a specific event where the performance of music with its esthetic criteria as its main goal (and a typically greater separation of musicians – "artists" – from the audience), the weaker the spiritual component is.

The program of the St. Wenceslas Festival shows "spiritual music" in a broad spectrum, from a castle chamber concert (in which it is difficult to find great spirituality) to an orderly pilgrimage of worshippers to a solemn mass. It seems that, where there is greater emphasis on the spiritual aspect, the participants – worshippers – want to join in, and that the easiest way is by singing. Therefore we also find here the characteristic features of Turino's "participatory" performance of music: simple, open forms, only approximate tuning, a more or less constant dynamic. Where the spiritual music is perceived mainly as art, we come across specialists, often instrumental virtuosos performing sophisticated music corresponding to high esthetic demands. We are tempted to say that religious ritual is replaced by concert ritual.

It should also be noted that instrumental music does not necessarily have to be connected only to the concept of "art." It is indeed true that the ideal of an unaccompanied human voice was and is considered the most suitable "instrument" for celebrating God not only in a chorale, but also in most synagogues. But Hobbs[53]

---

53   Hobbs 2010:71

points out, for example, Baroque organ preludes, which are mainly played in Protestant environments before the services: their melodic motifs, taken from Christian hymns, work like semiotic symbols and evoke in worshippers associations connected with the original text of the hymn.

If we tried to apply the Apollonian-Dionysian spectrum (which we also write about in connection with rebellion in the fourth chapter) to spiritual music, the Apollonian approach in Christianity clearly prevails. Yet it is not like that everywhere; the Pentecostal and charismatic churches mentioned in relation to trance are the main exceptions. We also find in gospel music, at least as Americans presented and taught it in Prague (with a gospel workshop), certain elements of ecstasy or, let us say, Dionysianism. No wonder, because gospel experts speak about the influence of Pentecostal churches.

But perhaps most distinctive for today's Prague is what we encountered during the vespers: some of the women sing Gregorian chants mainly as "art," while others express their faith through them – and the same is true for the audience. Perhaps it would also be interesting to try to find out something about the other reasons.

THOMAS TURINO ON MUSIC AS SOCIAL LIFE
Zuzana Jurková

After he thoroughly researched music in two very different places – the Peruvian Andes and Zimbabwe in the book *Music as Social Life* (2008) – Thomas Turino tried to understand why music is actually so often the basis of the most varied (and really the most dissimilar) social events.

For an explanation he uses a whole series of theories (we write in the third chapter, in the part about "The Macropoulos Case as a semiotic experience," about his application of semiotics to music) and theoretical concepts. The one we are going to speak about is constructed by Turino himself. He created four categories in which music is performed. Two of them relate to "live" music-making (participatory – and presentational), two to the creation of recordings (high fidelity and audio art). Each of these models basically differs both from the philosophical point of view and fundamental values and in the resulting sound.

For us, the first two are important. In the **participatory model** what is important is not so much the quality of the sound, but rather how the participants feel. Usually there is no difference between the musicians and the audience: instead, everyone takes part in the performance. Usually it is clear ahead of time that it will be an event of the socially interactive type, and if anyone finds himself here unexpectedly, he can feel a slight pressure to join in, without regard to his musical abilities. The musicians are most often, but not always, on a similar technical level. The success of the participatory performance of the music is gauged by the intensity of the participation, and one of the basic qualities of a musician is that, during the performance of his part (whether it be vocal, instrumental or, perhaps, dance), others are not excluded from participating. Here there is generally more room for various amounts of innovation or variation because, after all, it is a question of the musician taking advantage of the social music-making in which he is personally partaking.

As far as the **musical language**, which is the result of the participatory model of musical performance, is concerned, we will mention the main features. We will first examine the form. Musical theory distinguishes between two basic types of forms into which sound material is organized. The first of these is called the *closed* form. This prevails in Western (mainly art) music and its course is fixed in advance: the beginning, its course and the end are pre-scribed and its performance is always more or less the same.

The second type is the *open* form: this name on the whole indicates that the course of the music is not planned in detail and that the result depends on the momentary involvement of the participating musicians. Open forms are often composed of mostly short parts that can be repeated differently after each other and last various lengths of time. Common examples are the repetition of one of the "verses": or alternation of "verse" and "chorus" or two contrasting parts (ABAB, AABB, etc.)

What is essential is the interlocking of tuning, texture and dynamics. The precision of the tuning and demands on it are, according to Turino, lower in participatory music than in the presentational model. (I remember our inter-view with members of a folk male choir in Southern Moravia who not only sang together, but cultivated and produced wine and then enjoyed drinking it; they spoke about their founder, now an old man, who hears badly and thus sometimes sings somewhat off key. This statement, however, did not lead to any complaint, but to a conciliatory "Can we tell him?" Turino tells a similar story: a group of "his" Andes Indians from a mountain village was practicing new compositions for a town celebration. A friend from another village who longed to play with them joined them on the way to the celebration. Naturally, they didn't turn him down although his *sikuris*, Pan Flute, was tuned different-ly, giving off a nerve-wracking sound. Only after a weekend of playing when they were returning home did the main player complain to Turino: "It's a pity that his flute wasn't tuned a bit closer to us."

The relation between voices and instruments which resonate simultane-ously is called the texture. While there are individual parts in transparent texture that are clearly distinguishable aurally (which is much more typical for a performance model), the dense texture, common in the participatory model, includes various overlaps of the parts or their mixture so that it is hardly pos-sible to differentiate between them. In the participatory model one can rarely find dramatic contrasts such as sudden change of dynamics or tempo; gener-ally it is played aloud. Most interesting in this combination of tuning, texture and dynamics is, however, Torino's explanation. He calls this the *cloaking func-tion*. By this he means some sort of protective function which loud music with dense texture and only approximate tuning have in common for a beginner: it rids him of fear of making mistakes which either he wouldn't normally hear or that actually belong to the style. It therefore provides him with everything for him to become one of the participants.

In the performance model there is mainly one group of people - musi-cians, dancers - performing music for another group - listeners, onlookers. Both groups are separated; most often they stand or sit face to face, and this separation emphasizes other attributes such as the stage, the microphones, the lighting, etc.

The musicians in this model presume that the audience will listen to them quite attentively and thus they are prepared for the "performance" often with particular attention to details. The try-outs may be fundamentally different, depending on the leader/conductor... (This does not mean that the musicians of the participatory model never practiced, but that the rehearsals are repetitions of the numbers, without emphasis on details.)

Features of the **musical language** are in direct contrast to the preceding model: closed forms prepared in advance prevail; the beginnings and ends of the numbers as well as individual parts are clear. The texture is usually much more transparent because the details in directing the voices, etc., are what the listener notices. Gone is that protective function of the strong dynamic and "broad" tuning because here it would be counterproductive. While with the musician in the participatory model a willingness to provide space to others is above all appreciated, here "achievement," which often takes the form of virtuosity, is valued. The concept of a musical composition, sometimes even the whole program, resembles the idea of an artistic object.

Thus every model has a different goal – and consequently also different musical features. Nevertheless, they sometimess mutually intermingle. Turino gives the example of his own band playing zydeco.[54] The band plays in clubs where some come primarily to listen, but where the musicians' main goal is to encourage and accompany dancing. For the listener, then, they play various contrasting passages, e.g. a solo violin while, for the dancers, they try to keep a stable tempo. Before playing, they rehearse the beginnings and ends (so that they appear to be prepared onstage). Yet how long they play depends on how the situation develops. If there are passionate dancers, the musicians play until they feel that the dancers are tired. If, on the contrary, the dance floor is empty, the musicians play the most time-proven pieces that usually raise the people out of their seats. If they don't succeed (which the musicians consider as a failure), they begin to play compositions for listening. Torino's band has indeed taken over a few elements of the presentational model, but the basic features remain those of the participatory model.

---

54   Music of the Creoles of Louisiana.

GOSPEL WORKSHOP
GOSPEL NIGHT
22 JULY 2011, ST. ANNE CLOISTER, 7 P.M.
FREE ENTRANCE
Zuzana Jurková

I learned about Gospel Night from Monica and Joël, friends who came from France for a four-day *Gospel Workshop*: It would culminate in a Saturday evening *Gospel Showcase* concert. Friday's "Gospel Night" was part of the workshop and actually intended for its participants, which is why there was no particular advertising for it.

Monica says that they rehearsed at the Hotel Step in Vysočany and that the rehearsals alternated with lectures on various topics related to gospel. The whole workshop will end with a communal religious service. The instructors are American, like the leaders of the whole initiative. Probably two-thirds of the 250 participants who are going to sing in the final gala concert in Prague's Municipal House are from the USA. (There, afterwards, the individual serving as the conductor and emcee named another ten countries the singers were from: apart from Europe, e.g. Thailand). Today's "Gospel Night" can be understood, on one hand, as a time for familiarizing the mainly foreign participants with how gospel is sung in the Czech lands and, on the other hand, as a possibility of introducing Czech gospel choirs to a foreign audience. Perhaps it is also a certain compensation for the fact that, although family members were originally promised free tickets for the final gala concert, that offer was cancelled. Today gospel could be enjoyed for free.

The relatively small, beautifully reconstructed Gothic chapel of St. Anne's cloister is overflowing; people are also sitting on the floor and standing behind the back rows. Most are not dressed up, but wear comfortable clothes (most of the foreigners had been walking around town during the day); I see – and during the concert I also hear – a few small children, but mainly – like those in the performing choirs – they are people under forty, though there are also a few seniors.

A man and a young girl (Monica says that during the workshop she provided technical support) alternate as announcers; he is the conductor of, she a singer in *Touch of Gospel*, a Pilsen choir, which will perform later. Their role is limited to announcing the choirs and their conductors, and occasionally they add some technical instructions.

The first singers are *Voices of Joy*, the only Americans among the seven groups appearing today. Their conductor and pianist is Anthony Leach and their introductory song, without piano accompaniment, is a pure four-part piece presented by 17 singers, who surprise me with their moderation in dynamics and emotionality. After the concert, the people on both sides of me agree that they preferred this particular song (I guess that it was rather mainly the manner of their interpretation) to the rest of the songs in the concert.

> During the next number the atmosphere has basically changed: Tony sits down at the piano and something, almost ragtime, is heard: temperamental playing with decidedly syncopated rhythm. (I am somewhat surprised when I later note that he is playing from a score.) After a couple of measures a similarly energetic and enthusiastic choir, who seemed to exchange the disciplined ideal of polyphony for an ideal that was an expression of spontaneous joy, joins in. The singers clap to the rhythm and sway in synchronicity – on the second beat to the right, on the fourth to the left. The conductor/pianist sings a solo in which the choir alternates in a "call-and-response" way.

In the next numbers two young women with rich voices appear on stage as soloists; both sing into the microphone. Solo singing, amplified by the microphone (which allows for various delicacies of mood unheard during acoustic singing) and combined with some sort of general exultation, reminds me a bit of pop music.

After half an hour this group is replaced on the stage by the 16-member *Geshem*, introduced as the founder and mover of everything having to do with spirituals in the Czech lands. Though this may be an exaggeration, *Geshem* is the organizer of the SpiritualFest festival, which over the past few years has grown into a two-day international event supported by the Prague City Hall and the Ministry of Culture. A diplomat from the US Embassy or some African state can sometimes be seen in the auditorium of the SpiritualFest. In recent years the SpiritualFest has also been part of the Saint Wenceslas Festival.

For years I have also been witness to the ever more precise intonation, more sophisticated arrangements of songs (in which there now are passages without text, sudden changes of dynamics and tempo...) and even some sort of rudimentary stage action: walking while singing that they are ready to go, etc. All this corresponds very well to Torino's characteristic of a presentational model (see Tom Turino box, re: music as social life).

Of the ten songs that *Geshem* is singing tonight, nine are real spirituals; one – *I Paradisi* – is African, which is clearly of a different musical style as well as in a language I don't know. I am always surprised how often choirs, declaring their repertoire to be made up of spirituals, include African songs, the musical style of which is so different. This happens sometimes in the SpiritualFest, where the participants are explicitly challenged to maintain the style of African-American spirituals. In Prague it is explained as an unconscious mixture of songs of the "blacks," without regard to which continent the songs actually arose in. When, however, I experience the same thing during the *Gospel Showcase*, I think that this is probably – at least in the case of the American choirs – a deliberate "mixture." It is like when, in Khamoro, the Romani cultural festival, Indian musicians play semi-folk Indian music: a few decades ago it would not have occurred to anyone to connect it to the Romani culture. By having the Indians and Roma play side by side, the organizers demonstrate to the participants that they belong to each other.[55] *Geshem* have a few gospels in their repertoire; for example, the famous *O Happy Day*, which is on their first CD, *Wade in the Water.*

Actually the album *Wade in the Water* begins with one of today's spirituals, *It's Me, Oh Lord.* The structure of this song is ideal for improvisations and anyone can join in to this simple melody without regard to his/her musical talent. The song has two short, similar parts. One returns without change as a chorus: rhythmically succinct, descending in two steps and then again returning to the starting note, almost as if it were imitating the melody of urgent speech. That urgency continues to strengthen the repeated text. *It's me, it's me, oh Lord, standing in the need of prayer.* The second part includes verses/two measures, in which the soloist lists those who cannot pray for him (*not my brother, not my sister... not my preacher...* and here there is room for any long list). These two measures alternate with the musical figure of the chorus *standing in the need of prayer.*

This kind of structure is a direct example of the so-called open form (see Tom Turino box), a form generally used where there is not a completely predictable course of a musical event. And this was undoubtedly the case with original spirituals – not only that names or other current insertions were put into the changeable part of the text, but, in addition, the simple musical figure of the chorus provided room for musical variations.

Geshem sings in four-part harmony, exact not only in intonation, but also rhythmically and dynamically. You have the feeling that the chords are produced by one polyphonic singer; I know from my choir experience that the cost of such harmony is hours of rehearsing together and great concentration. In the places where only the choir sings (such as in the chorus) the melody is heard mostly in the high, soprano voice. The second part is sung by a soloist and she slightly embellishes her melody; the choir accompanies it only with wordless syllables which create chords. (During some performances of

---

55 Some researchers, e.g. Turino 1993, demonstrate that various social practices, including music, not only show how people imagine their past and their view of the world to be, but also show that it is a two-way process and that those different views are therefore constantly reforming with these practices.

this well-known spiritual the soloists alternate with the choir after two measures so that the ostinato *standing in the need of prayer*, stubbornly repeated by
the choir in the chorus and in the verse, impresses the listener in a way similar
to the short, repeated melodic figures, the "patterns," that are the basis of the
music of sub-Saharan Africa.)

Geshem sing ten spirituals during the designated half hour. Their structure
(chorus/verse) is similar and the way of arrangement and performance doesn't
particularly differ (it was one of the "canonical" ways in which spirituals were
sung at the beginning of the 20th century when their fame spread and the first
recordings appeared). In some, however, a fifth voice is added to four voices,
like an improvised voice. This individual sings more or less the same text as
the soloist or the whole choir, but, while the main voices generally begin on
regular beats, this one sometimes comes in a half-beat earlier, and elsewhere
a little later (this is greatly favored by those who enjoy jazz syncopations and
fans of African drumming since this element, the so-called off-beat, is typical
of them) the voice springs around more rapidly than the main melody, in unexpected melodic steps. It is as if it commented unpredictably from the personal
perspective on the predicted/predictable spiritual. This is the fifth, "liberated"
voice that some consider to be the decisive impulse for the birth of gospel.

Although the concert is hardly a third over, we have already heard two
main styles that will be heard tonight and tomorrow night: African-American
spirituals and gospel songs. (The next groups will sing only gospel.) I was surprised that the announcers did not comment on or emphasize the difference
at all even though, from the point of view of sound, there were very different
styles. Afterwards, however, it occurs to me that – as so often – the ears hear
mainly what the mind thinks in advance. And it is true that it is possible to
think of spirituals and gospel songs as having much in common.

Mainly they are the musical styles whose authors and primary users were
and are African-American Christians; styles that, however, spread to other
users and other listeners from their home environment of African-American
churches – and this understandably formed their further shape.

SPIRITUAL AND GOSPEL

The term spiritual is found in the literature for the first time in connection with religious singing of African-American slaves of the 18th century. It is, however, joined
to the adjective "folk" to avoid being unjustifiably identified with spirituals as we
know them from the latter third of the 19th century (since we know nothing about the
musical shape of folk spirituals). But already at that time it possesses one of its (later)
basic characteristics: an emphasis of those motifs of Christianity that resonate with

the situation of black slaves (eschatology, freedom from slavery...) Another feature of spirituals (which we reliably have from the first musical transcriptions from the end of the 19th and recordings from the beginning of the 20th centuries) is their musical shape. This follows the basic form structure of Euro-American folk music (verse / chorus), but on more subtle levels borrows elements of the music of sub-Saharan Africa. That is how the spiritual arose as a phenomenon that both reflected and expressed African-American uniqueness.

The shape of the first spirituals is inseparable from the environment of Protestant churches (the first independent one was the African Methodist Episcopal congregation in 1787) in which they were performed. Basic elements of the religious services were common prayer and singing, testimonies (that is, in the speaker's own words, the "proclamation" of what God did for him in life) and sometimes, but far from always, the sermon. As the participants testify, s/he who prayed often went from speaking to singing. (By the way, we can still hear this in some African-American churches.) The congregation chimed in, praying aloud. Everyone took part in the singing and many accompanied it with clapping, stamping and even dancing. Today, after more than a century, elements of that original community and reciprocity in a spiritual can still be heard.[56]

In the 1870s spirituals, until that time performed and accepted only within the milieu of African-American churches, also reached the concert stage. This is where their new shape and new history begins.

In very early recordings – from the 1920s – we can hear two ways in which spirituals proceeded: sung as solos, generally with piano accompaniment, or in four-part arrangements, to which, later, a fifth voice was added – the voice of a soloist, accompanied by complete four-part harmony. Some musicologists consider the addition of the fifth voice to be the musical impulse that began the birth of gospel.

One of the first real internationally successful (and in the US, especially in the 1950s, practically "unlistenable" due to his strong left-orientation) singers was **Paul Robeson** (1898–1976). As the son of a Methodist minister who still worked as a slave on plantations in the South, he embodied for the listeners the culturally acceptable voice of emancipated black Americans: a voice sufficiently manly and sufficiently mournful – so that it were possible in concert halls to imagine suffering slaves, while their songs would sound so very melodious.

At the same time (at least on recordings from the '20s and '30s) there still remain many remarkable elements of the African-American mix: apart from the above-mentioned syncopation, in listening carefully we notice traces of typical responsorial alternation which, however, should be performed by only one singer. When, for ex-

---

56   In Czech literature, Michal Bystrov (2001) writes in extraordinary detail about the spiritual
      Go Down, Moses, its history and social context.

ample, in *Sometimes I Feel like a Motherless Child* the slow, regular pulse of the main melody alternates with shouting *True Believer* off rhythm, it again returns to the original melancholy motif. This is similar to many later field recordings from West Africa, when the soloist improvises and forms his/her part in his/her own way, while the choir keeps the pulse returning, sometimes with a slightly varied figure.

Robeson undoubtedly had a great influence on the further spread of the spiritual. In recordings of the famous **Marian Anderson** (1897–1993), the first black singer in the New York Metropolitan Opera (in 1955 she sang Ulrika in Verdi's *Masked Ball*) which were made decades after Robeson's, one can hear both the same piano arrangement and, more strikingly, a similar way of singing: the deep voice itself tends to a certain mournfulness and pathos which so well tie in with most of the lyrics...

Marian Anderson became one of the stimuli for a discussion about American national identity: when she was denied an appearance in the hall of the patriotic Daughters of the American Revolution (DAR), not only did the First Lady of the USA, Eleanor Roosevelt, protest against this organization by leaving it, but the President, Franklin Delano Roosevelt, in his speech to the members of the DAR in 1938 changed the usual formula with which American presidents began their speeches, "My fellow Americans" to "My fellow immigrants." The change of emphasis in the original apparent all-inclusive formula pointed out those who are not considered Americans. One year later, Marian Anderson, under the auspices of the First Lady, festively sang before 75,000 people (plus millions of radio listeners) on the steps of Washington's Lincoln Memorial – spirituals.[57]

Another way spirituals were sung from the time when they broke away from the original milieu of African-American churches, the way *Geshem* follows, is part singing, most often without musical accompaniment (*a capella*). That is exactly what the spirituals of the first ensembles presented to the public, as they endeavored by this means to collect money for black students: the *Fisk (University) Jubilee Singers, the Taskiana Four, the West Virginia Collegiate Institute* and others. From listening to their old recordings it is quite clear that this is a profoundly prepared concert event in which spontaneity (the most varied clapping, stamping and also melodic variations...) is replaced by restraint and preparedness; through sophisticated four-part singing in which sometimes men also sang the highest voices, prepared changes of tempo and dynamics, a well thought-out choice of soloists who alternated with the choir... The spiritual as self-expression of the members of a religious congregation changed into a spiritual that provides consolation to the audience. The spiritual which, in addition, often becomes an instrument of expression of the social aspirations of its bearers.

---

57 Quoted from Reyes 2005.

GOSPEL

The beginnings of gospel style are connected to the movement of emancipated slaves from the rural South of the USA to the urban setting of the industrial North. There the music of African-American churches continues to have the same character as in the South, as discussed above: the call-and-response structure, the emotional way of performance accompanied by clapping, and heterophonic singing.

The distancing of gospel and spiritual styles from each other was rather gradual. The first important element starting in the early 1940s was the appearance of instrumental accompaniment of the singing. Until then, this was unusual in African-American churches because it was considered secular. The founders of the gospel style claimed to have been inspired by music outside of churches. Thomas A. Dorsey (1899–1993) often called the Father of Gospel Music, describes how, as a boy, he sold refreshments during vaudeville intermissions: *This rhythm I had, I brought with me to gospel songs...*[58] The famous Mahalia Jackson, another of the first gospel generation, admits to having a similar fascination with "worldly" music (along with music of the Pentecostal Church): *I remember when I used to listen to Bessie Smith sing "I Hate to See that Evening Sun Go Down," I'd fix my mouth and try to make tones come out just like hers.* Gospel music in the beginnings of Pentecostal Churches, i.e., in the first decades of the 20th century, was clearly the most closely connected with the folk spiritual in its style and feeling. The believers, influenced by the Holy Ghost, enthusiastically sang and danced to the accompaniment of instruments (such as trombones, trumpets and mandolins), which most of the churches disdained.

Today's popularity of gospel style, that type which today is the main musical language of African-American churches without regard to concrete denominations, however, first began in 1969 with the recording of *Oh Happy Day* by Edwin Hawkins. Its success is due mainly to two elements that were also present in the first concerts of a tour (and later recordings) of spirituals many decades earlier. One of them was the purpose, the second – relating to the purpose – the way of transmission. And this time, in the case of *Oh Happy Day*, it was not about a recording of "admiration, but about an attempt to raise financial resources for the *raise* (support) (the word *raise* in the history of spirituals and gospels appears repeatedly) of African-American students. The means were also adjusted to this purpose: here Hawkins used instruments of popular music of the that time as accompaniment – bongo, French horns and electric bass guitars. By the way, the project was successful not only as a stimulus for the new path of gospel, but also financially.

Thus the era of gospel began, transcending racial, religious and musical borders. Today you can hear a gospel whose language/style is close to R'n'B or jazz or rap or

---

58   Burnim 2001: 631.

funk or almost indistinguishable from pop music. Originally simple to remember, the predictable melodies are more complex today, the accompaniment often indistinguishable from secular music.

When, in 1932, the above-mentioned Thomas Dorsey participated in the founding of the *National Convention of Gospel Choirs and Choruses* in Chicago, this put into motion a movement that still surrounds gospel. The Prague workshop is only one of its small parts. Similar events are common, mainly in the US, but sometimes with much greater numbers of participants. The most famous of them, the *James Cleveland Gospel Workshop of America*, has been taking place since 1969 and today has about 20,000 musicians. Workshops are perhaps the most visible, but definitely not the only undertakings with a very similar aim to that of the *Fisk Jubilee Singers* and other groups singing spirituals: stimulation, support, and *raise*.

The Prague workshop is one of the events of the Ohio organization *Raise Productions*. There is written in the flyer that the participants receive:

Raise History: *Raise Productions* (RP) began serving the Columbus community in 1985... In 1989 *Raise* established "The Center for the Gospel Arts" to provide for gospel artists and the community. *Raise* has developed and implemented specialized curriculums and teaching resources... *Raise* has also developed performing groups which have performed throughout the United Sates and Europe, won Gospel Music Excellence Awards, produced musical reviews, plays, concerts and recorded several albums.

Raise Philosophy: *Raise Productions*... is not a church; it is a ministry. As such, *Raise* conducts its classes and services based upon Christian principles. While *Raise* is committed to the preservation and perpetuation of Gospel Music and African American cultural art form in scholarly and secular forums, our primary goal is to offer instruction in the Gospel Arts as a means of preparing musicians...for service within African-American churches or other Christian ministries.

Raise Vision: Since its inception, *Raise Productions* has always had the vision to establish an accredited educational and performing arts complex solely devoted to the instruction of African American Gospel Music, Ministry and the Gospel Arts...

As you can see, the idea of *raise* – support and exhortation – is always present in today's gospel; however, the word *raise* acquires a much broader meaning.

GOSPEL SHOWCASE
Conductor: Raymond Wise
Voices of Joy (Pennsylvania), Gospel Limited, Touch of Gospel, Maranatha Gospel Choir, Depot Lane Singers, Mohawk Valley Chorus, Hartwick College Choir (New York), Tebe Poem (Russia), Brno Gospel Choir & Geshem (Czech Republic)
Dr. Kathy Bullock, Dr. Anthony Leach – assistant choir masters

Czech National Symphony Orchestra
Smetana Hall, Municipal House
23 July 2011 at 7 p.m.
Tickets: 750, 450, 290 Czech crowns

Like most Praguers, I usually avoid the Municipal House; I have bad memories of arrogant waiters and crowds of tourists who, enthusiastic about the Secession architecture, block the wide sidewalk around it. Various masked figures dressed in Rococo costumes and selling tickets for one of the "Best of" concerts or *Carmina Burana* don't particularly attract me here either. I do remember some magnificent concerts I experienced here; not even the cathedral acoustics of the long auditorium with its high ceiling adversely affected them.

A quarter of an hour before the beginning, the area in front of the hidden entrance is bustling with activity. On the balcony over the entrance, a wind quartet is repeating a fanfare several times, which makes one aware that the concert belongs to the Prague Proms cycle, aimed at tourists in Prague's summer season. Yet, at the same time, it is rather prestigious.

Smetana Hall and its seating capacity of 1,200 seats is full. The audience is made up of every imaginable age group; compared to the audiences of the usual classical music concerts that often take place here, the average age of this audience seems relatively low. At the intermission I meet a few friends whom I wouldn't have expected to be here; they all say that family members participated in the workshop and are singing this evening.

The hall is still somewhat restless when, first, a strong and rapid drum roll is heard, and immediately after that two voices – a man's and a woman's. Both are deep; both are singing in an unknown language. The man more serenely; only a moment after him, the ornamented, deep, emotional woman's echo is heard. The majestic figure of a black woman with a striking head covering appears on the stage. But this lasts only a few seconds; the drum speedily settles down to a regular rhythm and the choir, the main participants of the concert, begins to fill in the ten rows above the stage. Over two hundred and fifty singers in black t-shirts and pants or skirts, a few more women than men. Their entrance, however, does not at all resemble the arrival of choruses of classical music that I have seen here: this time all the choir members clap, wave their

The combined choirs of Gospel Workshop

arms over their heads, shout and make their enthusiasm obvious. The audience behaves in the same way: clap, shout and sway to the rhythm. This will be repeated several times more over the evening.

As the choir arrives, a piano can already be heard (to the rhythm of the clapping and the drum) and the singers join in. The tune of the first song, described in the program as African, is simple and constantly repeated: ideally chosen for the lineup of some hundreds of people. The singing can hardly be heard through the clapping and drumming, but it is repeated over and over; after a few repetitions it moves one tone higher. The last few tones of the choir slow down and strengthen, then freeze on the final chord. The audience and singers burst out in applause with all their strength so that it is not clear who is actually greeting whom.

When the wave of enthusiastic applause dies down, the large orchestra seated on the stage begins to play, accompanying the gospel *Everybody, Let's Praise the Lord*. There are actually only two short melodic phrases - the first descending, the other ascending. What makes this piece in the program interesting - and evidently fun for the singers - is how individual groups exchange phrases or mutually complement them. At the end one can hear only two tones of the first word, something like "BOdy- BOdy- BOdy---," then "BOdy-BOdy", along with whooping from the choir which is how the others cheer on the group that is just singing.

After the second number another component of the program emerges: a commentary. The slight, black conductor, Raymond Wise, the main figure of the concert and the whole workshop, will present every number from now on. That in and of itself would not be particularly unusual, but although, as he immediately announces in his second sentence, he does not know Czech, he always reads us a Czech version of the commentary first and, only then, repeats the same thing in English. I presume that most of the audience, like me, hardly understands a word of his Czech and very much look forward to the English. The apparent struggle and occasional staggering through the reading (and, at the same time, some sort of anticipatory roguish winking: *Clearly someone whom you could understand would be able to say it, but it wouldn't be so much fun, would it?*) earn him something more than the audience's sympathy: the barrier between the stage and the audience is seemingly torn down. Wise's commentary contains a lot more than dry information. There is a certain degree of enthusiasm and naivety – as if he were trying to attract the attention of second-grade children. *There was a time when American blacks were not free and, with hopes for freedom, they composed songs. These songs are called black spirituals. We are now going to sing one of those spirituals to you... Gospel music is a celebration of God. When the Spirit is holy, we must raise our arms and cry and dance. We believe that we experience all this.* Such a path is, however, easily forgivable to those who, with obvious effort, wrestle with such a strange language as Czech, and every entrance closes a spluttered formula. *We hope you will like this song.* (Wow, I finally finished it.)

The spiritual the choir sings – *Done Made Me Vow to the Lord* – has a rather transparent two-part form which still reminds one of the African responsorial way, a form almost the same as *It's me, Oh Lord*, but with longer phrases. (Similar in form are the well-known spirituals of the *Swing Low, Sweet Chariot* or *Deep River* type). First, the choir hums the melody of the first, melancholic part – quietly, in unison and without words. Then it repeats it with the text with a little more urgency. During the third repetition the piano accompaniment is denser. Only then does the second part resound from above with women's voices, culminating in the third verse with exclamations in high tones. In the even verses the men interlace the melody with a repeated phrase in a lower position. Individual voices gradually become independent and vary the basic line, which sometimes disappears among them in places and then emerges again... Drums are added to this – at first unobtrusively; they drive the entire musical stream forward so that the mood is suddenly quite different from what it was at the beginning: energetically interwoven motifs, reminding me a bit of jazz. Then the whole dense liquid web slows down almost to a stop. The audience begins to applaud, but it is not yet over; the last phrase is heard in a maximally slowed-down, heavy tempo with the roll of the drums until the sustained final chord, with a soprano singing an unbelievably high note.

Then comes another gospel – *I Just Want to Say Thanks* (Wise: *This is a famous song in which we thank God for all he has given us...*), the instrumental overture of the orchestra and the melody of the song remind me of music of Broadway musicals. One could thus easily feel as though he were at another concert of the Prague Proms festival at which the music of musicals was played, regardless of the clapping that is heard again here. The conclusion is similar to the last number: heavy with the repetition of the main phrase "I just want to thank" with the support of drums and, into the applause, a high, shrill sound preparing for an even stronger final chord, which actually isn't the final one – the enthusiastically applauding audience is twice as deafening as the strongest choral and orchestral (this time, a real) full stop.

Next on the agenda is another "genre," that is, the involvement of the audience. Wise: *Gospel music is very lively and energetic. Yes. It is an artistic form in which everyone participates. We can sing and clap together. So, now YOU* (with an emphatic gesture to the audience). *So please stand up* (a gesture to get up from their seats. Most of the audience doesn't understand). *PLEASE, STAND UP!!* (Now the audience stands up; the choir on the stage applauds). *I'll give you four beats: one – two – three* (he is speaking Czech; when he mispronounces "three" the audience laughs) – *four. You will move to the right on the first beat, on the third to the left.* The drums give the basic pattern; a few rows of the audience slowly begin to move.

Further instructions have to do with clapping: on the second and on the fourth beat. With the support of the choir we master the job in a few beats. To the pulse of the rocking and clapping audience Raymond weaves in more and more complicated melodic phrases, which we repeat after him. I rapidly lose my admiration for the audience when I realize that it is actually the choir on the stage that is singing. But then our main role is revealed: we are to sing *Hallelujah!* It consists of four parts, but each part is sung on just one tone (which the conductor sings first). Now all of Smetana Hall is rocking in one rhythm, the polyphonic choir on the stage and in the auditorium repeat *Hallelujah!*; here and there someone (on the stage rather than below it) really raises his hands – as Raymond hoped at the beginning – and here he cavorts under the conductor's platform, waves his hands and in falsetto sings some sort of enthusiastic praises.

Then everything suddenly ends with an energetic motion (which, surprisingly, the majority obeys) and: *Fantastic, braaaavo, braaavo.*

We are back in an ordinary concert constellation. In gospel – *Lord, I Love You* – solos finally assert themselves. The same simple text is gradually sung over the basic melody of the choir by four women in four languages: Spanish, English, Russian and Czech. Each of the singers sings in a slightly different style. The Spaniard in more of a pop style, the Russian operatic... It occurs to me how different the people were – with different fates, opinions and cultures – who took part in the workshop.

At the end the choir switches over to Czech. (Now I understand why Monica asked last night about the pronunciation of the sentence Miluji tě, Pane můj [I love thee, my Lord].) The intonation of the text does not correspond to the intonation of the music, but I suppose that that didn't bother many people. The experience of singing together in a language that was exotic for most of them was probably more important than some accents.

There is one more famous spiritual on the program before the intermission – *I've Got the Robe* – whose melody is similarly minimalistic to *It's Me, but*, with a "Broadway" instrumental arrangement, clapping to the rhythm and repetition of phrases. When the intermission is announced, I cannot believe that it has been more than an hour since the beginning of the concert. Only now can I imagine that eleven songs, about which Monica said, "That's all we know," can fill up a whole-evening concert. But they do: without encores the concert lasted almost two and a half hours, while the second half was very similar to the first.

The gospel evening in the Municipal House that we just attended is an excellent illustration of what is captured in that spiritual musical style during its life. In musical language it is still possible to trace Afric(an-Americ)an roots in repeating figures (which, in connection with the music of Sub-Saharan Africa, are called "patterns") in occasional syncopated rhythm, in open form... African connection, by the way, often emphasizes the inclusion of some African (more or less Christian) song. Sometimes the music reminds one of jazz or pop or other styles which gospel encountered over the course of time. The manner of performing it is straddled between the (mainly older) practice of African-American churches, when the whole congregation participated in the musical component of the services, and concert performances with specific and rehearsed roles and course of events.

Not only the gospel text, but also the context – as is clear from the introductory word, advertising flyers and the course of the whole workshop, and most strikingly in the closing gospel religious service – demonstrates Christianity's central position. At the same time the singers and audience must have a sufficient dose of fun, which is so omnipresent in American public life. Besides, social "fun" reminds one of the time of early gospel when, in African-American churches, there was no strict barrier between the singers and the listeners.

The third basic element for gospel is a characteristic attempt of those who perform it to arouse, the *raise*. Well, what else than *raise* is proved by a gospel concert in a hall otherwise intended for classical music? And not only in a classical concert hall, but primarily in a "classic" manner: with a conductor in a tuxedo, a perfectly tuned large symphonic orchestra, with previously specified and rehearsed forms with prepared dynamics and tempo changes as well as soloists with classical singing techniques. Moreover, what else but an attempt at social uplifting, or, more precisely, a raising of social status is an attempt at founding an official college program dedicated exclusively to gospel, to that gospel that was originally spontaneous and collective music changing with each performance? It is naturally understood that institutional instruction itself bears rather different standards: instead of the most spontaneous involvement, technique, knowledge of theory (and, perhaps, also coming to class on time) will be evaluated. Gospel will not be alone. The same was true of "folk music" under socialism in Bulgaria and is true in Hungary today. Instruction in music academies is no longer a means of individual expression of a concrete musician or singer, but good or even better-learned "pieces" in a repertoire (mainly of a professional). This differs from before – which is, however, actually the fate of everything, including music genres.

SUMMARY
PRAGUE SOUNDSCAPE(S)

Zuzana Jurková

Prague Soundscapes is about the music in Prague listened to through ethno-musicological ears. From our point of view, ethnomusicology is more or less synonymous with musical anthropology and thus we seek the answer to that WHY in human society – in its behavior, values, and relationships. However, as is often the case in science, there isn't one universal theory or even one universal concept clarifying what exactly music is. What is basic is that, from the ethnomusicological perspective, it is not only sound, but also – actually primarily – the people who produce and listen to it and the way they produce and listen to it. It is the world around sound. The musical world.

Imagining it is not always completely simple and thus we begin with theoretical considerations which try to clarify our perspective. In the second part of the first chapter, then, we describe how we wrote this book. Each of the following six chapters is connected to one anthropological phenomenon which we are convinced is related to the shape of music. And actually these connections are the main theme of our book.

Prague and its soundscapes do not yet appear in clear contours, as a clearly profiled model. So our writing is also more a looking around the topic and that is why it is more an examination of the topic; it is similar to the groping of blind men trying to know and describe an elephant. The topics by which we are trying to introduce Prague – an elephant – definitely do not represent systematic categories (because we are unable to provide such profound systematicness).

At the same time, it is not a random ("aleatoric") choice of topics (although even such a choice would show something substantial). We set a few criteria. As mentioned above, our intention is to show music in Prague through the eyes and ears of an ethnomusicologist. That is why we tried, on one hand, to capture events which are at home here and, at the same time, those in which, at least from our perspective, musical language and a musical event are very explicable through the cultural values of the community. The third criterion was a certain diversity regarding presented styles as well as discussed topics in order to show Prague as multidimensional as possible. However, it is clear from the following pages that none of the topics is isolated, just as no music – whether we think about its language or an event – is untouched in today's Prague by what is happening around. This is exactly the interlocking that ascertained that we, groping blind men, are touching the same elephant. And that, with enough patience, contours will appear more and more clearly.

Besides a certain representativeness, appropriateness (homogeneity of musical style and its cultural context) and diversity, we targeted one more goal. In addition to Prague musical events themselves, we also intend to introduce ethnomusicology – a discipline which aims to understand people through music and music through people. Individual topics provided the occasion to introduce various theoretical concepts which are, in the history of (musical) anthropology, of different degrees of importance, but, in our opinion, relevant to a given soundscape.

We step into the Prague soundscape as anthropology and ethnomusicology used to do, that is to say, by focusing on "those others." However, this is not because we would consider the worlds of minorities and foreigners more interesting or more important than the others. But here it is possible to observe several basic phenomena that will also be important for other chapters. As for the material concerning Romani/Gypsy music, it is clear that the musical "world" arises through some sort of negotiation between musicians and listeners (whom Lévi-Strauss calls the "silent performers"). And here it is also apparent how musical language reflects those "negotiated" cultural values.

In the second part of the chapter we focus on recent migrants. We concentrate on the fact that their musical productions testify to attempts to join the new environment. And because what I/we belong to is an important component of personality we come close to the term "identity," that is, to the deep question of what music can express about who we are.

The next three chapters are interconnected. The first of them deals with **music in relation to social stratification and the specialization connected to it.** If Prague tries to (re)present itself by means of music (and mainly at the beginning of our research we were surprised at how little takes place in comparison to other metropolises), then it is through art music. The simplest explanation seems to be the emphasis on the presentation of Prague as primarily a historic city. The ideal intersection of this representativeness of art music and the emphasis on nationhood, which is always so present in the Prague space, can be, for example, a performance of the opera *Rusalka* by Antonín Dvořák (that Dvořák who – at least in the Czech imagination – conquered the New World, and a recording of his symphony even reached the moon, as the Czech media enjoy repeating) in the National Theater on National Avenue in the very center of the city at the most prestigious address. Here one can view the musical style of the opera genre through Lomax's *cantometrics* method: it almost perfectly corresponds to its characteristics of a stratified and specialized society. Although today *cantometrics* is considered mainly as some kind of historical curiosity, it would be a pity to disregard it, especially in connection to a topic that refers so much to history.

An accompanying feature of social stratification is usually **specialization**. While, until the beginning of the 20th century, in art music this specialization was manifested mainly in the sphere of interpretation, starting about 1920 the specialization also turns to the area of reception of art. "Modern" or "contemporary" art music becomes – because of its still unaccepted concepts – a preserve of specialists. The central figure in the introduction of these new concepts was John Cage. A beautiful illustration of the use of Cage's "new" approach to music, new sounds and emphasis on the specificity of place can be the "site-specific performance" of *The Lucid Dreams of Mr. William Heerlein Lindley* in the former sewage treatment plant in Bubeneč. A few dozen attendees confirm the "specialness" of such an event.

The second topic, the topic of **music and rebellion** is closely connected to the previous one through Turner's theory of *communitas* as a mode of social existence, complementary to a common stratified society. The theory of *communitas* can very easily be applied to the most famous phenomenon in the history of Czech musical rebellion, the group *The Plastic People of the Universe*. In the texts of the speaker of the group, Ivan "Magor" Jirous, can be found the concept of the **underground** as its *own special world existing apart from established society with a different internal charge, a different esthetic and consequently also a different ethic.*[1] Esthetics understandably correspond to a peculiar musical language; ethics, among others, with social humiliation and a certain local exclusion which can even be seen in today's punkers' events in the Modrá Vopice Club or on the Parukářka hill.

One everlasting question is related to musical rebellion: How rebellious is music if it keeps features of rebellious musical style, but fills stadiums with listeners – members of that very system against which the music protests (and here and there even with its representatives)? If (thanks to the functioning system) it fills the bank accounts of its performers? Quietly and from a very official and non-rebellious place – the New Scene of the National Theater – Tom Stoppard answers this question with his play *Rock ´n´ Roll*. A play which is, among other things, about the *Plastic People of the Universe*, a play in which not only in Prague performances, but also in premieres abroad, the *Plastics* play "live."

It is this last question which introduces the next chapter, which discusses the **commodification of music**, that is, a process by which music becomes primarily goods intended for earning money. We begin the chapter with Petr

---

1   Jirous 2008: 7.

Zelenka's entertaining (and mildly frightening) film "Mňága: Happy End." This opens the key topics of the chapter: the influence of money (financial corporations as are seen not only in the film but also in reality) both on the inhabitants of that world and on the shape of the music. The functioning of such a world is possible because of the new life philosophy of man (and also the understanding of music) as well as specific mechanisms connected with the dissemination of music. Part of it was described in the '30s and '40s by Theodor Adorno and, a half century later, the musicians of the KLF band made fun of them. Our snapshots confirm that these mechanisms are resistant to all ridicule – at least temporarily.

The variable which is the basis of the sixth chapter is technology, concretely electronically generated sound, which substantially changed the shape of music in many ways. From all of the forms of electronic music we choose two genres of **electronic dance music (EDM)**, freetekno and psytrance. In them we show two forms of an attempt to escape from that commercial reality described in the preceding chapter and to establish a non-commercial, non-anonymous, "free" world. A world created in closest symbiosis with technology – a sort of musical realization of Appadurai's *technoscape*. In connection with this attempt to escape, and also as a little bridge to the following chapter, we acquaint the reader with Judith Becker's book *Deep Listeners,* which is a very complex and unconventional way of dealing with the relations of music, emotion and trance.

The connection of **music to spirituality**, which is the subject of the 7th chapter, would be possible to discuss from many angles. We open it with a *harinam*, a procession of devotees of Hare Krishna through Prague. This event (by way of an unexpected link through techno music in a videoclip about the Prague Krishnas) connects this chapter to the preceding one. In addition, we can notice in the *harinam* several phenomena which are otherwise unusual in the Czech environment: objectivistic understanding of the effect of music, a public presentation of spirituality...

On the musical occasions of the autumn St. Wenceslas Festival we show the dichotomy of "specialization" vs. generality (laity) which in today's Christian context to a certain extent overlaps with the concept of "music as art" vs. "music as spiritual practice." The activity around a gospel workshop again opens wide another dichotomy connected with the performance of music, that is, (in the words of Thomas Turino) the participants vs. presentation model. The way of performing music reveals the prevalent reasons why music actually sounds the way it does. In addition there is here – mainly at a closing concert – a very evident snowballing of meanings or relabeling of the musical genre. And along with this changing of the meaning for musicians and the public the shape also changes. The eternal musical metamorphosis.

Although we did not create a sufficiently systematic theoretical model for the description of Prague musical worlds and the musical world of Prague, through the exposition of topics chosen on the basis of various criteria a few basic features emerged. The first of them is the blurring of various borders (in the concept of music, in style/genre, in the concept of musical sound...). This is a consequence of the merging of individual worlds or influences that cross the worlds, which is an unavoidable situation in a city – dense and dynamic – environment. It also justifies our concept of Prague as, to a certain extent, an integrated whole which we look at from various perspectives.

A second significant finding is that new "worlds" arise through the attempt of the inhabitants to separate – whether as a supporter of "new" music, which uses the language of concrete sounds until now unused; as an aggressively shouting punk rebel protesting against the system; as a dancer at a techno party, escaping from the world of commerce, anonymity and limits to his own autonomous world created in symbiosis with technology; or as a participant in a Krishna procession trying, with the singing of mantras, to extricate himself from this ephemeral world... From this perspective musical events of the new immigrants are the picture of a dynamic process in which its actors are looking for the shape of their own world. All of this corresponds well to the findings of a number of ethnomusicologists that music strengthens group identity by fostering internal values as well as separating them from the surroundings.

REFERENCES

Adamčiak, Milan. 1992. *John Cage 80*. Bratislava: Slovenská národná galéria.

Adler, Guido. 1885. "Umfang, Methode und Ziel der Musikwissenschaft." *Viertelsjahrzeitschrift für Musikwissenschaft* 1: 5–20.

Adorno, Theodor. 1941. "On popular music." *Studies in Philosophy and Social Sciences* 9: 17–48.

Anderson, Benedict. 1983. *Imagined Communities: Reflections on the Origin and Spread of Nationalism*. London: Verso.

Anderson, Benedict. 2008. *Představy společenství. Úvahy o původu a šíření nacionalismu*. Praha: Karolinum.

Appadurai, Arjun. 1996. *Modernity at Large: Cultural Dimensions of Globalization*. Minneapolis: University of Minnesota Press.

Assman, Jan. 2001. *Kultura a paměť. Písmo, vzpomínka a politická identita v rozvinutých kulturách starověku*. Praha: Prostor.

Autorský zákon č. 121/2000 Sb., §11 a §97.

Avellaneda, Veronika. 2010. "Psytrance coby žánr paralelní reality." Bachelor thesis. Fakulta humanitních studií UK.

Balog, Peter. 2009. "Freetekno jako protikultura." Bachelor thesis. Fakulta humanitních studií UK.

Barth, Fredrik. 1969. "Pathan Identity and its Maintenance." In Fredrik Barth (ed.). *Ethnic Groups and Boundaries*, 117–134. Oslo: Universitetsforlaget.

Bateson, Gregory. 1972. "A Theory of Play and Fantasy." In Gregory Bateson (ed.). *Steps to an Ecology of Mind*, 177–193. New York: Ballantine.

Bauman, Zygmunt. 2000. *Liquid Modernity*. Cambridge: Polity Press.

Bauman, Zygmunt. 2002. *Tekutá modernost*. Praha: Mladá fronta.

Baumann, Max Peter. 1996. "The Reflection of the Roma in European Art Music." *The World of Music: Music of the Roma* 1: 95–138.

Beck, Guy. 1993. *Sonic Theology: Hinduism and Sacred Sound*. Columbia: University of South Carolina Press.

Becker, Howard S. 1982. *Art Worlds*. Berkeley – Los Angeles: University of California Press.

Becker, Judith. 2004. *Deep Listeners: Music, Emotions, and Transing*. Bloomington and Indianapolis: Indiana University Press.

Bek, Mikuláš. 2003. *Konzervatoř Evropy?* Praha: Koniasch Latin Press.

Benedict, Ruth. 1934. *Patterns of Culture*. Boston – New York: Houghton Mifflin Company.

Benedictová, Ruth. 1999. *Kulturní vzorce*. Praha: Argo.

Berger, Peter L. - Luckmann, Thomas. 1999. *Sociální konstrukce reality. Pojednání o sociologii vědění.* Brno: Centrum pro studium demokracie a kultury.

Bělohradský, Václav. 2010. "Nesamozřejmé národy, samozřejmá Evropa." *Právo* 24. dubna: 10.

Blachut, Beno jr. 2008. *Věc Makropulos.* Program k představení. Praha: Národní divadlo.

Bloody Mary. Feministický zin. Praha.

Bowie, Fiona. 2008. *Antropologie náboženství.* Praha: Portál.

Brubaker, Rogers. 2004. *Ethnicity without Groups.* Cambridge - London: Harvard University Press.

Burchett, Patton E. 2008. "The ,Magical' Language of Mantra." *Journal of the American Academy of Religion* 76 (4): 807–843.

Burnim, Mellonee V. 2001. "Religious Music." In *The Garland Encyclopedia of World Music: The United States and Canada,* 624–636. New York: Garland.

Butler, Mark Jonathan. 2006. *Unlocking the Groove: Rhythm, Meter, And Musical Design in Electronic Dance Music.* Bloomington: Indiana University Press.

Bystrov, Michal. 2011. *Příběhy písní* (díl druhý). Praha: Galén.

Cage, John. 1961. *Silence.* Middletown: Wesleyan University Press.

Cage, John. 2010. *Silence.* Praha: Tranzit.

Chaney, David. 2004 "Fragmented Culture and Subcultures." In A. Bennett - K. Kahn-Harris (eds.). *After Subculture: Critical Studies in Contemporary Youth Culture,* 36–48. Praha: Slon.

Cole, Fred - Hannan, Michael Francis. 1997. "Goa trance." *Perfect Beat: The Journal of Research into Contemporary Music and Popular Culture* 3 (4): 1–14.

Dočkal, Tomáš. 2007. "Romská hudba: Romové a hip-hopová kultura." Master thesis. Husitská teologická fakulta UK.

Doubravová, Jarmila. 2008. *Sémiotika v teorii a praxi.* Praha: Portál.

Dummond, Bill - Cauty, Jimmy. 1988. *The Manual: How to Have a Number One the Easy Way.* KLF Publications

Drummond, Bill - Cauty, Jimmy. 2010. *KLF Manuál: Jak se dostat na vrchol hitparády.* České Budějovice: Jiří Březina.

Dvorská, Xenie. 1990. *Tradiční hudba Číny.* Doprovodný text k LP. Praha: Supraphon.

Erikson, Erik Hoburger. 1950. *Childhood and Society.* New York: Norton.

Erikson, Erik Homburger. 2002. *Dětství a společnost.* Praha: Argo.

Feld, Steven - Fox, Aaron. 1994. "Music and Language." *Annual Review in Anthropology* 23: 25–53.

Ficino, Marsilio. 1959. "De divino furore." In *Opera omnia.* Turin: Bottega d'Erasmo. Cited in Sullivan 1997.

Finnegan, Ruth H. 1989. *The Hidden Musicians: Music-Making in an English Town.* Cambridge: Cambridge University Press.

Fuchs, Filip. 2002. *Kytary a řev anebo co bylo za zdí.* Říčany u Prahy: Papagájův Hlasatel.

G bod. 2011. Občasník. Praha: Gender studies.

Geertz, Clifford. 1973. *The Interpretation of Cultures.* New York: Basic Books.

Geertz, Clifford. 2000. *Interpretace kultur.* Praha: SLON.

Gennep, Arnold van. 1997. *Přechodové rituály.* Praha: Lidové noviny.

Georgiades, Thrasybulos. 1961. "Sakral und Profan in der Musik." In *Münchener Universitäts-reden*, Neue Folge, Heft 28. München. Cited in Volek 1998.

Giddens, Anthony. 1991. *Modernity and Self-Identity*. Cambridge: Polity Press.

Goffman, Erving. 1956. *The Presentation of Self in Everyday Life*. Edinburg: University of Edinburg Press.

Goffman, Erving. 1999. *Všichni hrajeme divadlo. Sebeprezentace v každodenním životě*. Praha: Nakladatelství Studia Ypsilon.

Gonda, Jan. 1963. "The Indian Mantra." *Oriens* 16: 244-297.

Griger, Ján. 2007. "Acoustic Ecology – A Case Study of the Soundscape of Loreta Square in Prague." *Urban People* 9 (20): 83-97.

Havlík, Jaromír. 2000. *String Quartets Janáček/Novák* (doprovodný text k CD). Praha: Supraphon.

Havlíková-Kolihová, Lenka (ed.). 2007. *Tom Stoppard, Rock'n'roll*. Praha: Národní divadlo.

Heath, Joseph – Potter, Andrew. 2012. *Kup si svou revoltu!* Praha: Rybka Publishers.

Hebdige, Dick. 1979. *Subculture: The Meaning of Style*. London – New York: Routledge.

Hebdige, Dick. 2012. *Subkultura a styl*. Praha: Volvox globator – Dauphin.

Hemetek, Ursula. 1998. "Roma, Sinti, Manusch, Calé." In L. Finscher (ed.). *Die Musik in Geschichten und Gegenwart*, Vol. 8, 443-457. Kassel: Bärenreiter.

Hobbs, Gerald. 2010. "Christianity and Music." In Guy L. Beck (ed.). *Sacred Sound: Experiencing Music in World Religions*, 113-140. Delhi: Molital Banarsidass.

Hopkins, Thomas I. 1971. *The Hindu Religions Tradition*. Encino, California: Dickinson.

Hornbostel, Erich Moritz von. 1976 [1905]. "Die Probleme der vergleichenden Musikwissenschaft." In Klaus Wachsmann – Dieter Christensen (eds.). *Hornbostel Opera Omnia*, 247-270. The Hague: Martinus Nijhoff.

Howard, Judith A. 2000. "Social Psychology of Identities." *Annual Review of Sociology* 26: 367-393.

Hull, Geofrey P. – Hutchinson, Thomas – Strasser, Richard. 2004. *The Music Business and Recording Industry*. New York – London: Routhledge.

Jackson, William. 2000. "Ritual and Devotional Music: Southern Area." In *The Garland Encyclopedia of World Music: South Asia*, 259-271. New York: Garland.

James, Jamie. 1993. *The Music of the Spheres: Music, Science and the Natural Order of the Universe*. New York: Grove Press. Cited in Sullivan 1997.

Janáček, Leoš. 2003. *Literární dílo*. Brno: Editio Janáček.

Janáček, Leoš. 2007. *Teoretické dílo*. Brno: Editio Janáček.

Jenkins, Richard. 2008. *Social Identity*. London – New York: Routledge.

Jirous, Ivan Martin. 1997. *Magorův zápisník*. Praha: Torst.

Jirous, Ivan Martin. 2008. *Pravdivý příběh Plastic People*. Praha: Torst.

Jonáš, Jakub. 2010. "*Český punk v dnešní Praze*." Bachelor thesis. Fakulta humanitních studií UK.

Jónssonová, Pavla – Jurková, Zuzana. 2010. "The Makropulos Case as a semiotic experience." *Urban People/Lidé města* 12 (2): 291-307.

Jurková, Zuzana. 2008. "The Czech Rompop Scene: (Un?)surprising Continuity." In Statelova, Rosemary – Rodel, Angela – Peycheva, Lozanka et al. (eds.). *The Human World and Musical Diversity*, 76-83. Sofia: Bulgarian Musicology Studies.

Jurková, Zuzana. 2009. "Myth of Romani Music in Prague". *Urban People/Lidé města* 11 (2): 351–377.

Jurková, Zuzana – Seidlová, Veronika. 2011. "Hare Krishna mantra in Prague streets: the sacred, music and trance." *Urban People/Lidé města* 13 (2): 195–219.

Jurková, Zuzana. 2012a. "Environmental Aestetics and Urban Soundscapes – Lucid Dreams of Mr. William Heerlein Lindley." *Journal of Urban Culture Research* 4: 82–97.

Jurková, Zuzana. 2012b. "Listening to the Music of a City." *Urban People/Lidé města* 14 (2): 293–322.

Kalenská, Renata. 2010. *Evangelium podle Brabence*. Praha: Torst.

Klusák, Pavel. 2009. "Ticho bude jen pro bohaté." *Lidové noviny* 7. listopadu 2009: 30.

Kolářová, Marta (ed.). 2011. *Revolta stylem: Hudební subkultury mládeže v České republice*. Praha: Slon.

Kotík, Petr. 2010. "Má armáda musí poslouchat." *Lidové noviny* 5. června 2010: 30

Kovalcsik, Katalin. 2003. "The Music of the Roms in Hungary." In Zuzana Jurková (ed.). *Romani Music at the Turn of Millennium*, 85–98. Praha: Slovo21.

Kundera, Milan. 1991. "Improvisation en hommage à Stravinski." *L'Infini* 36.

Kundera, Milan. 1967. "Projev na IV. sjezdu Svazu československých spisovatelů."

Kundera, Milan. 2004. *Můj Janáček*. Brno: Atlantis.

Kundera, Milan. 2006. "Improvizace na počest Stravinského." *Host* 3: 14–23.

Kunst, Jaap. 1950. *Musicologica*. The Hague: Uitgave van het Indisch Institut.

Levenson, Thomas. 1994. *Measure for Measure: A Musical History of Science*. New York: Simon & Schuster. Cited in Sullivan 1997.

Lévi-Strauss, Claude. 1983. *Mythologica I: The Raw and the Cooked*. Chicago: University of Chicago Press.

Lindaur, Vojtěch – Konrád, Ondřej. 2010. *Bigbít*. Praha: Plus.

Linduar, Vojtěch. 2012. *Neznámé slasti: Příběhy rockových revolucí*. Praha: Plus.

Liszt, Franz. 1859. *Des Bohemiens et de leur musique en Hongrie*. Paris: Librairie Nouvelle – Bourdilliat.

Lomax, Alan. [1968] 2009. *Folk Song Style and Culture*. New Brunswick – London: Transaction Publishers.

Maffesoli, Michel. 1988. *Le Temps des Tribus. Le déclin de l'individualisme dans les sociétés de masse*. Paris: Méridiens Klincksieck.

Maffesoli, Michel. 1997. *Du nomadisme. Vagabondages initiatiques*. Paris: Le Livre de Poche.

Maffesoli, Michel. 2002. *O nomádství*. Praha: Prostor.

Merriam, Alan P. 1964. *The Antropology of Music*. Evanston (Ill.): Northwestern University Press.

Michels, Ulrich. 2000. *Encyklopedický atlas hudby*. Praha: Lidové noviny.

Mugglestone, Erica. 1981. "Guido Adler's The Scope, Metod, and Aim of Musicology (1885): An English Translation with Historico-analytical Commentary." *Yearbook for Traditional Music* 13: 1–21.

Muggleton, David. 2000. *Inside Subculture: the Postmodern Meaning of Style*. Oxford: Berg.

Nettl, Bruno. 1989. *Blackfoot Musical Thought*. Kent: Kent State University Press.

Murdock, George P. 1962-67. *Ethnographic Atlas. Ethnology.* Vol. 1-5. Pittsburgh: University of Pittsburgh Press.

Nettl, Bruno. 2001a. "Introduction: Studying Music of the World's Cultures." In Bruno Nettl – Charle Capwell – Philip Bohlman et al. *Excursions in World Music,* 1-18. Upper Saddle River: Prentice Hall.

Nettl, Bruno. 2001b. "Music of the Middle East". In Bruno Nettl – Charles Capwell – Philip Bohlman et al. *Excursions in World Music,* 46-73. Upper Saddle River: Prentice Hall.

Nettl, Bruno. 2001c. "Native American Music." In Bruno Nettl – Charles Capwell – Philip Bohlman et al. *Excursions in World Music,* 255-272. Upper Saddle River: Prentice Hall.

Nettl, Bruno. 2002. *Encounters in Ethnomusicology: A Memoir.* Warren (Mich.): Harmonie Park Press.

Nettl, Bruno. 2010. *Nettl's Elephant: On the History of Ethnomusicology.* Urbana: University of Illinois Press.

O'Dair, Barbara (ed.). 1997. *Trouble Girls. Women in Rock.* New York: Rolling Stone Press.

Ogden, Charles K. – Richards, Ivor A. 1923. *The Meaning of Meaning.* London: Routhledge and Kegan Paul.

Perplex. 2005. "Psychedelic Trance." *Ikarie* 12: 14.

Petrusek, Miloslav. 2006. *Společnosti pozdní doby.* Praha: Slon.

Pixová, Michaela. 2011. "Český punk za oponou i před oponou." In Marta Kolářová (ed.). *Revolta stylem: Hudební subkultury mládeže v České republice,* 45-82. Praha: Slon.

Pospíšil, Filip – Blažek, Petr. 2010. *"Vraťte nám vlasy!" První máničky a hippies v komunistickém Československu.* Praha: Academia.

Power of Open: licence Creative Commons ve světě a v České republice. 2012. Praha: Iuridicum Remedium.

Radostný, Lukáš. 2008. "Po stopách romského hip hopu." *A2* 27: 21.

Radulescu, Speranta. 2003. "What Is Gypsy Music? (On Belonging, Identification, Attribution, and the Assumption of Attribution)." In Zuzana Jurková (ed.). *Romani Music on the Turn of Millenium,* 79-84. Praha: Slovo21.

Radulescu, Speranta. 2009. "The Sonorous Image of the Gypsy in Post-Romantic Academic Music: Two Case Studies." In Zuzana Jurková – Lee Bidgood (eds.). *Voices of the Weak: Music and Minorities,* 103-107. Praha: Slovo 21.

Redfield, Robert – Linton, Ralph – Herskovits, Melville. 1936. "Memorandum on the study of acculturation." *American Antrhopologist* 38: 149-152.

Reich, Charles A. 1970. *The Greening of America.* New York: Random House.

Reyes, Adelaida. 1982. "Exploration in Urban Ethnomusicology: Hard Lessons from the Spectacularly Ordinary." *Yearbook for Traditional Music* 14: 1-14.

Reyes, Adelaida. 1999. *Songs of the Caged, Songs of the Free.* Philadelphia: Temple University Press.

Reyes, Adelaida. 2005. *Music in America.* Oxford: Oxford University Press.

Reynolds, Simon – Press, John. 1995. *The Sex Revolts.* London: Serpent's Tail.

Rice, Timothy. 2003. "Time, Place, and Metaphor in Musical Experience and Ethnography." *Ethnomusicology* 47 (2): 151-179.

Riedel, Jaroslav (ed.). [1997] 2001. *The Plastic People of the Universe: Texty.* Praha: Maťa.

Riesman, David. 1968. *Osamělý dav: Studie o změnách amerického charakteru.* Praha: Mladá fronta.

Ročenka OSA 2011. 2011. Praha: OSA.

Roszak, Theodore. 1969. *The Making of a Counter Culture: Reflections on the Technocratic Society and Its Youthful Opposition.* Garden City: Doubleday & Company.

Rouget, Gilbert. 1985. *Music and Trance: A Theory of the Relation between Music and Posession.* Chicago: University of Chicago Press.

Roux, Jean-Paul. 2007. *Dějiny Střední Asie.* Praha: Lidové noviny.

Rusalka. 2009. Programová brožura. Praha: Národní divadlo.

Schafer, Raymond Murray. 1994. *The Soundscape: Our Sonic Environment and The Tuning of the World.* Rochester, Vermont: Destinity Books.

Shelemay, Kay Kaufman. 1997. "The Ethnomusicologist, Ethnographic Method, and the Transmission of Tradition." In Gregory F. Barz – Timothy J. Cooley (eds.). *Shadows in the Field*, 141–156. New York: Oxford University Press.

Shelemay, Kay Kaufman. 1998. *Let Jasmine Rain Down. Songs and Remembrance among Syrian Jews.* London – Chicago: The University of Chicago Press.

Shelemay, Kay Kaufman. 2001. Toward an Ethnomusicology of the Early Music Movement: Thoughts on Bridging Disciplines and Musical Worlds." *Ethnomusicology* 45 (1): 1–29.

Shelemay, Kay Kaufman. 2006. *Soundscapes: Exploring Music in a Changing World.* New York – London: W. W. Norton.

Shelemay, Kay Kaufman. 2011. "Musical Communities: Rethinking the Collective in Music." *Journal of the American Musicological Society* 64 (2): 349–390.

Shobe, Hunter – Banis, David. 2010. "Music Regions and Mental Maps: Teaching Cultural Geohraphy." *Journal of Geography* 109: 87–96.

Small, Christopher. 1998. *Musicking: The Meaning of Performing and Listening.* Middletown: Wesleyan University Press.

Smolík, Josef. 2010. *Subkultury mládeže.* Praha: Grada.

Slačálek, Ondřej. 2011. "České freetekno – pohyblivé prostory autonomie?" In Marta Kolářová (ed.). *Revolta stylem: Hudební subkultury mládeže v České republice*, 83–122. Praha: Slon.

Slobin, Mark. 1993. *Subcultural Sounds: Micromusics of the West.* Middletown: Wesleyan University Press.

Slobin, Mark. 2000. *Fiddler on the Move: Exploring the Klezmer World.* Oxford – New York: Oxford University Press.

Skořepová Honzlová, Zita. 2010. "Ziriab – Arabic Music in the Czech Republic." *Urban People/ Lidé města* 12 (2): 399–417.

Skořepová Honzlová, Zita. 2012. "Acculturation Strategies in Musical Self-presentations of Immigrants in the Czech Republic." *Urban People/Lidé města* 14 (2): 369–384.

Sokol, Jan. 1998. "Jak se pozná posvátné?" In Milan Pospíšil – Marta Ottlová (eds.). *Sacrum et Profanum*, 9–12. Praha: Koniash Latin Press.

Sokol, Jan. 2004. *Člověk a náboženství.* Praha: Portál.

Stanovy. 2011. Praha: OSA.

Staněk, Luděk. 2012. "Žena x piráti." *Reflex* 7: 51–53.

Stárek, František – Čuňas Kostúr, Jiří. 2010. *Baráky: Souostroví svobody.* Praha: Pulchra.

Stewart, Michael. 2005. *Čas Cikánů.* Olomouc: Barrister + Principal.

Štědroň, Bohumír (ed.). 1986. *Leoš Janáček – vzpomínky, dokumenty, korespondence a studie.* Praha: Editio Supraphon.

Stone, Ruth M. 2008. *Theory for Ethnomusicology.* Upper Saddle River: Prentice Hall.

Stone Sunstein, Bonnie – Chiseri-Strater, Elisabeth. 2007. *FieldWorking: Reading and Writing Research.* Boston – New York: Bedford/St. Martin's.

Sullivan, Lawrence E. 1997. "Enchanting Powers: An Introduction." In Lawrence E. Sullivan (ed.). *Enchanting Powers: Music in the World's Religions,* 1–14. Cambridge, MA: Harvard University Press.

Thornton, Sarah. 1996. *Club Culture: Music, Media and Subcultural Capital.* Middletown: Wesleyan University Press.

Tomlinson, Gary. 1993. *Music in Renaissance Magic: Toward a Historiography of Others.* Chicago: Chicago University Press.

Turek, Pavel. 2012. "Boney M musí pryč." *Respekt* 18: 59–61.

Turino, Thomas. 1993. *Moving away from Silence: Music of the Peruvian Altiplano and the Experience of Urban Migration.* Chicago: University of Chicago Press.

Turino, Thomas. 1999. "Signs of Imagination, Identity, and Experience: A Peircian Semiotic Theory for Music." *Ethnomusicology* 43 (2): 221–255.

Turino, Thomas. 2008. *Music as Social Life. The Politics of Participation.* Chicago – London: University of Chicago Press.

Turner, Victor. 1969. *The Ritual Process. Structure and Anti-Structure.* New York: Aldine de Gruyter.

Turner, Victor. 2004. *Průběh rituálu.* Brno: Computer Press.

Vaněk, Miroslav. 2010. *Byl to jen Rock'n'roll? Hudební alternativa v komunistickém Československu 1956–89.* Praha: Academia.

Vladimir 518 – Veselý, Karel. 2011. *Kmeny: současné městské subkultury.* Praha: Bigg Boss & Yinachi.

Werner, Karel. 1975. "Religious Practice and Yoga in the Time of the Vedas, Upanishads and Early Buddhism." *Annals of Bhandakar Oriental Research Institute* 56: 179–194.

Wiseman, Boris – Groves, Judy. 2009. *Lévi-Strauss a strukturální antropologie.* Praha: Portál.

ZUZANA JURKOVÁ ET AL.
PRAGUE SOUNDSCAPES

Published by Charles University in Prague,
Karolinum Press
Ovocný trh 3–5, 116 36 Prague 1,
Czech Republic
http://cupress.cuni.cz
Translated by Valerie Levy
Proofread by Tamah Sherman and Daniel Morgan
Layout by Jan Šerých
Printed by Tiskárny Havlíčkův Brod, a. s.
First English edition

This publication was supported by the project
"Specifický vysokoškolský výzkum 2013-267 701"

Additional material available online:
www.cupress.cuni.cz

ISBN 978-80-246-2515-7
ISBN 978-80-246-2596-6 (online: pdf)